Nature- Speak

Signs, Omens and Messages in Nature

Dragonhawk Publishing Titles

General
Treasures of the Unicorn
More Simplified Magic
The Animal-Wise Tarot
Animal-Wise
The Animal-Speak Workbook
Ted Andrews' Animal- Speak Calendar 2004

Beginnings: A Dragonhawk Series
Music Therapy for Non-Musicians
Psychic Protection

Young Person's School of Magic and Mystery ®
Magic of Believing
Psychic Power
Dreamtime Magic
Star Magic
Spirits, Ghosts & Guardians
Faerie Charms
Healing Arts
Divination and Scrying
Word Magic
Ancient Powers

Nature-Speak

Signs, Omens and Messages in Nature

by

Ted Andrews

Dragonhawk Publishing   Jackson, Tennessee

A Dragonhawk Publishing Book

Nature-Speak

Signs, Omens and Messages in Nature

Copyright (c) 2004 by Ted Andrews

First Edition

Book design by Ted Andrews

Author Photographs by Margaret K. Andrews

ISBN 1-888767-37-5

Library of Congress Catalog Card Number: 2002108334

This book was designed and produced by

Dragonhawk Publishing

Jackson, TN

USA

Acknowledgments

Several months before my father died, I visited my mother and him for a weekend. His cancer was spreading. While I was visiting, I drove him to the hospital for a check-up. It was one of the few times in our life that we really talked. During the drive, he apologized for not having been able to do more for my brothers and sisters and me. I think he was a bit offended when I chuckled, but then I explained to him that he had given us the best gift we could have ever imagined. He moved us from the city to a home that was surrounded by woods, fields, ponds, creeks and farms. I was six at the time and it was an environment filled with imaginative possibilities and adventures. It was in those woods that I learned of the spirits of Nature and for that I am ever grateful to Dad.

This is also for Grandpa Sims who showed me what a naturalist was long before I even knew there was such a thing. He could make almost anything grow. I still see his long fingers working the dirt in his garden every time I take a shovel in hand. And every spring I think back to all the years when I dug up his garden for him to prepare it for planting or took a walk in the woods with him.

Outside of the family though there have been others who revealed the wonders and spirits of the plant world. This is also for Victoria Parotta who revealed the medicine and power of herbs. Her teachings in herbology are still with me and for more than 25 years now, her teachings have remained a foundation in my healing work.

This book is also dedicated to Debbie and Bob Brill and everyone at Brukner Nature Center. Every day there brought new opportunities to learn. I have always been amazed at the depth of their knowledge and their ability to teach the wonders of Nature. My time there is one of the most treasured periods of my life and helped crystallize my work with animals.

And most of all this is for the Master Gardner Kathy, who never fails to point out the tiniest wonder of the plant world that I might otherwise have just walked by. Her knowledge of plants and herbs still amazes me and her perception of the small and subtle astounds me regularly.

Table of Contents

Table of Contents

Introduction

The Soft Voice of Nature

Every evening during the summer, my grandfather would sit by his garden, watering his plants. If you were quiet and sneaked slowly down the hill, you could hear him talking softly to them. (If you weren't quiet, he turned the hose on you.) He had a green thumb and I believe he could make anything grow. I was always amazed at how much he seemed to know about plants and animals – whether in our yard or the nearby woods.

Occasionally friends and family would ask him to find a tree from the woods to transplant to their yards. On those times, he would take one of my brothers or me to the woods with him to do the digging. He always walked ahead of us, and I remember hearing him muttering softly and touching various trees as he walked. Sometimes he'd pause, studying the tree, and then shake his head and move on. This would continue until he found just the right tree. Most of those trees are still alive today – and that was 40 years ago.

When I got older and asked him about it, he would laugh or get gruff and change the subject. Although he would never speak of it directly, by observing him I got my first lessons as a naturalist. I also got my first confirmations of what I always suspected. *Plants and animals can and do communicate with us.*

I am neither a botanist nor a biologist. Although I do consider myself a naturalist, this doesn't quite define my relationship to Nature either. So what does define it? It is a question that I am frequently asked and for which there is no simple answer. If I must be classified (which honestly is something I have always tried to avoid – enjoying the idea of being enigmatic and all), I am what some traditions would call an animist or, more preferably, a spiritist.

In anthropology animism is the belief that all of Nature – the elements, the plants and the animals – have spirits. These spirits are closely connected to humans. Fetishes (feathers, skins, stones, seeds, etc.) of Nature were protected and honored because they were bridges between the spirit of the plant or animal and the human. Often these beliefs became superstitious, and many even believed that harm to the fetish would in turn result in harm to the human. Superstitions aside though, it has never been difficult for me to believe that the Divine – no matter how we define those divine forces – manifests in this world through many more avenues than merely the human one.

Animism – sometimes called spiritism – is complex. At its core is the recognition that everything in the phenomenal world is truly alive and has spirit. This includes not only humans, animals, and plants, but also non-biological expressions of the natural world as well, such as stones, rivers and cultural artifacts. We do not have to believe that everything in the world has a creative intelligence, but we should be able at least to recognize that there is some spiritual force associated with and /or connected to everything.

Spiritism is the belief that not only is the nonhuman world alive, but it also possesses articulate and at times intelligible spirits, which can perceive, communicate and interact with us. It is the belief that everything has a spirit associated with it. It is the belief that the Divine manifests through all things of the natural world in unique ways. It does not just manifest only to and through humans or only in church buildings for an hour every Sunday. The Divine lives, manifests and communicates perpetually throughout the world of Nature.

When we understand this, then the elements of Nature take on greater spiritual significance than we may have ever imagined - whether those elements are plant or animal. When learning, guidance and even divine messages are not limited only through those of "our kind", our world is no longer the same. It fills with a myriad of new possibilities. And the most mundane elements and experiences of life take on meaning.

On an intuitive level, we always know there is significance to our experiences in Nature, even if we don't understand them. Biologists and zoologists try to rationalize these significances. Philosophers try to theorize about then, and the religious have always tried to spiritualize them. So where is the truth of their meaning? Do we need to become more animistic, as with many primitive societies or should we focus strictly upon the scientific?

The traditional biologist and/or zoologist will often only explain aspects and elements of Nature in terms of its science. Nothing else is possible, unless it can be proven or scientifically verified. This has great value, but it is not the complete explanation. We must also combine the science of biology with the mysticism of animism or spiritism without becoming superstitious or myopically rational.

The scientific and the mystical are not truly at odds when it comes to Nature and its meaning in our life. They support and promote each other. Early shamans, priests and priestesses knew this. They were mystics, magicians *and* scientists. They studied the plants and the animals, learning their characteristics and qualities. They also honored the spirit that was expressed in and through the animals and plants.

On an experiential level, it is difficult to imagine a life cut off from the creative wonders of Nature. Our spiritual imagination responds in a unique way to creatures and plants, but in order to understand these experiences we must also learn to blend science with spirit. We can study the metamorphic processes of plants and understand them scientifically, but we should also marvel at the handiwork of the Divine in such a creation that can alchemically transform itself from seed to flowering plant.

People have asked for years when I would write a book that did for plants what *ANIMAL-SPEAK* and *ANIMAL-WISE* did for the animals. Always my answer was, "Oh, it's in the works." And it has been, but there is a time for everything. Just as there are natural rhythms within Nature, so there are within our own lives. Like a seed, this book needed to germinate, sprout and come to fruition in its own time. I have found through my own work with Nature that it is always best to follow my own rhythms when writing and producing books. When I do, the books are usually more apropos, more timely and ahead of trends and thus much more successful.

Understand though that I am not a biologist or a botanist. I am a spiritist and a naturalist. So how does this qualify me to write something on plants? As most people know, animals are my primary focus, but you cannot deal with wildlife successfully without also discovering and learning something about the habitats in which animals live - that myriad of plants and landscapes. It is integral to their lives. It reveals as much about them as what the focus of our own energies and daily activity reveals about us. We cannot explore one without the other. The relationship of plants and animals that share habitats is often symbiotic.

In addition, most of my life has involved communicating with spirits of one kind or another – including those of Nature. In all of these communications, I have always gone out of my way to confirm the legitimacy of these often-intangible messages in some pragmatic and tangible way. Indeed, a good part of my life has been spent learning to recognize, translate and understand spirit communications and then help others to do so as well.

As much as is possible within the confines of this text, I have tried to combine the scientific with the mystical, for it is key to understanding the messages of Nature. My approach is universal – drawing upon my own naturalistic and mystical experiences and education. I have tried to incorporate the science with the spiritual - biology with mythology. I have tried to seek out the common threads running through all traditions about Nature. I have provided outstanding characteristics and scientific qualities of plants. I have tried when possible to provide significant myths of the various plants. I have tried to show how they work together. By reading the descriptions, you should come to a clearer understanding of how the plant's qualities, characteristics and spirit reflect its keynote and how its spirit speaks to us. You should have a clearer idea of what the plant's message is for you.

From the elements to the animals, from the plants and trees to stones and minerals, the natural world is one of our most powerful sources of spirit, wonder and wisdom. Every tree has its own magical story. Every plant has healing and every animal has spirit. Every cycle brings opportunity for change and growth. Familiar and exotic fragrances that tease and delight fill the air. The songs of birds awaken and soothe. The colors of plants, flowers and trees stir emotions and resonate subtly with our body and mind. And the appearance of an animal causes our spirit to soar. Nowhere does the spirit of the Divine manifests more clearly than within the natural world.

Nature is probably our greatest healing resource. From the plants, we gain medicines and beauty. From the trees, we get fruit and strength. The stones gift us with color, light and electrical frequencies of health. And the animals guide, teach and protect us. We are blessed by Nature. It touches each of us in personal and special ways.

Nature reminds us that there are things much greater than the affairs of humans. When we are unbalanced or if life is unsettled around us – whether through erratic psychic activities or day-to-day life aggravations – we can do no better for ourselves than to seek out the embrace of Nature. It is my hope as you explore the world of Nature that you will find a childlike surprise and delight in the green things that grow around you. For it is in the surprise and delight of things that grow that we find the hidden gifts of the Divine, whispering softly to each of us every day.

<u>Special Note</u>

Throughout this book are descriptions of how people have used various plants (flowers, trees, herbs, etc.) in the past and even still use them today. Some of these uses are spiritual, magical, psychological and/or medicinal. These descriptions are not prescriptive in any manner whatsoever, and no herbal or natural remedy should ever be employed medically (physically or psychologically) by anyone without first consulting a qualified physician. This book is not a textbook of prescriptive remedies or medical advice. Its purpose and function is to provide a new perspective on the spirit, energy and qualities of the natural world and show how we can benefit from a new relationship with it.

Part One

Nature-Speak

"The rounded world is fair to see,
Nine times folded in mystery:
Though baffled seers cannot impart
The secret of its laboring heart,
Throb thine with Nature's throbbing breast,
And all is clear from east to west.
Spirit that lurks each form within
Beckons the spirit of its kin;
Self-kindled every atom glows
And hints the future which it owes.

- Ralph Waldo Emerson *Nature*

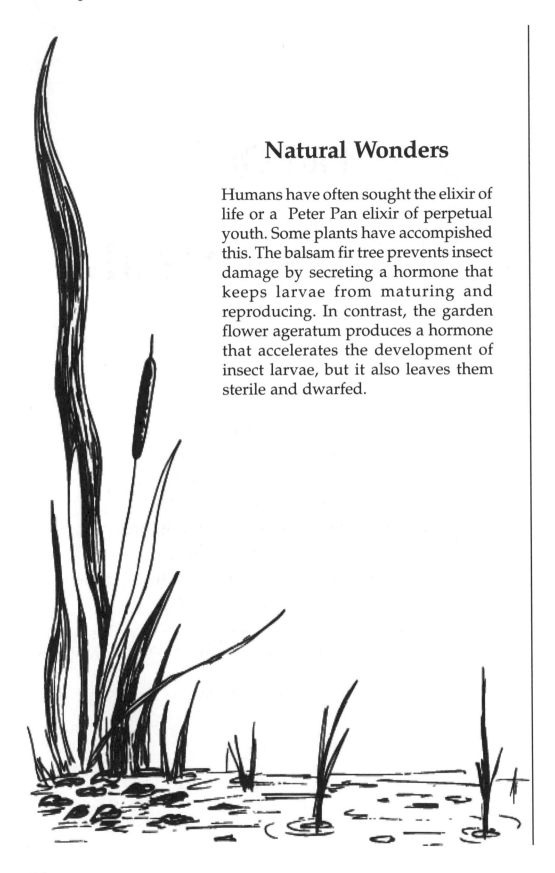

Natural Wonders

Humans have often sought the elixir of life or a Peter Pan elixir of perpetual youth. Some plants have accompished this. The balsam fir tree prevents insect damage by secreting a hormone that keeps larvae from maturing and reproducing. In contrast, the garden flower ageratum produces a hormone that accelerates the development of insect larvae, but it also leaves them sterile and dwarfed.

Chapter One

Initiation Through Nature

We are walking down the street and the fragrance of honeysuckle brushes over us. The flash of a yellow daisy catches our eye in the grass. We spot a tiny flower blooming among dead brush and brambles. We keep seeing the same type of bird perched in the same type of tree every time we walk in Nature. The scent of pine swirls around us as we step out the door. We dream of journeying through the desert. We have a vision in which we walk through an opening in an oak tree to another world. A storm rolls in every time we start a new project. A part of us knows that these experiences have meaning, but is Nature truly speaking to us?

Nature is the most powerful realm of magic and spirituality upon the Earth. It is the source of primal energies and great spirits. Within it are most of life's lessons and most of life's answers. There are teachings about life, death and rebirth. There are teachings of creativity and the development of survival skills, applicable to our modern world. Within Nature are revelations for solving problems and accomplishing tasks that seem impossible. Through Nature we can learn respect, nurturing and trust in our perceptions. It is a reminder of our greatest possibilities and our greatest magic. It is our greatest guide while we walk the Earth.

This is truly a magical time to be living. It is a powerful, dynamic, growing time for both individuals and the planet. It is a time that many can use to bring ancient energies and myths to life within new scenarios. Because of increased awareness of other planes of life, opportunities to tap greater physical and spiritual resources surface daily - for the tearing down the old and building the new. It is a wonderfully exciting time of change, and if the changes are to be constructive, then a new understanding of life must arise with effective and beneficial methods for exploring it. The key to this is found within Nature.

Gifts of the Earth

Native Americans recognize that they are a part of Nature, not a ruler of it. They acknowledge a stewardship role with the natural world. Plants and animals are companions, healers, teachers, spirit messengers and even younger siblings needing protection at times. As such, they are given the respect that one gives to any member of the human family. To them everything in Nature is related. All life is sacred and thus everything that comes from the Earth is a gift, including the signs and communications.

Choctaw collected gifts of acorns, chestnuts and berries. The Natchez were great fishers and hunters and recognized their catch as gifts. The Tuscarora grew corn, considered a very sacred gift of the Earth. Native farmers practiced crop rotation to honor the Earth. It kept the nutrients strong after harvesting, and it was a show of respect for the harvested gifts of the Earth. Young women were taught prayers to thank the Earth for what was dug up and harvested. Nothing was taken without first offering a prayer.

To the Cherokee, ginseng is a powerful healing plant. It grows wild in the mountains but it can make itself invisible to anyone unworthy of gathering it. Women were instructed to show respect for the plant by leaving the first three plants untouched and to say a prayer before digging up the fourth, leaving a bead as a gift to the plant's spirit. By performing such honoring and appreciation, the Earth spirits are encouraged to continue their gifts of food, guidance and even protection.

Every season brought its wisdom and gifts, which guided people and enabled them to survive. Each plant and animal has its purpose and everything in Nature has a consciousness and spirit. Among native peoples, everything that comes from the Earth must be honored. When it is, the gifts become more sacred and the communications become more clear and powerful.

We must try to understand its language – to relate to Nature in a new way. Every society taught that the only way the Divine (no matter how you define that divine force within the world) could speak to humans was through Nature. And the only way humans could understand what the Divine was saying to them about their lives was by studying Nature – especially the plants and animals that caught their attention. The modern, civilized world neglects its ability to understand communications from Nature and fails to recognize and read the signs. But no matter how much we cloak ourselves in civilization, this ability remains dormant and alive within each of us - because we will always be a part of Nature. And Nature is speaking to us all of the time.

Plants and animals are messengers, guides, brothers and sisters. They are living gifts of the Earth. This simple truth is a part of our spiritual heritage that we have forgotten or neglected. Among the Native Americans and other indigenous groups, this sacred heritage is still strong. And it is by drawing upon this foundation - and others like it - that we can reconnect with Nature's gifts once more in powerful new ways.

Throughout the world, people have always looked to Nature for healing, spiritual guidance, signs, communications and omens. Learning to read and work with the forces of Nature is a true initiatory path to understanding the world, to finding direction in all daily activities and to uncovering our greatest potentials in a truly balanced manner.

For many in today's modern world, this approach to Nature will be difficult to accept, especially in our scientific and rational society. It is the stuff of superstition. And yet, even in this modern world, the average person still looks for signs daily. Does he love me? Will I get the job? How will I do on my test today? What kind of day will I have? I hit all green lights, so this must be a good day.

There are answers to most of our questions in life, including the spiritual ones – if we know how and where to look. As we learn to honor and listen to Nature once more, her gifts and communications will unveil themselves to us. We will find both guidance and protection. We will discover new healing, new inspiration and even new dimensions.

Signposts

What am I supposed to do in life? How do I really know what choices I should make? Imagine if we could get answers to our most important questions in life. Imagine if we had signposts to guide us throughout our life. Well, the truth is that we do. Yes, we have all come into this world to grow and develop and learn in ways unique to each of us. But we do not have to go through life blindly. There is guidance and direction for each of us.

Throughout our life, we each have a unique resonance with certain things, people, activities and even aspects of Nature. These rsonances often serve as signposts for us. Signposts are things to help us make proper choices, decisions and actions. These signposts spark our intuition and stimulate awareness so that our path can be more creative and productive in life. They help our decisions and choices be more effective and beneficial. These resonances are established before we are even born into this world, because once we take physical form, we forget what it is that we have come to do. Without this forgetting, we would not develop our creativity and grow. So these signposts - these natural resonances and triggers - are established before birth as a gift to us throughout our life.

There are ordinary and extraordinary signposts and encounters to help us in life. We encounter a person who helps us at just the right time. We experience a dream that gives us a creative idea. An animal appears in our life in an unusual way, and thus we discover a way of solving a problem. We have an encounter with an angel or spirit being. The fragrance of a flower awakens the exploration of new healing techniques. Our signposts in life happen in a myriad of dramatic and subtle ways, but they happen for everyone. The problem is that most people do not pay attention to them or do not recognize them for what they are.

There are times throughout the year when our intuition is stimulated more strongly so that we can recognize the signposts of our lives. We will discuss these times in part two of this book. But more importantly, there is a realm in which we can always find some guidance and direction - regardless of who we are. It is a realm of signs, messages, omens and even spiritual intiation. If you have ever asked: Why am I here ? What am I supposed to be doing? What is the right decision to make? What is my path in life? Then you have come to the right place.

In the realm of Nature, there are a myriad of signposts to guide us throughout life. This book will help you recognize your own signposts in Nature. It will help you to find guidance and answers to the above questions and more.

Benefits of Working with Nature

We are related to everything in Nature, and we must begin to imagine, think and act as if we understand that relationship. If we persist in this effort, the doors of our awareness re-open. We are the stewards. Just as we may have had to watch over younger brothers and sisters, so too must we do so with the natural world. We can begin by imagining the plants and animals as younger brothers or sisters. We do not have to believe that they have creative intelligence, but we should be able to recognize that some spiritual force – some archetypal energy – works through it. And in time, we should become aware that there are specific spirits that work with and through that element of Nature.

When we first begin to work with Nature and all of its inherent energies, some tremendous benefits come to us. First and foremost, it shifts our attention away from the physical world and its problems to the magnificence and wonder of the Divine within our lives and ourselves. We begin to recognize that there are many wonderful dimensions to life - some much less tangible than what we may have ever experienced, but just as real.

We begin to experience a great increase in psychic and astral phenomena. Dreams become more colorful, lucid and even prophetic. Our own psychic sensibilities will heighten, manifesting in a variety of new ways. Healing avenues open for many areas of our life. We discover the healing properties of herbs and plants. The colors and fragrances of the natural world soothe the emotions and even awaken past memories and ancient wisdoms.

Encounters with beings of other realms will occur. We awaken to the wisdom of animals, and we discover the reality of the Nature spirits, so often relegated to the realm of fiction. Nature is one of the safest realms for opening astral doorways and developing conscious astral projection. We will learn to use the natural world as a gateway to other realms, laying strong foundations for opening consciously and safely the doorways to their phenomena. Through Nature, we learn to open and close doorways to those more subtle realms at will. Shamans around the world have done this for ages, and we will explore several of these techniques later on in this book.

Yet another benefit is that we begin to realize that shamanism has its place in the modern world. It is not relegated to indigenous societies and cultures. Shamanism is an experiential growth process. The shaman though maintains a true sense of connectedness to all life. The individual is able to visit both the heavens and the underworld and is able to learn from all life forms – plant and animals – by communicating with their spirits. Pursuing our spiritual quest and unfolding our innate powers through reconnecting with Nature begins with changing our perspective about Nature. It begins with recognizing that Nature truly is one of the most ancient and powerful paths of initiation, providing tremendous guidance and great magical and spiritual blessings.

Special Blessings of Nature

In Nature, we can find guidance about all life's mysteries and all issues in our individual life circumstances. The following are some of the revelations we can find in Nature, along with special abilities that we can develop through following the spiritual path of Nature.

Practical Life Revelations:
Insight into imbalances, needs & problems
Insight into our relationships
General health insights
How to face fears and doubts
Revelations about our true potentials
Creative direction and inspiration
Lessons of faith and patience
Benefits of our sacrifices
How to fulfill obligations
How to overcome obstacles and accomplish tasks
Seeing cause and effect connections
How to initiate new, successful endeavors

Spiritual & Magical Gifts
Enhanced psychic perception
Increased ability to read signs & omens
Healing with herbs & spiritual healing through the forces of Nature
Knowledge and use of natural cycles/rhythms
More tangible spirit contact
Control of the elements
Past life connections
Future life vision
Control of weather & ability to alter the climate of your life
Plant and animal communication
Journeys into other realms
Alchemy

Nature as an Initiatory Path

Today there is a greater revelation of the ancient mysteries than at any other time in history. The glamour and secrecy of older esoteric traditions are dissolving. Opportunities to take higher initiations are available to all. The latter years of the 20th century renewed interest in more compatible work with Nature, including work with the elemental and devic beings. There is increased blending of consciousness with and realization of higher beings and dimensions. Mysticism and spirituality are melding with psychology, physics, biology, botany, engineering and other sciences. New sources of energy and new methods of healing are surfacing daily. All of these inspire greater interest in things beyond and behind the tangible and visible.

If we are to take the fullest advantage of this wonderful time, we must reexamine some of the accepted paths and methods for unfolding higher consciousness. We live in a time that demands a fully conscious union with the spiritually creative, supersensible world. This cannot be fulfilled by mere clairvoyance or by demonstrations of psychic ability. There are laws and principles that govern the raising of consciousness, not the least of which is personal responsibility. Unfortunately, we live in a "fast food" society. People like things quick and easy. They want to pull up to the drive-in window, get their stuff and drive on - even the psychic and spiritual stuff. And it is easy to forget in this modern world where so much information is available that what is psychic is not always spiritual. What is occult or metaphysical is not always uplifting, and what is appealing is not always useful.

The purpose of spiritual studies is not psychic power, but the purpose is to develop the ability to look beyond the physical limitations. Its purpose is to learn the creative possibilities that exist within limitations while at the same time, transcending them. Its purpose is to help us rediscover the wonder, awe and power of the divine and to learn how that power reveals and reflects itself within us individually. And nowhere is that purpose, awe and wonder found more clearly than within Nature.

The qualities essential for accelerating our growth and spiritual evolution are innate, although this idea is often unrecognized or believed to be only for the "gifted few". Even when this innate ability is recognized, there is still needed an effective system or a means to release it. In our modern world, there are a myriad of individuals providing maps. How then are we to know which map is best for us to follow through this labyrinth of spiritual explorations? It is difficult at times to know. But while many traditional initiatory paths are no longer available to the average person, there is one path still open to everyone - the mystical path of Nature.

Whatever system we use as a guide to explore other realms inside of us or outside of us should fulfill certain criteria. Such a system should be easily understood, and if based upon an older Mystery Tradition, it should be living and growing, adaptable to the modern world and to us within it. The system should be capable of awakening our inner potentials without overwhelming us in the process. Finally, it should enable us to experience the universal energies that fill and touch our lives daily. The ancient initiatory path through Nature fulfills all of these criteria.

Unveiling the Mysteries

When we choose to walk the path of Nature, we open ourselves to initiation. Initiation has taken on many meanings in recent years, but simply put, it is a beginning. It is a beginning of new perceptions. It leads to an awakening of deeper levels of consciousness.

Any initiation, whether in the form of a new job or in a new study, reflects a cycle of life, death and rebirth. This cycle of life is at the heart of all worship and unfoldment, and nowhere is it found more clearly than within Nature. Birth, death and rebirth are repeated literally and symbolically in all growing things throughout the natural world. These mysteries and their rhythms provide clues and mirrors to our own higher forms of consciousness and existence. In working with the initiatory path of Nature, we are deliberately acknowledging and inviting these cyclic energies to play more important, vibrant roles in our lives. We are choosing to place our own individual life rhythms into the more universal and powerful rhythms of Nature.

New life and transformations have to be earned. This is the law of sacrifice operating in death and rebirth, and reflected continually throughout the Green Kingdom. A plant may die, but its seeds struggle forth to take root, work its way through soil and sprout – extending itself. Leaves and flowers die off, to be reborn again in a new cycle. The old is laid down for the new.

In that process, though we begin to see the hidden divinity that lives in humanity, in the Earth and in the universe. We begin to understand the hidden significances of our own lives. We begin to see the significance of everything and everyone. We begin to see that which was hidden. We begin to see the signs, omens and messages that speak to us daily.

The Hero's Journey

Nature is a true spiritual path, which teaches us to look into our environment and into ourselves for our answers, magic and miracles. It is the hero's journey, but with less trauma and turmoil. It is a path of initiation, which embraces the solitary seeker and which awakens four of the more powerful archetypal aspects of ourselves - the hero, the magician, the warrior and the wise one.

Hero tales often provide pictures of the spiritual journey we each must take if we wish to open to higher initiations, to our greater potentials and to the mysteries and energies of the universe. Almost every major myth or heroic tale starts with a younger individual (**the hero**) leaving home to seek a fortune in any of a multitude of forms. Often it involves going off into the wilderness or away from civilization and back to Nature. Sometimes the hero chases a deer into a strange forest and sometimes the hero becomes lost in a wilderness, wandering and searching.

These tales often have older characters who, when met along the road, offer advice and assistance. Sometimes it is the spirit of the wilderness itself, but the elder or spirit represents those who work as mediators between the physical and spiritual worlds and who become available (showing up in our life) as we expand our awareness and open to new possibilities. They reflect **the magician** within us. In the ancient tales and myths, how the seeker or hero acts upon their advice and messages (**the wise one**) determines the future and how progress is made.

One of the common forms of the hero's quest was the entering into service of a mighty king or queen, symbolic of a greater force - or even our own higher self. Being of service is part of becoming the spiritual **warrior**. In our case, we are choosing to re-enter the service of Nature. We are taking back our role of stewardship. When we commit to that, then the magic and wisdom of Nature opens gently but powerfully within our life. And these four archetypes begin to unfold within us.

We are all of these together. We are the Hero of our life. And we are also The Magician, The Warrior and The Wise One, who help us accomplish what we have set out to do. Sometimes we are more one than the other. Sometimes it will be easier to be one than the others. All of them though are necessary. All are part of who we are. And all are awakened on the initiatory path of Nature.

The Hero Archetype

In stories and myths, the hero has many adventures into unknown territories, facing tests and gaining magic and wisdom along the way. If the journey is successful, the hero is transformed with something to benefit the world around him or her. If unsuccessful, the journey must be undertaken again. The hero learns by the decisions that are made and what results from those decisions. Most problems arise when the hero hesitates or doesn't make decisions or choices. Making decisions and choices is what the hero must learn to do. Since you are the hero of your life, part of your initiation is realizing that your decisions and your choices will affect you, your life, those who are closest to you and in some way the world around you. This is reflected continually through the natural world. For example, a mule deer rarely follows the same path to a water source. It may end up as someone's meal if it does. If it chooses not to follow the same path, it has a greater chance of avoiding predation.

When we learn to make decisions – right or wrong – we are being the heroes of our life. This doesn't mean we must make them by ourselves, but we still must learn to make them. Through signs and messages, Nature guides us in those decisions and choices and even helps us see the effects of them – both short and long range.

The Magician Archetype

Every aspect of life has its magic, but nowhere is magic more evident than within the natural world. Acorns transform themselves into mighty oaks. Flowers and leaves die off, disappear and then are reborn again with cyclic rhythms. The mysteries of life, death and rebirth play themselves out in a multitude of ways. Nature teaches us creative ways of working with all activities and endeavors and how to accomplish them more successfully. Nature shows us how to be the magician in our life.

Through the magic of Nature, we become more creative and imaginative. We can learn shapeshifting to project personal power, magnetism and a dynamic energy in all we do. Look how animals display to attract mates and ward off threats. We can learn to enchant to bring love into our lives. Look how flowers bloom with brilliant and subtle colors and fragrances, inviting insects to them, stimulating pollination. We can learn how to camouflage activities and even become invisible. We can learn how to sow seeds and bring our endeavors to fruition, at the most appropriate and beneficial time. On the initiatory path of Nature, we will discover these forms of magic and more.

The Warrior Archetype

Nature also connects us to the warrior archetype. This archetype teaches us endurance, persistence and assertiveness. Nature reminds us that without these qualities, real magic is not likely to happen. Real success does not occur. Learning to assert is part of life. Knowing when to assert and how strongly to assert is sometimes difficult to determine. Often it is a trial and error process. When we learn nature-speak, there is much less trial and error.

The warrior energy is what pushes us to get things done. It is the job of the warrior to carry it all out. The warrior perseveres, doing what must be done. The warrior teaches us discipline that we need to pull all of our energies together. Often in Nature, rootstocks will extend and branch out until they find a place to push up through the earth. Othertimes, they wait, absorbing more nutrients and/or storing them for the main. For many plants, without this root persistence and efforts, the growth cannot occur or is limited. Without this same process in our efforts, the goal at hand will not be accomplished. The warrior is the one who knows that there is work and effort in all endeavors. Through this archetype, we learn to be strong, focused and persistent.

The Wise One Archetype

Successful survival in Nature often has much to do with adaptation - adjusting and changing to the world more successfully. There are always things in life that we cannot control. Because of this, things do not always work out the way we plan. We might have to adjust and adapt. The wise one archetype teaches us adaptation to the given circumstances to accomplish and succeed in the best way possible. Through signs, omens and messages, Nature shows us how best to do this.

Wisdom is the ability to apply knowledge and understanding successfully. The wise one in us must be flexible and adaptable, with the ability to alter our course a bit to accomplish what we wish. Sometimes this means combining the faith of a child and the experience of an elder. It is through this archetype that we become a keeper of knowledge. We seek answers in Nature and we determine how to use them to accomplish our tasks. One area of Nature that falls into this category is found in the healing qualities of plants and herbs. Healers were often the wise ones of a community. They knew how to use plants and herbs for a variety of healing activities. For example, if there were nosebleeds or open wounds, many healers knew that the yarrow plant would help. Yarrow contains a chemical that promotes the clotting of blood. It has been used often as a treatment for slowing or stopping the flow of blood.

Nature's Call to the Quest

As we open to the world of Nature, these four archetypes will come to play within our life more strongly. The hero archetype will provide direction along our life path. The magician archetype will help us be more creative in all endeavors. The warrior archetype will show us how to persist and place our efforts more effectively. The wise one archetype will help us draw on our knowledge and experience to adapt to circumstances and energies that arise. As we open to these archetypes through the signs, omens and messages of Nature, we will find ourselves - as many heroes have found themselves - on a sacred quest.

For most heroes, the call of the quest in tales and legends (and in real life) is a call to adventure and excitement, but it is not always recognized for what it truly is: *a time of growth and emergence into responsibility and maturity.* It is a time of transition and a time of dynamic growth - growth that can entail some very strong emotional highs and some very intense emotional lows. It is a time of serious self-assessment (sometimes forced). Traditionally, the individual must examine the circumstances, people, situations and beliefs of his or her life. He or she must examine what has been lost, stolen, broken and/or no longer necessary, in order to clean it out once and for all. This makes room within the hero's life for that which is more beneficial. We experience what Nature herself experiences periodically. Natural fires cleanse brush and dead growth, so that stronger, more beneficial growth can occur, triggering a new cycle.

Many enter into metaphysical and occult practices as a means of escaping their daily lives. They look for these mystical practices to solve their problems. Many see the spiritual path as leading up into some blinding light into which all of their troubles and problems dissolve. In reality, metaphysical and mystical practices are paths to find the light within so that we can shine it out into our lives. If an individual has difficulty handling the situations daily life, invoking spiritual energies - even those of Nature will not necessarily make things easier.

More often, the spiritual energies serve to intensify the daily, mundane circumstances of life - forcing a reconciliation or resolution of daily troubles and problems. Our own fears, doubts, limitations and perspectives - whether self created or imposed upon us by society - create barriers to accessing and expressing all of our highest capacities. Because of this, the hero's path through the realm of Nature is one of the safest and least traumatic. Nature awakens all of the same forces as other initiatory paths, but it provides balance and healing throughout. It provides continual guidance for reconciling and resolving troubles and problems. And nothing is as soothing and balancing to the emotions, psyche and soul as the embrace of Nature, as it touches all of our senses.

When we start any spiritual journey, everything is usually goodness and light, which is as it should be. This is the strengthening process, preparing us for greater tasks and mysteries to be undertaken. When we start a major path of study, we are proclaiming to the universe: *"I am ready to take on greater work and responsibility, and I am taking it on in full awareness of what that entails!'* And this holds true for the spiritual path of Nature.

When we open to the world of Nature, the result is illumination. Illumination is a higher form of consciousness, which changes the mind, enhancing all of our perceptions. This in turn opens us to initiation and the revelation of the Mysteries of Life – all of which are encompassed within the natural world. And the first step is learning to understand the language of Nature - to develop the art of reading signs, omens and messages that come daily to us from the natural world.

Seven Rules to More Magical Encounters

1. Practice seeing and questioning as a child does. Be fascinated and filled with wonder about everything in Nature.

2. Be a naturalist first. Magic and spirit flows out from this and without the naturalist part, the magical shaman cannot be.

3. Take trips regularly into Nature, at least once per season. Each season brings its own unique offerings and has its own lessons for us.

4. Find one special place for you to sit and observe regularly, a place that you can visit throughout the year.

5. Observe and be curious about everything. Notice what is going on around you., making notes or sketches of what you observe.

6. Be unobtrusive when out in Nature. Learn to be silent. Try not to talk. Just observe, contemplate and note activity.

7. Make your home environment attractive to wildlife. Hang feeders. Put up birdbaths and fountains. Have a variety of plants.

Exercise

Establishing Relationships

Benefits:

- **Appreciation of Nature**
- **Subtle recognition of communications from Nature**
- **Opens the heart to the blessings of Nature**
- **Increased opportunities to connect with the spirits of Nature.**

Many speak to me of wanting to attune more personally to plants, animals and Nature. They often ask if I do intensive, one-on-one work with individuals – if I take personal students under my wing. My answer is always "no". The reasons for this are many – most having to do with me not having much free time as it is for my own personal studies, teachings and writings. And the negative answer has nothing to do with "wanting to keep the secrets to myself".

Although many may believe I have some special secret or gift for attuning to Nature, it is nothing more than taking the time and energy to do so. It has to do with opening the senses and heightening the powers of observations. There are no magickal tricks, per se. I did not find tablets from some divine source with secret Nature communication knowledge inscribed upon them.

We live in a society in which people remain indoors for most of their activities. How many people do we know that have treadmills placed in front of a window so they can watch the outdoors from indoors while they run? Granted, weather does affect how much we can get outdoors, but there is no way to truly open to communing with Nature without being outdoors.

That doesn't mean our houseplants and pets have no benefit and can't help us, but if we truly wish to connect with Nature on a deeper level, we have to spend time outdoors, even if only in one's own backyard.

Fresh air is essential to our overall health, but it is essential for spiritual reasons as well. It opens the pores and the senses. It strengthens them and cleanses them. Being outdoors regularly is critical to heightening our senses, whether we live in a city or rural environment. And even if we live in the city, which houses a tremendous amount of plants and wildlife, we can do a variety of things outdoors to help open our senses more fully and encourage greater experiences with Nature.

Remember, Nature talks to us all of the time, and if we start listening and paying attention, we can gain some wonderful insight into our activities and our life processes. Throughout the rest of this book are exercises for getting answers and guidance through animals and nature, but there are a number of things we can do to help re-establish our relationship with Mother Nature and strengthen the communications from her.

The following list provides simple ways of opening to the plants and animals within your own living environment. It is a way of inviting the Nature's messages more strongly into your life. It will heighten your senses. You will become increasingly more aware through senses other than sight.

Perform some of these, and you will not only find yourself spending more time outdoors and experiencing increasing natural wonders. By connecting with one aspect of Nature, it becomes increasingly easier to connect with all other aspects.

1. Involve yourself with some aspect of Nature more personally.

We cannot expect to open communication with the natural world if we do not spend some quality time in it. Plant a garden. Allow an area of your yard to grow wild so that the wild can take up residence within it. Become an amateur naturalist. Do some bird watching. Create a pond. Seek out marshlands. Take night hikes. Try to identify birds by their calls. Take up herbology. Try to identify trees by their leaves. Volunteer and support nature, centers, zoos and other environmental organizations.

Take regular walks in Nature. You will be surprised at what you will encounter and experience with walks around your neighborhood or in parks. For many years, I lived in the city, but I always ran and walked my dogs around a certain route. About a year and a half before I moved, my wife discovered a family of albino squirrels in area that I had passed by countless times without ever noticing. There are tremendous natural wonders – even in the city – but there is no chance of encountering any of them unless you get outside. And what you encounter will change with each season!

2. Study Nature.

One of the best things to do to open to the natural world is to learn more about it. Study a different plant each week. In one year, you will have learned a significant amount about 52 plants. Begin with plants found around your home or those that have always fascinated you. Keep a log on unusual and amazing facts about them. Go to the library get several books on the plants found around your home. Learn to identify them. Look for what is unique about the plant. What is its growing cycle? Has it ever had any medicinal or magical properties?

3. Meditate out in Nature.

Send thoughts and prayers to Mother Nature, asking for signs and communications. Quiet the mind in your backyard or a nearby park and pay attention to what you feel, smell, hear and see. Feel yourself become one with Nature. Try and feel the heartbeat of Nature resonating through you and your own heart beating in rhythm with it.

Choose different environments for your meditations. Mediate under a tree or next to a pond. Sit quietly and contemplate the riverbed. Feel the warmth of the sun on a stone as you sit calmly. Lie back in the grass, breathe deeply the sweet air and fragrance. Feel your body upon the Earth, balancing, grounding, and healing.

Perform walking meditations, especially at dawn and dusk. Feel the sacredness of the Earth and the softness of all life. With each step you will find yourself more attuned than ever before.

4. Listen for and acknowledge Nature's daily greetings to you.

When you are outside, even when just stepping out for a few moments, try to pay attention to what stands out for you. It may be a crow cawing to you. It may be a fragrance from a tree. Nature usually greets us in some way every time we step outside through one of our senses.

The more you acknowledge it, the stronger the greetings become. If a bird speaks as you step out, mimic its greeting back to it. If a crow caws, caw back. If you are uncomfortable doing this, then just say something like, "Hello, friend crow." If the fragrance of a tree or flower catches your attention, greet it in return.

Some people are uncomfortable doing this, worried about what others might say or think. I usually operate under the assumption that most people think I'm a little "weird". (I know; it is hard to believe, isn't it?) If I am out walking and my neighbors see me saying "hello" to a tree, they usually just roll their eyes, pull their kids inside and wait until I move on. But I don't worry about their response. I am being courteous and answering the greeting.

5. Read Nature tales and myths from different traditions and countries.

In every society, there were individuals whose task it was to keep the ancient mysteries alive and to pass them on by word of mouth. These people were the storytellers. Through myths and tales, they guided individuals into new wonders and new possibilities. They parted the veils of mysteries.

Myths and tales touch us on many levels. They provide a tool for life direction and they nudge us to ever-greater exploration of life's mysteries. They open us to possibilities. Through tales and myths of the natural world, we open more fully to the colors of the archetypes they represent in our life.

By reading the Nature tales and myths from different parts of the world, several things will happen. First, you will begin to recognize common teaching about the natural world. Second, you will begin to see some of the spiritual qualities and thoughtforms that are associated with the elements of Nature – the plants and animals.

6.   Honor Nature.

When we choose the path of Nature, we must begin to develop a new relationship with it. We must learn to perceive the natural world from a different perspective. We have to see it as full of life, consciousness and spirit. Educate yourself about plants and animals.

Leave the natural state unchanged. In your home environment you can do this, in public environments you should not. There have been more than a few complaints across the country of individuals who have painted ancient symbols on great stones in national parks and moved stones around to make miniature medicine wheels. Regardless of intent, it shows ignorance and disrespect for that environment.

Plant a promise tree. A tree is a living creature. It eats, rests, breathes and even circulates its "blood". It also provides a home and shelter for animal life. It provides shade and prevents erosion of soil. It is critical for habitat, and thus the planting of the tree is the planting of a promise to be a guardian of animals and nature.

As your care for and nourish the tree, the care and nourishment of nature toward you will grow stronger. And even if the tree should die, your efforts will not be for nothing. In Nature, even the dying trees provide shelter and food for insects and other plant life. When working with Nature, every effort is a promise from you to Mother Nature. And she always rewards the efforts with communications that become increasingly clear.

7. Be ever grateful.

Appreciate the natural world. Be a caretaker of the environment. Reuse and recycle. Take pictures, not souvenirs. Don't waste or take for granted. Leave a gift. Native Americans offer sprinkles of tobacco or corn meal. Plant trees wherever you can and offer prayers.

That feeling is a feeling of gratefulness. When we have encounters they stir that wonder in us, and that stirring makes our day a little brighter and more fulfilled. That feeling we get is an expression of gratitude.

When we breathe deep in the morning and enjoy the sweet air, whether we speak it or not, that appreciation is an expression of gratitude. Our excitement at spotting the hawk perched on the telephone pole or the woodpecker drumming on a nearby tree is a form of gratitude. If we take time to enjoy those moments, we express our gratitude.

The more we appreciate the little experiences of Nature and animals, the more frequently they come into our life. The experiences grow, increasing our wonder even more.

Honor and Appreciation

Native stories speak of an ancient time when the plants, animals and humans lived together in harmony. When humans invented knives, bows, and other tools, the balance shifted.

The animals held council and the deer decided they would send rheumatism to any human who killed them without first asking forgiveness. Little Deer, who was swift as the wind, was chosen to enforce this. When a deer was killed, Little Deer would run to the place of death and ask the animal's spirit if the hunter had asked for forgiveness.

If not, Little Deer followed the hunter back to his village and crippled him with rheumatism. In time the people learned prayers asking that the spirit of the slain return in the body of a fawn.

Exercise

My Nature Journal

Benefits:
- **increases understanding of plants and animals**
- **improves observation skills**
- **crystallizes the spirit energy behind encounters**

When we begin keeping a record of encounters in Nature and follow it up with some study, we become naturalists. The Nature Journal is a log of your encounters. It is a personal field guide for you to observe and note activity and ultimately apply its meaning to your life. It is a record of your plant and animal messengers - your signposts. It can even be used for dream encounters as well as all waking encounters involving aspects of Nature.

This journal or field guide is an important aspect of moving to a deeper level of understanding the spirit behind your encounters. It is what helps us develop the mindset that *everything has significance*. More importantly, when you record your experiences, they truly become yours. Each experience becomes a drop of wonder in your life and this makes your own well of magic deeper.

When we explore the significance and energy associated with our experiences then we are becoming more than just a naturalist. We are becoming animists or spiritists. Animism in anthropology is the belief that all of Nature has spirit and these spirits are closely connected to humans. Animists recognize and believe that everything in the phenomenal world is alive and has spirit. These spirits are often intelligent and have the ability to communicate and interact with humans.

Spirituality is not determined or limited by knowledge, reason or creative intelligence. Remember that our teachers are not merely the human ones. Our learning and guidance can come from sources other than human. Divine messages are not limited to coming to us only through those of "our kind". When we realize this, our world is no longer the same. Your Nature Journal helps crystallize this for you.

The journal activity should be used for all significant encounters and journeys into Nature. It should have two parts. The first is for notes of what you observe and it should have space for follow-up research information and conclusions - possible meanings of the encounter. You may want to have space to make sketches of elements that stand out.

Although some people use separate notebooks for both, I recommend using just one. Simple is always better. A good spiral notebook is simple to use and easy to carry. Adapt it to suit your own needs. In time, you will adjust it anyway, finding the way of noting and recording that is best for you. You will surprise yourself how much more you will notice and remember when you record your encounters.

Take your time when in Nature. Sit under a tree. Sleep in the grass; meditate next to a spring or pond. Take the time to enjoy Nature and appreciate its wonders. The communications will simply flow like a soft voice that fills the heart. And the path will open wide.

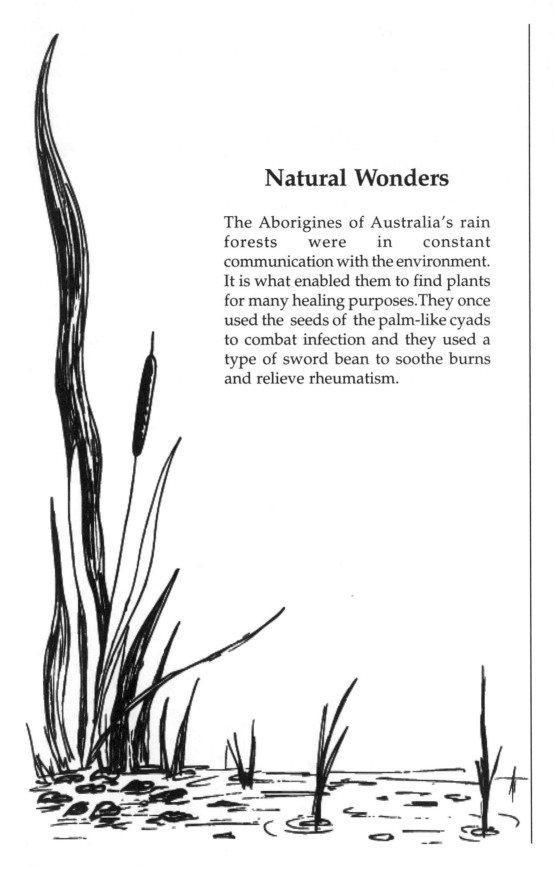

Natural Wonders

The Aborigines of Australia's rain forests were in constant communication with the environment. It is what enabled them to find plants for many healing purposes. They once used the seeds of the palm-like cyads to combat infection and they used a type of sword bean to soothe burns and relieve rheumatism.

Chapter Two

How Nature Speaks to Us

The Green Kingdom has great significance and symbolism for humans. It mirrors and reveals the truths of our lives. Plants breathe, grow, adapt and defend themselves, just as humans do. They communicate, perceive, and react – just like humans. They reproduce and they impact the world around them.

But plants do so much more. Plant life sustains the living world. Plants produce oxygen and food. They stimulate the senses, heal, and inspire. Plants are alchemists - providing lessons of growth, synchronicity, and relationship. They are forecasters of change in the weather and changes in the environment and they have unique rhythms, powers and cycles. Plants are very self-sufficient. Without plants, animals could not exist. They are the fabric of our landscapes. They travel and they colonize. They are the life-givers and life-support of the planet.

Plants are often taken for granted in the modern world. To many, they are little more than part of the view, but they are actually unique among all life forms. They alone contain chlorophyll, which allows them to derive energy directly from light (photosynthesis). They are living symbols of the Earth's life force and they have been the focus of worship in times past. Most gods and goddesses throughout history have had some plant associated with them. In the Scandinavian tradition, Yggdrasil was a sacred ash tree, the great Tree of Life associated with the god Odin. To the Native Americans, corn and tobacco are sacred plants of the Earth.

The Green Kingdom is an environment from which we can gain tremendous spiritual insight and wisdom about our lives and our potentials. In fact, everything we encounter in Nature has the potential

*"All signs and messages
in Nature
work to accomplish 1 of 3 things:
First,
to stir a sense of wonder about
the world around us,
Second,
to help us solve and handle the
problems and issues in our life
and Third,
to awaken and quicken us to
new potentials and creativity."*

of being a powerful symbol, which can direct us in our activities and endeavors. In order for this to happen effectively, we must come to look at Nature in a new way.

There are two steps to understanding the communications of Nature. The first is recognizing the signs, omens and messages and the second is learning how to translate them. In order to recognize the messages from Nature, we must develop our senses and in order to translate the messages, we must develop some understanding of symbology.

As just stated, recognizing the messages begins with developing all of our senses. Nature communicates to us through our physical senses of sight, sound, smell, touch and taste. The whispered rustling of pine trees may stand out for us. We may catch the fragrance of honeysuckle or dogwood. We spot a tiny larkspur along our path, where we had never seen it before. There is a sweetness in the air. A cardinal sings to you throughout your entire time in Nature. What stirs and touches your senses is a message to you.

Nature also communicates to us through our intuitive sense as well. Of all of these, most people assume the intuitive part will be the most difficult. On the contrary, this happens naturally when you spend time in Nature. Your intuition sharpens. It is one of the subtle gifts of Nature. There may not be something tangible that we experience but our thoughts keep returning to that cedar tree we passed, for example.

A lot of the time, the intuitive part comes into play frequently during the translation of the message. We are just impressed with an answer. Translating the messages usually requires some introspection and awareness. We don't have to learn deep meditation techniques for this to happen. Quiet sitting (the Confucianism technique of quiet contemplation) will usually elicit the answers and insight we are looking for.

The "Aha!" Response

We must learn to apply the message to our own life or it has little pragmatic importance. Sometimes this involves trial and error. Not always is the message obvious, and often it is multi-dimensional. Its message may very likely apply to several areas of our life, but if the message is truly important, Nature will give it to us several times and sometimes in several ways.

Think of interpeting your Nature encounters in a way similar to interpreting your dream experiences. Dream imagery and symbology can have multiple meanings that apply to several areas of our life. A dream of a family quarrel, may indicate an actual quarrel with someone in your family. It might also indicate that you are quarreling with yourself about a decision you must make. It might also indicate that something you are eating is quarreling with your body's health. And all of these interpretations may apply to you.

Our subconscious might also send us several dreams in the same night, centered around the same issue. It uses a different scenario in case we didn't quite get the message the first time correctly. For example, we may dream of quarreling with the family. We may have a second dream that night in which we are on a vacation and everyone around us is arguing and preventing you from enjoying your vacation. There may even be a third dream in which you are struggling to swim across a lake to the safety of your home. All reflect emotions in turmoil and that are affecting your peace and that of your home. There are always common threads running through these dream series.

Signs, omens and messages from Nature are often very similar to dream communications. Our subconscious mind will stimulate the senses so that we notice in Nature what is important to us or some aspect of our life. The encounter or experience will provide insight into several areas of our life simultaneously. Let's say, for example, that you are struck by the whispery sounds of the breeze through the pines, while you are out in Nature. You remember an old folk warning about telling secrets around a pine tree. It will whisper it to all the other pines and before long, the secret is out. The message could very well be a caution about revealing anyone's secret. Keep confidences. It might be telling you also that there is some whispering going on around you at work. If you've been suspecting this, Nature may have just given you the confirmation - even though that wasn't your primary focus. Messages in Nature are often multidimensional.

And just as several different dream scenarios in one night can provide different ways of looking at the same issue, if the message is important, Nature will present us with several experiences or encounters to help ensure that we get it. These experiences will have a common thread. For example, let's say that you are having difficulty asking for a raise at work. You are not sure if you should go for it and if so, you also are not sure how to go about it. As you are walking in Nature, you spot a great blue heron soaring down and lands softly in a pond. You watch as it spears a fish and then stands calmly in the water. You continue your walk and you come across an area that is covered with acorns. You see the oak from which they had fallen.

What happens when we try to examine both experiences in relation to asking for a raise? They seem entirely different. In the first, we see the heron, gliding confidently down, spearing directly and then standing patiently. This could reflect a need to be straight, direct and calm in your approach to asking for the raise. Just glide in and do it. The acorns provide even more insight. Great oaks come from tiny acorns. This could very well be an encouragement for you. Make your request. If you don't, the acorns won't ever grow.

The question though always arises as to how we know for sure that our interpretation is correct. If you have found that it applies to an area of concern within your life – even if it is not the answer you wished, it is very likely correct. It almost always means the first thing you think it means and it always means a little more. And when you have hit on where the communication applies in your life, there will come with it the "Aha!" response. We just know it. This is called an epiphany. It is a sudden illumination. They are also what I call my "frequent forehead-slapping experiences". If it is a true message, it will always have a kismet, fate, or synchronistic coincidence about it. But remember though that the message is usually multidimensional. And even after having the "Aha!" response, the communication can probably be applied elsewhere in your life as well.

Symbolism of Nature

Symbols express that for which we have no words. They touch both objective and subjective realities. They span the world of thought and the world of being and symbols bridge the rational and intuitive levels of our being. They provide a means of understanding and interacting with the true world of hidden realities within us and our life. They open us to that which we have either ignored or been unaware. They are a means for the conscious mind to recognize and discern information from the subconscious mind, which attends to everything that goes on in and around us.

Symbology is the language of the unconscious, and each of us at some point will need to learn more about it if we are truly to read the signs, omens and messages of Nature. If we intend to step out on the path of controlled evolution through the magic and power of the natural world, we must become aware of Nature's significant symbols within our lives. To many this might seem to be buying into the superstitious or a belief in the supernatural. In fact, the opposite is true. As you will discover throughout this book, learning to recognize signs and communications from Nature is not supernatural at all. It is a very natural part of life.

Symbols are derived from archetypes or universal energies found throughout the world and thus at some point in our use of them, they lead us back to those archetypes. The archetypes are the manifesting energies of the universe. The archetypes are the points where the abstract divine forces begin to take upon themselves actual substance, form and expression. It is within the Green Kingdom that archetypes unveil themselves most powerfully, particularly through the plants, animals and activities of Nature.

Everything in the natural world is potentially symbolic, with the ability to reflect something about the hidden forces at play within our life. In other words, at the core of everything we encounter in Nature (and in all of life for that matter) lies some archetypal force. For example, a flower opening its buds and blooming reflects the energy of emergence and new beginnings of an archetypal Journey. A storm may reflect the intense emotions we are battling with and thus are tied to the archetypal Adversary - forces we must direct, overcome or control for change to occur. The opening, hidden at the base of a tree, may reflect something about the potential of a new idea or endeavor, since all openings are reflections of the archetypal Feminine - the creative and birth giving energies.

There was a time in which humanity saw itself as part of Nature and Nature as part of it. Dreaming and waking were inseparable. Animal, plant and human were inseparable. The natural and the supernatural merged and blended, as did the symbolic and mundane meanings of the elements of Nature. Shamans used the symbols and images of the natural world to express this unity and to instill a transpersonal kind of experience. Modern initiates are creative individuals that intuitively see possibilities for transforming ordinary data and everyday experiences into new creations and inspirations. They process information in new and creative ways.

Two Ways of Learning

If we are to accomplish this as well, we must be able to learn in new ways. We must be able to relate to the world around us in new ways. Inside each of our skulls, we have a double brain with two ways of knowing and learning. The different characteristics of the two hemispheres of the brain have a dynamic role in releasing higher potentials into our daily life expression - especially when working together. Each of the hemispheres gathers in the same sensory information, but they handle that information in different ways.

One hemisphere (often the dominant left in Western society) will inhibit the other half. The left hemisphere analyzes, counts, marks time, plans and views logically and in a step-by-step procedure. It verbalizes, makes statements and draws conclusions based on logic. It is sequential and linear in its approach to life.

On the other hand, we do have a second way of knowing and learning. This is right-brain activity. We "see" things that may be imaginary - existing only in the mind's eye - or recall things that may be real. We see how things exist in space and how parts go together to make a whole. Through it, we understand metaphors and symbols, we dream and we create new combinations of ideas. Through the right hemisphere, we tap and use intuition and have leaps of insight - moments when everything seems to fall into place but not in a logical manner. The intuitive, subjective, relational, wholistic and the time-free mode is right hemisphere activity. It is this activity, which is stimulated through any contact with the natural world.

Because of our innate connection to Nature, plants and animals have always played a particularly strong role in our unconscious symbology and continue to do so today – even if it is unrecognized. Understanding the relation between the archetypal forces and elements in Nature that we experience in our daily lives is critical to leading a magical existence. It is also critical to reading accurately the signs, omens and messages that come to us through Nature. We must be able to recognize the symbols of Nature, along with their inherent archetypal forces and meanings, and work with them. These symbols are the tools we use to build perception of the spiritually creative worlds and their hidden energies playing within our lives. It is how we recognize signs and omens and can interpret them accurately. And this we accomplish most easily through Nature.

Symbols, visualization and creative imagination are often a part of developing higher potentials. The symbols and images assist us in accessing that part of our brain and mind which bridges into deeper levels of perception and consciousness. We accomplish this most easily through symbols and images of Nature because they are such a strong part of our most primal self. Because we are an integral part of Nature, patterns from Nature speak to our intuitive consciousness. The symbolic patterns that speak softly to us allow us to know what has or will come to pass and even what directions we should take in various areas of our lives. When we recognize this and can apply this awareness to our own unique life circumstances, we are developing what I term *nature-speak*.

The key to empowering our life is setting up conditions that create a mental shift to a new way of processing information. Through the techniques in this book, you will learn to delve into parts of the mind and its perceptions that are often obscured by the endless details of daily life. Through the proper use and understanding of Nature's images and symbols, you will create a bridge that begins the process of unveiling the hidden to you. You will begin to see underlying patterns and you will access greater potentials and manifest them within your daily lives. You will begin your journey to becoming the modern initiate.

Seven Major Archetypes of Carl Jung

Archetype	Characteristics	Common Symbols in Nature
Self	ego, individual	home environment; complete meadow, forest or habitat; individual trees,plants. totems; seeds; eggs; outdoor temples
Feminine	mothering; birth; beauty; receptivity; acceptance; creative/intuitive	cave; holes in trees; tunnels; blossoming plants; archways, bushes, nests; eggs; pods, ponds & lakes; night; moon; water; female plants and animals
Masculine	fathering; initiating; organizing; fertilizing	seeds; pollination; tall trees; sun; stems; fire; mountains; daytime; male plants & animals
Heroic	facing difficulties; overcoming; healing healing	healing plants and herbs; immature plants & animals; storms; annual plants; new growth; survival adaptation; struggling plant growth
Adversary	agent of change; unexpected; tearing down; obstacles	stinging & thorny plants; storms; overgrown areas; swamps; natural disasters; erosion; struggling plant growth
Death/ Rebirth	ending & beginnings; sacrifice; crises; new life	marshlands; seasonal cycles; perennial plants; bogs; environment changes; border areas; natural intersections
Journey	movement; development; aging;	pathways; hills & mountains; rivers & streams; deer trails; wind; growth; perennials

Doctrine of Signatures

From the elements to the animals, from the plants and trees to stones and minerals, the natural world is one of our most powerful sources of spirit, wonder and wisdom. Every tree has its own magic and story. Every plant has healing and every animal has spirit. Every cycle brings opportunity for change and growth. The air fills with familiar and exotic fragrances that tease and delight. The songs of birds awaken and soothe. The colors of plants, flowers and trees stir emotions and resonate subtly with our body and mind. And the appearance of an animal causes our spirit to soar. Nowhere does the spirit of the Divine manifests more clearly than within the natural world. Nowhere does the Divine speak more often to us than through the images and symbols of nature.

As much as is possible within the confines of this text, I have tried to combine the scientific with the mystical, for it is key to understanding the messages of Nature. My approach is universal – drawing upon my own naturalistic and mystical experiences and education. I have tried to incorporate the science with the spiritual - biology with mythology. I have tried to seek out the common threads running through all traditions about Nature. I have provided outstanding characteristics and scientific qualities of plants. I have tried when possible to provide significant myths of the various plants. I have tried to show how they work together. By reading the descriptions, you should come to a clearer understanding of how the plant's qualities, characteristics and spirit reflect its keynote and how its spirit speaks to us. You should have a clearer idea of what the plant's message is for you.

One of the best ways for understanding how these messages come to us through the plant kingdom is by working with the Doctrine of Signatures. This doctrine teaches that the use and message of a plant are hidden in the form of the plant itself. The form of the plant is the signature, reflecting a hidden energy that manifests through its form. In times past, the plant's physical form provided clues to its healing purposes. For example, plants with a yellow sap were cures for jaundice. Plants with red flowers or coloration were good for the blood.

While use of this doctrine can be traced to ancient China, during the Middle Ages, its application to medical practices became widespread in Western culture. There existed at this time a general belief in the unity of Nature and a belief that everything in Nature was placed there for the good of humans. Religious leaders even taught that God provided visual clues to the medical use of the plant in its form.

Physicians and healers used this physical signature of plants to determine remedies for a multitude of illnesses. Famous individuals, such as Nicholas Culpepper and Paracelsus (Phillipus Aureolus Theophrastus Bombastus von Hohenheim), promoted the use of this doctrine in treating patients. In fact, many names of plants tell us how the plants were used to cure. For example, lung and breathing imbalances were treated with lungwort and bloodroot was used for general diseases of the blood.

The application of this doctrine to healing was not always successful or accurate. And it was often quite complicated. It usually involved the erecting of an astrological chart of the patient and working out the plants most suitable for the individual, according to his or her chart. The application of the Doctrine of Signatures to understanding the communications from Nature though is much more accurate and not nearly as complicated.

Modern metaphysicians know this doctrine as the Principle of Correspondence. The Principle of Correspondence states: *"As above, so below; as below, so above"*. There is always a correspondence or link between the phenomena of the various planes of being within the universe. All planes and dimensions affect each other. What happens on one level has impact upon others. We cannot do something on one level without it affecting us on another. What we do on one level will play itself out on other dimensions. There is a corresponding energy. Thus, everything in Nature reflects a force of the heavens and everything in the heavens reflects itself in Nature.

This is why so many societies had their own versions of sympathetic magic. An action on one level can be focused to release a corresponding energy on another level. For example, many shamans poured water out ritually upon the ground to bring the rains. They recognized the corresponding impact of a properly focused rite.

The ancient Hermeticists used this principle as a means of prying aside the veils to other worlds and dimensions. By observing the physical and reflecting upon higher correspondences, they could understand some of the spiritual forces impacting upon physical life. Through this principle, we can pry aside some of the obstacles that hide the subtle dimensions and forces playing within our lives. Through this principle, we can discern the hidden forces in our own life. By attending to what we experience in Nature and examining the characteristics of what captured our attention, we open ourselves to tremendous guidance in the form of signs, omens and messages.

The Meaning of Colors in Nature

Nature is filled with colors and the plant kingdom has some of the most unique coloration, combinations and variations. All colors in the plant world have meaning for us and we should always explore their meaning when they stand out for us. They are a major characteristic in the interpretation process and they provide strong clues to energies at play in our life. The following provides guidelines to the major colors and their meanings.

Black

Black is found commonly throughout Nature in both the plant and animal kingdoms. In the plant kingdom, black is most often accent coloration or a color of the stem or bark. It is more common in the fungus and mushroom groups of plants, but wherever it is found, it is often associated with mysticism, magic and new birth. It is a color of quiet strength and protection. It can indicate a need for secretiveness and sacrifice. Black is also associated with the feminine energies, the creative and intuitive. When found with other colors, it often indicates a grounding or even a more mundane energy or issue at play.

Blue

From blue birds to a variety of moths to a multitude of flowers, herbs and even fruits, blue always stands out when encountered in Nature. Regardless of the shade, this is a color reflecting truth and happiness in some area of our life. Blue brings energy of expressiveness and increased perception. If the blue is capturing your attention, be careful about loneliness or faultfinding. It reflects a time for interactions that are more social and for trusting your perceptions. It reminds us to maintain calm and to trust that all will be well. It is quieting and soothing.

Deeper shades of blue appear when healing is needed – on both physical and spiritual levels. It can indicate a need to reign in our nerves. If we do not trust our intuition, indigo and darker shades of blue will catch our attention in Nature. When it appears with lighter shades of blue, we may need to deal with some aspect of depression (either in us or in someone close to us) and there may be a need for a little more social activity.

Brown

Brown is one of the most common colors of Nature. Whether found in animals or in plants that catch our eye, it is always a reminder to stay grounded. This color often denotes a time of practicality and strength. It can also reflect a tendency to be overly critical at this time. When plants and grasses are turning brown, we need to examine how we are using our resources. Are we allowing them to dry up? Are we using them freely? Do we need some fresh water (activities, creativity, etc.) in our life?

Brown is always a reminder to keep our feet on the ground. It is a time to be practical and apply common sense to situations going on around us. It can be a reminder to take care of the mundane things in our life.

Green

Green is the color of Nature and it is found throughout the plant and the animal kingdoms. It usually reflects something about growth, abundance and healing in our life. It can confirm that we are on the right track and growth and movement is occurring in its proper time and space.

Brighter greens and even toward the blue range, provide positive clues in regards to friendships and relationships, especially in regards to issues of trust and faith. It is a healing and often presages a renewal in a relationship.

Yellow-greens can indicate a need to move through some emotional imbalances and uncertainties. This yellow-green can indicate that things and activities may be premature or that some healing in some area of your life is necessary.

Gray

Gray is in both the animal and plant kingdoms as well. Traditionally, this is a color of ancient teachings and clarity of mind. When it stands out for us, it reflects a need to trust in the imagination or a need to keep it in balance. Gray is the color of clouds and fog, so when it captures our attention, it can reflect things are hidden from us at this time. It can even indicate that people around us are hiding things from us. Do we need to be more careful about what we reveal and to whom?

Gray is also tied to dream activity and when it stands out for us in Nature, we should pay very close attention to our dreams. Revelations and answers are coming through them, especially any dreams involving some aspect of Nature.

Orange

Orange is the color of warmth. It is most often found among the flower, insect, bird and reptile kingdoms. Its appearance most often reflects that new energy, new creativity and new joy are at hand. Now is the time to balance your worries and recoup your energies.

Orange moves us to act. It is time to seek out new activities, especially if they are ones we will find enjoyable. We will have the energy and time to pursue creative activities, if we initiate them now.

Peach shades are often indicators of a need for a little more protection. Is someone being overly sensitive? Are we allowing emotions to get out of control? Do we need to be a bit more protective of our emotions?

Red

In Nature, this color is striking, wherever it is found. It is a color of sexuality, passion, strength and it is attention-getting – often warning others away or drawing them near - whether plant or animal. When it captures our attention in Nature, it always indicates strong energy around us and our life. Traditionally, red is associated with love, passion, sexuality and even anger and revenge.

With this strong energy around us, we may need to be careful about impulsive and aggressive behaviors. It might also indicate that we need to be a little more creative and showy in our endeavors. This is not a time to hide in the back. Red always catches the eye. Maybe this might be the time for you to catch the eye of someone. Maybe this is the time to pursue something you desire. The energy to do so successfully is strong.

Darker shades of red can indicate that we need to be more careful about how and where we express our physical energies. Are we overextending ourselves?

Pink is used to treat skin conditions in color therapy, and our skin is our largest sensory organ. Pink in Nature often contains a message about sensitivity or lack of it. Lighter pink shades in particular can indicates oversensitivity around you. Are you or someone around you being immature and overly sensitive to the truth? Pink reflects issues of compassion and of the heart and in Nature, it can help soothe emotions.

White

Found in all of Nature's kingdoms, white reflects the energies of truth. It is soothing to our spirit and even indicates the presence of spirits about us in some area of our life. When white appears predominantly, we may have messages coming to us soon from the spirit world.

White is always a reminder to follow our creative inspirations. If it is capturing our attention in Nature, we may need to look at how we are or are not expressing our creativity. Now would be a good time to follow any creative pursuits.

If we have doubts about issues or activities or even people in our life, white is a color that reminds us to be patient. The doubts will soon be alleviated. We will get our answers.

Yellow / Gold

When yellow and gold colors appear strongly to us through Nature, it indicates issues of communication are at hand. Now is the time to trust in your inspirations and avoid being overly critical. It can even indicate that new learning opportunities (formal or informal) are at hand. Their appearance is usually an encouragement to take advantage of them, especially if the yellow leans toward the lighter lemony shades.

Yellow and gold often reflect a renewal of enthusiasm in some area of our life. The pressures will be lifted and the joys will return. Lemon shades and even lemon fragrances encountered are indicators of a cleansing that is in process. This may be a health or an emotional cleansing – for you or someone close to you in some area of your life.

The Meaning of Numbers in Nature

Some plants are found in small clusters, while others remain solitary. The number associated with your encounter is significant - whether it's the number of times you encounter something or the number within an encounter. A study of numerology will provide further insight

One - time to initiate; new beginnings; take charge - leadership role may be upon you; be careful about coming on too strong or domineering.

Two - time for a partnership or dealing with a companion; has the energies of the dreams; issues of intuition and cooperation at hand; be careful about meddling.

Three - time of magic and new birth; creative imagination is very active and should be worked with; express yourself but be careful of gossip.

Four - time for a new foundation and for patience in laying it; issues of groundedness and stability are at hand; focus on the practical and avoid being too stubborn.

Five - time of change and movement; lots of activity is at hand and will require versatility; make your moves but do not become scattered.

Six - time to focus upon yourself, your home and your family; energies and issues of feeling safe within your personal environment are at hand; control your worries and be practical.

Seven - time to seek out and explore the spiritual and mystical energies at play in your life; trust in the wisdom of your animal guardian; issues of trust surface; be careful of where you put your faith.

Eight - time of power is at hand; issues of money (a symbol of power in our society) are prominent; be careful about being careless or greedy; trust in your own power to do.

Nine - time of healing and completion; issues of endings and new beginning surface; energies of transition and leaving the past behind; be careful about being overly sensitive.

The Heartfelt Intuitive Connection

Being reflective in and about Nature will help you to develop a heartfelt connection to the natural world and everything in it. If you wish to develop greater harmony with Nature, ensuring stronger and clearer messages, there are some specific things you can do to help accomplish this. They will enhance your sensitivity. And they actually help attracts birds and other animals, create empathy and patience and they can be practiced day or night.

1. Enjoy your experiences in Nature. Look and experience first. Don't worry about the messages. Don't talk about your experiences with another person while you are out in Nature. Just experience and enjoy.

2. Don't worry about the names of plants and animals. It labels them but there is much more to their essence. I found when I quit focusing on identifying and naming everything I experienced, the clearer the communications become.

3. Try to see Nature from new angles. Try to see through the eyes of the forest or field. Lie down and look up through the trees; get the perspective "from the Earth". Imagine yourself as part of the Earth. Cover yourself with leaves and sticks, leaving the face uncovered. Climb a tree occasionally - if you are able. I still climb trees. I've always enjoyed it, especially the views that open up.

4. Mark landmarks. What stands out for you? Occasionally look back the way you have come. You will be surprised at what you will see that was originally missed.

5. Make mental notes and guesses about what you see and experience. Note how many shades of color, what kind of plants and where, how many different bird sounds, etc.

But above all enjoy your experiences!

Exercise

Cloud Readings

Benefits:

- **Aids in understanding symbols**
- **helps develop clairvoyance**

Remember lying back in the grass and looking up at the clouds? How many different things can you see in the clouds? Like a Rorschach ink blot test, clouds will take on many formations and the images that you see can give you answers to questions. Nature often speaks to us through the clouds

Cloud readings are one of the oldest forms of divination. It was common among the Celtic people and the Druids. By looking at the formations and how the clouds moved, someone's fortune could be determined by them. Several years ago, I was attending the International New Age Trade Show in Denver. One of my books, *ANIMAL-WISE*, had been entered into the Visionary Book awards contest. On the bus from the hotel to the awards banquet I was doing some cloud gazing out the bus window. I was quietly wondering whether my book would win an award that night. I saw four very large dragon cloud formations. In the East, dragons are good luck. They reflect good fortune and great power. That night my book won four awards, including Book of the Year.

Cloud readings are a wonderful way of learning to understand symbols. Years ago, I used to participate in a lot of psychic fairs. In the spring and summer, many of these were held outdoors. At times I would do cloud readings on people just to do something different. I would take the person's hand in mine and then look to the clouds. I would then look for images that related to the person. We can do this for other people and for ourselves.

RORSCHACH INK BLOTS
What do these remind you of?

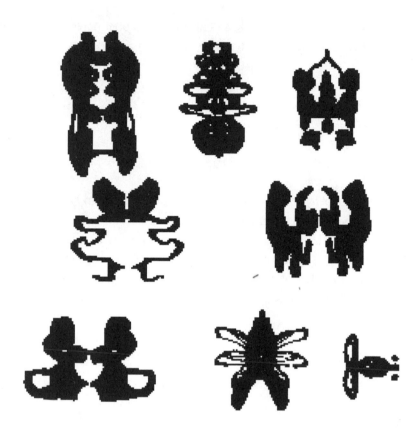

Inkblots are made by dabbing ink onto paper and then folding it in half. The mind tries to make sense of them, and so what you see can be quite revealing about you and your life. In Nature are many unusual forms and patterns, and they will also register upon the subconscious mind. If you have a question or problem, take a walk into Nature. The images and symbols of Nature significant to your problem will register upon you and providing an answer or some guidance for us.

1. Pick a time when there are plenty of clouds. It's particularly fun if you can lay back in the grass.

2. Close your eyes and think of a question or a problem. Sometimes asking the "cloud and air spirits" for help is beneficial.

3. Stay relaxed, and as you look to the clouds, pay attention to any formation. The subconscious will help you to recognize images that relate to your questions.

4. Ask yourself some questions:
   - *What does that image mean to me?*
   - *Is it positive or negative?*
   - *What else could it mean?*

5. Trust in any emotions that you feel. Remember that you will see and feel what your subconscious mind knows you can relate to. With every cloud divination you strengthen your ability to work with your symbols and subconscious. You develop your psychic power and by learning how to use this technique you've got a tool you can use anywhere as long as there are clouds in the sky.

*"Most people look for the sacred
in the unusual
and the often dramatic,
supernatural experience.
But the irony is that
the Divine mysteries
are found in the ordinary,
the mundane
and the natural aspects of life -
softly whispering to us."*

Exercise

The Sacred Walk

Benefits:

- **Develops awareness of Nature's communications**
- **Grounding and stabilizing;**
- **Puts life and situations into perspective**
- **Calms fears;**
- **Heals and blesses**

Every tree, plant, stone and animal has its own qualities, its own energies. We can not walk through Nature without realizing the life and energy within every aspect of Her. One of the most beneficial ways to eliminate stress and to strengthen our our connection to Nature is to take regular sacred nature walks. Choose a park or woods in your area. Even city parks are beneficial for this. Try to choose a place where there are trees and natural trails (no concrete walkways unless it is all that is available). Try to pick a place that also has a stream, river or lake nearby.

By choosing a place with trees, meadows, and natural water, we balance all of the elements within the body. Our own earth, water, air and fire become balanced and strengthened.

Plan to have at least an hour for this exercise, and I highly recommend it be a gift for you at least once per week. The best times are early morning and dusk because a greater variety animal life is more active and more likely to be experienced. If it cannot be done at these times, any time will provide benefit.

Treat your walk as something sacred, a spiritual realigning of your body and its essence with Mother Nature. Do not anticipate what you should expect to encounter. The idea is not to try and encounter anything in particular. The idea is to try and merge with Nature, to awaken and heal our senses and energies. Try to plan your walk so that it gives you time in different types of environment – open areas, trees, water, etc.

As you step out along the trail you have chosen, feel the earth beneath your feet. If your area has only a concrete walkway or bike path, step off of it onto the earth itself periodically, so that you have direct contact with the earth. If it is warm enough, at some point take your shoes and socks off so that your skin touches the earth directly.

Notice whether the earth is soft or hard. By doing this in the beginning, we will notice changes in the terrain more naturally as they are encountered. Know that with each step you are grounded and stabilized, no matter what the terrain. Know that this groundedness and stabilizing will touch all aspects of your life when you leave.

Periodically along your walk, pause and breathe deeply, inhaling the fragrances and the air. Notice how sweet it is and how good it feels to breathe the air of Nature. Know that with each breath your aura becomes cleaner, freer of stress. It becomes more vibrant.

Listen to the sounds around you. Can you hear the song of birds? The humming and buzzing of insects? Listen to the sound of your feet on the earth. Every sound awakens your own inner symphony. It makes us more alert and perceptive.

As you walk along your sacred path, stop whenever something catches your attention. The flash of sunlight on the water, the brightness of a flower, the dance of a butterfly. Quietly note the colors that stand out for you and know that you are absorbing all of the colors of Nature into you with each step you take.

Feel the sun and the air upon you. Feel it energizing you, increasing your circulation making you more vibrant. Touch things as you walk. Let your hands brush the leaves of a tree. Feel the roughness and strength of trees. Feel the daintiness of a spring beauty, so tiny and yet powerful enough to grow among such diverse life.

Step to the water's edge. Hear the stream and feel it. It may even whisper to you. Feel your own blood moving in rhythm with it. Feel yourself cleansed by being in its presence. Know that you are healed.

As your walk draws to a close, note how much more alive your senses are. The air is sweeter, the colors brighter, the sounds crisper – all because we have grounded and energized ourselves through Nature. Feel all of your elements balanced and healed.

Make a mental note of anything that stood out for you on your walk. Before the day is over study some of its significance. The symbology of it will often provide wonderful insight into things occurring within our life. Offer a small prayer of thanks for the blessing. Know that the benefits will grow throughout the day and with each return visit.

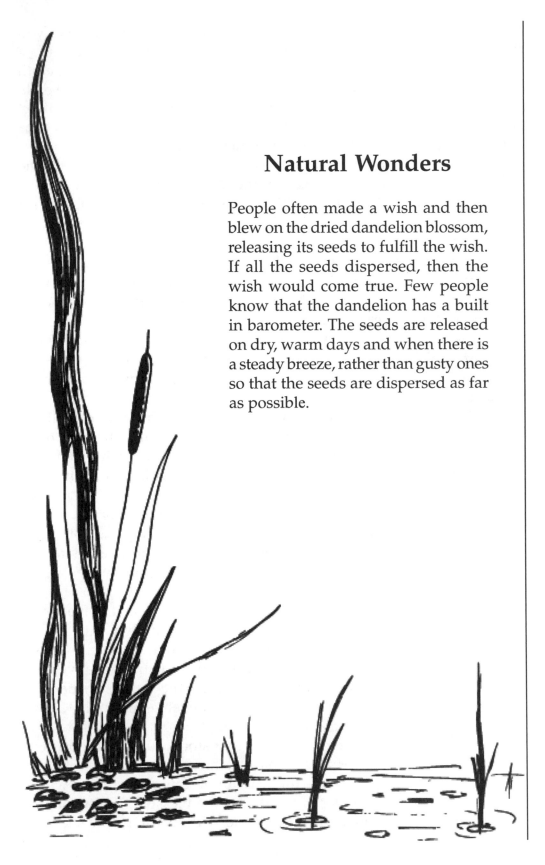

Natural Wonders

People often made a wish and then blew on the dried dandelion blossom, releasing its seeds to fulfill the wish. If all the seeds dispersed, then the wish would come true. Few people know that the dandelion has a built in barometer. The seeds are released on dry, warm days and when there is a steady breeze, rather than gusty ones so that the seeds are dispersed as far as possible.

Chapter Three

Reading Signs &Omens

Study of the stars. Dream interpretation. Reading tarot. Consulting the I Ching. Dowsing with a pendulum. Gazing into a crystal ball. Looking for signs in Nature. Throughout the ages, people have always tried to divine or know the future. Every society has had its practices – from the earliest of times through the Biblical era and even into the immediate present. Some of the methods have been very strange and some are still in practice today.

Divination is often defined as fortune telling. It is the gaining of some knowledge as if coming from a divine source. It is the art of learning to recognize and interpret signs, omens and messages. Although there are many types, forms and expressions of divination, there is one that everyone can and should learn to use. It is the art of nature-speak. Nature-speak is the ability to read signs, omens and messages from Nature and all of her elements. This includes the plant and animal kingdoms, as well as general landscapes and even weather phenomena.

Because we are still a part of Nature, learning to read the signs and messages is one of the easiest and most rewarding of the divinatory arts. When we use the methods and tools of nature-speak to read and interpret the signs and messages of Nature, we will begin to understand what and why things are happening in your life. These messages will help us to solve problems. They will help us to be more creative and to make better decisions and choices. They can even reveal our future possibilities.

Intuition, psychic power, signs, omens and prophecy are all part of divination. They all deal in some way with knowing the hidden aspects

Seers, Prophets & Oracles

Clairvoyants (clear-seeing) and true seers trained their natural ability "to see" that which was not readily visible to the average person. It could be auras, spirits and even events yet to unfold.. Prophets and seers have been found in many societies and many traditions. Most people are familiar with some seers who have taken on almost mythical proportions., such as Merlin, Moses and Ezekial.

Probably the most famous seer, Michel de Notre Dame (Nostradamus), in the 16th century described his technique of altered consciousness in "Preface `a Mons Fils". His prophecies were written in the form of poetry. His accuracy at predicitng modern events, including the rise of Hitler and the world wars is quite remarkable.

One of the most famous modern prophets and seers was Edgar Cayce. Born in Hopkinsville, Kentucky, most of his seeing focused on health problems. Through his abilities, he treated over 30,000 patients, providing accurate readings on health, personal and even social matters.

Most prophetic lore is is often disguised in complex symbolism. In more ancient times, schools of prophets and oracles existed. Many were located in special environments. The Delphic Oracles of Greece were srrounded by sacred groves. Some were located near volcano chasms and others in caves. It is interesting to note though that the most powerful oracles and seers were usually strongly connected to the natural world.

of life. Some people roll their eyes and make fun of this possibility – especially at the idea that Nature speaks to us. Others are afraid of the possibility. What if you find out something bad is going to happen and then can't change it? But most people want to know. And the realm of Nature is one of the safest environments for anyone to explore the world of spiritual signs, omens and messages.

Signs, Prophecy and Divination

We pick the petals from a daisy, softly chanting, "He/she loves me….He/she loves me not." Do we consider this true prophecy though? Is this how we read signs in Nature? No, not really. Although in the modern technological world many people sneer at what appears to be "superstitious nonsense", most of us do experience prophecy or some aspect of it daily. Prophecy is embedded within our lives and probably always has been throughout history. Look how many people seek patterns in the stock market every day. And how many of us adjust our activities based upon weather reports?

Throughout the ages, there have been many unusual methods and some very disciplined techniques for forecasting the future. Ancient Mesopotamia, Egypt, Babylon and China read the stars. Ancient Rome eviscerated animals and examined their internal organs for signs. Divination is the use of a tool or system by which predictions and even prophecies can be made. Even today, a multitude of people use divination tools such as runes and tarot cards with varying degrees of success. The tools help us to shift awareness so that we can perceive hidden energies and patterns around us. For most people, creating that shift in consciousness in order to make the perception is the difficult part. When we work with messages from Nature, that shift occurs naturally and with little effort. It is the one realm of divination at which everyone can succeed.

When we are in Nature, we relax more quickly and the more intuitive aspects of us, which have been cloaked in civilization, become free. Because we are part of Nature, our innate abilities become more viable through any contact with the natural world. This doesn't mean that we must sojourn into some primitive area of Nature. We don't have to be in the wild for our more natural instincts to awaken. We just need to be around some aspect of Nature. Plants and trees are with us in city, suburban and rural environments. We can create indoor gardens. Even sitting quietly among a few plants that are strong and alive will accomplish this for us. Remember that we are part of Nature and there is an instinctive resonance with it – no matter how long we have ignored that part of us. Nature is speaking to us all of the time.

One of the problems all people go through is learning to trust in their perceptions and interpreting the intuitive / psychic messages and signs correctly. Is the message what really is or just what we want to hear? Divination through nature-speak helps us with this. We become more objective and trusting of our insights and perceptions. The more we look for the signs, the clearer they become.

Most people know of me through my work with animals, totems and reading the signs of nature. When I need an idea about how projects are unfolding and how the rhythms are playing in my life, I take an answer walk through Nature, looking for signs. By paying attention to what stands out on the walk, I gain insight. To understand how this is possible we must understand two basic principles at play in the process.

#1. All things are connected.

Everything is connected to everything else. Every person is connected to every other person. Every event is linked to those of the past and to those of the future. Everything relates to everything else. This is also known as the Law of Correspondence that we discussed in the previous chapter. There is no such thing as coincidence. Every action has a reaction. Everything we do and think sets energy in motion and shapes what will unfold somewhere within our life. If we do one thing, something else will result from it.

The difficulty though is figuring out how things relate. True divination comes from recognizing what the connections are or will be. Sometimes the connections will be obvious. Other times though it takes a great deal of effort before we figure out these connections or why things happen the way they do. An encounter with a skunk may be alerting us to be careful of our boundaries. On the other hand, it may also indicate that we may need to take a bath. The appearance overnight of a group of toadstools/mushrooms, may just reflect that the excessive rain has created an extremely moist and fertile environment for them. But because mushrooms act in almost the reverse manner of normal plants, their appearance might indicate that it is time to recycle ideas and activities and take an entirely different perspective in some situation around us.

#2. All things are possible; some are more probable.

Not everything you perceive or divine is set in stone. It is often a reflection of possibilities. Your impressions, dreams, images, visions and psychic perceptions are usually *probable* patterns that are very likely to unfold. Some events are more probable than others. In nature-speak, the subconscious mind helps you to see aspects of the natural world that are important to your life or to some specific area within it. Because the subconscious mind can't speak, it accomplishes this through symbology. Certain elements of Nature will stand out for us or register with us – a color, a fragrance, a sound, a plant, a tree, a stone, an animal, etc. The subconscious mind stimulates attention to something around us - especially when we are out in Nature.

People who rant against fortune telling usually throw up the idea of free will. How can we know the future if we have the free will to change it? We always have free will. As long as we are living in the physical world, there are going to be some events and situations that we are not going to be able to change or to know about entirely. If we can divine probable outcomes though or gain some fresh perspective, we can take actions or make choices that will make outcomes more favorable to us - and far less traumatic. And something as simple as a walk through Nature reveals tremendous insight.

Signs, Omens and Superstitions

Ecology is the study of the interaction between living things and their environments. The ability to read Nature within whatever environment we find ouselves is what enables us to recognize signs and omens. Signs and omens are usually non-verbal messages. Omens indicate a particular destiny or likelihood of events. Omens border upon an almost instinctual perception with the natural elements. Thus, any changes in nature can reflect changes that are likely to occur in our own life. As you spend time in the natural world, you will begin to see relationships and patterns in Nature, and their relationship to your life.

The difficulty though is being able to define and apply the message or sign to your own life. For this to occur effectively, you have to see the relationships without forcing the correspondences. It begins with recognizing that nothing happens by accident or coincidence - all things, all plants, all animals, all people have significance for us.

It is easy to become superstitious. Most people see superstitions and omens as the same things. The recognizing and accurate interpeting of signs and omens occurs through a strong base of knowledge of the environment and the plants and animals within it. When we have that, then the changing elemnts within our natural environments will more directly reflect the changing elements in our life. The changes, activities and elements that stand out for us can be interpreted from a strong knowledge base and with reason. It is important to remember that correspondences in reading signs in Nature do not need to be forced - nor should ever be - when there is a strong foundation of knowledge.

Superstions, on the other hand, are beliefs or notions in the significance of an event or thing that is not based upon knowledge or reason. Superstitions often involve irrational fears and behaviors and actions that are taken to avoid "bad luck". The correspondences between natural elements and our own life are not formed from a base of knowledge.

Let's say , for example, that you are in a work situation that has recently become stressful. There seems to be a lot of gossiping, tension and arguing. You are thinking about quitting. You take a walk in Nature to relax and to look for some direction in handling this situation. On the first part of your walk you hear blue jays, screeching at each other and they remind you of some of your co-workers. you stop, watching and listening. The screeching continues until one of the jays flies off. And the woods quiet. As you move on, the jays return and seem to follow you, screeching at each other - or possibly at you.

As you continue on, you keep catching the fragrance of pine trees, even though they are not yet visible. You begin looking for them. Not far off the trail you see several tall pines. You step off the trail and move toward them. There is no pathway to them and it is tangled and overgrown. As you fight to get to them you see a small clearing among the pines. You finally reach it, and as you sit in the clearing, you reflect on what may be the answer. But you are not even able to relax among the pines. The jays seem just as noisy and numberous as when you started.

Jays are often thought to be harbingers of bad luck, as well as being thieves and bullies. To a superstitious person, the jays screeching might indicate that the gossiping and arguing in the work environment is going to continue. It may even follow you no matter what action you take or where you try to find peace - even in a new job (the pine clearing). Its just a sign of troubled times and bad luck. And there is nothing you can do about it.

To someone with a knowledge base though, it may reflect something a bit different. Jays are just doing what they do. They are vocal opportunists. And they are plentiful in Nature, surviving in a variety of environments. Maybe Nature is telling you that even if you move to a place that seems to be more peaceful, you are still likely to encounter "jay-like" people - similar situations to what you are currently in. Maybe Nature is saying that instead of trying to leave, you must find a new way to deal with the situation, because this kind of activity is found everywhere. Take a lesson from the jays here. Use this as an opportunity to develop some new people skills you have not yet tried.

The most common misinterpretations occur because of our own fears, but knowledge always conquers fear. The correspondences between Nature and our own life will deepen as your knowledge base grows. The relationship between what you are experiencing in Nature and what you are experiencing in your own life do not need to be forced. Just be careful not to allow your desire to divine the future to override common sense. It is easy to read into Nature what we want t o read and not what truly is. Many want to see everything in Nature as a supernatural sign. The events and observations that are unusual, out of context of normal patterns or not part of your daily contact will often have the most significance for you. Although it is usually safe to assume that events and elements within Nature can and do reflect something about your own life, only a true knowledge base will allow those mirrors to be clear. The dictionaries of Nature's elements throughout this book will help you get started with this.

Recognizing Signs

So how do we begin? How do we know whether the plant or element of Nature that has caught our attention has particular significance for us? It's not always easy and nor is it always obvious. Learning anything new takes time, effort and patience. Developing a new relationship demands even greater time, effort and patience.

We begin by first recognizing and accepting that the aspect of Nature has caught our attention for a reason. Our subconscious mind stimulated us to attend to it for a reason. Accept that some force, some archetypal energy is expressing itself to you through it. By studying and learning about the aspect of Nature, we understand more of its spiritual significance to our life and us.

Maybe it is a specific message for us. Maybe its appearance provides a clue to resolving a problem. Maybe it appeared to provide a course of action. Maybe it has the particular quality we need to develop at this time in our life. Maybe its appearance is just to remind us to keep a sense of wonder alive. Maybe it means all of these things – and more.

In understanding the language of Nature and in developing that new relationship with it, we must develop the mindset that *everything has significance.* That significance is not always going be crystal clear, and it may affect us on many levels. But everything we experience has some importance and significance for us. If it got our attention, it has meaning.

One of the best things we can do everyday is to spend 5-10 minutes quietly outside. We do not have to pray. We do not have to meditate. Just sit outside. At the end of those 5-10 minutes, what aspect of the natural world stood out for you? Was there a particular fragrance, sound, tree, flower, animal that stood out? At the end of the day, look back over the day's events and then study something about that aspect. It won't take more than 2 weeks and you will begin to see the connection. Nature is talking to us all of the time, and we must learn to listen anew.

Anything that catches your attention has significance. Nature's signs and messages come to us primarily and initially through the physical senses:

> *What color do you notice most strongly?*
> *Does a fragrance catch your attention?*
> *Does a flower, tree or plant stand out for you?*
> *Are there any physical sensation (tingling, cold, warm, itching…?*
> *Is there a particular sound that catches your attention?*
> *Does an animal cross your path?*
> *What is most memorable?*

How do I know if what I experience is a message?

Does every aspect of Nature have meaning?" Yes, it does have meaning. All Nature (animal, mineral and vegetable) encounters have meaning and significance. Not all of them are direct messages to us about something in our life, but they do have meaning. Sometimes the meaning is just environmental. It is a reminder of the beauty surrounding you and available to you. It is often telling us to take time to smell the roses, to attend to the wonders around us. Listen to the haunting songs. See the beautiful colors. Smell how sweet the air is.

There are two kinds of encounters: the ordinary and the extraordinary. Seeing a bird or the same trees as you step out the front door may be an ordinary encounter, just a general reminder of the wonders of Nature. Many times our encounters are little more than an ordinary (if there really is such a thing) environmental encounter. If the plants and animals are a part of our living environment, our seeing them may not have a specific message. This does not mean they aren't significant though. They can remind us to pay attention to what we may have been ignoring. They keep a sense of wonder alive within us.

An extraordinary encounter is one that is much more. A flower grows where none was planted. An acorn falls off a tree and hits us in the head. One color appears to dominate our attention when out in Nature for more than a single day's time. The air brings us the same fragrance every time we are outside for a week. We dream every night for a week of a desert. Every time you turn on the TV over several days' time, someone is talking about roses. Extraordinary encounters are more striking, more extensive and repetitive and often they come with a sense of what I call the "wow" factor. We can have a variety of encounters, and when we have several of them within a close time frame, we should pay attention. The archetype and/or spirit of that aspect of the natural world is manifesting in our life and our own subconscious mind is trying to make us aware of it

It is sometimes difficult to tell the difference between Nature encounters that are part of our own living environment and those that may actually have a more specific import to us at the time. Experience is the key, and sometimes it is just developing that "inner knowing". Two tangible signals can help us though. First, look for unusual and out-of-the-ordinary encounters. Secondly, if the aspect of Nature is a more direct message or sign we will encounter it in a variety of ways, all within a relatively short time frame. If the aspect has significance for us, we will experience it in different ways and on more than one occasion. We may dream of it and then see it on TV, in stores, magazines and in other ways - all within a few days.

Understanding the Signs and Messages

Recognizing the sign or message is actually the easy part. Understanding it is the difficult part. The subconscious mind controls over 90% of our body's activities. It also monitors and registers everything that goes on around us. If there is an aspect of the natural world that can answer our questions or guide us, the subconscious tries to make us aware of it.

This seems simple enough, doesn't it? Well…not really. There's a small problem. The subconscious cannot speak. It can't use language, so it has to find other ways of communicating to us. It usually communicates to us is through symbols and images. It sends us images through dreams, through certain tarot cards, through imaginings, etc. It makes us notice images and symbols in Nature that it thinks we will understand and be able to use for guidance. Our task is to interpret them.

Learning the language and significance of our Nature encounters is not always easy. This book will help, but the answers are not always readily apparent. Learning any language can be time consuming, and when it comes to a symbolic language, we must guard against superstition.

The difficulty initially though is determining the significance of our encounters. Is this aspect of Nature just part of our normal environment? Or does it have a more direct message for us? And if it does, how do we interpret its meaning within our lives? This is not always easy.

All symbols and images – even those that capture our attention in Nature - will be personal. The image has a meaning that is unique to you. An acorn may be "the seed from which grows the mighty oak" to many people, but maybe as a child, someone threw an acorn at you and hit you in the head. To you the acorn represents pain and possibly an attack by someone. The subconscious knows this and it will use this image to alert you.

Interpreting signs and messages accurately requires practice. You must keep track of what you think things mean and how you feel about them at the time. If they prove themselves out, then the next time that you have a similar communication, you will have a better idea of how to interpret it.

Always begin with what the image means to you. The subconscious will try to make you notice images and symbols that it knows you can relate to. Then ask yourself some simple questions. What do you think about when you think of this thing? What does it bring to mind? How does that fit with what is going on around you? What emotion does it stir in you? Trust your first impression. It will usually be partly accurate. Then consult other possibilities. How would other sources (including this and other books and people) interpret these symbols or images? What do they mean to others?

Focus on what the message is and not when it will happen. Determining the timing of possible events is one of the most difficult areas of psychic development. When things happen is not as important as what is likely to happen when we are learning. Determining what the message is should be our focus. With time and practice, you will begin to get an idea how to figure out when.

Sometimes it will require more effort to determine the meaning. Most elements of nature that stand out will apply to our life on more than a superficial level. They are frequently multidimensional, reflecting things going on in our life on several levels. By studying the element and its qualities in relation to people and issues in our life, we begin the process of determining its significance Begin by asking four significant questions and then proceed to the more in-depth exploration of the meaning:

· When we have the encounter in Nature, what were we focused upon at that time? What were we doing and/or thinking about at that time? What was most on our mind?
· What have we focused most upon in the couple hours prior to the encounter? In the previous 24 hours?
· What major issue(s) are currently present within our life?
· Are there new things you are starting? Have you already take up some new endeavors or activities? Are you about to do so?

In-Depth Guide to Interpretation

When we have significant encounters, it is because that aspect of Nature has something to teach us. It has caught our attention to show us how to accomplish a task, resolve a problem or remind us of what we are capable. Learning to interpret the message effectively will save us a lot of frustration in our endeavors. We increase our chances of success tremendously.

Study the general species of the plant or animal encountered.
All elements of Nature of the same type have qualities in common. All insects go through metamorphosis. All trees have trunks and protective bark. All plants have chlorophyll, creating energy from light. All roses

are soothing to the emotions. All mushrooms reproduce by spores and not by budding. These qualities speak generally to you about something going on in your life or something you should be doing.

Examine the aspect of Nature specifically.

Every individual plant or animal has unique qualities and characteristics that set it apart from the rest of its species. Some require interplay with insects and other animals to seed and reproduce. Some are bisexual. Each has its own unique coloring and applications. Some are annuals (living for only one year) and others are perennials (returning year after year). What would that say about problems or new endeavors in your life? The aspect of the natural world that has caught your attention has qualities specifically beneficial for you and for what is going on in your life. Study it. The information in the dictionaries of this book will help you with that, but do not limit yourself solely to this information.

Examine what is happening in your life.

Look for issues, problems, new activities that you are involved in at the time of the encounter. Are you undertaking new tasks, making changes or moves, trying to solve conflicts and problems? Make a list.

Apply the qualities to what is happening in your life.

Learning to apply a plant's or animal's characteristics and energies to your life and yourself takes practice. It involves analysis, reflection, intuition, some trial and error and even some testing as to whether it truly applies. One of the best ways of doing this is to do some kind of analysis. It doesn't have to be intricate. It can be simply a list of the plant's characteristics along side of a list of issues, activities and endeavors currently on-going within your life. It can also be a bit more formalized, as part of your own personal animal messenger field guide, as described in the Nature Journal exercise earlier.

Getting Simple Answers

*Ask for communications whenever
you start something new.*

When you start something new, take a few minutes to meditate or pray, asking for guidance from some aspect of Nature to watch over the activity. Ask that it make itself known so that you can honor it. When we start to ask, we get our answers.

Be specific in your questions. The more specific you get as to what you should do, the better and more specific the answer will be. When you start applying these answers and when you then study that aspect of Nature, you will gain even more insight and you will start to recognize more and more subtle communications and meanings

Take answer walks in Nature.

If you have a problem, take a walk to find out your answer. Remember, Nature is talking to us all of the time. Most of the time, we miss the communications. If we have a problem or need some guidance, sit and meditate upon it, praying for Nature to provide us with a message. Then take a walk in the woods or in a park. Even take a walk in your neighborhood. Do not talk to others. Reflect on your problem or situation. Make sure the walk lasts about a half an hour.

At the end of the walk, what aspect of Nature stood out or kept appearing? Was a particular fragrance? Maybe you kept smelling pines. Pine fragrance is calming to emotions and feelings of guilt. It may be telling you that you are getting too emotional about the problem. A study of the plant or tree will provide some clues as to its meaning. Was there a particular bird or animal that caught your attention? Maybe there was a blue jay calling off and on. Blue jays often indicate assertiveness and reflect proper and improper uses of power. It might indicate a need to take advantage of the opportunity or to assert yourself more. Do not worry that you might be imagining it all. The particular aspect of Nature would not be catching your attention or coming to mind if it did not have significance for you.

Exercise

The Silent Walk

Benefits:
- **Learning to recognize communications of Nature**
- **Develops the intuition**
- **Strengthens relationship with Nature**
- **Increased knowledge of plants and animals**

The silent walk is a powerful exercise for attuning toNature and the myriad of wonders within it. It is potentially the most powerful exercise we can perform. It is an act of sacred sharing, honor and openness. I included this exercise in my book *The Animal-Speak Workbook*, but it is such a powerful exercise for connecting with Nature that I am including it here as well.

The skill lies in walking in silence, abandoning all words, vocalizations, and any trappings of civilization that are likely to make unnatural noises. The silence and harmony of this activity, especially when performed at dawn or dusk, creates an acute awareness that we share the world with all living things. And ultimately, it will gift us with Nature encounters that fill our hearts with blessed wonder.

This exercise should be performed at dawn or dusk because these are sacred times, times in which the spiritual and physical intersect. They are times when the human and the animal walk through similar corridors. They are also times in which animals are often more active and visible and the spirits of plants, flowers and trees are more discernible.

Prepare for this by giving yourself at least a half-hour of meditation time prior to the walk. The focus should be on quiet attunement to Nature. Choose a location that is somewhat secluded – where there will be no traffic. Old country roads that are seldom traveled and overgrown are good. Choose a park or nature center that has easily-followed trails. Plan on walking a half-hour to forty-five minutes out and then turn around and come back.

Open to the spirit of Nature as you walk. Imagine stepping into Nature as stepping into a new dimension where sights, sounds, smells, etc. have a sacred meaning. Imagine this natural world as a sacred place, an open-air temple, inhabited by spirits. Imagine the spirits of plants and trees. Think of them as greeting you with their colors, textures and fragrances and sounds.

Nature (plants and animals) will sense the energy of a single person or a group, thus the preparatory and solitary meditation. It recognizes disharmony and even unconscious and unintentional disrespect. If animals feel a peace, a harmony that is soft and unthreatening, they do not run away. They do not hide. The animals experienced may move away at your approach, but they do so without the frantic fear that they demonstrate most often when humans approach. They will retreat a few steps at a time, stopping to look over their shoulders, just to satisfy their curiosity. The colors and fragrances of plants will be soft but very strong at these times, standing out more clearly.

If you walk under trees or by bushes, gently touch them. Sense their energy and response to you. Enjoy the beauty and wonder. Try to experience with all of the senses, noting sounds, colors, fragrances and more. Walk slowly and calmly. And remember that you are entering a sacred realm - not as an outsider or possessor of the land but as a distant relative, a cohabitant.

This exercise requires control, sensitivity and a subtle appreciation. It will enhance attunement to the presence of animals not readily encountered or readily visible. Through experiencing Nature in silence, we discover everything is an expression of the Divine Life – including ourselves.

One of Nature's greatest gifts is her endless willingness to teach us about our possibilities and ourselves. Through sacred silence, we experience the wonders and beauty of the environment more intimately, and we begin to realize that every creature and element of Nature mirrors the magnificence of our own soul.

Part Two

Sacred Rites
Of
The Seasons

"To everything there is a season
and a time for every purpose under Heaven.
A time to be born and a time to die;
a time to plant and a time to harvest.
A time to kill and a time to heal;
a time to tear down and a time to build…"

- Ecclesiastes 3: 1-3

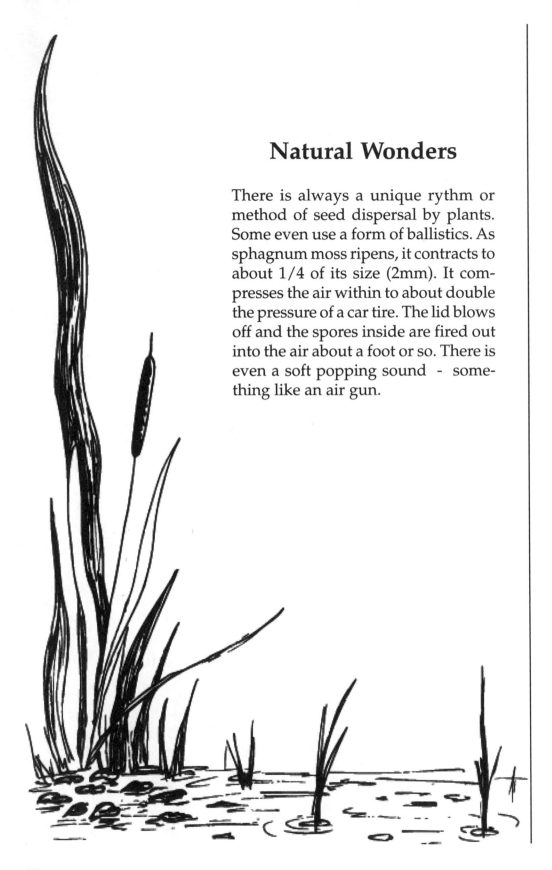

Natural Wonders

There is always a unique rythm or method of seed dispersal by plants. Some even use a form of ballistics. As sphagnum moss ripens, it contracts to about 1/4 of its size (2mm). It compresses the air within to about double the pressure of a car tire. The lid blows off and the spores inside are fired out into the air about a foot or so. There is even a soft popping sound - something like an air gun.

Chapter Four

Magical Rhythms

There are rhythms to life that are stronger than our own. Most ancient and magical traditions realized this. They created ceremonies and initiatory rituals to tap into those rhythms to help strengthen their magical endeavors in the natural world. Some of the most powerful magical rhythms and possibilities occur around the times of the solstices and equinoxes. Every society has taught, at one time or another, the sacredness of the seasons. The ancient mysteries involved teaching the rhythms and cycles of Nature and how to align with them more harmoniously. They also included teaching how to align with the spirits of Nature more easily through celebrations of the sacred seasons.

Each season brings with it a corresponding change in energy that plays upon humanity in very real ways. Within the schools of the ancient mystery traditions, the students would learn of the sacredness of the seasons and the power that was available at such times. Part of our task in unfolding our highest potential will involve aligning our energies with the energies and rhythms of the universe. We must learn to recognize them, align with them and then utilize them to enhance our own life circumstances. If we wish to truly unfold our magical selves and make them stronger, we need to work with the rhythmic power of the seasons.

There are many ways of looking at the year. We can look at it as beginning January 1 and ending December 31. We can look at it as following the planting and harvesting rotation; beginning with the spring, moving through the summer and fall, and culminating with the winter. In many of the ancient societies, the year followed a different course. The year would begin with the autumn equinox, move to the winter solstice, the spring equinox, and then culminate with the summer solstice. As you will learn, this latter rhythm is reflected in Nature. And when used properly, it creates what is called a "Year of The Soul" a time of

*Rhythm is the pulse of life and
it affects all physical energies.
It is found in all life.
It is the heartbeat of Mother Earth.
It is the heartbeat of humans,
animals and plants.
It was almost unthinkable
for an ancient shaman,
medicine person or healer
not to have
a drum or rhythmic instrument
to connect to
the forces of Nature.*

greater opportunity for new soul growth.

In general, the four-day period leading to and including the end of one season and the beginning of the next is a "Holy Interval." It is an intersection of two energies. This creates a vortex, which thins the veils between the spiritual and the physical worlds. This thinning of the veils functions dynamically within the lives of any student of the mysteries. At these times, certain energies can be accessed that cannot be reached at other times of the year. This four-day interval, marking the ending and beginning of the different seasons, is a time when the spiritual forces ascend in their play upon the earth. Each season marks a time when a particular manifestation of the spiritual force of the universe becomes dominant and it influences every atom of life upon the planet. It plays itself out most visibly within the natural world, as a continual reminder to us of what is possible.

The Year of the Soul is a year of concentrated growth and change resulting from aligning with and utilizing the energies available each season. Yes, everyone has years in which there occurs greater soul growth than at other times. It is the task of the true student of the Mysteries though to make each year a Year of the Soul. Each seasonal change then brings with it a new spiritual impulse that will plays within our lives – touching each of us at the atomic level of our energy and providing opportunity for growth and unfoldment.

At each turning point of the year, the gates of the inner spiritual temples and worlds open up to the Earth and release a fresh outpouring of spiritual force upon it. The more we become aware and celebrate such times through our connections with the natural world, the more we can take advantage of those forces to accelerate our growth and enhance our lives. Behind all physical phenomena lie specific archetypal spiritual forces, which is why Nature and the physical sciences were sacred in more ancient times. The ancient wisdoms included religion, science, art, and astronomy. The movement of the stars and the changes of the seasons all reflected specific interplays of energy between the divine worlds and the natural world. Nature is the way in which the Divine has always spoken to humanity.

The four seasons sound forth a call to come higher. They are temporal doorways that heighten our sensitivty to signs, omens and messages in the natural world. They are times for giving birth to new expression of our divine energies, higher clairvoyance and initiation. They are times, which serve to help awaken and utilize the universal energies alive within the natural world for dynamic impulse within our own growth process. And we accomplish this most easily in the world of Nature.

Mundane & Spiritual Aspects of the Seasons

The atomic structure of all life is affected uniquely with each change of the season. Each season has its own spirit or feel to it. A quickening occurs. This quickening gives play to conditions in each person's life for personal opportunities of growth, expression, and transition. Communication with other beings and dimensions occurs with greater ease and occurs more widely. Knowing which energies are in play with each season and how they manifest within the earth environment is the first step to learning to direct them and manifest their effects more dynamically within our lives – to accomplish our own goals more easily and effectively.

Plants and animals face unique conditions with each season and adapt to them accordingly. Seasons do affect plants and animals and how likely we are to have encounters with them and what their messages will be. Examine how the plant or animal that has appeared to you adapts to the season you are in. Most of the time, this adaptation will work for you in your own endeavors throughout this season.

Autumn

The beginning of the Year of the Soul is the autumn equinox. In the natural world, autumn is the time of year when animals prepare for the winter. The plants and animals that come into our life during this time of the year provide clues as to the best kind of preparations we can make for the upcoming winter. Animals instinctively know that food will become hard to find, so many animals store food to eat later in the winter. Most grow a thicker fur to help stay warm or build a winter home or den more suitable for the months ahead. Migration occurs for some species and amphibians and reptiles begin to burrow underground so that the frost can't reach them. Mating occurs in a number of animal species, such as deer, elk and bear. This allows birth to occur late winter and early spring, when the year moves into a more food-abundant time.

In the plant kingdom, trees shed their leaves and many perennial plants lose their outer stems and blossoms. Annuals will begin to die off. There is also a new burst of growth from the "late-bloomers". These late bloomers are often yellow flowers, such as the sunflower, asters, some thistles and goldenrod. The dying plants or parts begin a process of decomposition that ultimately will promote healthy soil and future new growth.

In the fall, the energies play upon humanity, facilitating receptivity to a new spiritual impulse to our lives. It is a time for the harvesting of the old and a time of sowing seeds for the new in our lives as well. Often the messages that come to us through Nature at this time of year will help us in making choices and taking actions along these same lines. Nature is the way in which the Divine has always spoken to humanity.

The fall season is the best time of year to initiate changes. It is the time of the Hero starting the journey. It is the best time to shed the old and start the new. It is a time of sowing seeds to start anything new. It will make new starts stronger and make them more likely to succeed. It is also the ideal time to sow the magical seeds for abundance. The seeds you sow in the autumn will come to fruition for you by the following autumn season - if you work with natural rhythms.

Winter

Winter is the time of the holy birth. Plants and animals face many of the same problems in the winter. Water may be difficult to find; food is in short supply. In addition, warm-blooded creatures must conserve heat, and they must have shelter. Winter migrators build new homes. Metabolisms adjust to conserve energy. Hibernating amphibians wait out the winter by breathing through their skin. How an animal survives the winter often provides directions as to how best we can manage through that season or when we feel winter has come upon us, whether it is by the calendar or not.

Many flowers have left behind pods and dried seed heads. These seeds of autumn germinate and begin expand. Throughout the winter, these pods and seeds begin an alchemical change that will lead to new growth. Sap runs slower, conserving energy. Plants become outwardly dormant, patiently waiting for the warmth of spring to trigger a new release of energy and life.

Many think of winter is a bleak, colorless and lifeless period. The sounds and appearances of wildlife may be less, but that makes them even more precious in the winter. Winter still has many colors if we look. Although not as striking as in other seasons, there are subtle nuances. There is always more than meets the eye during the winter. It is the time of death, hibernation and rebirth. Insects have laid eggs that will be dormant until spring. Plants have stored resources and their root systems wait patiently. There is much invisible activity and it is a reminder to us to be patient in new endeavors. They too need time to germinate properly so that they can sprout forth at the most opportune time.

The winter is one of the best times to tap your inner, magical self.

The energy that is playing upon the Earth during this season makes it easier to meditate and access our psychic ability. Dreams become more vibrant. It is a time though to slow down outer activity, but it is an ideal time to open to contact with spirits guides and angels. It is a strong time for the Magician in us.

Spring

Spring is a time of new growth and resurrection. In the spring as the days become longer, animals become more active. Animals prepare homes for young to be born. Migrant birds return to their breeding grounds. Cold-blooded creatures emerge from their winter hibernation as their body temperature rises with the surrounding warmth. Animals, active or appearing in the spring, often herald a coming forth, and provide clues how to initiate new activities.

In the plant kingdom, wildflowers are the first to appear and are usually growing close to the ground, which provides protection for them against the changing weather patterns common to the spring. Spring beauties begin to appear in damp woods and nearby clearings, heralding a song of promise. Bloodroot begins to emerge from March to May. This plant is a relative of the poppy and is found only in rich leaf mold or nearby streams .Its reddish green stem is a reminder of new blood flows stronger in our life with the new season. Violets, the most common symbol of springtime, appear – as do the mayapples.

In the spring, this force resurrects itself into a new form of expression within our lives. The seeds of the fall that germinated in the winter now begin to burst forth and grow. The spring comes in with an energy that can help us become more of the Warrior. It is a time to assert our efforts and do what we have to do. It is a time to take things to the next step. Creative energies are strong and it's a great time to expand on those things we started in the autumn. It is the time to help our magic along by doing what we can in the physical.

Summer

The seeds then come to fruition in the summer, ripening for the yearly harvest that will come again in the fall. The energies of the previous autumn are fulfilled and consummated in the summer.

In late spring and early summer, many animals give birth to eggs or young. The young must be fed and guarded, and adults are kept busy day and night frequently. Examine your animal's activities during the summer and pattern your own after it. You will find less frustration.

Those animals, which appear in the summer often, reveal the best ways to help things grow and become stronger.

Flowers are in full blossom, showy and tall. The delicate, spring wildflowers of woods don't stay around as now fully clothed trees and foliage block the sunlight from them. A few species still blossom in the open fields and at the edges of clearings. Fruit ripens. Plant life reaches its maturing cycle.

The summer is the culmination of the Year of the Soul. It is a time when we may have to adapt a bit to get the harvest – the results- for what we are working. It is a strong time for the Wise One inside of us. It is a good season for psychic development and for connecting with spirit guides – especially those associated with nature. Any work that we do with relationships of any kind will be easier during this season.

The changes of the seasons are temporal doorways that heighten our sensitivity to signs, omens and messages. They awaken our intuition, making signs & messages much clearer. They stimulate epiphanies.

Magic of the Seasons

Season Keynote	Beneficial Activities

Autumn Equinox

"Beginning the Hero's Journey"
(usually between Sept. 21-23)

endings and beginnings; new starts; clean out old; harvest and abundance; start new changes.

Winter Solstice

"Awakening the Magician"
(usually between Dec. 21-23)

slow down outeractivities; deeper meditations; strong angel contact; intuition; healing; new birth; emotions and dream work.

Spring Equinox

"Asserting the Warrior Within"
(usually between Mar. 21-23)

creative fires; cleansing; greater self-expression; expand new endeavors; new opportunities; rebirth.

Summer Solstice

"Becoming the Wise One"
(usually between June 21-23)

abundance; love; new relationships; uncovering mysteries & magic; contact with nature spirits; awakens hope and psychic vision.

Yearly Cycle of Energies in the Body

All of the ancient traditions teach that both masculine and feminine energies exist within each of us. The task of the spiritual student is to learn to balance and express them creatively within their life circumstances. The early alchemists taught that true illumination and at-onement would be formed from a union of the sun and the moon - a union of the masculine and feminine energies. On one level, this can be seen as a union of the subconscious and the conscious. On another level, it is the union of the centers of light within the body (the chakras) - specifically those of the pituitary (brow) and the pineal (crown). Within these two crown jewels is divine work consummated. And they are key to recognizing signs and omens and to developing accurate prophecy.

The pineal gland is the seat of the masculine energy of the individual. This is known in esoteric tradition as the Sun-Seed. It is the active part of our energy system - necessary if our divine capabilities are ever to be expressed within the physical world. For its full power to be experienced and expressed, the individual must be sufficiently dedicated and spiritualized - and wise enough to know how to activate and use it.

In the course of a year, the masculine energy flows throughout the body, making an annual circuit - similar in many ways to the path of the sun through the heavens. As this flow moves throughout the body, it activates and stimulates other energy centers and currents in accordance with the various seasons.

After the summer solstice, it begins to flow and move. By the time of the autumn equinox, the masculine energy has reached the heart chakra center of the body, helping to attune the energies of the physical body to the rhythms and energies of Nature, as they play upon us and within us at this time of the year.

After the autumn equinox, the masculine energy begins to move. By the time of the winter solstice, it has reached the solar plexus center of the body, stimulating it into greater activity. In the ancient mysteries, this center was termed the "manger" of the human body, or human temple. It is the point of lower birth and illumination, which must always come before the higher birth.

By the time of the vernal equinox, the sun or masculine energy is moving upward, again touching the heart center. In the autumn, it stimulates the heart for a cleansing, but by spring it is stimulating the heart center for a higher expression of its creative forces.

By the time of the summer solstice, the masculine force of the body rises once more to its uppermost position, located at the pineal, to provide greater opportunity for higher illumination. By paying close attention to one's own rhythms and by focusing meditation at these times in directed manners - as we will learn - this circuit is radiated with new life and powers that restore vitality and vibrancy to the body, soul, and spirit.

We have feminine energies within us as well. Just like the masculine, they also make a circuit throughout the body. The feminine energies do not follow the course of the sun, but rather the moon. Each phase of the moon brings a shift and movement of the feminine energies within the individual. It renews itself month by month, but in the course of a single year, this feminine energy can be accumulated through various practices, to give a dynamic power and force to one's life on all levels.

The seat of the feminine energies is the pituitary gland. It will follow a circuit monthly, reflecting the path of the moon around the earth and through the twelve astrological signs. At the new moon, the feminine energy is at home in the pituitary gland (brow chakra). At the quarter phase following the new moon, it moves down to the throat chakra, stimulating this center of higher expression. At the time of the full moon, the feminine energy reaches our center of generation (the base or sacral chakra). This is a critical time. It releases tremendous amounts of energy into the system of the individual. If unaware, this lunar seed power can be easily dissipated and lost through misuse of energies. Through proper meditation, it can be conserved and then lifted once more to the pituitary during the rest of the month. If this is done over the course of the year, a tremendous reservoir of energy accumulates. This can then be used for great alchemical changes in our life and us. It also awakens greater vision and intuitive sensitivity.At the quarter phase following the full moon the feminine energy is drawn back up to the throat chakra, hopefully more energized through its contact with the lower center. Then once more at the time of the new moon it reaches its home at the pituitary.

Many ancient traditions and societies have used the time of the summer solstice to link the male and female together. The feminine energies accumulated over the previous year are united with the masculine energy over the previous year. Through special meditation techniques, the energies are linked at the point of the third ventricle of the brain, the bridge between the pineal and the pituitary. A rainbow bridge is formed that opens up full spiritual consciousness and illumination.

This is the point of the higher manger - the higher birth. The masculine and feminine energies - through the pineal and pituitary glands - are parents in a union that creates new life for the individual - physical and spiritual. The Holy Child within is born.

Angelic Powers of the Seasons

All life is hierarchical. Humanity often does not recognize this due to a myopic view of life. Part of the purpose of the ancient mystery traditions was to open this sight. All traditions taught that there are spirits and even the celestial beings of light, known as the angelic hierarchy, who assist us. Those students who are willing to accelerate their growth and evolution will have the responsibility of extending awareness from individual life rhythms, to the more universal. This will entail a greater understanding and working with those life forms and energies that extend far beyond humanity itself.

Four of the great angelic hierarchy serve as governors of the four seasons. They assist us through each season so that the energy can be experienced in the most beneficial manner. We will explore them more fully in the next few chapters on the sacred rites of the seasons. These four are:

Michael - Autumn Season
Gabriel - Winter Season
Raphael - Spring Season
Auriel - Summer Season

There are others of the angelic hierarchy that also work to assist humanity. They do so in accordance with the rhythms of the seasons and the months in the natural world. Their activities have been carried on since humanity first inhabited the earth. They have gone by many names through the ages, but for our purposes we will refer to them as angels of the zodiac. Unfortunately, few are, or have been, aware of their functions. Their activities were taught to the students of the mysteries in many societies, but to the general public they were less identifiable, or were often attributed superstitious characteristics. They were often thought of as vague spirit forces at play each month.

Astrology is a guide to the interaction of the celestial beings from the higher kingdoms within our own lives. They impact us in subtle, but real, ways. Your astrological chart reveals the relationship between individual planetary and celestial entities and you. The zodiac on one level is a symbol of twelve creative ministrations of the celestial beings, known as angels, within our lives through Nature. The twelve signs of the zodiac reflect twelve great "patterns" of angelic influence. These beings of light called angels work through the signs of the zodiac during the course of year, to effect changes of energy upon the planet and all life. As the individual becomes more attuned to those rhythms, the communion with the beings behind it increases, and the individual's life is filled with blessings. These angelic beings diffuse their energies through the universe and our solar system through the signs of the zodiac and the planets. The more we align with them, the more we can utilize their influence. Just as the seasons reflect the play of cosmic energies in particular patterns upon all life, the months within the season (and their astrological signs) reflect angelic influence that assists in directing that universal energy in ways that can be more effectively used by the us.

Each season brings its own corresponding energy change that manifests most clearly in Nature Each month within that season also has its pattern, directed by the angels of the signs, falling within the particular season. Each season has its predominant energy pattern. Those of the angelic hierarchy who work through a cardinal sign of the zodiac assist the individual in generating the power of the particular season into his or her life. Those of a fixed sign in the zodiac assist the individual in concentrating that newly generated energy, and those of the angelic hierarchy, which works through a mutable sign of the zodiac, assist the individual in distributing the energies of the season into the most appropriate areas of his or her life.

It is important to understand the intimate relationship and influence upon us through the angelic hierarchy of the various signs of the zodiac and the months in which they are most active. They influence everyone in varying degrees but they are experienced and felt most strongly within natural environments. We become more sensitive to them.

Signs of the zodiac in which we have a lot of planets, or particularly those associated with our birth, our ascendant and our moon will have a greater influence upon us as well. We will be more susceptible to the influence of the angelic hierarchy at such times. Thus we need to be aware of how each group directs energies into our lives to assist us in our evolution, and particularly in unfolding our greatest potentials.

Autumn (purification and preparation)

1. The angelic hierarchy working through the sign of Libra assists in generating greater energy for purification and preparationfor the new.

2. The angelic hierarchy working through the sign of Scorpio assists in concentrating the energies of purification and preparation for the new.

3. The angelic hierarchy working through the sign of Sagittarius assists in distributing the energies purification and preparation for the new.

Winter (giving birth to feminine energies)

4. The angelic hierarchy working through the sign of Capricorn assists the individual in generating energy that is more feminine, birthgiving and creative.

5. The angelic hierarchy working through the sign of Aquarius assists the individual in concentrating the generated feminine energies of new birth and creativity.

6. The angelic hierarchy working through the sign of Pisces assist the individual in distributing the newly generated and concentrated creative and birthgiving energies.

Spring (expression of the masculine energies)

7. The angelic hierarchy working through the sign of Aries assists in generating more dynamic expressions of masculine and initiating energy.

8. The angelic hierarchy working through the sign of Taurus assists the individual in concentrating the newly generated masculine and initiating energy.

9. The angelic hierarchy working through the sign of Gemini assists the individual in distributing and expressing the generated and concentrated masculine and initiating energy more productively.

Summer (union of the masculine and feminine)

10. The angelic hierarchy working through the sign of Cancer assists the individual in generating the ability and opportunity to unite the feminine and the masculine for a new expression.

11. The angelic hierarchy working through the sign of Leo assists the individual in concentrating the force of the united energies of the feminine and masculine for a new expression.

12. The angelic hierarchy working through the sign of Virgo assists the individual in distributing and expressing the new birth of energies, culminating from the union of the feminine and masculine forces.

Exercise

Angelic Spirits Throughout the Year

Benefits

- **Improves attunement to Nature**
- **Develops awareness of spirit influence throughout the year**
- **Increases sensitivity to Natures rhythms**

How then does one make oneself more receptive to the influence of this hierarchy as it operates within our lives? It is not as difficult as it seems. It is important, though, to become "ever watchful" as all the masters have cautioned their students. Pay attention to everything within your life. Remember that the occult significance of everything is "hidden" and must be searched out.

The input of the celestial beings within our lives is more available now than at other times. The meditations throughout this book and "the seasonal rites" in the next four chapters will not only explain the spiritual Mysteries of Nature more specifically, as they are reflected within the seasonal changes, but they will help attune the individual to those energies of Nature and to those of the angelic hierarchy, devas and spirits assisting Nature.

Take time each month to reflect upon the season and upon the sign of the zodiac with its corresponding group of celestial beings. Reflect upon their functions. Doing this at the beginning when the sun first enters the new sign is beneficial, as is repeating it at the end of the month, when you can look back over the events of that time period and draw correlations. Remember that they play upon humanity in a pattern that can be discernible for everyone, but they also will behave in a manner specific to you, as you have your own unique energy system.

As the sun moves into a different sign of the zodiac every 30 days or so, there are new influences felt upon the earth. They are subtle and often unrecognized, but we do experience them. Although we will explore these influences more thoroughly in the next few chapters, this exercise will help you in very simply and effectively opening to those influences and empowering your connection to the spirits of Nature.

The astrological zodiac reflects 12 great patterns of angelic influence within our lives every year. The energies are there and changing month to month, whether we are aware of them or not. The angels that work with those energies are there also. The beings of light that we call angels work through the signs of the zodiac throughout the year to create changes upon the planet. As the sun moves into each new sign of the zodiac, a new group of angels comes into play. The signs of the zodiac are call signals to the angels affecting us during the month of that sign.

As you begin to open up more to spirit and the rhythms of Nature throughout the year, you will be able to recognize and work with these monthly angelic influences to help shape your lives more effectively. To help you with this, I have provided some basic information on how the angels can help us throughout the year, based on astrology. These angels can be called upon anytime throughout the year, but they are most effective during their specific month. The symbol or glyph for the sign of the zodiac is a call signal to the spirits and angels of that sign. Meditating with it is like ringing their doorbell. The other information will help you see what is best to focus upon during that month.

The classical composer's music, when meditated with, will help open the doors to the angels of that sign more clearly. Playing it softly in the background invites the angels into your life. Most of the music can be checked out of the local library. Do not worry if you cannot find the specific musical composition. Choosing something else by the composer will still help.

Guidelines for the Angelic Zodiac

1. Read through the information for the sign of the zodiac whose month you are in.
2. Decide how you would like the angels of that sign to help you and with what.
3. Create a sacred space, preferably outside where you can sit quietly and be undisturbed.
4. Close your eyes and visualize a doorway in front of you. In the center of the door is the symbol for the sign of the zodiac.
5. Imagine yourself touching that symbol. As you do it begins to glow

and the door opens. On the other side is an angel for the month.

6. In your mind, greet this spiritual being and ask for its help. Carry on a conversation with this angel. Don't try to control it. Just let it happen.

7. Then imagine the angel embracing you. Feel the angel's energy pouring into you and your life. Thank the angel.

8. The door closes and then fades from view.

9. Perform a grounding exercise.

10. This works best if done two days in a row near the beginning of each new sign. It can be done anytime though throughout the month for extra help.

♈ Angels of Aries (March 22-April 21)

- Angelic Keynote: new beginnings
- Music: Johann Sebastian Bach (Brandenburg Concertos)

Aries angels assist us in new endeavors. They help us to become more assertive and develop self-control. They assist in developing greater effort in creating our magical personality. They also help us to overcome obstacles. They are the keepers of magical beginnings.

♉ Angels of Taurus (April 22 – May 21)

- Angelic Keynotes: life and freedom
- Music: Peter Ilich Tchaikovsky (Swan Lake)

Taurus angels help us with change and new expressions of our abilities. They assist in overcoming selfishness in those around us or us, and they create opportunities to follow higher aspirations. They stimulate creativity and help us to experience more of the pleasures and beauty in life. They are the keepers of magical fertility.

♊ Angels of Gemini (May 22 – June 21)

- Angelic Keynotes: faith and devotion
- Music: Edvard Grieg (Hall of the Mountain King)

Gemini Angels help us develop the power of silence while also helping us communicate better. They help us hear our inner, psychic voice and can reveal the Faerie Realm. They teach us the power of humor and versatility. They are the keepers of the magic of thoughts and words.

♋ Angels of Cancer (June 22 – July 21)

- Angelic keynote: spiritual vision
- Music: Gustav Mahler (Eighth Symphony)

Angels of Cancer help us with things of home and family. They help us to develop our psychic ability and help us control our emotions. They often come to us through dreams and visions when called upon during this month. They help us create powerful sacred spaces. They are the keepers of magical places and times.

♌ Angels of Leo (July 22 – August 21)
- Angelic keynote: power and creativity
- Music: Achille Claude Debussy (Afternoon of a Faun)

Angels of Leo help awaken our own dynamic creativity. They can help find what is hidden and help reveal it. They are beneficial to call upon when leadership abilities are necessary. They are the keepers of the magic and power of creativity.

♍ Angels of Virgo (August 22 – Sept. 21)
- Angelic keynote: patience, inspiration and organization
- Music: Johann Sebastian Bach (Gounod Ave Maria)

Angels of Virgo help awaken our magical sparks. They help us find the meaning in confusing life situations. They bring wisdom. They inspire ability to organize and can outline steps to improve our health. They help us learn patience and understanding, which leads to wisdom in whatever field we pursue. They are keepers of the magic of knowledge.

♎ Angels of Libra (Sept. 22 – Oct. 21)
- Angelic keynote: balance and beauty
- Music: Giuseppe Verdi (Nabuco)

Angels of Libra help us to maintain balance when life begins to rock us. Calling upon them helps bring justice and calm into our life. They help us to see the inner, hidden beauty in others and ourselves and stimulate artistic inspiration. They teach us what needs to be done for harmony. They are the keepers of the magical power of **art.**

♏ Angels of Scorpio (Oct. 22 – Nov. 21)
- Angelic keynote: transformation
- Music: Franz Liszt (Hungarian Dances)

Scorpio Angels awaken deep psychic perceptions. They inspire us to seek out hidden knowledge and can reveal secret activities around us. They help keep the spirit strong in times of difficulty. They help us transform things in our life that need it. They stimulate strength and help us to problem solve. They are the keepers of the magic of desire.

✗ Angels of Sagittarius (Nov. 22 – Dec.21)

- Angelic keynote: applying wisdom
- Music: Ludwig Von Beethoven (Ninth Symphony)

Sagittarius Angels help expand our perceptions. They reveal immense possibilities – if there is proper focus. They can reveal the wisdom of everyday events. They help us to trust our own inner wisdom. They are the keepers of the magic found through sacred quests.

♑ Angels of Capricorn (Dec. 22 – Jan. 21)

- Angelic keynote: persistence in dreams
- Music: Charles Wakefield Cadman (Shanewis)

Capricorn Angels awaken our dreams and our ability to go within ourselves. They show us how to climb to the top, through proper effort and persistence. They show us and help us with our responsibilities. They can awaken astral travel, teach the importance of blending the earthly with the spiritual. They are the keepers of the magic found in pursuit of dreams.

♒ Angels of Aquarius (Jan. 22 – Feb. 21_

- Angelic keynote: science and magic
- Music: Franz Schubert (Symphony in B Minor)

Aquarius Angels help us blend the old wisdom with the new sciences. They stimulate new thought and new ideas to old concepts. They inspire new approaches to problems and difficulties. They heighten our intuition and show us how to blend new science and old magic. They are the keepers of the magic in tools.

♓ Angels of Pisces (Feb. 22 – March 21)

- Angelic keynote: healing and sacrifice
- Music: Georg Friedric Handel (The Messiah)

Pisces Angels awaken the healing power within us. They show us how sacrifice does not mean the same as suffering. They stimulate spiritual vision and psychic ability. They can reveal our karma (what we have come to do and how it can best be done). They help us to move forward on faith. They are the keepers of the magic and power in spiritual visions

Angelus Preposterus

Extant literature often describes unusual angelic and spirit ceremonies. The following chart provides the specific month in which a particular angel has been invoked in more ancient times for less than honorable purposes. The angel could only be called upon for this purpose with the proper ritual and only during that particular month in its season.

Aries - Machidiel (invoked to send a maiden or man of your desire - kind of an angelic matchmaker)

Taurus - Asmodel (fallen angel invoked to punish others)

Gemini - Ambriel (invoked in spells to ward off evil or conjure evil - twin purposes)

Cancer - Muriel (called upon to procure a magic carpet)

Leo - Verchiel (invoked for the power to rule - Lord's Day rite)

Virgo - Hamaliel (had dominion over water and was invoked in love charms by those thirsting for love)

Libra - Zuriel (invoked as a cure for stupidity)

Scorpio upon - Zophiel (God's spy – fallen but not evil, called to spy on others)
Riehel (invoked to finds lost objects)

Sagittarius - Adnachiel / Anakimel (invoke to call forth giants who were the offspring of fallen angels and mortal women)

Capricorn - Haniel (companion to Ishtar, invoked to help transport the person to other worlds)

Aquarius an - Cambriel (invoked as a personal guardian, like angelic body guard)

Pisces - Barchiel (The"lightning of God" was invoked for success in games of chance)

Exercise

Angel of the Season
Talisman

Benefits:

- **Angelic protection**
- **Illuminating and strengthening to the aura**
- **Strengthens connection to seasonal energies/ forces**
- **Heightens perception of signs and messages**

Talismans are objects that we carry or wear that have magical qualities to them. They are also called charms. They are imprinted with a specific magical energy or purpose. They can also be symbols of specific magical energies we wish to attract. The St. Christopher medal and the rosary are two such talismans. Anyone who wears a cross about the neck is using a talismanic image. It is a physical reminder of one's beliefs. Talismans serve as reminders and stimulators of creative forces.

Many of the oldest charms are derived from stones, feathers and herbs – things of nature. We know today that crystals have a form of electrical energy. Different crystals have different frequencies, and thus can be used for different things including helping us connect to spirits. There are many books available on how to use stones and crystal for protection and other purposes, so we will not be examining them here.

Talismans serve several purposes. They remind us of our magical connection to the mysterious dimensions of the universe and Nature. They help us to recognize and to connect with those forces, and they help us bridge to those magical forces of the universe.

But how do they work? They are imprinted with energy of a specific type, that we can carry or wear to give ourselves an extra boost when we need it. One way of looking at it is to think of it as a portable sacred space. By wearing it, its energy envelops us. The drawback though is that its effectiveness is limited by how much we have charged it and how much we draw upon it. It's like a battery that serves a specific purpose for a time, but that battery can run down and will need cleaning and recharging.

The most effective talismans and amulets are those which are personally made. The process is very simple, but you must focus on why you are making them. The more significance you associate with the images and symbols you use, the better they will work for you. You must know what everything on the talisman represents.

We will create a simple angelic amulet that we can wear for angelic protection. It will envelop us in angel energy and remind us of our connection to them while we wear it. You will need the information on the symbolism of the four major archangels for this talisman.

Talismans and amulets can be made of various materials: parchment, wood, paper, cloth. Clean cotton is easy to work with. One side of our angelic amulet will have symbolism associated with a particular archangel for each season, and the other side will be personalized. It can have your name or some symbol that represents you. Be as creative as possible.

During the Holy Interval of each seasonal change, wear this to help strengthen your own alignment with the archangel, overseeing the forces of Nature throughout the coming season. Wearing it during the sacred rites of the seasons, described in the next four chapters will also benefit your connection to the forces of Nature coming into play with the new season. You can also wear it throughout the season or whenever you are out in Nature, to further empower your connection to Nature and to heighten your perception of signs and messages that are important to you.

1. Choose an archangel to work with. You can even include all of them on the talisman.

2. Take your cloth – either white cotton or the color associated with the archangel you have chosen. Draw on it a double circle, each about two inches in diameter about a half an inch apart.

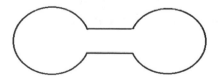

3. On one of the two circles in the center draw the sigil, or name signature of the archangel. This is a symbol representing the name of the angelic being. It is derived from old Qabalistic teachings and magical working with the Hebrew alphabet. You may wish to draw the sigil in the color associated with the archangel or even sew it on using appropriate colored thread. It is one of the most ancient and power calls to these archangels.

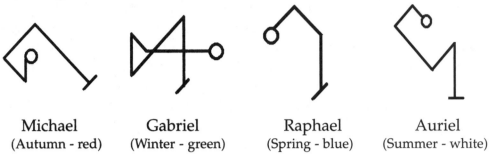

Michael	Gabriel	Raphael	Auriel
(Autumn - red)	(Winter - green)	(Spring - blue)	(Summer - white)

4. Arrange other symbols that you find comforting around it. In the sample, I used the phases of the moon, to represent angelic protection in all phases and at all times.

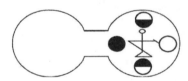

5. On the other circle draw or sew symbols personal to you. In the example, I used the Dragonhawk Publishing logo.

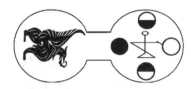

6. Cut the talisman out of the cloth. Do not cut the circles out separately. Leave them connected by a half-inch square section of cloth. Fold the talisman at the half-inch square section and align the two circles so that the markings and symbols are facing out.

7. Before sewing the two circles together, you may wish to place something in between them. Herbs, incense, oil, a small crystal, anything that may help and also reflect your purpose.

8. Sew around the edges of the circle, binding the front and the back together. The half-inch square now forms a loop through which we can slip a necklace of some sort and wear the talisman around our neck.

9. It is important to stay focused on the task. Once you start, do not stop until finished. See and feel it coming alive, activating its corresponding archetypal forces. Visualize the symbols as you work on each step, and see each symbol awakening energy to help you.

10. At its completion, perform a small blessing and meditation ritual with it. Smudging it or running it through cleansing incense is even more effective. You may want to put a drop or two of essential oil or flower elixir to amplify its effects. Angelica flower elixir is good for this.

11. Place the talisman over your head. Feel its energy come alive. Feel the archangelic influence surrounding you and embracing you. I recommend keeping it in your magic chest when it is not needed or being worn.

12. Putting it on at the beginning of your seasonal meditations, Nature walks and other magical practices is a wonderful way of opening up the veils to the spirit world of Nature. Taking it off and placing it back in your magic chest is a way of closing the veils and grounding yourself.

Front of Talisman   Back of Talisman

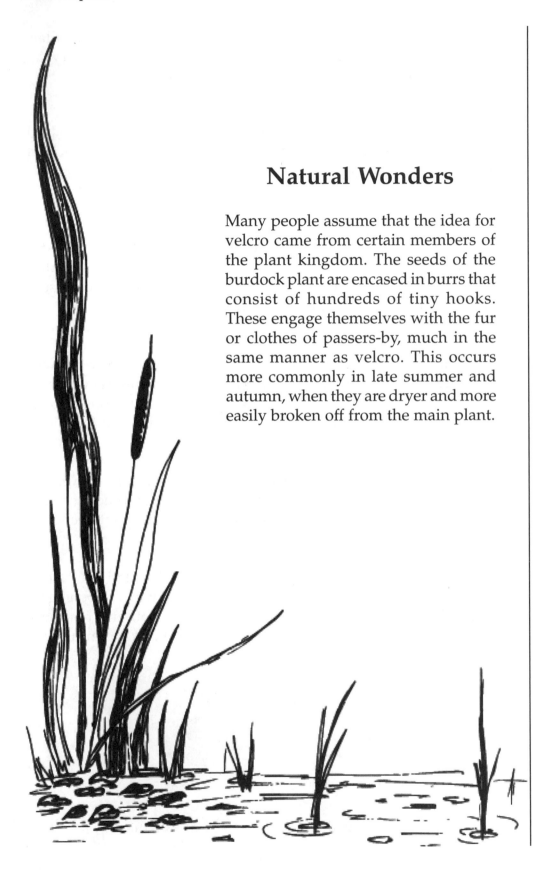

Natural Wonders

Many people assume that the idea for velcro came from certain members of the plant kingdom. The seeds of the burdock plant are encased in burrs that consist of hundreds of tiny hooks. These engage themselves with the fur or clothes of passers-by, much in the same manner as velcro. This occurs more commonly in late summer and autumn, when they are dryer and more easily broken off from the main plant.

Chapter Five

Rite of the Autumn Equinox

Nature's energies and its spiritual forces affect us in varying ways with each season, manifesting subtle changes and opportunities for those who are aware. Autumn is the time in which Nature's energies facilitates the process of purifying one's life and for the planting of new seeds and endeavors. The fall season is a time to determine new values, and to make new decisions and goals. It is a harvesting and assessment time for what has passed in the previous year, and it is a time for setting new goals for the coming year. It is a time in which the energies influencing all of humanity are most appropriate for purifying the mind and for transmuting that which would hinder the full and highest expression of the divine within us. This enables the energies that are set in motion through the rest of the year to be fully taken advantage of.

The autumn season holds an energy that aids in purifying and transmuting the lower, for overcoming obstacles and in preparing our creative life forces for regeneration. It is a time for harvest and spiritual recapitulation. It is a time for shedding the old to prepare for the new. It is a time of transition and to initiate transition. If attuned to properly, it manifests opportunities for needed changes and needed purification.

The fall season sets in motion an energy that facilitates communion with the angelic hierarchy that can build over the course of the year. (As we will explore later within this chapter, many of those of the angelic hierarchy work with the rhythms of the seasons and through the various signs of the zodiac to facilitate the growth of humanity.) This season also provides opportunity to balance the physical and the spiritual. Our dreams often reveal much during this season about measuring and determining our values. The season also brings some degree of testing

*"Within Nature
is the adventure
of the occult -
that which is hidden.
Through the sacred quests and
cycles of the seasons,
we discover
that we are not part of the world.
We are the world."*

one's judgment. There is a reaping of past sowing, along with opportunity for sowing next year's harvest. Whatever seeds are sown in the fall season will come to fruition by the following fall.

How these energies will interact specifically in the life of the individual will vary; thus it is important to be as watchful of events in one's life at this time as one can. These energies perform in such a way that, during the three days prior and the day of the autumn equinox, everyone's etheric bodies are drawn back into alignment with the physical. This provides opportunities for healing, balancing, and greater strengthening of the physical. It also opens the etheric realm to more conscious sight. This is augmented tremendously through journeys and visits to Nature. It is a time of preparation so that the gifts of the Divine Feminine can be conceived more easily within the winter season. It is next asserted and expressed through a new vibrancy of the masculine energies in the spring, and then united with the Divine Masculine to give birth to the Divine Child within us during the summer.

The autumn equinox opens the cycle of the Year of the Soul for one who wishes to attune to the true mysteries of Nature. The force playing upon the planet varies with the season, each manifesting subtle changes and opportunities for those who are aware. It is like planting a seed that over the following seasons and months will germinate, take root, sprout and then be harvested.

The Spiritual Mysteries of Autumn

The atomic structure of all life alters its vibrational frequency with each change of the season. This creates opportunities for growth, expression and transition in each person's life. Communication with other beings and dimensions occurs more widely and with greater ease. Knowing the energies in play at each season is the first step to learning to direct them, to manifest their effects powerfully within life. Learning to attune to these energies has been part of many mystery traditions.

Behind all physical phenomena lie specific spiritual archetypes, which is why the physical sciences were sacred in times that are more ancient. The wisdom of Gnosis and Sophia comprised religion, science, art and especially astronomy. The movement of the stars and the changes of the seasons all reflect specific interplays of energy between the divine and the physical. Each month is a miniature duplication of what occurs within the course of a year. The four phases of the moon reflect the four seasons - a continual reminder to keep the sacredness of the seasons alive.

To the Western world, the mysteries of Egypt were handed down through Greece and its masters (Orpheus, Pythagoras, Plato, Aristotle, etc.). The Greeks recognized that humanity was strongly affected by two stars. These two stars are more visible at the changes of the seasons. The first, Sirius, is more active at the time of the solstices, and the second, Alcyone, is more active and visible at the time of the equinoxes.

The ancient Egyptians ascribed to the autumn equinox the origin of all evil. This is, of course, symbolic. It is the time of the sacrificing of the present for the future. The autumn is a time of transition, a time, which offers opportunities to change, purify, and transmute the conditions of one's life. Each student of the ancient mysteries must approach the sacred festivals of the seasons from his or her own point of evolvement. In more ancient times, the autumn was a time of serious recapitulation. It is the ideal time to assess the past year's experiences and determine changes still needed. It is a time to plant new seeds for the coming year.

The energy of the autumn equinox is felt weeks before the actual event. When the sun enters the sign of Virgo, it is the time of the Immaculate Conception, a concept found in a number of mystery traditions besides the Christian. The earth and any individual upon it can prepare themselves for a new cycle of growth within his or her life. As the sun moves into Libra, energy begins to affect the whole surface of the Earth. The energies of plants are drawn inward. Within us, energy is drawn inside to cleanse the heart, so that a new birth can unfold at the time of the winter solstice. Then, within the course of the rest of the year, this birth will be brought out into greater expression.

The autumn forces become active, in a manner that triggers opportunities for transition. Its energies create a time to determine new values and make new decisions. It is the harvesting time for what has previously passed; a time for purifying the mind and to begin the process of transmuting that which needs transmuted. Because of this, the three days prior to and the day of the autumn equinox are the most powerful, but every day of the fall is the time of holy preparation.

During this time of the year, the energies can assist us in the following ways:

-   In purifying and transmuting the lower.
-   In overcoming obstacles and sewing new seeds
-   In opening the inner temples of awareness.
-   In cleansing and purifying the heart chakra, the seat of much karma.
-   In more easily turning our attention from the outer to the inner worlds, thus aligning with spirits of Nature and the angelic kingdom.
-   In determining what still needs to be transmuted for the greatest growth in the coming year.
-   In developing harmony between the laws of love and karma.
-   In initiating a time of weighing, measuring, determining values, and decisions for the physical and spiritual life of the individual.
-   In manifesting opportunities to reap the rewards of past sowing, and to sow seeds for the future.

For anyone who begins aligning with the force available at this time of year, it will serve as a catalyst. Throughout the season on the lower consciousness, it will be a testing time for the soul. For all who do align with its force, though, it brings the individual opportunities for preparation, the development of judgment, and opportunity for renunciation. For some it may bring the "test of Abraham" - a willingness to give up that which is most sacred. It is important to keep in mind that when the tests are passed, there is always spiritual compensation and there is always special assistance and spiritual guidance during this time. That guidance and assistance is strongest through contact with Nature.

Michaelmas & Angels of the Season

Spiritual guidance comes from two main sources during the autumn season. First, there is the dynamic assistance of the governor of this season, the Archangel Michael. He provides protection and balance to those who align with the power and mysteries of Nature through the yearly cycle of the soul. The second surce of guidance comes from the hierarchy of angels working through the signs of the zodiac.

In orthodox Christianity, the Feast of St. Michael falls at the time of the autumn equinox. As we will see, this is most appropriate, for we need someone of great strength to assist us in balancing and transmuting our lives. The work of Michael has always been for purity and transmutation. Initiation is now open to all, and Michael is the Initiate Companion of every student of the Mysteries of the Holy Grail, which are the Mysteries of Alchemy, the Mysteries of Transmutation, the Mysteries of Nature.

Michael is the Prince of Splendor and Wisdom, the great protector. He is also called the Prince of Light. He brings to all the gift of patience. Michael is often given the title of "Dragon Slayer." This has great significance in regard to the process of "Meeting the Dwellers upon the Threshold". This is a process of facing those aspects of ourselves that we have ignored, pretended didn't exist, hidden or just denied. One must remember, though, that Michael did not slay the dragon. Michael drove the dragon to the depths of hell. Dragons are not meant to be slain. They are meant to be controlled and transmuted.

This great being of light has a long occult tradition concerning his influence in the evolution of humanity. He has been a part of almost every society's scriptures and esoteric lore. He was known as Marduk of Babylon who slew Tiamut, Apollo who slew Pytho, and St. George who slew the dragon. To the ancient Hebrews he was the "countenance of Jehovah." Esoteric tradition teaches that Michael hovered over Christ Jesus at Gethsemane, assisting him in transmuting the earth streams of hate and despair into currents of love and healing. The Chaldeans worshipped him as something of a god: "Who is as God." He is believed to be the author of Psalm 85 and is in the Dead Sea Scrolls. He was also guardian at the times of Lao Tse, Confucius, Buddha, Zoroaster, Pythagoras, Ezekiel, and Daniel. Lore and tradition also speaks of how Michael oversaw the teaching and training of Arthur and the knights of England to perpetuate those mysteries.

Michael works with others of the angelic hierarchies to transmit divine consciousness into the minds of humanity through greater knowledge. A group of the angelic hierarchy, working through the planet of Mercury assists him in initiating the more advanced of humanity into the higher truths necessary for spiritual leadership in the times to come. They work to teach individuals self-mastery, and they work to teach us to leave and re- enter the physical body at will (conscious out-of-body experiences). To the early Egyptians and Greeks, Mercury was considered the "captain of the planets." Mercury touches every sign of the zodiac in its revolution around the sun in the course of one year. It is a symbol of illumined reason, which Michael comes to stimulate each autumn.

In some esoteric traditions, Michael is associated with the planet Saturn. Saturn is the Great Mother, the Great Teacher. One tradition speaks of how Saturn is where the Spiritual Hierarchy for this solar system gathers, and it is Michael who oversees it. In many traditions, he has been known by different names, serving a variety of functions on the behalf of humanity.

The student of Ancient mysteries would do well to spend time meditating upon Michael and his work, particularly upon the images of the Flaming Sword and the repelled Dragon. The dragon is the lower self, the untransmuted elements of the soul, and Michael aids in transmuting such. To those aligned with the full power and significance of this season, Michael assists in the great overcoming. He acts within your life to assist in purifying so that greater illumination of the intellect will occur. He works to help the individual manifest opportunities to transmute the dragons of their lives.

Angelic Hierarchy of Autumn

Angels of Libra

This group of the celestial hierarchy work to assist us in unfolding our latent spiritual potentials. Its symbol is a scale - the balance - the lesson of polarity in the ancient Mysteries, including the Gnostic Christian tradition.. They work upon the astral and etheric bodies of humanity. They oversee what is often called the "Trial Gate of Choices." They assist us during this month to awaken intuitive perception as to how best to balance our life. Messages in Nature during this month often reflect this. Their messages through the natural world reveal to us conflicts in spirit and personality. They guide us in expressing fiery passions in a more balanced manner. Their messages and signs through Nature also stimulate increasing ability to weigh opposites and attain balance through higher expressions of love. They guide us in opening and moving through human love to devotion and aspiration and on to higher understanding. They awaken the search for balance.

Angels of Scorpio

These beings of light work to keep the human spirit strong. During this month, the signs they provide in Nature give instruction and assistance in transmutation of our own energies - the most advanced work of the spiritual initiate. Transmutation is a stage of initiation. These beings assist the student of the Mysteries in learning to re-orient the self to the life and energy of the soul. They will guide us as to the best ways to manifest opportunities for new endeavors and stages in our life. Their messages in Nature reveal how best to demonstrate increasing sensitivity. During the fall season, they reveal any lack of unity, any selfishness, or any conflict or duality in our life. They often reveal how to become a spiritual fighter so that a higher unity may manifest through the course of the year.

Angels of Sagittarius

In the final month of the fall season, the angelic hierarchy working through Sagittarius comes into play. It is their task to awaken in us a more directed and focused light. They assist us in developing our own beam of light that will illuminate our environment and activities in the months ahead. Their messages in Nature often direct us away from the untrained and materialistic aspect of our lives - especially when they come to the forefront during this time. They assist us in developing freedom in thought and single-pointedness and guide us in the besty ways of overcoming purifying lower ambitions. Their messages in Nature often help us to recognize and overcome self-centeredness in any area of our life. One of the paths that may open to the true student of the mysteries is that known as the "Path of the Beneficent Magician." In this path, the individual learns to work with the law of supply and to become the true "sower" in all of its esoteric significance. And this is one of most important lessons found within Nature.

Autumn Tales

One of the best ways of opening to the the energies and rhythms of the season is by reading and even meditating on myths, tales and stories that reflect those energies. Take a day periodically throughout the fall season and and read some of these tales outside. They can even be used in meditation prior to your "answer walks" to help you connect with Nature's messages more clearly.

Imagine yourself as the hero/heroine of the story, and watch how the power of words magnifies the the messages of the unspoken language of Nature.

- Myths and tales of dragons and fantastic creatures
- Tales of the Archangel Michael slaying the dragon
- Tales of St. George and thedragon
- Greek tale of Ixion
- Masonic legend of Hiram Abiff
- Biblical book of Ruth
- Greek tale of Persphone
- Egyptian tales of Horus
- Tale of Parsifal and the Grail Knoghts
- Milton's *Paradise Lost*
- Biblical tale of Jopseph being sold into slavery
- Nigerian tale of "Nana Miriam"
- Apache myth of "Wild Pony"
- Native American tale of "Changing Woman"
- Grimm's tale of "Snowdrop"
- West African tale ""The Great Mwindo Epic"
- Arabian tales "Voyages of Sinbad"
- Greek tale of the "Odyssey"
- Native American tales of "Grandmother Spider"
- Any hero tales and myths

Exercise

Rite of the Autumn Equinox

Benefits:

- **Increases ability to call upon Nature for protection**
- **Invites opportunities to clean out what is no longer beneficial**
- **Opens doors to practical healing wisdoms of the natural world**
- **Invites change and new beginnings**

This exercise, if performed on the three days prior to and the day of the autumn equinox, will release energy into our life that will manifest opportunities for purification and preparation. This time frame is one in which the veil between the physical and the spiritual is the thinnest, and it is easiest to access energies for awakening Nature's Mysteries throughout the rest of the season. It can also be repeated as the sun moves into the other signs of the zodiac associated with the autumn season (Scorpio and Sagittarius).

If this meditation serves as a catalyst for too many or too intense changes within your life, it can be softened through meditation and focus upon Michael - particularly upon the image of Michael extending to you the Flaming Sword of Spiritual Law and Discrimination. It is an image, which will invoke extra assistance, strength and balancing. It will also invoke stronger and clearer messages from the natural world. Keep in mind, though, that the more we purify and prepare through the fall, the more we will give birth to throughout the rest of the year.

This meditation will also stimulate opportunity for change and opportunity to sow new seeds. Before you participate in it, make sure that you want to trigger such within your life. There is an old saying: "Be careful what you ask for, for that is what you will receive." This is an exercise, which asks and invokes the spiritual energy of the autumn season to act more dynamically within your life.

The most effective time to perform this exercise in this four day Holy Interval is at a time of intersection - dusk or dawn, prior to sleeping or upon awakening. On the day of the equinox, perform it as close to the actual time as possible. It will have a powerful effect. If you cannot do so at these times, at least find some time to do it each of the four days.

Four is the number and rhythm of a new foundation. This is a foundation of new energy that you are invoking into your life to use in the coming year to awaken and express greater potentials and creativity. Feel free to adjust the meditation to yourself. We each must approach the energies of the seasons and their mysteries from our own point of perspective and evolution.

Preparations
1. Make sure you will be undisturbed.

2. If you choose to meditate with candles, use candles in the colors of autumn - brown, green, russet.

3. Ears of corn and corn husks (such as are often found in Halloween decorations), add to the energy and symbology of the meditation.

4. This can be an effective meditation to perform outdoors, at dusk.

5. The images are powerfully invoking to the archetypal energies of Nature as they manifest through the autumn.

6. Allow yourself to relax, and as you do, feel yourself lifting slowly and gently up toward the heavens. The stars are brilliant, filling the dark night sky with diamond sparkles. In the distance is one star, which stands out among the rest. It scintillates with a brilliancy that shimmers and pours streams of light down below it.

Meditation
As you float gently through the heavens, your eyes trace the path of light from this one great star to the earth beneath. There on top of a high mountain, overlooking the earth, is a temple. The light from the star outlines the four columns that separate the inner from the outer. From your height, it appears in the shape of a cross, with one column standing in each of the four directions.

You begin to feel yourself gently descending, and ever so softly, you come to rest in the soft grass outside this grand temple. You stand before the doors. Emblazoned into the massive frame above it is a large flaming sword. As you step to the door, the sword begins to glow brighter and a sound fills the night air, making the earth and yourself tremble.

You step back from the door, and as you do, the earth on either side of it rips open and two large trees burst forth. The limbs and branches stab in every direction, twisting and entwining, until the door to the temple is barely visible and virtually impassable. The trees are growth gone astray. There is no form or shape. They twist and entangle, knotted together, preventing any further growth. They have grown wild and are beginning to suffocate the growth of each other.

The sounds soften and then there is silence. You stand before the blocked doorway of the temple, unsure what the next step should be. Within that silence comes the answer. A soft light begins to form between you and the trees. It is a soft pastel red that grows into a mighty column of light extending from the earth into the heavens. A gust of wind blows across you, and the column shimmers, shrinks and there stands before you a beautiful being of great strength and light. The eyes are steely and strong. Dressed in robes of the colors of autumn leaves-russets and reds-he holds your attention. Within his hand is a sword, which is more light than substance. Mingled with the energy of his essence, you cannot help but feel the strength about him. You wonder how he is able to control such force, and he smiles as if reading your thoughts.

He waves his hand at his feet and a great hole within the earth opens. You can see deeply within the heart of the earth and beyond. There within the depths was a powerful and magnificent dragon of red and gold. With each breath, light and energy of primal force pour forth from it towards all life upon the earth. Michael raises the Flaming Sword over this primal energy as it rises up and softens and surrounds him, pours through him and out from him in blessings of strength and love to all.

"We each must face our own dragons. We each must face that which we most fear. As we learn to transmute our dragons we give birth to light and love. As we learn to wield the Flaming Sword of spiritual law and discrimination within every aspect of our lives, we control the dragons rather than being controlled by them."

He waves his hand over his feet again, and the image disappears. You look at him, drawing strength from his gentle words. He steps to the side of the temple doors. "Before all are the trees of Life and Knowledge. Before you enter into the inner temple, the trees must be pruned, trimmed. Just as a bush is pruned in the autumn so that it may grow greener and more fruitful in the spring, so must your life be pruned. Look upon these trees and see within their tangled mess what must be pruned and trimmed from your own life for greater fruitfulness."

You gaze into the two trees, tangled and knotted. You see the people and situations, the habits, behaviors, attitudes, and knowledge that is blocking your own growth. As you look upon the two trees, you see all that you must do to untangle your life. You begin trimming and pruning the tree, one branch at a time. The task seems great - even overwhelming.

"We are never faced with more than we can handle."

The soft words break the reverie and fill you with encouragement. "Now look again."

You look at the trees once more. No longer are they entangled and knotted. They are trim, full and green. There are blossoms, hinting of the fruit they will bear in the future. The doors to the Inner Temple are no longer obstructed. Slowly they swing open, and a golden light and a chorus of song surrounds you. You see an altar upon which rests an equal-armed cross. In the middle of the cross is a large white rose. A light shines down upon it from above, and you remember the star whose beam of light led you to this temple. Before the altar stands a magnificent being of shimmering rays of blue and gold light. He turns, acknowledging silently your presence. He slowly raises a Golden Chalice - the Grail of Life - to the heavens in silent prayer.

The door closes slowly, leaving you only with the joy of a memory that has emblazoned itself upon your heart. Michael - stands before you, his look tender and loving. "With strength, we all must prepare that we may enter the inner temples of the mysteries of the Divine. There was a time, though, when each had to accomplish it alone, but that time has passed. Today there is guidance and strength from many sources for those who will open their hearts."

He raises his flaming sword and softly touches your breast with its point. He closes his eyes and intones a word both foreign and familiar. You feel your heart seared with the light of the Flaming Sword. You look down upon your breast, and you see within your heart center your own Sword of Truth aflame.

"When you touch the heart and when you imagine the Flaming Sword within, I will come. For as you awaken to the Divine within and learn to express it without, you become a Son or Daughter of the Flaming Sword."

His sword grows blindingly bright, encasing you in light, and then fades. As it does, you find yourself alone outside of the Temple, but you feel the warmth of the Flaming Sword alive within your heart. You look to the sky and see the one star that led you to this moment. As you look upon it, you feel yourself lifting up gently once more into the heavens, carrying forth the energy of purification and preparation for entrance into Nature's inner temples.

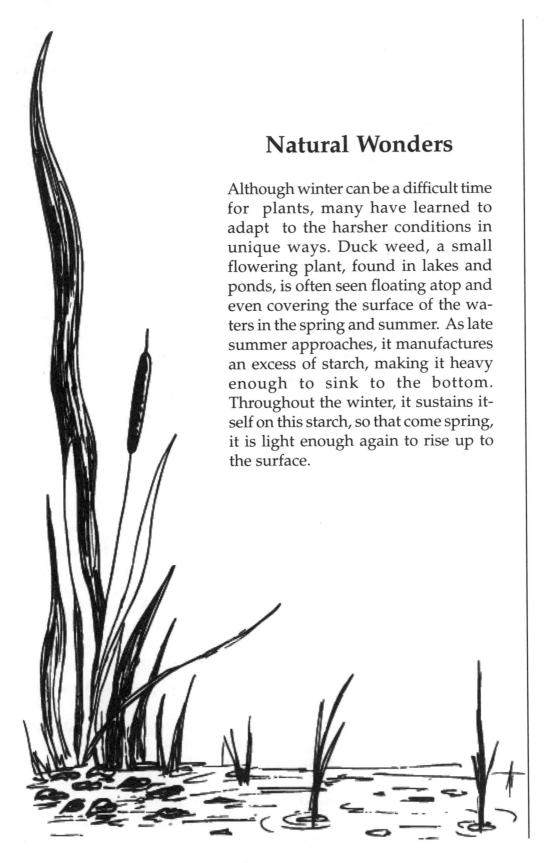

Natural Wonders

Although winter can be a difficult time for plants, many have learned to adapt to the harsher conditions in unique ways. Duck weed, a small flowering plant, found in lakes and ponds, is often seen floating atop and even covering the surface of the waters in the spring and summer. As late summer approaches, it manufactures an excess of starch, making it heavy enough to sink to the bottom. Throughout the winter, it sustains itself on this starch, so that come spring, it is light enough again to rise up to the surface.

Chapter Six

Rite of the Winter Solstice

As the sun moves into the sign of Capricorn in the Northern Hemisphere, the winter season begins. This movement brings with it a change of energies that touches all life. The energies of the planet now work to bring the etheric and astral energies of humanity and the planet in alignment with the physical.

This time of year love is preeminent. The spiritual energies of the heavens converge upon humanity through the realm of Nature to awaken the feminine powers within us all. Because of the alignment that occurs at this time of year, along with the awakened feminine energies, many of those of the angelic hierarchy and devic beings of the earth are more easily perceived. They are beheld and sensed by many - if only through the dream state. This will be explored later in the chapter on "The Rite of the Winter Solstice."

The energies of the winter solstice and those of all festivals celebrated at this time of the year are connected to humanity's life of healing, new birth, and creativity. This season deepens the life feeling, which flows to us through the astral. It can release opportunity to bring peace to the soul and new birth to inner potentials. It strongly plays upon the hearts of all.

This is a time of year in which the Inner Light is kindled in spite of outer darkness, and thus it is a powerful time for revelation through dreams and meditations. It is a time to go within us to free ourselves from separateness. It is a time in which the feminine energies are stirred in all life upon the planet, so that their seeds can sprout within the darkness and begin their growth toward the light. .

*"As the sun moves
into the sign of Capricorn
in the Northern Hemisphere,
the winter season begins.
Because our feeling nature is
heightened during this time,
we can experience the beings
and spirits of the natural world
more clearly than
at any other time of the year...
but especially when we
spend time in Nature!"*

The spiritual forces of Nature affecting us at this time of the year brings opportunity for healing and the expansion of consciousness for those who would open more fully to it. It is a time that opens perceptions of what must still come upon us in the growth process. It opens a vision of what we must still face within ourselves if we are to give birth to the higher. Spending time in Nature now re-awakens your inner dreams and visions.

This is actually a time for withdrawal from outer activities, so that we can give birth to the light within our own darkness. To bring new life from the darkness of the womb is the goal of this season, and the purpose of the quickening of Nature's spiritual energies at this time upon humanity. These universal rhythms converging upon us are keyed to enable anyone who is seeking to awaken the interior gifts and light.

This energy is most appropriate for learning how to balance our emotions and to use our astral energies constructively. This is a time to cleanse the heart and the astral so that the profound feminine mysteries can unfold within our lives - the birthing capabilities within each of us. The energies at this time stimulate introspection and inspire seriousness for greater depths of meditation. Anyone wishing to succeed in meditation and dream work - or those who have difficulty with them - could choose no better time to initiate efforts along these lines. This is augmented tremendously when done in Nature. This is a time when doors open to approach the angelic hierarchy more easily. It is a time in which the universal energies facilitate illumination, forgiving and forgetting petty resentments and great wrongs, and it is a time for new initiation.

Spiritual Mysteries of the Winter Solstice

The winter solstice is connected to humanity's life of feeling. When it is rightly understood, it deepens the life feeling, which can be found within each of us, and it overflows into the astral energies. It is a time, which can bring great peace to the soul. The energies affecting humanity are most appropriate for awakening the Divine Feminine within at this time. And this is reflected most profoundly in Nature, for it is when seeds germinate.

This is a season often associated with modern Christianity, but the significance of this time of the year has been celebrated in many ways throughout the world. The solstice is a time in which the sun turns northward. In the Northern Hemisphere, it marks the shortest day of the year – with the sun shining longer each day thereafter throughout the winter season. In Egypt and Asia, the winter solstice was a time of celebration, a festival connected to the victory of the sun over darkness- a time when light triumphs over darkness upon the earth. It is the light of the inner potential - the Divine Feminine. Hanukkah, the Hebrew Festival of Lights, and Christmas, celebrating the birth of Jesus, are two modern feasts reflecting ancient celebrations at this time. Many still enjoy the lighting of the Yule log at this time of the year. This is the ancient rite of the rebirth of the Divine within the fires of the Mother Goddess.

All life is touched by the energies playing within and upon the Earth at this time of the year, especially when we connect with Nature. The astral plane is brought into alignment with the physical, facilitating the communion and ministrations of the angelic hierarchies with humanity. The inner heart, cleansed and prepared through the autumn season, can now give birth to a new expression of energies, which will germinate and unfold through the rest of the year. Nature's energies amplify this dynamic play of energy, creating a quickening on an atomic level within all of humanity. Few are untouched by the energies of this time of the year. Each has the ability and the opportunity to attune to this energy more intensely and thus give greater birth to the inner feminine potentials and energies through contact with the natural world..

The winter solstice triggers a time in which the Inner Light is kindled in spite of outer darkness. It is a time to give birth to and awaken the higher self. If celebrated properly, spiritual impulse is born anew within us, adding light and strengthening the love principle within our life.Compassionate ones have always entered the earth plane at this time of the year to serve as guides to humanity. Guidance through signs and omens in Nature is extremely strong during this time as well. This is a time of the year best suited to learning the ancient significance of the "Feast of the Interior Light." It is a time of dedication and the renouncing of the false. It is a good time to step away from outer activities. It is a time best suited to turning inward and attuning to the mystic rhythms of Nature, set in motion with the winter solstice.

Unfortunately, society has created an attitude of participation in continual gatherings and outward celebrations. This is contrary to the energy and rhythms of this season. The energies playing upon humanity stimulate great introspection and facilitate meditative states of awareness, and time should be given for these. The energies touching all at this time of the year present opportunities to awaken the seeds of inner potentials that we most desire to unfold. It is a time to reflect upon the miracle of heaven and earth uniting, coupling within the dark to give birth to new life. It is a time, which gives each individual opportunity to light the light that shines eternally within the darkness.

During this time of the year, the entire angelic hierarchy draws close to the earth and they pour forth their spiritual force upon it. Nature spirits and devas come forth a little more tangibly. Overseen by Gabriel - the archangel of tenderness, mercy and love - this force brings expansion of consciousness beyond the confines of the physical world for those who learn to attune to it.

There is awakened the opportunity to develop love as a power within our lives. All of the souls who will incarnate within the coming year draw close to the earth at this time to share in the angelic and devic blessings. They draw near to their prospective mothers, and those mothers who attune to this season can become aware of their presence. At this time of the year all the world is basked in flows of love, and for those who open to these touches and rhythms, the Great Star Call can be felt. For the student of Nature's mysteries, these energies will open the doors of approach to the Angelic Hierarchy. It is a time of illumination and the beginning of igniting the Star Body of the Soul. For those with a dedicated mind and heart, December should be a joyous month, one attuned to angelic and devic bliss.

This is a time of dedication. If the preparatory stages through the autumn have been followed, the winter solstice will initiate a time when new life begins to be experienced. Signs and messages in the natural world direct us to the best avenues and activities of new birth for the months ahead. It opens a variety of opportunities:

- We will begin to realize that he or she is a true child of the Divine and will never again be without inner guidance.
- It is a time in which spirit can begin to have dominion over the physical.
- It can lead to the state of true Initiation and the seeing of the star shining within our heart and the heart of the Earth.
- It opens new clairvoyance, and the individual can see what must still be done to become the true spiritual Initiate.
- The etheric plane and all of its energies become more open to us, revealing spirit guidance - especially from those of the Nature realm.
- We can learn from the devic and angelic beings that are more accessible.
- We open to spiritual insight that penetrates all of our Earth experiences more deeply.
- We can open to the Divine Imagination so that we can give birth to our own light in all aspects of darkness within our life.

The Occult Significance of Christmas

The season of Christmas is prepared for in orthodox Christianity four weeks prior to the winter solstice. This period of time is known as Advent. In other mystery traditions though, the last four weeks of the autumn season - prior to the winter solstice - were also times of greater and more intense purification and preparation. They involved the final efforts of purification before opening to the Divine Feminine energies of Nature, which dominate the winter season. It is a time, which awakens fresh revelations about our spiritual development. These revelations often comie to us through signs and messages from the natural world.

The Annunciation

Aligned with the first week of Advent, the focus of the spiritual disciple should be on cultivating purity as a power. Physical, emotional, mental, and spiritual purity will unfold the higher faculties that open one to the Divine Feminine energy that plays upon the Earth most strongly throughout the winter season.. It is what assists us in consciously perceiving the celestial realms and the glorious beings that inhabit them and who manifest in Nature through the holy days of winter. The Annunciation in Christianity was the moment when Mary became aware of the presence of Gabriel and he announced to her the role she would play in the Christ Mysteries. Developing purity as a power can open us to that same kind of revelation. Spending time in Nature at this time of year helps purify the aura and facilitates our own revelations.

The Immaculate Conception

The Immaculate Conception is associated with the second week of Advent. For those who open to the seasonal rhythms, there is a growing realization of wisdom and ove within our own lives, regardless of outer appearances. The last weeks of autumn are times when things begin to appear very lifeless. But it is just appearance.This week holds the promise of attainment for us. Though seeds become dormant in late fall and early winter, they will begin to germinate and develop throughout the winter months. If we visit Nature this week, we will receive signs of this in our own life. This mystery involves the ultimate realization that nature is a reflection of the Divine, and becausewe are part of Nature, we possess the seeds of divinity. But it is up to us to prepare and to conceive that expression of divinity within the unique circumstances of our own lives. Messages from the natural world at this time often provide guidance on the best ways of expressing our gifts within our life throughout the coming months.

The Holy Birth

In ancient traditions, including the true Christian Mysteries, the third and fourth weeks of Advent were times to focus on the Holy Birth. These are the last two weeks prior to the actual winter solstice. Birth only occurs through a union of the male a and female. In Nature, it is the seed beginning to germinate or the plant preparing for new expression and growth in the months ahead. This is symbolic of lifting the Holy Child within each of us from the manger of the lower self to its rightful place within our lives. On another level, it is the raising of energies along the channel of the spine to the heart and up to the head. – to the third ventricle of the brain where the higher birth of illumination occurs. It is the mystery of learning to follow the star seeds of our own higher nature.

Mystic Midnight Sun

This brings us then to the time of the Mystic Midnight Sun - the winter solstice. In the Egyptian and the Persian Mysteries, at the hour of midnight, the priests would gather around them their truest disciples and teachers, and would speak of the great mystery of the victory of the sun over darkness. They would teach them the mystery of the immortal soul becoming victorious over the animal forces of nature and the re-awakening of the consciousness. It was a celebration of confidence, trust, and hope. This was known as "seeing the sun at midnight."

At this point the astral plane and the angelic hierarchy begin to open the floodgates to infuse the earth with the angelic power. This flood of energy reaches its highest point on midnight of Christmas Eve. (Interestingly enough, this is a day in traditional Christendom dedicated to Adam and Eve, reflecting the occult principle and mystery of polarity often portrayed within the true Christian teachings.) This energy remains pouring forth upon the Earth for thirteen days, through January 6, the time of Epiphany. In other mystery traditions, the Epiphany was a time of baptism into new life and initiation. It is a time pregnant with possibilities - like a seed in Nature, preparing to burst forth.

One of the powerful acts we can perform for ourself is to spend some time in Nature on the day of the winter solstice.There are special meditations that can be used during these days to open what has been called the Christed Imagination. They will awaken an awareness of what must still be done. During this time the soul may pass through deep-even cathartic-experiences, and close attention to dreams will provide insight. The visions and guidance that cxomes through that comes from concentrated work in Nature during this holy time can open us to an awareness of what we still must endure inour evolution. We can open to what we personally must do to bring light into our life circumstances.

Gabriel & the Angels of the Seasons

Gabriel is the archangel of love and hope. He is the governor of the winter season, working with the angelic and devic influence upon the planet during this season. It is the task of Gabriel to assist in the purifying, elevating, and spiritualizing of humanity. He is the initiator of the mysteries of Love-primal creative Love.

To the neophyte, he brings experiences of love consciousness through the lower emotions - beyond the confines, though, of friends, family, and benefactors. At this time of the year, he works to stimulate a greater appreciation of the divine essence within all. He works to develop the power of love within the life of the individual - a power that has no emotional or sensory thrill. It is the power of Love that is offered as an attribute to be attained.

To those who work to attune to the rhythms of the winter season - especially through special times in Nature, Gabriel helps reveal the significance of the "Nativity Mysteries", that have been taught in many traditions as a step toward initiation. On the supreme mystery night of the year, he works to open the tender sweetness of the angel song, and he activates the feminine element in all beings upon the planet, as he has charge of all nurturing throughout Nature.

Gabriel is the guardian of the sacred waters of life - the seed and the egg in the male and female. He is also overseer of the sign Cancer – the direct opposite of the sign of Capricorn, which inaugurates the winter season.

The lily is the symbol. Sometimes the white rose is substituted for it - as they are often interchangeable. It is the task of Gabriel to assist in the process of linking of the male and female. Gabriel assists us in this so that we may give birth to the Holy Child within. The lily is a symbol of purity and self-control, the norm for any true disciple of any mystery tradition. It is a symbol, which invokes angelic influence - particularly that of Gabriel during this season. It stimulates the energy of the throat chakra and all of the centers of the head, so that the creative power of the 'Word" can be - unfolded and expressed within each person's life.

A wonderful exercise is visualizing the lily forming within the body. Its stem extends up the spine, and at the point of the throat, the flower unfolds, encompassing the head. This activates the Light Body or what could be called the "Lily of Light" within one's life. This will gradually awaken the true significance of the Immaculate Conception, a key to the ending of illness and the other limitations of birth. This exercise activates the ability to conceive with Love as a force.

Angelic Hierarchy of Winter

Angels of Capricorn

The angelic hierarchy of Capricorn helps inaugurate the winter season. They work to help teach humanity the true importance of the astral body and how to mold and shape its energies. They assist us in balancing the emotions and awakening our inner potentials. They stimulate introspection and insight and they inspire a new seriousness for greater depths of meditation and realization.

These beings assist us in opening the initiatory process to the Feminine Mysteries. They assist us in clearing a way to the "mountaintop" - to transfigure the soul. They awaken opportunity to conquer death in some form within their life - and thus open to the mysteries of new birth. Death and birth go hand in hand, and this is part of the lesson of the Feminine Mysteries being awakened at this time of the year, and mirrored in the world of Nature. To the undeveloped individual, everything will only have an outer, earthy significance, but to one developing, the depths of life situations will reveal themselves through signs and omens in Nature. These beings assist humanity in that process.

Angels of Aquarius

The second month of the winter season is one that can more directly align us with the group of celestial beings that work through the sign of Aquarius. This group will oversee much of the initiation in the "Aquarian Age", which is upon us. They strongly influence our etheric body, working to make it more receptive to the higher influences, especially to the guiding spirits of Nature. They stimulate clairvoyance, so this is an excellent time to develop and exercise one's leaning toward it. Time spent in Nature during this month will often stimulate vision of Nature spirits.

Angels of Aquarius help those of higher initiation to fashion "The Golden Wedding Garment" of the New Testament scriptures - the soul body. In Christian Gnosticism, those who would meet the Christ within the etheric realms must weave this garment through fulfilling obligations, life tasks, and responsibilities.

During this month, they assist us in transmuting superficiality and selfishness, which can block the manifestation of our creative and birth-giving energies. Those who are just beginning development often are stuck trying to be all things to all people. For those who open fully to their assistance at this time of the year, there will grow a dedication to the soul. And there will be revealed a greater understanding of the mysteries of the vital functions of the body and how the elements of

Nature affect them. These beings assist us during this time of the year to awaken our own divine light - that ever shines within the dark. They help awaken the light that heals and nourishes.

Angels of Pisces

The last of the months of the winter season is influenced by a group of the angelic hierarchy who work through the sign of Pisces. These beings hold the key to perfected humanity. They help us realize the way to end the darkness of various areas within our life circumstances. In Nature, this is a month in which seeds begin to break open and sap begins to flow stronger. Many elements of Nature herald the coming of new life for us.

This group of beings assist us in bringing our physical body more under the balanced control of the masculine and feminine. During this month, there is a call to the depths within. It is a time for healing - physically and spiritually, and any time spent in Nature facilitates this healing. They assist us in transmuting self-centered dreaming to a vision that is dedicated to the higher service of humanity. Dream activity, in fact, often involves scenes of the natural world., and many signs and messages from them in Nature encourage us in expressing ourselves.

Throughout this month, those of this hierarchy work to reveal the karma of our life to us. Those revelations are usually more clear through time spent in the natural world. There arisse increased guidance for balancing our life and greater revelations of our destiny. These beings work to assist us in lifting our psychic energies into a higher, spiritual force. Those of this sign work to open initiation into the Nature - more fully awakening the creative, intuitive and birth-giving forces of the universe to those who are receptive. At the very least, for those who open to the path of Nature as a guide during this month, they will reveal the path of initiation yet to be walked by you throughout the rest of the year.

Winter Tales

One of the best ways of opening to the the energies and rhythms of the season is by reading and even meditating on myths, tales and stories that reflect those energies. Take a day periodically throughout the winter season and read some of these tales outside. They can even be used in meditation prior to your "answer walks" to help you connect with Nature's messages more clearly.

Imagine yourself as the hero/heroine of the story, and watch how the power of words magnifies the the messages of the unspoken language of Nature.

- The Hebrew tale of Judah Maccabbee
- Biblical events in the life of Mary and the birth of Jesus
- The illumination of Rama of India
- Roman tale of Cybele and Atis
- Egyptian tale of the birth of Horus to Isis
- Persian tale of the Birth of Mithrus
- Greek tale of Kronos dethroning Uranus
- Scandinavian tale "East of the Sun, West of the Moon"
- Hassidic tale "Magic Mirror of Rabbi Adam"
- French tale "Master and His Pupil"
- Grimm's tale "The TInder Box"
- African Byshmen tales of "Praying Mantis"
- South African tale "Mbega the Kego"
- Egytpian tale "promises of the Three Sisters"
- Mayan tales of Ix Chel
- Kiowa tale "Pasowee, the Buffalo Woman"
- Chinese tale"The Pear Tree"
- American foldtale "Rip Van Winkle"
- Celtic tales of Cerridwen and Morgan Le Fay
- Tales of magic, birth and compassion

Exercise

Rite of the Winter Solstice

Benefits:

- **Stimulates dream activity**
- **Awakens a deeper connection to the spirits of Nature**
- **Helps open vision of hidden activities of plants and animals**
- **Promotes healing**
- **Opens visions to the healing powers of Nature**
- **Stimulates great creativity and intuition**

This exercise should be done from the night of the winter solstice through the Night of the Mystic Midnight Sun. It has a powerfully healing effect upon the individual, and it will plant seeds that will sprout within one's life by spring. These seeds are seeds of abundance, prosperity, love, and illumination.

This exercise uses a symbology that will assist us in aligning with the dynamic rhythms of this season and to be more receptive to the angelic and devic ministrations throughout it. It can have a significant effect upon our dreams, and thus we should pay close attention to them throughout the season. It will also open a new vibrancy to the meditative experience, and it will manifest opportunities over the following months to give greater expression to the energies of love, illumination, and intuition. It will manifest opportunities to bring your own light out in the coming months. It will, of course, be up to you to take advantage of such opportunities.

Preparations

1. Make sure you will be undisturbed.
2. Use candles of a color appropriate to this season. Red and green are traditional, but black and white are powerful also for winter solstice celebrations.
3. Have a single white taper candle that you can hold in your hands-for the beginning of the meditation.
4. Have a rose (preferably white, although the red rose is an outer symbol of the inner white rose) that you can place upon your lap throughout the meditation. If possible, also have a Christmas lily. You may interchange it with the rose.

Meditation

Light the single white, taper candle. As its light begins to shine within the darkness of your meditation area, focus upon the flame. Then close your eyes, and remember how the flame looked. Imagine that flame coming to life within the heart/solar plexus area of the body. When you can feel and see that flame of light within you, softly extinguish the candle. Be aware now of the small flame of light that shines within the darkness. As you do you hear the gentle words: "At last, my child, come up higher."

You focus upon this inner flame, and allow yourself to float upward into the night sky. See and feel it. The sky is black except for one lone distant star that shimmers in the distance. You feel yourself floating toward it, and as you draw closer, you see that the star hovers over a large temple, set high upon a mountain, looking over the earth. You follow its trail of light down until you come to rest before it.

Soft light bathes the entire temple, and although you were here at the celebration of the autumn equinox, it appears so much different now. The two trees are trimmed, and you can see that the temple is great in size, more so than you remember. It has twelve sides, and the star above it makes it shine a luminous white. Raised above the temple is an equal-armed cross against a five- pointed star.

The door is closed, but through the window, you can see that a shimmering white mist fills the inner temple. In the center stands the altar and above the altar is a spotless white cross. Where the poles of the cross intersect is a single white rose. Around the outside of the altar are circular tiers of seats. They are filled with those dedicated to service. These are the "Compassionate Ones" - and they are both familiar and unfamiliar.

They are uniting their spiritual forces and directing them toward the unfoldment of that single white rose. Their voices rise in waves of harmony that fill the temple and carry to the outer - world. As their song touches the rose, it unfolds petal by petal, giving off a golden hue. The light from this rose pours forth through the twelve windows of the temple, suffusing the landscape. The light surrounds and fills you. You are enfolded within its light. You feel yourself being cleansed of selfish desire and your mind fills with clearness and the brilliance of a diamond. You close your eyes and feel the energy as it heals and nurtures.

As you open your eyes, there is standing before you a beautiful being of great light and gentleness. The light is a soft emerald that touches your soul. Within his hand is a lily of great luster and you know that this is the one called Gabriel.

The door behind is now open, revealing the workings of the Inner Temple more clearly. Gabriel reaches forward and touches the crown of your head in blessing. You are filled with a love that goes beyond comprehension. You feel it pouring down through you, overflowing into your heart. You look down and you see the inner flame that brought you here shimmering. It dances, shifts, and forms itself into a soft white rose. Gabriel then takes you by the hand and leads you into the doorway of the Inner Temple.

"You have opened your heart to the ministrations of the Servants of the Light. Hour by hour they will pour forth their energies. You are being shown so that you will remember and someday lead others to this point."

The voice speaks softly within your mind and it touches your heart. Your eyes fill with love for this magnificent being and the inner cross and rose grows even more lustrous, pouring forth greater energy out of the temple and down the mountainside to the world below.

"With each expression of love, the entire world is touched. At this time of the year the great beings of light shall ascend and descend,, surrounding the Earth and pouring forth energies to touch and awaken the hearts of all upon the Earth."

Your eyes are drawn to the ceiling. It is open to the night sky and to the Great Star above. From the star to the temple, streams of light ascended and descended, the angelic hierarchy working to suffuse the earth with streams of love.

"These streams will touch all parts of the earth. Some are directed to the foulest areas of the earth. Some are released to the battlefields. Some become the benedictions at hospitals. Many are balms for hearts laden with sorrow. Some serve to help new souls re-enter the earth life stream, and others to assist those newly released from the body through the transition you call death. These are the labors of love for the world."

Gabriel turns toward you, and he touches your heart.

"Look within the inner white rose of light and see the love that is your divine heritage." You look into your own heart at the rose. Petal by petal it unfolds, and as it does, you see what you must do to become the true child of the Divine. You see the vision of the Divine potential within you. As you lift your eyes from this vision, the temple is gone. Gabriel is gone. At your feet lays a red rose, a gift and an outer reminder of that which lives forever within the heart. You raise your eyes to the night sky, feeling yourself being drawn up to that distant star. The music of the inner temple sounds softly within your mind, and your heart is filled with the song of the angels.

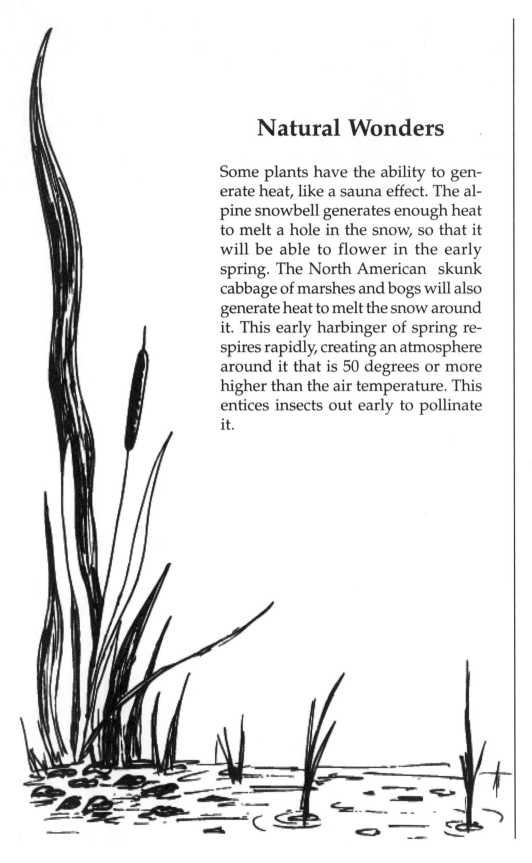

Natural Wonders

Some plants have the ability to generate heat, like a sauna effect. The alpine snowbell generates enough heat to melt a hole in the snow, so that it will be able to flower in the early spring. The North American skunk cabbage of marshes and bogs will also generate heat to melt the snow around it. This early harbinger of spring respires rapidly, creating an atmosphere around it that is 50 degrees or more higher than the air temperature. This entices insects out early to pollinate it.

Chapter Seven

Rite of the Vernal Equinox

As the sun moves out of the sign of Pisces (water- feminine) and into the sign of Aries (fire-masculine), that which we were cleansing and giving birth to through the winter can now be given greater expression. The shift of energy upon the Earth at this time of the year marks a time for greater expression of the masculine energy within all of us. It is a time to unveil and assert our creative aspects more dynamically and productively - a time to resurrect our innate gifts from the darkness.

The creative force within each of us stirs into greater outward expression. Aries is the sign of creative fire, of new beginnings. Much esoteric significance has been attributed to this time of the year - from the resurrection of Tammuz in Sumeria to the resurrection of the Christ within the Christian Tradition.

The keynote for this season is creation and expression of the new. This is reflected in Nature. New seeds begin to sprout. Sap runs and flows, stimulating new growth. Flowers and leaves begin to bud. The natural world begins to resurect itself. For us, the rhythms are excellent for initiating new endeavors and manifesting opportunities for such within our life. It is a time in which the energies propelling us are excellent for initiating a new order to one's life. Spring's energies are strengthening and developing in the physical. They facilitate initiating change and the beginning of the balancing of the masculine and feminine within us.

In Western Orthodox Christianity, sorrow and mourning has come to be associated with this time of the year. Focus has been upon "Crucifixion", whereas it should be upon "Resurrection" which reflects the true energies playing upon the planet now. There is an impulse to resurrect our lives-if only out of the doldrums of winter. This is found throughout the Earth and most apparent in the natural world. It is the

*Throughout the spring season,
creative forces are stirred
into expression.
There is an impulse throughout
Nature to resurrect itself.
As we spend time in Nature
during the spring season,
this impulse will even impact
our dream activity –
making it brighter
and more colorful,
revealing how
we can begin anew.*

time to focus upon the conscious transmutation of our lives. The living waters of life (Pisces) are flooded with new radiance (Aries), and if the cleansing and preparations have been accomplished through efforts in the previous two seasons, this new radiance can effect changes in all avenues of our life. It awakens the "magic green fire" of Gaelic legends – the alchemical force one of the greatest forces found within Nature.

Spiritual Mysteries of the Vernal Equinox

The Ancient Mysteries call forth a return to Nature's rhythms on an intuitive level. Spirit and Nature in Harmony! The earth seasons are designed to promote specific evolutionary needs. The autumn is the seed planting time; the winter is the gestation of the seed and the taking root. The spring is the bursting forth of those new seeds to release new aspiring life to be harvested in the summer. These are always reflected in the hidden mysteries of Nature.

The spring equinox opens the veil between the physical and the spiritual so that a resurrection in our lives can be inaugurated. The keynote of this season is creation. It is the drive to move our lives upward, like a seed pushing forth out of the earth into the air. The spring is the time when the creative powers we have been nurturing through the winter can be expressed to initiate a new world of opportunities for ourselves.

It is at this time of the year that the sun leaves the water sign of Pisces and enters into Aries, the creative fire sign. Fire was always regarded as something mysterious. Many traditions speak of how fire first belonged to the gods. Plentiful are the myths of the ancient firestealers and the creation of humanity. It is an element, which consumes and changes-it is both destructive and creative.

Aries is the fire sign of new beginnings, and much esoteric significance is attributed to this time of the year. The ancient Hebrew tradition speaks of how God fashioned the world at this time and that Moses led the Israelites out of Egypt in the spring. Resurrection myths, associated with the spring season abound - from Christ Jesus to Osiris of Egypt, Adonis of Babylon, and Tammuz of Sumeria. In the Roman Mysteries, people celebrated the death and resurrection of Attis at this time of the year.

This is the time for the fires of the new. The spring is the beginning of the alchemical process of the seasonal changes. Because much of humanity has lost the sensitivity to attune to the seasons, it is increasingly important for the student of the spiritual mysteries to recognize that each season, each day, and even each hour has its own peculiar quality. We must learn to attune to them to take advantage of them. We are being exposed to a universal cycle of influence.

While the winter season is the time of the Feminine Mysteries (the water element), the spring season is the time for the Masculine Mysteries (the fire element). The time of the equinox is the time of the alchemical and magical blending of water and fire. The living waters within us are flooded with a new radiance so that they can be expressed more fully within our life circumstances. This is the time, which releases energies that manifest opportunity to understand the mystery of polarity. We understand the importance of balancing the masculine, and feminine so they can eventually be blended to create new life. Spiritually and physically, this is a time of great creative expresson. In the Northern Hemisphere, the creative forces begin to grow. There is a fresh outburst of exuberant life and it holds many opportunities for those who align with its rhythms and forces:

- It is an excellent time to initiate a new order within your life.
- It is an ideal time for burning out the old – the burning of the dross - so that the new seeds have room to sprout and be given new expression.
- It is also a time in which the veil between the physical and the spiritual is thinned, creating opportunities to access and invoke dynamic spiritual energy into one's life.
- Its energy can be used to accelerate our own growth or to open new patternsofr it throughout the rest of the spring.
- It is an excellent time to invoke energy that will assist you in making things new within all areas of your life.
- The inner temples are more accessible so that the secrets of life can be more deeply attuned to.
- It is a powerful time for releasing fiery healing energies.
- For the advanced disciple it is an ideal time to fashion the soul body so that the individual can function consciously in the spiritual world.

For the true student of the spiritual mysteries, it is during the spring that the energy is available that facilitates the undergoing of discipleship. The individual must learn to roll away the stones of personal and sense limitation and come forth, bringing the Inner Light out into the external world. At this time of the year, the individual can open to the path of probation and learn to access the vibrant force of the planet to heal the self and others – especially through the world of Nature. (Opportunities to discover the healing power and magic of plants often open as a doorway to those who have been seeking.) Any study of the healings performed by ancient masters can assist the individual in understanding the intricate play of energy within humanity's life.

This is the time to focus upon conscious transmutation. It is the ideal time to assert the will force over the personality. It is a time to balance polarities. This balance is necessary to comprehend the significance of the greatest symbol of this season. That is the symbol of the Holy Grail. The Mystery of the Grail is intricate and has many levels. For most involved with the Nature's mysteries, initially it is the blessing of both the male and the female.

The Occult Significance of Eastertide

The entire initiatory path of the Christian Mysteries is outlined during Eastertide. Easter is still the one holy day determined by the stars. It falls always on the first Sunday following the first full moon of spring-after the vernal equinox. Gnostic and esoteric tradition tells us that only the highest initiates are able to participate in the Mysteries and energies that occur at the equinox itself. That may have been so in the past but no longer is that so.For everyone, the celestial energies of the equinox can be celebrated at least in a "reflected" manner at the time of the full moon. (Students of astrology will recognize that the moon reflects the light of the sun, and thus has significance to the time at which Easter is celebrated.)

We have an ideal opportunity during Eastertide to access energies to transfigure our lives. It is a time supervised by the Archangel Raphael - the Keeper of the Holy Grail. It is his task at this time of the year to help open the senses so that the soul can truly see and know what the individual in this path must do.

This is a celebration that can assist us in our ever-upward spiral. It is a time of great angelic celebration, a time when we can connect more with the angelic and Nature's messengers so as to resurrect our own lives. It is a time in which new teachers are often awakened to their tasks and purpose. It is a time in which those who have such a leaning can discern the esoteric power of music and flowers.

Raphael and the Angels of the Seasons

Raphael is the overseer of the season of spring. The sun or the returning sun sometimes symbolizes him. He is the angel of brightness, beauty, healing, and life. The name literally means "God has Healed." He instructs in the art of healing, especially through the elements of Nature and thus the caduceus is often his symbol as well. He works to help humans link the heart and the mind in the healing process.

Information about Raphael originally came out of the Chaldean tradition, but he is also one of three great angels named in post-Biblical lore. In the Biblical Book of Tobit, he is companion and guide to Tobias, the son of Tobit. At the end of their journey together, he reveals that he is one of the "seven holy angels" that attend the throne of God.

In the *Zohar*, Raphael is charged to heal earth and "through him the earth furnishes an abode for man, whom he also heals of maladies." He is also the angel of science and knowledge, and he was the preceptor of Isaac. One legend tells how Solomon prayed to God for help in the building of the Temple. God answered with the gift of a magic ring brought to the Hebrew king personally by Raphael. The ring, engraved with the five-pointed star had the ability to subdue all demons, and it was this "slave labor" of demons that enabled Solomon to complete the Temple.

Raphael is the keeper and guardian of the most sacred symbol of the Christian Mysteries - the Holy Grail - throughout the Piscean Age. He works to awaken the Great Quest - the quest for our true spiritual essence and how best to manifest it within this life. He bestows valor and grace upon humanity, and with a group of beings of light known as the Malachim, he is the chief bestower and bringer of miracles, coloring our lives with wonder. It is from his influence and this group known as the Malachim that our individual Holy Guardian Angel comes, to teach us and guide us as we begin to take more conscious control of our evolution.

Angelic Hierarchy of Spring

Angels of Aries

The beings of light working through this sign of the zodiac work to stimulate a "Call to the Great Overcoming" - the conquest of the personality by the spirit. They stimulate and awaken energies of self-sacrifice and transmutation. In the unaware or undeveloped person, there seems to manifest only undirected experiences in life - often because the signs and communications are not recognized for what they are. For those working toward advancement though, these beings stimulate greater effort toward developing the personality. .

In the spiritual disciple, these angelic beings will awaken recognition of the "Plan of the Divine" and work with it through strong signs and communications from the natural world. They assist us in merging self-control with wisdom. Depending upon our development, the energy may be experienced through instinctual reaction, a higher form of desire, or directed will. They help us to tap the forces of Nature to stimulate new opportunities and growth within our own life.

Angels of Taurus

This group of the angelic hierarchy has a dynamic purpose in the manifestation of the energies during the spring season. In more ancient times, festivals for the living were often celebrated in the month of May. This angelic hierarchy works with us during this time. They stimulate opportunities for change and new expressions of our abilities and desires. They assist us in the overcoming of selfish desire and the awakening of higher aspiration. And they bring opportunities to follow such aspirations.

These beings awaken a light and love of the Earth, especially in all manifestations of Nature. They open us to the empathic languages of plants and animals. We begin to feel what they are expressing. Because of this, it is one of the most powerful times to explore the natural world and open to its wonders.

It is also their task to assist us in developing control over how we use our own light. Is it for our own ego or the good of others? They also assist us in developing discrimination, discernment and removal of glamour from our own life circumstances. Seeking out guidance in the natural world will help us with this during this month. As the glamour is removed, we are able to penetrate into the new spheres of illumination and vision. They assist any of us, who wishes to do so, to attune more closely to all life within Nature - animal, plant, or mineral kingdoms. They assist in the development of language skills in the natural world.

Angels of Gemini

As the spring season enters its last month, the angels of the sign of Gemini come into greater play upon the Earth. Theirs is the task to begin to awaken the polarity that is a part of the natural world and us. This is reflected within its glyph (II). This includes working to unite the soul with its physical form more intimately. They help equalize the masculine and feminine - so that they can be united to create new life.

.

Before they can unite - as is reflected in the sign of Cancer (the two swirls moving together), the polarities must first be established and balanced (symbolized by the glyph of Gemini). Because of this, contact with and time spent in any realm of Nature facilitates this process. Nothing is more grounding and balncingthan Nature.

This month, and the work of these celestial beings during it, produces change in consciousness in regard to all areas of life. They work to reveal the light that exists in spirit and in physical form. For those who align with them through Nature, the evolution is traced from service to oneself to service to others and on to service to the "One Light beyond all Lights." They help the individual to develop discrimination in the art of relating to others (including those of the natural world) on both physical and spiritual levels.

Spring Tales

One of the best ways of opening to the the energies and rhythms of the season is by reading and even meditating on myths, tales and stories that reflect those energies. Take a day periodically throughout the spring season and read some of these tales outside. They can even be used in meditation prior to your "answer walks" to help you connect with Nature's messages more clearly.

Imagine yourself as the hero/heroine of the story, and watch how the power of words magnifies the the messages of the unspoken language of Nature.

- Egyptian tale ofthe Resurrection of Isis
- Biblical events in the death & resurrection of Jesus
- Babylonian tale of the resurrection of Adonis
- Roman tale of the death & resurrection of Attis
- Sumerian tale of Ishtar & resurrection of Tammuz
- Goethe's *Faust*
- Greek tale " Jason & the Quest for the Golden Fleece"
- Native American tale of White Buffalo Woman
- Chinese tales of Kwan Yin
- Hassidic tale "The Healing Tree"
- European tale "Snow White and Rose Red"
- European tale of "Rumplestiltskin"
- West African tale "Fire Children"
- Egytpian tale "Promises of the Three Sisters"
- Grimm's tale "Boy Who Went Forth to Find What Fear Was"
- Kiowa tale "Pasowee, the Buffalo Woman"
- Chinese tale"Li Chi and the Serpent"
- Italian tale "Jump into my Sack"
- Japanese tale "The Ugly Son"
- Tales of descent, rebirth and healing

Exercise

Rite of the Vernal Equinox

Benefits

> **Opportunity to heal**
> **New Birth and transmutation**
> **New endeavors open up**
> **The spirits of Nature become more tangible to us**
> **Stimulates change and movement in our life**

This meditation has a dynamic impact upon our life when performed at or around the time of the vernal equinox. It releases energy into our life, which manifests opportunities for change and movement. It stimulates choices and decisions that help us to grow. The opportunities will arise; whether or not you act upon them is a matter of free will.

This meditation opens to us a play of energy that will allow us to begin to express, in the outer life, circumstances that we have been nurturing and developing through the winter season. It awakens new insight and stronger intuition, and it may call for a testing of our inner goals and desires. Are they really what we wish to have manifest within our life, or are we just dabbling for the fun of it? The energy of this season, activated through this meditation, will bring you face to face with this question. It is important to follow your heart. Do what you know in your heart is right for you - that which you have been nurturing through the winter. If unsure, seek the answer in Nature.

This meditation in the spring opens contact with new people and opportunities to extend yourself in all areas of your life. Your own attitudes and perspectives will only limit you. This releases the energy of new beginning - initiating new activities, new people, new learning, and new spiritual growth and unfoldment. It initiates a clear realization and expression of the inner potential you knew you had all along. All that is necessary is the faith and the courage to follow through upon them. We are never given a hope, wish, or dream, without also being given opportunities to make them a reality. The only thing that can shatter that possibility is compromise. This is not a time to compromise, but rather to go forward with what you have already sown!

Preparations

1. This is most effective to perform during the three days prior to and the day of the vernal equinox.

2. Make sure you will be undisturbed.

3. Repeat the meditation again at the time of the full moon that follows the vernal equinox.

4. For those into the Christian tradition, performing this exercise on Good Friday, the Saturday before Easter and especially in a sunrise meditation on Easter Sunday can be very powerful and transforming.

5. Repeat it at other times during the Holy Interval between the vernal equinox and Easter.) Meditating with fresh flowers at this time enhances its effect.

6. Pay close attention to the events in your life that occur day- by-day and week-by-week throughout the spring season. This will help you to understand the seasonal power of the spring as it manifests energy within your own unique life circumstances.

Meditation

As you begin to relax, the awareness of your present setting fades. A cloak of darkness surrounds you, and you feel strangely safe. As you look within the darkness, it begins to lift. You see yourself upon the breast of a small hill that overlooks a still river. Its waters are black and deep. The sky above is filled with dark gray, swirling clouds. The trees and bushes are bare and gray. Across the river sits an ancient temple-in ruin. It is dusk, and the sun is going down behind you, taking the last of the daylight with it.

You are standing upon a path that leads down to the dark river below. It is lined with people on both sides who are painted and dressed for mourning. You walk silently between them, unsure how to respond to their sadness or even if you should.

At the river's edge is a small barge, and raised up on it is an altar, draped in black. It reminds you of an open sarcophagus, and the thought does not comfort you. Next to the walkway stands a tall figure dressed in black. Upon his breast is the symbol of a golden chalice, encircled in a field of blue. On the barge itself, next to the open sarcophagus, stand three hooded figures - silent and stoic. You step onto the barge, searching their shielded faces for some indication of the events to follow. Silently they assist you in stretching out upon the altar, and you are draped up to the chin in black silk cloth. Embroidered into it is the figure of a giant phoenix rising from the fires and ashes.

The barge is shoved off from the shore and at a nod from the guide with the chalice emblem, one of the other three draws from beneath his cloak a white rose, and the second brings forth a great sword. The sword is touched to the rose, and it turns a fiery red. It is then dropped into the water beside the barge. The water bursts into flame, igniting the entire river. The flames surround the barge - water and fire together, neither extinguishing the other. When your guides are sure that you are fully aware of the fires, the black cloth is pulled up and draped over your head.

Again the darkness. You are alone. You can see and hear nothing. You know the fire is burning in the water, but you do not know how it will affect the barge. Will it consume the barge? Will it consume you? You force yourself to breathe deeply and relax. Somehow, you know that you may stop if you wish. You also know that the trip must be made sometime. As always, the choice is up to you.

Within your mind you hear the words, "Thy will be done," and the decision is made. All is silent. You are left to your own thoughts on the sacredness of your own life. Your mind begins to look back upon the events of your life. You look back at all the people and events you have encountered. All the changes you have been through within your life float before your eyes, showing you how you have become who you are at present. You see those whom you have hurt and those who have hurt you. You see and feel the love you have given and the love you have lost. You see your life intertwined with the lives of so many, each one adding to the essence of creativity that you now are.

You remember all of the unfinished tasks and all the things you promised yourself that you would do. You see all the illusions of life that you have encountered, and all the blessings you have received. You remember the abilities you have manifested in the past and can give birth to once more. You see the dreams and hopes and wishes you have yet to fulfill, and there arises within you a realization that the opportunities for such are never past. They are ever at hand!

There is a slight bump, as the barge touches a shore. It draws you from your reverie. You arch your back, feeling the stiffness that has settled. It lets you know that a great length of time has passed. Slowly, you draw the black cloth off your face. The waters of the river are no longer on fire.

It is predawn; the sun has not yet risen. And your guides are gone.

You see that you are on the distant shore from whence you began. Up the slope, you can see the outline of the ancient temple. You raise yourself from the altar and step off the barge onto the earth. You climb the slope toward the distant temple. As you reach the crest, you see that magnificent temple standing in luminous glory. No longer is it in ruins. The two trees bordering the door are full and green, and you look about you. All of the earth is green again. The trees and bushes are budding with new life.

It is then that the first rays of the sun streak the horizon to the East. With that, the temple door opens wide, inviting you in. At the altar in the center are your four guides, but no longer are they dressed in black. Theirs are the color of the great beings of light, for your guides are the archangels of the seasons – Michael with his flaming sword, Gabriel with the white rose, Auriel in luminous white with a companion unicorn, and Raphael in the middle, holding high above his head the Great Chalice of Life.

The temple swells with the music of harmony and life. All who had mourned are dressed in brilliant shades of rainbow light, and as they sing forth their song, the sun rises over the horizon. Its light fills the temple, breathing new fire and life into all. It touches and fills the Holy Grail, radiating and reflecting out upon the earth. A flock of birds soar above you. In the distant fields, a magnificent unicorn appears in the clearing and the sounds of Nature come to life.

You look back toward the river and you see the golden sunlight reflecting and filling the waters with new radiance and a fire of light, not flame. As you turn back to the altar, Raphael turns to you, holding aloft the Golden Chalice. He raises his eyes to the heavens and the light pours forth over you. It spirals in and through you, and you are renewed. You are born afresh. Your aura is ignited with new radiance and you can see it in its true glory. It is infused with a cross of radiant light that shines out from you like a great star in the heavens that will shine upon all within your life. It shines in harmony with Nature and all of life.

You close your eyes in gratitude and prayer, lifting your thoughts and your heart to the divine through the song of the Inner Temple. As you open your eyes, the temple lifts from around you, but you feel its impress within you still alive. Its energies will grow like the rising sun, and your life will be fused with creative fires.

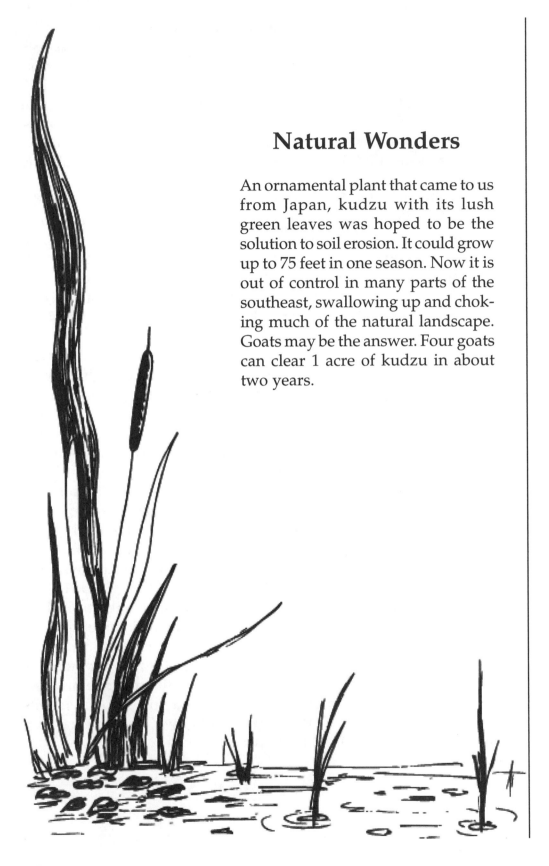

Natural Wonders

An ornamental plant that came to us from Japan, kudzu with its lush green leaves was hoped to be the solution to soil erosion. It could grow up to 75 feet in one season. Now it is out of control in many parts of the southeast, swallowing up and choking much of the natural landscape. Goats may be the answer. Four goats can clear 1 acre of kudzu in about two years.

Chapter Eight

Rite of the Summer Solstice

The summer solstice marks the high point of the "Year of the Soul." For a brief time, all four planes of life are aligned with the physical - the spiritual, mental, astral, and the etheric. Because of this, there is a more direct flow of spiritual energy available to us within the physical. It is a time that provides opportunity to consummate a phase of our spiritual growth. It is a time in which separateness can yield to unity in any area(s) of our lives. And this is experienced most strongly when out in Nature.

The summer solstice is a time when the forces of Nature reach the peak of their annual cycle, and the spiritual forces of Nature stirs their magnificent play within our life. The keynote is transformation and transmutation that instills greater spirituality. The energies available to us at this time of the year facilitate communion with our devic and angelic brethren more easily and more intimately.

This is the time of the blending of the male and female within us for greater expression and a higher birth. The glyph of the sign of Cancer provides much insight into the esoteric significance of this blending. The winter is a time of stimulation of the feminine within us, and the spring is a time of the masculine. Summer is the time of bringing the two together to give birth to the Holy Child residing within each of us. This is a time to ascend to a new form of life expression for us if we utilize these rhythms.

This is the time of the Mystic Marriage - the linking of the male and female, the bridging of the pineal and the pituitary (crown and brow chakras) to open ourselves to new realizations of our true essence. If understood and accessed properly, these natural impulses will stimulate tremendous illumination. Autumn releases the forces of purification and preparation, and winter releases the forces of love - the feminine. Spring

"Enchanted worlds still exist
and the doorways to them
are hidden within Nature.
These doorways
may be more obscure
than in times past,
but we can still seek them out.
Every flower has its fairy,
every tree has its spirit,
every woods has its
Lady of the Woods and
caverns do lead to nether realms.
At the change of seasons,
Nature reveals the doorways
to those whose hearts are open."

releases the force of will - the masculine power, but summer releases the Power of Light! It is a time of the light within that only occurs through the renewing of the mind. Light brings beauty and vision, and it is both of these, which are keynotes of the summer.

In the quest of the spiritual student, there must be alignment and attunement, not only to the energies of an entire incarnation, but also to those of the yearly cycle. Within the ancient mysteries, attunement to this cycle is necessary for higher initiation. The individual, by attuning to these mysteries and to their rhythms throughout the year, brings his or her physical and spiritual energies into alignment, and can thus use that alignment for illumination, revelation, and true unfoldment.

Spiritual Mysteries of the Summer Solstice

The summer solstice is that point in the year in which the energies of Nature reach their culmination, and it is the time in which Nature's energies touch the body, mind, and soul of all living things most powerfully. This is the time of the Mystic Marriage, the uniting of the male and female to give birth to the Holy Child within us.

This is the time of the year to establish a relationship between ourselves and the divine forces found upon the Earth, and all of those who have aligned with it. It is the time to awaken spiritual ecstasy. It is the time in which contact with the angelic hierarchies -including those of the Faerie Realm - can occur most easily and most intimately. Greater concentration is required, as there is often more outer world activities which can distract us. But it is a time in which the alignment of the more subtle planes of life with the physical provides greater access.

Magnetically, the physical, etheric, astral, mental, and spiritual planes are drawn into alignment on the three days prior to and the day of the summer solstice. The physical and subtle bodies of humanity are also aligned at this time. For one who works with these energies, a new and more stable alignment can be established, which will open for even greater growth as the next Year of the Soul is unfolded.

For those who align with the rhythms of the seasons, the summer solstice can trigger a time in which much can be accomplished:

-       It awakens great spiritual inspiration and can stimulate the development of conscious vision of spirits and other planes.

-       There arises greater opportunity to link with others who - like you - are involved in the spiritual mysteries.

- There will manifest opportunities to create harmony and unity in various areas of our lives.

- There can arise a revelation of the path that will lead to a higher initiation of your own abilities in the year ahead.

- There increases greater opportunity to work and commune with the Nature Kingdom and those beings that work with humanity through it. On Midsummer Night (the solstice), the year's work of the Nature Spirits is completed. This is a time in which the Fairy Realm is opened for those prepared to see.

- This time releases energies that manifest opportunities for confidence, strength, and hope.

- It provides opportunities to balance all the elements of the Earth and the physical body.

- There occurs a general expansion of the faculties and intuitive energies.

- It is the ideal time to renew the mind and attune to the highest realms through a merging of the brow and crown chakras - the male and female forces. This will ultimately awaken the opportunity to become a channel of Light.

The Occult Astrology of Summer

Cancer is the mother sign of the zodiac. It is the sign for manifesting the new waters of life. It is a sign for giving birth to a new polarity and expression of polarity. The two swirls that comprise the glyph for this astrological sign reflect the blending of the male and female into new expression.

Easter and the vernal equinox bring with them the lessons of death and rebirth. The cross - the predominant symbol of the spring season - is an indication of the juxtaposition of the poles of the masculine and feminine energies within us all. As we learn to realign and balance those poles, they become parallel columns, creating a doorway by which we may enter into the inner mysteries of new birth and new expression. Gemini, the sign that ends the spring season, has as its glyph the twin columns standing parallel rather than juxtaposed. Once balanced, then the process of blending can begin - as reflected within the sign of Cancer which follows Gemini.

As the sun enters the sign of Cancer, there is a stimulation of varying intensities of a new expression of the divine within. This stimulation affects people differently, according to the sensitivities developed. This varying intensity is reflected through the three planets that are associated with Cancer in esoteric astrology. These three planets influence all of us in unique ways, giving impulse to new processes of energy manifestation within our lives. These processes are those of generation and regeneration. These three planets also reflect the three levels upon which the influence of the summer solstice can affect us, in accordance with how attuned we become to the energies of this seasonal change. These three levels can be on a physical level, a soul level, and/ or on a spiritual level.

The moon, which rules Cancer, affects everyone most strongly on a physical level at this time of the year. Most people respond to this lunar influence, involving themselves in new physical activities, etc. The moon is a symbol of the physical energy of generation. The planet Jupiter and its affect upon us is also stimulated when the sun enters into the sign of Cancer. How it specifically affects us can be determined by its placement within our astrological chart, but during this time of the year its influence will be felt on a more subtle level. Anyone engaged or wishing to engage in a creative or artistic endeavor can open to great inspiration by attunement to the energies of this time of year. This is the primary effect of Jupiter upon individuals as the sun enters this astrological sign. Jupiter has ties to that aspect of soul awareness within us that helps us to bridge the physical with the spiritual. It increases and expands the energies of the etheric body, thereby opening the individual to greater vision and inspiration. The more we attune ourselves to these rhythms, the greater the effect upon us. And they are heightened through our connection to Nature.

The esoteric ruler of the sign of Cancer is Neptune. Neptune is the planet of initiation, and when the sun enters this sign the influence of Neptune and the energies of initiation can be attuned to and invoked within one's life. The influence of Neptune is felt by all, although it is not usually consciously recognized. Neptune is the planet of regeneration, and those who are capable of undergoing a new birth will feel the pull of initiation. Neptune is a planet associated with the sea, and much of the Christ teachings occurred around the Sea of Galilee. The fish, a symbol for Neptune, was a symbol of the Christ Mysteries as well. The influence of these three planets and the angelic hierarchy that works through them has been described in extant literature and scripture. Even the Biblical scriptures reveal this hidden influence: "Except a man be born again, he cannot see the kingdom of God. . . except a man be born of water (moon in Cancer) and of the spirit (the Jupiter influence on humanity through Cancer), he cannot enter the kingdom of Heaven (the Neptune influence on humanity through Cancer)." (John 3:5)

The archangels associated with the planets of this sign also provide insight. Gabriel is the archangel of the moon. He is also the ruler of the season that begins in the sign opposite Cancer - Capricorn(winter). Auriel is the governor of the summer season, but Auriel also is known to work through the influence of the planet Jupiter to awaken the soul qualities of inspiration within humanity. In the Gnostic tradition, it is the Christ who is most commonly associated with Neptune, the esoteric ruler of Cancer. Working through the influence of Neptune, the Christ works to stimulate the divine feminine into greater and purer expression in all people.

Cancer is the sign of the Madonna, the woman with the moon under her feet and with a crown of twelve stars. It is also the sign of the prodigal son, the return to new birth and to new expressions of the divine . Cancer is the sign of birth and the principle feminine sign of the zodiac.

The Cherubim are the angelic beings associated with this sign. They are the guardians to the sacred places upon the planet and to all the sacred waters of life. These sacred places have been called by many names, such as "The Holy of Holies," "The Ark of the Covenant," "the Holy Grail" etc. Cherubim guard the sacred secrets to the sexual force. These sacred places we must learn to build within ourselves and within all expressions of our energies by becoming one of the "pure in heart." It is this task which is most accessible to us at this of time of the year.

As the sun moves through the rest of the summer, it is the task of the students of Nature to maintain the equality of polarity. This is accomplished through self-authority and self-triumph. This is the season that enables us to prepare for the Rite of Mystic Marriage within the inner temple of the soul.

Auriel and the Angels of the Season

Auriel is the governor of the summer season, working to help spiritual energies become diffused throughout Nature upon the Earth. Auriel is known as the angel of beauty and vision. Auriel is also considered the tallest of the angels, with eyes so clear that they can see across eternity. The name Auriel means, "God is Light." Sometimes called the Son of the Star, this has ties to a name by which early Christian Initiates were known. Auriel brings with the summer season beauty and an awakening of vision. One who opens to the ministrations of Auriel during this season can behold the streams of life that are infusing everything in the natural world.

The colors associated with this great being vary according to tradition. When contacted through work with the nature spirits and devas, the traditional colors are yellow and black. At the highest vibrational aspect, the color of this being's raiment is a combination of crystalline white and ethereal blue, filled with the silvery stars of the Madonna. During the summer months these colors veil the earth, especially at the time of the summer solstice.

Contact with Auriel opens one to the fairy kingdom and to fairy vision. This vision usually begins with the appearance of glimmering lights and then subtle forms. From here the vision of the figures of the angelic hierarchy begins to open. Through work with Auriel one can open to true etheric vision on a fully conscious level.

One tradition speaks of Auriel as being the teacher of the Biblical prophet Esdras. Auriel awoke within him the gift of spiritual vision whereby he was able to see Christ face-to-face and prophecy. Working with Auriel will awaken our own spiritual vision, which can be developed into true prophecy - especially in recognizing the signs of Nature.

Like Michael, Auriel is often associated with the Flaming Sword. Invoking Auriel was a means by which individuals could manifest the appearance of this Flaming Sword. This is the sword of discrimination and comprehension of spiritual law. In the ancient grail legends and scriptures, this sword was also interchangeable with the lance or spear which shed the blood of Christ Jesus while upon the cross. Through work with Auriel during the summer, the spiritual force symbolized by the sword is awakened in those aspiring to lead a life of initiation. It is a symbol of the divine force, which animates all creation, and it represents the power that the ego has acquired through its many incarnations. When awakened through work and attunement with the seasonal cycles, it can be used to heal and to bless, but only as long as there is a true willingness never to inflict wounds even if it means that you will receive the wounding yourself. What one hurts, one must heal, and what one kills, one must bring back to life.

Auriel was once known as the "Fire of God" and some ancient works ascribe the process of alchemy to this being. Anyone who works with Nature, nature spirits, and the alchemical processes of life could do no worse than to meditate upon and invoke the aid of this great being.

Auriel rules the summer season, the point at which the energies of Nature reach their peak and also begin their decline toward a new cycle. This is the process of alchemy: birth, death, and rebirth. It is the assistance of Auriel that enables us to see these laws operating within our own unique life circumstances, so that we may truly transform ourselves in the manner that is best for ourselves.

Angelic Hierarchy of Summer

Angels of Cancer

The summer begins when the sun enters the sign of Cancer. This is the high point in the Year of the Soul. It is the time of the Mystic Marriage, the time to initiate the process of blending the masculine and the feminine- to fertilize the egg so that new life will spring forth. The mysteries of the sexual energies - applied both physically and spiritually - is in the hands of this group of celestial beings. They are the guardians of the holy places of the planet. They guard the Holy of Holies, the Mystery Tombs and Pastos. They teach humanity to use, rather than abuse, our most treasured possession - the holy water and the sacred seed of life. They work to assist the individual in developing the intellect into higher intuition. They work for the development of purity and chastity in esoteric manners that permit the highest transmutation of the fires and waters of life. They work to reveal to the individual who is receptive, the light within all substance - a light that is always stimulated through contact with the natural world.

Angels of Leo

When the summer sun moves into the sign of Leo, those of its angelic hierarchy become more active. It is their task to awaken in us the power of life. They assist humanity in learning to apply the newly born power of love that arises from the united male and female. They help us learn that everything is connected and that we are all part of the same family - not just the human family but the family of Nature as well. They stir greater expression of individuality during this month, and a greater will to illumine and a will to rule. Theirs is the task of assisting humanity in acquiring self-knowledge and self-mastery through the balance of the male and female forces of life. To those who are receptive to their influence, they awaken the ability in the individual to reflect the divine out into the lives of others. They learn to overcome the lower self and to express the higher, to find the hidden and to reveal it for all.

Angels of Virgo

The last of the groups of the angelic hierarchy working through the summer are those associated with the sign of Virgo. Theirs is the task to awaken even further spark of consciousness that in the following Year of the Soul will be given still greater expression. They open the individual to the true meaning and purpose of wisdom - Sophia. They open the doors of initiation through service and sacrifice. They awaken greater ability in synthesizing the essence of our experiences, so that they can be trans- formed into true soul wisdom. They assist us manifesting opportunities for change.And through signs from Nature, we learn how best to make that change. They have the ability to teach the individual how to blend the light of the Divine with the Light of Form, as found in all things of the natural world. In the undeveloped or unaware individual, the force simply germinates, but as one becomes more advanced and works toward unfoldment through the teachings of Nature, we become increasingly creative and our light is no longer hidden.

Summer Tales

One of the best ways of opening to the the energies and rhythms of the season is by reading and even meditating on myths, tales and stories that reflect those energies. Take a day periodically throughout the summer and read some of these tales outside.They can even be used in meditation prior to your "answer walks"to help you connect with Nature's messages more clearly.

Imagine yourself as the hero/heroine of the story, and watch how the power of words magnifies the the messages of the unspoken language of Nature.

- Shakespeare's *Midsummer Night's Dream*
- Biblical tale of the ascension of Jesus
- Greek tale of Theseus and Hyppolyta
- New testament story of the Marriage Feast at Cana.
- Egyptian tale of Sheikh Ramadan and Destiny
- African tale"Mirimi Giants who ate People"
- Greek tale " Jason & the Quest for the Golden Fleece"
- Native American tale of White Buffalo Woman
- Chinese tales of Kwan Yin
- Native American tales of Changing Woman
- English tale of Arthur and the Knights of the Round Table
- European tale of "Cinderella"
- German tale "The Goose Girl"
- Native American tale "Deer Hunter and White Corn Maiden"
- Korean tale "The Toad Bridegroom"
- Chinese tale "The Magic Pear Tree"
- Japanes tale "Urashima"
- Native American tale "How Men and Women Got Together"
- Chinese tale of "Tien Hou"
- Tales of fairies, marriage and following dreams

Exercise

The Rite of the Summer Solstice

Benefits:

- **Contact with the spirits of Nature**
- **Healing opportunities**
- **Abundance and fruition of dreams**

This powerful meditation has great potential for setting in motion a harvesting within one's life that creates new birth on many levels. It manifests an energy that opens a probing of how you came to be. It may manifest a testing of your ability to place Divine will first. There will begin to unfold increasingly through the summer months an understanding of there being a reason for who you are and where you are – even if you do not know the specifics.

This is an exercise, which will increase the intuitional faculties. You will become aware over the following months of the effects you have on other people. Others often comment about something "different" about you, even though they cannot put their finger on it. It has to do with the new energy being born within your auric field.

The qualities of idealism, devotion, and the following of a higher calling become more important. There may manifest a testing or confronting of hypocrisy. There will occur a release of pressure in your day-to-day events. Intuition, inspiration, fertility, compassion, and an expanded vision will awaken and grow through the summer. There will unfold a greater connectedness to Nature and to others, and it is not unusual to have individuals from your past step back into your life as a way of proving to yourself how much you have changed.

Dream activity becomes vibrant. This dream activity can often ~ reveal past life information important to where you are going. There will begin to unfold through the dreams glimpses of what the higher can bring.

Preparations

1. Make sure you will be undisturbed. Perform this meditation three days prior to and on the night of the summer solstice. It can be repeated periodically throughout the summer.
2. Have cake and ale, bread and wine, or any Eucharistic combinations available - a physical participation and grounding of the spiritual energies you invoke through this exercise.
3. This is a powerful exercise to do in a group situation, or it is powerful also if done with a partner of the opposite sex. (Make sure the individual is one with whom you have a good connection.)
4. Keep an air of celebration about this. You are participating in the celebration of new life - a new birth.

It is powerfully effective if performed outdoors, as the summer solstice is the high point of the forces of Nature in their yearly cycle. There is almost always a full or new moon at or around the time of the solstice. Make sure you perform this exercise then for the maximum results.

Meditation

Relax and breathe deeply the fresh summer night air. As you relax, allow your eyes to close. Feel the warm embrace of summer soothe and nurture you. Feel and imagine being lifted into that summer night sky and carried gently to the top of the high mountain that is now becoming familiar. As you allow your- self to be gently lowered before the beautiful Temple, imagine yourself as coming home. It is like a reunion or a wedding which draws all together.

As you stand outside the temple doors, you notice the trees on either side are still full and green. Over the past year there has been growth, and you can already see where there may need to be future trimming. These thoughts pass quickly as you look up into the night sky. It is filled with shades of deep blues and purples.

There is but one constellation visible, and one star among it shines brightly. Although you do not recognize the constellation, somehow you know that this is the star called Sirius. The Egyptians named it for the union of Isis and Osiris.

The door to the Inner Temple opens, and you bring your attention to the event at hand. You step through the doorway, and you find the temple seems much larger than you ever remembered. You are surprised to find yourself wearing a robe of white with images of emerald ivy and rich grapevines embroidered along its edge. The robe is tied at the waist with a silver cord, with a buckle inscribed with the symbol for the sign of Cancer.

A magnificent being of fire and light steps forward, its eyes embrace you, and it calls you by name. You recognize Auriel and are humbled. Auriel steps behind you and places upon your shoulders a cape of deep blue silk.

You step further into the Temple and look about you. The ceiling has a window in the shape of an equal-armed cross that opens the Temple to the heavens. In the distance you can see that one star shining down through it. The light casts its gleam in the shape of that cross upon the floor of the temple.

Around the temple, in tiers, sit men and women, alternating from all ages and all races upon the planet. These are the masters of the ancient schools of wisdom. Behind them sit all of those who, like you, are on the path to self-knowledge. Auriel steps forward and with a motion shows you to your seat.

Once seated you turn your attention toward the altar in the center. There in front stands a priest and priestess. They are dressed simply in robes of deep blue, and there are silver streaks in their hair. You hear your name spoken softly, and you see that they have fixed their eyes upon you - acknowledging you as they have with all who are present. Their eyes hold your attention. They are older than time, and they are filled with a mixture of pride, pain, love, and despair.

They turn to the altar and together lift Golden Chalice from it and raise it high over their heads. Together they sing out a word that is foreign and yet touches your heart. His voice is deep and hers crystalline and in harmony. In the four directions appear great columns of light. In the East a column of blue and gold rises and then forms the figure of the Archangel Raphael. In the West, a column of emerald green rises and then shimmers into the figure of the Archangel Gabriel. To the South, a column of brilliant red fire rises and then forms the figure of the Archangel Michael. And then to the North a column of crystalline white brilliance shimmers and before you is the Archangel Auriel.

Their voices are lost in a sound that begins to fill the temple. A light streams forth down from the star above, blessing the chalice. A wind blows through the temple, and you have never felt more alive than at this moment. . You never knew that the heavens had a song, but it is that song that fills you now. The temple fills with the force of this sound, and you surrender to it, are drawn within it and recreated by it.

And then there is silence.

As you become aware of the temple ceremony once more, you see yourself in ethereal form, standing before the High Priest and Priestess. Then from out of you steps the other half. For every male, there is the female, and for every female there is the male. They live within us all.

Auriel steps forward, and the priest and priestess stand aside. You watch as Auriel takes the hand of the female you and places it within the hand of the male you. Auriel holds the two hands together and then breathes upon them, binding them together for eternity. You watch as your male half and your female half turn to each other and embrace. The two forms seem to melt into each other - blending, changing, swirling - until there stands a single figure with the essence of both. In the shimmering light around them you see faintly the sign of Cancer. You shiver and you feel the blended essence of both once more within you. You feel stronger, more clear and focused. It is as if you can truly see now.

The priest steps forward and pours wine into the Golden Chalice. The priestess breaks the bread into pieces for all in attendance. As the bread is passed around, with its taste comes the awareness that you will never again lack for loving guidance. And as the wine is blessed and passed around, its taste fills your mind with the thought that in love there is no division of faith.

These are part of the High Mysteries that as yet you have only seen through a veil. You feel a gentle touch upon your shoulder. It is time to leave. The rest you are not ready for. Auriel leads you to the door and the twin columns formed by the trees. You are filled with a sense of peace.

Auriel steps forward, embraces you, and kisses you gently upon the head. With the kiss comes a feeling of exquisite joy. Gently you reach out with your heart and your mind, daring to touch this magnificent being, aware of a new power within you. For a moment the intensity is too much to endure, but for a few brief seconds you find yourself at one with this great being of light and you know your life will never be the same. The door to the Inner Temple closes, but you know it will never seal you out. You know it will be a part of all aspects of your life forever, as you bring it alive within your life!

Part Three

Symphony of the Land

"In Xanadu, did Kubla Kahn
A stately pleasure-dome decree:
Where Alph, the sacred river, ran
Through caverns measureless to man
Down to a sunless sea.
So twice five miles of fertile ground
With walls and towers were girdled round:
And here were gardens bright with sinous rills,
Where blossomed many an incense-bearing tree,
And here were forests ancient as the hills,
Enfolding sunny spots of greenery."

- Samuel Taylor Coleridge "Kubla Kahn"

Natural Wonders

No one knows for sure how many species of plants actually exist, but it is estimated that there are at least 1/4 of a million flowering plants alone. It is believed though that we are losing an average of about 3 species of plants every day from a variety of landscapes. While Hawaii accounts for less than 1/2 of one percent of the United States landmass, it is home to 1/4 of all US endangered species. In fact, 1/3 of all species of birds lost worldwide, were lost in Hawaii.

Chapter Nine

Reading Landscapes & Terrains

As I worked to put this book together, I wondered how many environments and their plant and animal species would be around in the next century – or even the next decade. How much wildlife will we lose? How much more deprived of the natural world will people become? Will experiences with Nature be limited to books, films and recorded images of Nature's wonders? Or will there be natural areas still accessible to the average person?

Yes, natural extinction has occurred for eons, but that is more of a changing of the guard. Better adapted species take the place of those lost. But in the last century, most plant and animals species lost to us have been lost due to human cause. Right now, half of all rainforests will be gone in a few more years. While we can't restore what is gone, we can develop a new relationship with Nature before more of it is lost to us. And its wisdom and blessings lost along with it.

We can begin by developing a new perspective on Nature. We truly are the Stewards of the Earth, whether we choose to believe it or not. No one else upon this planet has the capability to destroy or preserve the natural wonders. It is therefore our responsibility, so we can start by relating to plants as we do our homes. Care for them and their environments. Protect them. Treat them respectfully, as we do your own furnishing. Recognize animals as younger siblings, needing protection at times. Embrace all environments as sacred temples in which the spiritual and wonders of the life play out everyday in microcosmic splendor.

Sacred Directions

Many societies attributed special qualities and energy patterns to the four directions of North, South, East and West. Where the landscape faces, where the plant or animal appears in relation to you, can help you pinpoint the lessons as they apply to your life.

The South is the area purification and awakening the inner child. The West is the place of visions, dreams and new journeys. When I moved in 1997 to my farm, I moved South and West of where I was living. The move has allowed me to pursue more dreams and to reawaken my spirit and creativity on many levels. But it has also involved cleansing the old way of doing and pursuing.

What direction does your home face? This will tell you much about the issues and energies at play around your home life. In which direction do you travel to work? Working with the directions can help bring some enlightenment to old issues and to new enedeavors.

The East is the direction of healing and creativity. The sun rises in the East, so it brings illumination. It awakens intuition and new birth, opening opportunities for new learning. The East often reflects issues of strength of will, communication and expression.

The West is the direction of visions and dreams. To the Native Americans it is the direction for sacred quests and journeys, stimulating the imagination and creativity. The West awakens the feminine, higher compassion. Its energies help with spiritual renewal and the achievement of goals.

The South is the direction for cleansing and purification. It stirs the energies of faith and strength. It awakens the inner child and provides guidance in overcoming obstacles. It stimulates playfulness and change around us. It brings energies of protection and resurrection. It brings to light issues of self-sufficiency and trust.

The North is the direction of teaching, sacred wisdom and knowledge. It has an energy that brings balance and abundance. It awakens issues of thankfulness and trust, and its energies help us to draw upon our inner treasures and develop empathic intuition.

Landscapes, Terrains and Habitats

There is a variety of ecosystems in Nature, and although we may speak of them distinctly and separately, they are all connected to each other. Birds, animals, insects move between them. A variety of plants grows within and connects them. Together they influence the elements of air, wind and rain. These ecosystems are also landscapes and/or environments. Within those individual landscapes are varying terrains, habitats and a multitude of individual plants and animals.

For our purposes, we will refer to a landscape as to an outlay of land that is visible, a particular environment. It can be a patio, a backyard, a garden or part of a park that we choose to walk in. It is the general panoramic view of the scenery before us. Terrain is a description of the natural features within that landscape. For example, the landscape may have a rocky terrain or be comprised of rolling hills. It can be barren or fertile, cluttered and dense or eroded. There are many possibilities of terrains within a landscape.

A habitat is an area of Nature within that landscape that is livable for plants and animals. While plants and animals prefer certain types of habitats, one that is truly viable must have a number of features: appropriate climate, a varied terrain, food (especially plants), water and safe places to build homes. In any habitat, there can be thousands of plants, animals, insects and microorganisms. In general, more variety in terms of plants and animals within a habitat indicates better health of that environment

Plants and animals develop traits that help them to survive a specific habitat. This ability is adaptation to the environment. The beaver has special "goggles", layers over the eyes, fur that is waterproof and webbed feet, which enables it to survive in its watery environment. The hog nosed snake has an upturned nose that helps it dig out prey in the soil. Pine needles have a wax-like substance on them hat allows dew and moisture to slide off easily to water the roots. Corn roots can grow at a rate of 2-4 inches per day for three or four weeks. The root tip secretes a weak acid, which breaks down surrounding soil particles. This releases minerals from the soil that the plant will eventually absorb.

In interpreting Nature's signs and omens, we must remember that everything is significant and everything in some way relates to our lives and us. All things are connected, thus an element of the landscape that catches our attention is related to an element within our own life. Different landscapes reflect different states of being. The difficulty is in distinguishing between predominant elements and incidental ones. As we begin to explore and assess the general landscape and environments for signs and messages, we will see what we need to see. We will notice what is important to our lives and to us. Aspects of the landscape, certain features and elements within it, will stand out for us as significant and symbolic messages.

The art of reading and understanding these signs, omens and messages in Nature accurately is a three step process. We can read signs and omens with any one of these methods individually, but when we combine them, the signs and omens will become clearer. The messages will be more accurate. And Nature will even begin to reveal our destiny. These three steps are:

1. Assessing the landscape and terrain (provides a general overview)
2. Assessing the habitats
3. Assessing individual plants and/or animals that catch our attention

Step 1 - Assessing the Landscape and Terrain

The landscape and terrain reflects the general overview of your life or some aspect within it. Your home environment reflects the basic energy at play around you. Often when we first reflect upon the landscape, the terrain is what stands out first. The terrain reflects the natural features found within a landscape. It provides clues to the terrain of your life in some way. For example, a terrain, which is flowing and balanced (with a variety of elements), reflects a flow and balance at play in most of your life circumstances and activities. One that is dense and overgrown may reflect that the individual is overwhelmed, is taking on too much activity or even is not dealing with life situations appropriately. The landscape and terrain are symbols of something within our life.

Carl Jung said that symbols are not manufactured but are discovered through primal inner sources. Landscapes are living mandalas, filled with symbols that stimulate those primal inner sources imprinted upon the deeper levels of our consciousness. The landscape is a psychic transformer, helping us to connect through its symbolic characteristics with our missing parts, with answers to our questions and with the guidance and direction we need. It provides a general guide to the energy patterns at play around us. Landscapes and all of their elements miniaturize archetypal energies, so that we can experience and relate to them. We are put in touch with these energies through our senses when out in Nature. In other words, everything we notice or assess about the landscape will provide insight into some pattern of our own lives.

168

Begin by taking note of its geometric shape or the shapes that seem to stand out most strongly within it. All landscapes have some geometric form or shape to it. They do not always take the shape that is regular, but it does have some form that visually we can identify. We can look out and assess its shape generally: it seems oval-shaped, it seems rectangular, or it has a rolling and waving form to it. This shape or the portion of it that we are focused upon will reveal much about the energies at play within the environments of other parts of our life.

To understand how this is possible, we must realize that geometric shapes alter and focus electro-magnetic energies. They amplify, diminish, shift or direct energy, eliciting a response in the environment and impact upon those in their vicinity. Individuals sometimes have difficulty believing that geometry and form (natural or architectural) really has an effect upon us, but look at your home environment. In which room(s) do you spend the most time? The angles of that room may be affecting your electro-magnetic energy patterns, being more soothing to them. Look at the angles and shapes of the rooms you spend the most amount of time in and the angles and shapes of rooms that make you feel the most uncomfortable. When out in Nature, are there certain terrains that are more appealing to you? Are there parts of your yard that are more healing? More stimulating? More uncomfortable?

Think of your landscape (your room, your yard, your neighborhood) as a mandala. In the East, a mandala is a visual doorway between worlds. It is a tool for focusing energy and concentrating the mind in order to pass through the usual and often subconscious blocks and fetters. In Eastern philosophy, they are known as yantras. In the Native American tradition, they are known as medicine shields, They can be a mixture of symbolic pictures or geometric patterns designed to elicit a specific effect or to send a particular message.

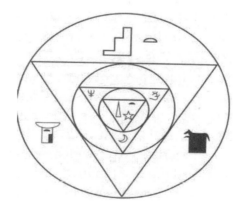

Mandala for stimulating dream activity

A mandala is designed to draw our consciousness more fully into some concept. It is a vehicle for bringing us back in touch with the universe or some aspect of it. It stimulates the intuition. and affects the emotons. It is a tool of integration and transformation, a form of action and interaction with us. If we learn to perceive the landscapes we encounter as living mandalas, they will arouse our intuition and guide us through doorways of integration and transformation. We will find is a source of answers. Nature becomes a mandala oracle.

Learning to look at your own landscape (home, yard, and environment) as a mandala is a powerful way of opening to the language and messages of Nature. The landscape is a symbol of a specific energy at play within it. Because we are part of that landscape, it reflects a specific play of energy within the landscape of our life circumstances.When you look at a particular landscape in relation to some question or for some guidance in an area of our life, ask yourselves some simple questions:

What emotion do you feel in rersponse to the landscape?

Every landscape will stimulate an emotional response in us. And the same landscape can affect different emotions at different times, depending upon where we are and what is going on within our life. Try to define the emotion you feel from the general landscape. How does it make you feel? Is it stimulating? Relaxing? Does it make you tense or excited? Does it inspire? Always take a moment to just feel. Close your eyes, breathe deeply and sense how you are feeling? Try to pinpoint the emotional response to the landscape because it provides a strong clue to the overall energy at play.

What does the general shape and outlay of the land tell you?

Use the chart on the opposite page to help determine the meaning of the general space and form. Keep in mind that form in Nature is always irregular. In Chinese feng shui, the idea is to create symmetry in landscapes so that there is a more harmonious flow. This is accomplished by planting to create an illusion of symmetry. But even in irregularity, we can attribute some basic shape or form to the landscape.

Does the environment seem balanced? Do straight lines cut across the landscape? In feng shui, fences, wires roads that dissect may intercept the flow of natural energy or create disruptions in it. There should be both horizontal and vertical features (trees, clearings and ponds). This reflects a balance of female and male, a balance of receiving and giving. Remember that what you notice or what stands out for you is the message.

Examine the edges. Gradual changes are much healthier than sharp. There should be smooth transitions, reflecting a more gentle flow

Geometric Shapes and Their Meanings

Circles are the most natural and perfect shapes in nature. It creates an energy of wholeness and health. The circle is the womb, and it helps establish a union between human and divine, inner and outer, upper and lower. It awakens energies to resolve problems and difficulties more easily. Spiral circles are the most common geometric shape found within the natural world. It is the spiral of life, death and rebirth. It even reflects the spiral of the DNA molecule. Its shape stimulates t he energy of change and transformation for good or bad. It is powerfully healing and its shape helps reveal the karma of present life situations. It stimulates creativity.

Crosses and intersections are power points. Wherever there is an intersection, there is a thinning of the veils between the physical and the spiritual. It is catalytic in its balancing effects. It balances opposites, creating polarity – the balanced male and female with all of their symbolism. It can reflect the intersection of waking and dreaming – stimulating more vibrant and lucid dreams.

Crescent shapes enhance the healing of emotions and stimulate greater expressiveness. They awaken intuition and the imagination.

Diamond shapes are activating and stimulating. They awaken creativity and inspiration. They can have a powerful affect on dreams, making them more colorful and are often reminders for us to pursue them.

Polygon shapes (many-sided) have unique energies. **Five-sided** landscapes are balancing and grounding. It activates the energies of the individual, strengthening creativity and individuality. It can awaken a concentrated force of spirit, reflecting spirit over the elements, reason over matter. **Six-sided** landscapes have an energy that touches the heart and issues of the heart. It activates energy of balancing opposites in a healing manner. Six is the number of home and family and these energies are stimulated strongly in landscapes with this number of sides. **Seven-sided** landscapes manifest some gentle and dynamic healing energies. Seven has always been a mystical number and its energy affects all of the major systems of the body and works to bring them into balance. It is soothing to the emotions and is especially amplifying to the healing energies for children.

Squares and rectangles are grounding. They creates an energy that is calming, one that provides stability and a foundation. It brings together a merging of inner and outer forces for a stronger foundation. Although their energies are similar, the rectangle energy has a bit more activity to it. It amplifies the initiation of new activities in a more solid fashion. It is also stabilizing.

Triangular shapes amplify and diminish energy flows, depending upon whether it is upright or reversed. It stimulates emotions and it can bring unresolved issues and events to a head. Inverted triangles reflect the yoni or feminine energies of energy. If you are noticing abrupt changes, you may expect the same in some area of your life.

Does it look healthy?

A healthy landscape has four layers - ground, plant, shrub & tree. Anything missing, may reflect something missing from your life as well. It can also show us where to more successfully put our efforts and energies. Does the landscape look barren or fertile? If there are areas of barrenness, it might be telling us about missing aspects within our own life. Elements that would help make the landscape healthier can often reflect things that will make our own life healthier as well.

Dense and tangled landscapes have more animal species than simple, clear ones. On the other hand, tangled landscapes may indicate a density that is choking off new growth. A cluttered terrain is often symbolic of other things. Clutter can be an actual mess, but it also can reflect the state of our mind and emotions. Debris can prevent movement and a flow of creativity and health. Erosion areas can indicate that something is slowly washing away. We may need to establish new roots or plant something new to create a stabile ground foundation in some area of our life. Natural barriers may indicate problems or walls that we may be heading toward in some area of our life.

Overgrown and entangled landscapes often reflect either the idea of devouring, being swallowed up or the idea of being encloked in protection. Are we losing ourselves in something? What are we entangled in? When vegetation seems to swallow up the environment, we may want to look at issues surrounding digestion - literally and figuratively. Do we need to look at some health issues concerning our digestive system, or is there something going on in our life that is hard to digest.In the South, kudzu seems to swallow up everything it with which it comes in contact. Are there issues that the South is having difficulty digesting? It might bear examination.

What is the general terrain?

What kind of terrain does it have? Rocky, flowing, barren? Is it overgrown, dense and cluttered? Are there varying types? What do those terrains indicate about the flow of energy into your life?

Terrain predominantly comprised of mud or animals encountered at times when mud is prevalent (after rains, etc.) are very significant. Mud is the union of earth and water. This combination reflects transition and transformation. Mud is the substance of birth. It is the medium for the emergence of matter. - This landscape reflects that there is a new stimulation occurring in some area of your life.

Mud can also be a reminder to recharge and strengthen our connection to primal earth. The plants and animals that appear may provide the clues to how best to accomplish this. Mud usually reflects the opportunity for new germination within your life. On the other hand, excessive amounts of mud can warn of the same thing. Are you bogged down in a particular area of your life? Are your emotions bogging you down? Are you stuck in old emotions and unwilling to grow and move on?

Rocky terrain can reflect many possibilities, all colored by the plants and animals within that area. Rocks have been depicted in story and myth as obstacles that need to be climbed over. They are often symbols for the true self. Of course, different rocks and stones have different meanings-each with its own unique qualities. Rocky terrains, especially high upon mountains, were often considered the dwelling place of gods and goddesses because they were so inaccessible.

On the other hand though, they also can reflect solidness, stability, and sturdiness. They can be a point from which we can gain a new perspective. Many people can't resist standing or climbing rocks to gain a view of the sur- rounding terrain. In learning animal-speak, we begin by looking at the animals. But we do not stop there. If we truly want to understand how the Divine is expressing itself to us through Nature, we should also examine the environment in which the totem is discovered, along with its natural habitat if it is different from where it was encountered.

Reading Landscapes With

When the use of geometric shapes is applied to living environments, it is called feng shui, which has become so popular lately. Feng shui is the ancient Chinese art that helps us to live harmoniously with our environment. It is art that uses ancient wisdom to assist in arranging furniture and buildings to achieve the greatest harmony with Nature. This Chinese practice is based on principles of design, ecology, mysticism and architecture. Feng shui evolved from the simple observations that people are affected, for good or ill, by their surroundings. The Chinese, as with many societies, saw a dynamic link between landscapes and humans. They believed that Nature reacts to every change and that reaction resounds within the life of the human.

Feng shui is a language of symbols associated with landscapes - rural, city, towns, and even in the rooms of a home. To the feng shui person, the shape of the landscape could leave an imprint upon an individual's life, affecting the character or the prosperity. It can be read and interpreted in very significant ways that need to be considered if we are to become fluent in speaking and understanding the language of Nature.

Feng shui principles can be applied to a room, a patio, a garden, a backyard and even larger landscapes. And it can be a wonderful tool for reading the landscape. In feng shui, the environment takes on a symbolic quality. For example, round or square openings, symbolizing heaven and earth, are good features in gardens as they allow a view of the world beyond and open up to infinite possibilities for movement and change. Mountains could be watchdogs or dragons, rivers could be serpents, and hills could be barriers. Trees could reflect longevity and protection, and flat, riverless plains are often considered devoid of energy. Looking at the symbolic qualities of the landscape can reveal much more information.

Chinese Feng Shui

This process can be applied in both rural and city environments. In the city, high buildings replace mountains, and roads replace rivers. The size, the shape, and the colors of buildings and skyscrapers affect the natural flow of energy and reflect much about what kind of energy will manifest in your life. The directions of roads and the angles can help define this as well.

For a number of years, I lived in a home that had a slight hill behind it. At the top of the hill was a line of apartment buildings that were like the vertebrae of the dragon. Separating the apartments from my home on this hill was thick foliage and trees of rich green, which would indicate to a traditional feng shui person that this is a spot of high energy. It is a spot where a variety of animals gathered - raccoons, opossum, crows, woodpeckers, owls and a variety of other birds and small mammals.

Unfortunately one year, the city demanded that the apartment owners clear out the trees and foliage. Though they gutted the area, it took little more than a month before it was green and growing wild again, in spite of their efforts to seed it with plant life that could be more easily controlled. Even new trees were stretching upward, all attesting to the positive flow of power in this area. It simply reinforced the impression that the dragon my home was nestled against was both very powerful and very beneficent.

A study of feng shui will provide some wonderful insights into the landscape of your life and its significant symbols and meaning to you. And while at one time, few books were available on the subject, today there is a multitude that we can draw upon.

175

#2   Assess the habitats.

When we decide to explore habitats, whether it is to observe animals or to study plants, it is best to learn one habitat at a time. Animals usually frequent specific habitats, and although some species of plants are found in a variety of habitats, other plants can be found only in specific kinds. Animals are intimately aware of their environment and notice changes within it. We should do the same. By repeated visits, throughout the year, we will notice more and more subtleties in animal and plant life.

Find a place to sit and try not to disturb the environment. You do not need to wear camouflage. Natural clothes are fine, but avoid smoking and wearing perfumes or colognes. Keep your movement slow. Sit with the sun at your back so the animals have to squint to see you. Keep the wind in your face so that your smell will fan out behind you.

Early morning and late in the day are the best times to explore habitats for animal encounters. Visiting habitats at night can provide a tremendously wondrous experience. Cover your flashlight with a red filter. You will still be able to see and many animals see red as black and will not notice the light. Practice using your peripheral vision. Shift your vision from directly in front of you to surrounding areas every few minutes.

For plants, visit habitats at different times of the year and different times of day. The shifts in seasons and the shifts in daylight will make species of plant life stand out more clearly. With each change of season, there will be subtle changing in the green environment. Some flowers only bloom in the spring, while they can still get sunlight. Tree foliage will eventually fill out, blocking the sunlight and preventing the blossoming at other times of the year.

Study one area of the habitat at a time. Make a list of plants or things observed. Some people choose to make drawings of the environment. Either way provides a record that you can refer to with each visit thereafter. It will help you to note the changes. Take along a good field guide to help identify species of plants.

Change your focus regularly. My wife and I frequently give each other whiplash when exploring or walking through Nature. I am usually looking up, studying the trees, birds and distant edges. I am often grabbing her and pointing to something I see. My wife who is a Master Gardner is usually focused on the ground and is often grabbing me to point out an unusual plant. Shift your vision and perspective. Occasionally brush away leaf litter to look for new growth.

Do not be afraid to imbibe the senses. Note the colors. Breathe in the fragrances. Touch the plants and trees. As always in Nature, take only pictures and leave only footprints. A number of habitats and landscapes are in the following chapter. It will provide some guidelines and insights for you, but always begin by asking yourself some questions:

What kind of habitat is it and what does it reflect?

Remember though that every habitat has its own unique qualities. For example, wetlands are areas of breaking down the old for new growth & reproduction, and forests are environments of practical applications & healing. Within them are found sources of wood for paper, aromatherapy, color therapy, and more.

Is the habitat diverse with a lot of elements?

The more diversity there is, the healthier the habitat is. Most animals spend most of their time in areas where there needs can be met. Most animals depend on a variety of habitats to meet their needs – old and young growth, clearings, water, etc. Dense and tangled habitats usually indicate more species – plant and animal. It may also indicate a tangling up of emotions, activities, etc. in your own life. In general though, habitats with a wider variety of plant life are usually healthier.

#3   Assess specific plants and animals that catch our attention.

Everything about the plant or animals that catches our attention has significance for us. Where it is encountered, its unique qualities, its color, its fragrance (in the case of plants), its behaviors (in the case of animals), everything about it has significance. In my books *ANIMAL-SPEAK* and *ANIMAL-WISE*, I have thoroughly covered the process of how to begin understanding the significance of animals in Nature.

Throughout the rest of this book are guidelines for doing so with the plant kingdom as well. It involves combining the scientific with the mythological. Use the doctrine of signatures as a guide to understanding the symbology of the plant within your life. Use the descriptions in the dictionaries provided in this text as a starting point. But do not limit yourself to this. Do your own study and explorations.

Exercise

Creating
Sacred Space

Benefits:

- **Strengthens your ability to tap into your psychic senses**
- **Develops your attunement to Nature**
- **Heightens all of your perceptions of signs**

Every area in Nature is like a sacred temple, each with its own unique energies, reminding us that there are a myriad of ways to worship and celebrate. Even those areas of erosion remind us of neglected things we have allowed to run off or slowly disappear, sacred and mundane parts of our life. Finding or creating places in Nature to meditate, pray or just do "quiet sitting" in the tradition of Confucianism is one of the most empowering things you can do in Nature to open to her heart and soul language.

Have you ever been some place where there was a great sense of peace? Ever be so relaxed or into something that you lost track of time? If so, you have experienced a sacred place and time. There is a shift away from "normal" thinking and feeling. Sometimes this experience is referred to as an altered state of consciousness. This just means that our focus has shifted. One of the keys to learning to shift to our magical and psychic self at will is to create or to find a sacred space. Sacred spaces shift our attention and focus from the normal daily activities to magical ones. They help us to hear the inner voice more clearly. And most psychic experiences have to do with listening to the inner self. This is accomplished most easily and naturally through Nature.

Sacred spaces create powerful magical intersections in our life. They are places and times where the inner and outer worlds meet. They are intersections where the physical and spiritual can come together. They are where the past, present and future flow together to help us understand how they each affect the others. They are where psychic perceptions become stronger and more normal. Through sacred spaces the veils that separate worlds and creative wonders become thinnest.

To begin developing your ability to read signs and omens in Nature, you need to create a sacred space, a place that you can use for all of your psychic and magical explorations. It is an actual place in the outer world that connects you to your inner world of magical abilities. It can be as simple as the corner of your room or a corner of your yard. You should have space enough though to sit, and you should be able to close out distractionsSacred spaces can be anywhere and any time. It is up to you though to make them sacred and special. You must create that bridge between worlds and to new possibilities.

Here are some guidelines that will help:

- **You do not need a large space.**

    A corner of a room or a corner of a yard where you can spend a half hour or so undisturbed and quiet is all that is necessary.

- **Create an altar or sacred center.**

    This can be a desktop that is cleared or a fold out table for indoor space. It does not need to be large. On it you will be able to set special items that help you shift your awareness from the outer to the inner. For outdoor spaces, it can be a table, a log, a large flat stone or even a campfire area.

- **Have a special cloth that you only use for your magical work.**

    This is sometimes called an altar cloth. It should cover part of the surface or easily spread out before you. Upon it you can set items that are helpful and special to you. This works indoors and outdoors, but I have also found that a covering of leaves when outdoors is very effective.

- **Have aids to help you.**

    Candles, incense, whatever is comfortable and special for you are wonderful aids to create sacred space. They set a mood. The lighting and dowsing of the candles also signals the doors opening and closing. Some will tell you that you need to mark the space more magically, but for our purposes nothing more is needed than what is given here. Remember to take care when using any flame outdoors. A small campfire in a protected area is a powerful aid and fabulous for shifting consciousness.

- **Make it a special time through clothing and special preparations.**

    Use a meditation or prayer shawl (a special blanket, towel or cloth that you use only for this). Each time you use it in your magical practices or have it with you, you charge it with magical energy. When you use it outdoors in Nature, it absorbs the energies of Nature surrounding you. Eventually all you will have to do is wrap it around you, pull it up over the head or even just sit on it, and it begins to shift you from normal everyday type of thinking to your creative, psychic and magical part. It connects you back to those same energies of Nature.

    I have several meditation cloths that I sit on or drape about my shoulders and head. I use them according to my purpose. One is for healing and one is just for meditation. I also have a special meditation rug – my magic carpet. It is about 2 feet by 3 feet. In all of my meditations, I unfold it and sit upon it. I have one I use indoors and one that I take outdoors with me for when I wish to sit on the ground or meditate beneath a tree.

- **Create a portable sacred space if necessary.**

    It can be as simple as a candle and a cloth that you take with you and use for your work. I do a lot of work outdoors, so I have a box of sacred things that I use in those activities. I just carry them with me.

    When you have set up your sacred space, light your candle(s), your small campfire or just lay out your meditation blanket, rug or shawl. Take a seated position. Breathe deeply, relaxing. Just focus on being as comfortable and as relaxed as possible. Send warm soothing thoughts and energy to every part of your body.

    As you begin to relax, notice how the atmosphere in that habitat changes. It is softer, calmer, and more peaceful. The colors soften. Fragrances of plants around you grow stronger. This is the shift into sacred space. Close your eyes and just enjoy the quiet sounds of Nature..

*"Intersections in the natural
world are doorways
between realms.
They are sacred portals
that open us to times past
and times future.
They awaken
the mythic imagination
and can be catalysts
for making changes in our life."*

Exercise

Spirit Keepers of the Green Kingdom

Benefits:

- **Opens us to the hidden forces of Nature**
- **Brings contact with the spirit teachers & nature spirits**
- **Opens doorways to the secrets of Nature**
- **Manifests surprise blessings and opportunities**
- **Stimulates lucid dreaming;**
- **Promotes healing of the past**
- **Stimulates movement & growth**

Of all the magical exercises associated with Nature that I have done and still do, this exercise is one of my favorites. I try to do it around the time of the full moon and at least once per season. If endeavors and things in my life are blocked, this exercise helps to release the energy for movement. It realigns me with the rhythms of Nature and it openes me up to the sacred Spirit Keepers found in all natural environments. It can awaken stronger contact with all spirit teachers, and especially the nature spirits. This exercise is filled with images and symbols to awaken our inner self on many levels.

1. If possible, perform this exercise outdoors in a safe and secluded spot, one of your sacred areas. If performing it outdoors is not possible, it will still be effective when performed indoors. If you do perform it indoors, make sure you will not be disturbed. Choose a candle and fragrance to help you set the mood.

2. Perform a progressive relaxation. The more relaxed we are - especially when out in Nature - the more powerful the results and the stronger connection to the plants, animals and spirits of Nature.

3. Feel the rhythm of Nature. Breathe deep the fragrance around you. Listen to the soft rustling of leaves andthe sounds of birds in the background. Allow your eyes to close, and in your mind's eye, visualize yourself on a garden pathway not far from where you are seated. You are surprised that you had not noticed it before...

The grasses are soft and rich beneath your feet. The summer flowers are bright around you. Your home is behind you, and you are standing upon a path that leads down to a green meadow. As you step out into the meadow, you see a pool of clear water. At the far end of the pool is a waterfall. You move toward it and you feel its spray, cool and misty on your face. As it splashes into the pool, all reflections are distorted. The sun is warm upon you as you stand next to the water.

You tilt your head, listening to the environment. You are surprised. There is no other sound other than your own breathing and the splashing of the waterfall. There are no sounds of life. you realize that since you have followed the path, there have been no sounds of Nature. This garden meadow looks pleasant enough, but where is all of the life? It appears to be all form and no substance.

As you stand next to the waterfall, you notice a small cave half-concealed behind it. You step carefully behind the waterfall and into the inner darkness of the mouth of the cave. What little light there is comes through the opening by the waterfall. It shimmers through the splashing water, casting dancing shadows about the cave.

The air inside the cave is cool and damp. The floor is moist from the mist of the waterfall. The only sound is that of the splashing until you step further into the cave. You begin to detect a soft sound, a second splashing – only like waves against the shore.

You move deeper into the cave, leaving the light of the entrance behind you. The ceiling begins to slope down, causing you to hunch. It is more difficult to see and you move more by feel than by sight. The sound of the waterfall becomes softer, fading, while the soft rolling sound of gentle waves against a shoreline becomes stronger. Still you move further into the cave. At the far end you discover a second opening. A pale light comes from the other side, illuminating this opening for you.

This opening has not been used in ages. It is thick with cobwebs, and you gingerly peel the silken threads back. You step through the opening and find yourself in an open beach area next to a large river. It is nighttime here, and only the light of a distant moon illuminates the area. Next to the water's edge is a small boat.

You step carefully down to the edge of the river. It is black and it stills as you approach. The full moon reflects off of its surface, emphasizing its black depth – as if to tell you that these are the waters from the womb of the earth - from which all life came forth.

You look out across the river. A vague outline of an island is barely visible through the soft fog that surrounds it. It is then that you notice the man. Tall and broad, he looks at you with piercing eyes. He motions to the boat, inviting you silently. You hesitate, a little fearful of this strange figure. He gestures a second time. Still you hesitate.

"We are never given a hope wish or dream without also being given opportunities to make them a reality."

His voice is soft, deep and gentle. It touches a chord within you. You step forward and into the boat. The dark man steps in and stands in the back. With one of the oars, he pushes the boat from the shore. The trip is silent as he maneuvers the boat through the dark waters. Your only comfort is the soft reflection of the moon upon the water's surface. Soon you move into the fog. It blocks your view of the shore and of the island. You are cloaked in it. Not even the moonlight penetrates. It is so thick that you are not even sure that you are moving. It is as if you are hanging in a cloud – stuck in limbo. You look toward your guide, but his face is stoic, showing no expression. He merely goes about the business of working the oars as if you are not even there.

Then you feel a soft bump, and you know you have reached the island. The guide motions for you to stand. As you do the fog begins to thin. He steps from the back of the boat and into the water. He wades to the shore and then offers his assistance in stepping out onto the shore. It is then that you notice the medallion of wings, encircled in a wreath, that hangs around his neck. He nods in acknowledgement of your noticing, and then he steps back.

Before you is a path leading up a slight incline out of the mist of the black river. It is lined with trees on either side. You hear what seem to be whispers from those trees and catch subtle movements out of the corners of your eyes. As you climb to the top, you find yourself at the entrance to a large clearing in which is an open-air temple. It is lit by torches and the full moon, which is now directly overhead. The air is sweets with the fragrance of exotic flowers and herbs.

In the center of this temple is an old stone altar. You walk closer, and upon the altar you see a mirror, engraved with the images of plants and vines, a small bowl of water and a medallion with wings, just as your guide had worn. Across the front of the altar, chiseled into the stone are all of the phases of the moon.

From behind the altar, as if appearing from the shadows, step three women. One is a young child. The second is what appears to be her mother, and the third is an old woman. All three wear robes of gray. The old woman has an insignia upon her robe of the dark of the moon. The mother has one of the full moon, and the child has one of the new moon.

These are the creative forces of the Earth and the moon. These are the feminine energies, the true guardians of dreams. They are the Ancient Spirit Keepers of Nature. You are not sure how you know this, but you do. It is familiar, as if it is a replay of a long-forgotten dream from childhood.

The child steps forward, lifts the engraved mirror from the altar and stands before you. She extends the mirror to you.

"When we first begin to open to new realms and new possibilities through the world of nature, we are all like children. These new realms and possibilities need to be nurtured and coaxed. We must learn the language to open fully to its wonders. The mirror is a tool that you can use to see how all life - plant, animal and mineral - reflects itself within your life. It is a tool to help you see the night reflected within the day, the inner within the outer, the magical within you."

With these words, she places the mirror within your hand and melts into you. You feel her essence alive within you, a bridge to the magical energies of the Nature coming to life within you like a child. You hold the mirror up and gaze at your reflection. Within your reflected image, you see the image of the child. She smiles at you. She is holding your favorite flower, and you cannot help but smile back, feeling a new sense of possibilities awakening.

The mother steps forward and raises the bowl of water from the altar. She holds it in front of you and you can see the moon reflected upon its surface.

"All cups, all bowls, all cauldrons contain birth-giving energies. From out of the cup of life comes the new. Out of the depths of the water comes new birth. Ponds, lakes, rivers, streams and even the waters of the Heavens are a source of life and replensishment for all plants and animals. As you learn to touch the subtle, magical areas of Nature, you will stir the magical waters within you. Only then can you truly bring them out and drink of them fully within your day to day life."

She then places the bowl of water within your hands, and like the child, she melts into you to become a part of you. You realize that the creative and magical exists throughout Nature and because you are a part of Nature, those same forces exist within you. You look into the water of the bowl and you see your reflection overshadowed by her. And you realize that your abilities will allow you to give birth and re-create your life. And you feel yourself being brought into the rhythms of Nature and its powerful ebb and flow.

As you look up from the bowl, the old woman stands before you. Aged and wrinkled though she may be, she has a vitality about her that is eternal. She is like an ancient tree with roots that extend deep into the earth and which has weathered many a season. Her eyes pierce deeply, seeing all within you and yet loving you regardless of it all. She holds in her hands a necklace of leather, upon which is the medallion of silver wings, encircled in a wreath. She holds it out to you, and you lean forward, lowering your head. She places the necklace and medallion about your neck.

"We three are the guardians of Nature. We are the Spirit Keepers. Every plant, animals and stone contains some spirit and part of our task is to watch over them and to guide those who are worthy to their wisdom. These wings will be a sign of your willingness to honor and open to those mysteries.

"There will come a time when these wings shall become wings of light. With them you shall be able to fly from one dimension to another, from night to day and back to night – all in the twinkling of an eye. With these wings you will open Nature's doorways to other realms with all of their wonders to explore. They have always been open to you but these wings are the reminder and the promise of our desire to work with you to fulfill your dreams. They are the promise of magic, which is born out of love through every season of the year. They are the promise of dreams fulfilled found in every expressions of life found within the world of Nature."

In her face you see the young child. Then it shifts, becoming the mother, and then once again it shifts, returning to the face of the old wise woman. There is a sparkle of amusement in her eyes. She smiles warmly upon you, and gently cups your face in her hands. She places a kiss upon your brow and melts into you.

You raise your face to the night and to the moon above. You feel the ancient energies alive within you. Never have you felt so connected to Nature. You feel the pulse of life in every plant and animals around you. You feel your own heart in rhtyhm with the Earth's heart. You feel them awakening your magic and your dreams. You close your eyes and offer a silent prayer of thanks for the magic and wonders of the natural world, which are about to unfold within your life.

As if in response to your prayer, a beam of light issues forth from the moon above. It forms a rainbow bridge of light back across the river. As you step upon this bridge of light to leave the ancient temple,part a part of you remembers an old myth. It is a myth about walking upon the path of moonbeams, the path to your heart's desire. And it is this thought that is strongest with you as you follow the path back to where you began this journey.

You cross this bridge of light, and it empties you into the cave. The cobwebs are gone, and you hear the waterfall in the distance. You move quickly back through the cave and out from behind the waterfall. The sunlight greets you warmly and you step down to the pool of water. You breathe deeply of the fresh air, and you feel as if the cobwebs have cleared from your life – just as they seemed to disappear from the cave.

You pause, taking another deep breath, but your breath catches. A flock of birds fly overhead. A fish jumps in the pool beside you. You look across the meadow, and a deer walks serenely into the open. You smile. The fragrance of spring flowers and new mown hay swirls about you. The garden meadow is alive! And there is life and sounds of life all around you now. Where there had been no sign of life, now it is everywhere. you were seated when this journey first began. You breathe deeply, feeling the Ancient Spirit Keepers of Nature strong within you and around you. You breather deeply, allowing the images to slowly disappear. You realize though that they fade from the inner world only so that they may now be born into the outer life. Allow yourself to stretch and become grounded before moving.

To further enhance this exercise's effects, you might wish to write your responses down in your Nature Journal. To help you ground you can also take a walk in nature to anchor these energies strongly into your life. Study something about the flower that the young girl held. Pay particular attention to signs from Nature over the next few days.

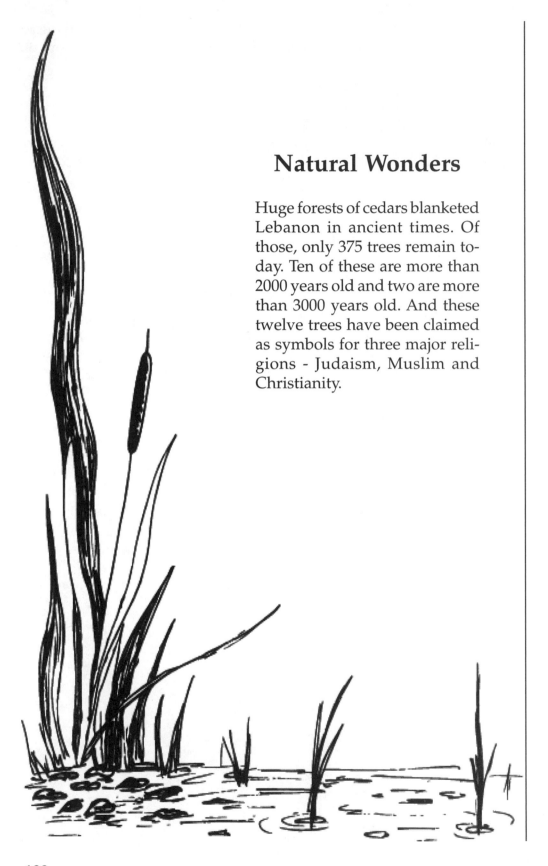

Natural Wonders

Huge forests of cedars blanketed Lebanon in ancient times. Of those, only 375 trees remain today. Ten of these are more than 2000 years old and two are more than 3000 years old. And these twelve trees have been claimed as symbols for three major religions - Judaism, Muslim and Christianity.

Chapter Ten

Dictionary of Landscapes

As mentioned in the previous chapter, one of the ways in which you can come to understand Nature and what she says to you through plants and animals is by examining the symbolism of the habitats. The landscape, the habitats, the countryside in which we observe and experience plants and animals can add much to our understanding of the role they will play in our life as totems and as signs. Keep in mind that the inner, spiritual forces often unfold as forms within Nature. This means then that a mountain crest has much greater significance than just being the top of a big hill.

Different worlds - different landscapes - reflect different states of beings. We can discover much about our own state of being by orienting ourselves to the landscapes within our life. Some study and reflection on important elements of the various landscapes and environments in which we find ourselves will reveal general patterns of energies, lessons and even future possibilities likely to unfold around us.

Determining the overall pattern of energy at play around us should always involve reflecting on three specific things about the landscape.

1. Begin by examining the shapes and contours of the environment.

Each environmental landscape has its own unique qualities. Wetlands, for example, are areas where there is a breaking down of old growth so that new growth can occur. Beaches and dunes are areas of adaptability. The type of landscape will also reveal more specifically about lessons and issues currently at play within your life. The dictionary that follows in this chapter will help with some of this.

Dances with Horses

Dancing and playing in an open field and meadow at the winter solstice is wonderful way of celebrating the return of the sun and of inviting the energies of creativity, balance and fertility back into your life more strongly. Doing so with a horse, as in the above photo, amplifies these energies tremendously in journeys throughout the coming year.

We have already mentioned how shape and form reflects certain energies and qualities. The overall shape will reveal much about the overall pattern of energy at play in some environment of your life – work, home, relationship, etc. Examine the landscape in which you live. Reflect on its symbolic qualities. Is it soft and rolling? Is it harsh and dry? Does it have balance?

2. *Then examine the plants and animals common to that landscape and which stand out for you.*

What is the predominant element(s).Most environments are homes to unique and special plants, trees and even animals. In most landscapes certain plants, trees and animals will always stand out for you. Study them specifically, but in relation to the landscape. They can often provide clues as to how little things in our lives relate to the whole pattern of energy at play.

Some of the plants indigenous to specific types of environments are provided in the descriptions that follow, and a study of them specifically will provide insight as to how specific elements of your own life may be influencing your overall environment. For example, cacti are common to many desert areas. They are plants that have learned to adapt to harsh temperature changes. If we find ourselves dreaming about, living in or visiting desert-type environments, then a study of the cacti can show us how we should adapt to live or accomplish tasks more successfully in that environment. Identifying the specific type of cactus will help pin point the skills most beneficial for us at this time in that area of our life.

3. *Pay attention to the edges of various environments.*

In most traditions around the world, edges have often been magical borders and boundaries – places where worlds and dimensions intersect. Although in fact, edges are areas that often support wildlife and plants that depend on several types of environments for survival. They are often the busiest zones of growth and change in an environment, signs showing up there first before appearing in the actual environment. Because of this, edges can be a tremendous source of omens and future castings – of things about to unfold. Plants, shrubs, bushes, animals and other border markers can be significant in letting us know what is happening at the edges of our own life. They can reveal things that haven't manifested yet but soon will. They can reveal subtle influences on us that we may not have recognized.

Landscapes and their elements not only serve as signs and messages but they also serve as catalysts, helping to trigger patterns of energy within our life. To understand how this can be, we must remember that we are an energy system. All living things have an energy field surrounding them. This field is most often referred to as an aura. It can be comprised of a variety of energy types and frequencies. The human body's aura is comprised of sound, light, electrical, magnetic, thermal energies and more. All energy fields and all auras – human and otherwise – have specific characteristics. Two of these in particular are essential to understand how environments and habitats can be catalysts as well as messages.

Every aura has its own unique frequency, its own fingerprint. No two are ever exactly alike. In humans the food we eat, the air we breathe, our activities and all aspects of our life come together influencing our energy system. All of the elements of our life that affect our physical, emotional, mental and spiritual health affect our aura, making it unique to us. The same is true of habitats. All of the elements of it come together to make it a unique energy system. And every type of habitat has its own unique aura and we will explore a number of these later in the chapter. (For information on the aura and its all of its characteristics, you might wish to refer to my book *How to See and Read the Aura* through Llewellyn Publications.)

One of the most important characteristics of any energy field or aura though is that it will interact with other energy fields and auras. Because of the strong electro-magnetic aspects of the aura, we are constantly giving off (the electrical aspect) and absorbing (the magnetic aspect) energy from everyone and everything we encounter. This includes not only other humans but also all living things - especially plants, animals and habitats.

Most people know that being around Nature is balancing and cleansing to our energy. We feel better after being out in Nature. There is also much truth to the idea that hugging a tree is healthy for you. Our energy field interacts with that of the tree, resulting in specific effects. As we will learn later in this book, each tree has its own unique and powerful energy field. For example, sitting under a willow tree for five or ten minutes will alleviate headaches and body pains. Pine trees are very cleansing and balancing to strong emotions, especially feelings of guilt. I have a wonderful pine tree in my front yard that I am often sitting under an hour before my family visits and several hours afterwards – bless their hearts.

Just as different trees can be hugged for different effects, encounters with other natural elements - such as plants, flowers and habitats - can serve as catalysts. They all have unique effects upon us. The stronger the element and the longer the contact with it, the greater the energy exchange. It then becomes a catalyst, affecting us and our life on some level.

Habitats, because they comprise so many elements, living together, can have a strong catalytic impact. Spending intentional time in a particular environment during one of those temporal doorways (changes of the seasons discussed earlier), when signposts and catalytic energy is more available, can elicit a variety of changes for us throughout the season. It will set certain energy patterns in motion around us throughout that season. Thus if we spend time in an environment that has a particular energy to it, it will trigger a resonance within us, serving as a catalyst, for healing, change, cleansing, inspiration, peace, joy, strength or a variety of other possibilities – depending upon the kind of habitat and its elements.

The following list provides a starting point for you in the process of understanding the meaning and influence of various habitats, but keep in mind that the descriptions are only sketches. Entire books could be written on each type of environmental landscape and its characteristics. If you find yourself dreaming about, spending time in or even living in these environments, a study of them will reveal some of the prominent issues and lessons for you. Even just visiting these environments and spending some time in them will activate their energies around you. It can herald an awakening of those lessons, issues gifts and patterns awakening and important at this time in your life.

Beaches and Dunes
Keynote: adaptability to unique challenges; healing; doorways to the spirit/ faerie realm opening

Beaches are mystical and powerful environments. In many traditions, they are doorways between the world of spirit and the world of humans. They are intersections where powerful forces can be encountered. Beaches and shorelines are doorways to the Faerie Realm and the world of spirits. They are natural intersections, whether it is a creek bed, a sea shore, river bed or lake shore or beach. Traditionally, any intersection in Nature is a place where there is a thinning of the veils between the physical and spiritual world. At these places, encounters with less substantial life and energies are often experienced. It is in-between, neither of the land nor of the water. These "Tween Places" are sacred doorways. Many folktales and faerie tales speak of amazing encounters at these Tween Places.

Spiritual doorways aside, beach and dune habitats are more challenging than most. Plant life must contend with winds, salt spray, high temperatures and dry surfaces. Plants that survive here have unique qualities and adaptability. Beach grass, though it seems sparse, has runners underground, protecting its roots and anchoring it through the harsh conditions of beaches and dunes. This is often a reminder to keep ourselves grounded when opening to new realms and to protect our own roots, while we extend ourselves out into new and challenging areas.

Dunes are also areas of extreme life. The plants found there help hold the sand in place. In order for them to survive, they have adapted in unique ways. Some beach and dune plants have fibers that reflect the sun and trap the dew. Others tilt their leaves away from the sun to reduce evaporation. This is often a reminder to be selective and discriminating in our activities in challenging environments and not overextend ourselves.

Although beaches and dunes often seem barren, there is a multitude of life – plant and animal. Multitudes of shorebirds are common, as are a variety of crustaceans, turtles and other wildlife. A variety of grasses and some trees are also common, including palm and mangrove. Poison ivy grows frequently in this environment. In fact, poison ivy can grow anywhere. Later in this book, we will discuss the powerful qualities of this plant. Always examine the plant or plants that seem to dominate the particular beach or dune area. It will provide tremendous insight and guidance. Sea oats, bayberry, lichen, holly and even oak trees are common in these environments.

Physicians often recommended that recuperating patients make a trip to the beach or shore to facilitate the healing process. This environment is still one of the most healing and balancing we can find. And it is one of the most beneficial for recovering from illness. As mentioned, beaches and dunes are areas of sometimes harsh conditions, but they are areas of primal elemental forces. When we are ill, our own elements have become out of balance. Beaches and dunes contain all of the elements of Nature in a primal form. There is the sun and the element of fire. There is the ocean or sea and the element of water. There is the land with the element of earth and the ocean and sea breezes with the element of air. Spending time in this environment brings our own bodily elements back into balance. This environment can benefit everyone at times and we should seek to spend some time there periodically. For those who may not have access to these primal energies at the ocean or sea shore, lake and river shores can also provide this same balancing, in a less primal manner.

When beaches and dunes show up in our life - through where we live, in dreams or even visits – it reflects a time in which we need to balance some elements within our life. Visits to the beach are often invitations for healing and balance. They can also reflect that the spirit realm is opening and visits to this type of habitat can be a catalyst for inviting that opening. This environment reminds us to find creative and unique approaches to the challenges in our life.

City and Suburban Environments
Keynote: **adaptability; finding our foundation; community and social issues**

In modern society, most people find themselves living within city or suburban environments. Almost every decade brings changes as to where people desire to live. For many years, people moved out of the city to suburban areas. In fact, many downtown areas became desolate at times. Then came the drive to resettle the city. People moved back out of the suburbs, often because the suburbs did not fulfill their dreams the way they thought it would.

Whether you live in the city or the suburbs, the lessons are very similar. And neither environment will prevent you from understanding Nature and from developing the ability to read signs and omens. City and suburban dwellers are often trying to establish a foundation for basic dreams – career, home and family. We often find ourselves making decisions and choices based upon what we feel we need in these environments to help fulfill our dreams. Both environments bring us into a mix of social issues that impact upon our life. Of course, both cities and suburban communities do have their own unique lessons as well.

City environments generally have less accessible natural areas. Yes, there are parks, but yards are smaller and trees and plants are often tiny islands among concrete. Because of this the natural areas are more precious, and the importance of connecting with Nature is often more critical for the city dweller. This scarcity of readily available natural environments makes many people adamant about their indoor plants, window gardens and more.

Every city has its own unique lessons and everyone who lives within a particular city will experience similar lessons and issues in varying degrees. Examine the shape of your city. What does its shape reflect? Do government offices face East, West, North, or South? (Remember that directions are symbolic of qualities.) Does your home in the city face the East, West, North, or South? What is the symbolic shape of your house or yard? What are the most common issues discussed or recurring year after year within your city? These issues are also reflected somewhere within your own personal environment as well as in the community. For example, if appropriate health care is neglected consistently in your community, it is likely you may be neglecting your own personal health care or that of someone in your immediate environment. Extra care should betaken not to neglect it.

To the feng shui person or anyone skilled at reading landscapes, rectangular or square shapes are often best. They reflect balance. What do the street patterns closest to you seem to reflect? A backyard higher than the front is usually more auspicious. Is there plant life or trees flourishing near your home? This reflects healthy energy. Remember that cities and homes have their own metabolism. Those living within them will take on many of the same characteristics of their home, their yard, their neighborhood and their city. They will embody and reflect the qualities of these landscapes.

Cities often contain many lessons associated with community and learning to live with variety, flexibility, and adaptability. In city environments, we must balance sociability with maintaining boundaries. We must be able to adapt to a wider variety of people – economically, racially, religiously, etc. Examine the variety of people, conditions and such within your environment. Examine your own ability to adapt and relate to a variety of people and circumstances.

Cities also have their own indigenous plant and animal life. Many city neighborhoods have trees planted specifically by the city government. Those trees are often planted for their durability, beauty and those animals that survive and live in the city are also very adaptable. Be careful about making biased judgments about city animals. Even the rat can have wonderful, symbolic characteristics. In Chinese astrology, the rat possesses characteristics that range from humorous to meticulous to initiative and success. As with any animals, city animals should be examined for all their characteristics.

Many people are amazed to discover when they move out of the city to suburban and even rural areas that the wildlife is not as evident. In the city, the habitats are not as large, so greater numbers of animals have to share the plants and trees, and thus they are more visible. In more suburban and rural areas, the animals are more naturally hidden. But this also makes encounters more significant. With plant life, there is likely to be a greater variety in the suburban and rural environment and so there is greater ability to define the message more easily and specifically.

Suburban environments allow for greater creativity in working with Nature and with the lessons of our life. There is greater contact with a wider variety of plans and animals on a daily basis. Messages and signs are often more elaborated. Because of this, there is a greater responsibility to work with them. Examine the shape of the yard and the direction it faces. It will provide some insight into the primary lessons and issues that will arise while living in this environment.

Although the pace is slower than in the city environment, the lessons are often similar – if not identical. Only the intensity of the lessons differs. Because of close confinement within city environments, issues are more readily apparent. In suburban areas, community issues do not have the "in your face" impact, sometimes experienced in the city environment. But the same issues of how to lay foundations, adaptability and community are still present. City and suburban environments often indicate that in community is at the forefront of both the gifts and issues at play within our life. You may need to become more selective as what "communities" you choose to belong. Regardless of the community, there are blessings that can only come through developing that sense of community.

Desert
Keynote: **ability to use resources available; hardiness in struggles; purification; spiritual revelations**

The desert has often been a symbol of purification and testing. Many tales and myths speak of individuals getting lost in the desert. They overcome harsh trials, find true direction for their lives, and unfold their inner gifts. In Biblical writings, spending "40 days and nights" in the desert was often a phrase for spending an indeterminate time in the harsh environment to purify oneself and prepare for an initiation. It is an environment of harsh conditions and great subtle beauty.

To many the desert is an area of little life and much death. In reality, it is full of abundance that is just not readily visible, but the desert is an environment of often extreme conditions. The sun beats down and reflects back because of near bare grounds. At night, the temperatures drop dramatically, since no heat is retained. The air is dry and so is the soil. Those plants and animals that live in parched deserts must have adaptations that enable them to hold onto water in the face of drying winds and hot sun. The lack of water is one of its most obvious aspects of the desert environment. Even early peoples recognized the need for adapting and adjusting to this unique environment. The Hohokam people knew the importance of water when living in the desert and they developed a system of canals to supply water for drinking and farming. And this was nearly 2000 years ago

Animal and plant life have to adapt in unique ways to survive successfully within or around desert environments. Some animals in desert environments estivate. This is a form of "hot weather hibernation", utilized during the day to lessen the impact of the heat. Other animals go into seclusion and only come out at night. The "sidewinder" rattlesnake uses an unusual side-slithering pattern of movement to avoid being burned and to facilitate movement upon shifting, hot sand. Eggs of freshwater shrimp in desert areas only hatch when rains come and this may take as much as 25 years. Of all the desert animals though, the Harris hawk demonstrates one of the most unique ways of adaptation to the desert environment.

Harris hawks are not loners like so many birds of prey. They breed in small groups and hunt in teams. Then they share the prey. Their hunting parties are usually family groups. This group hunting is an adaptive behavior. Because of the hot sun and harsh conditions, this type of hunting prevents less stress and overexertion by an individual. Harris hawks live in desert areas where prey is often larger than in other environments. It is also scarcer. So in order to survive as a species group hunting was adopted over the years. One of their more amazing behaviors is their stack perching. In the desert, there are few trees to perch on, and so the Harris hawks will often stand and perch on each other shoulders on top of cacti. Harris hawks perch atop each other and developed cooperative hunting techniques to be more successful in hunting less abundant animal life.

Plants can grow anywhere, no matter how impoverished or imbalanced the soil and climate might be. Plants can be found in almost every environment with leaves, root structures and chemistry adapted to fit the conditions. Nowhere is this more evident than in the desert. Desert plant life typically has shallow roots, which spread widely to benefit from the dew. In cacti and other succulents, spines replace leaves. This is common in arid environments. It curtails water loss, and discourages grazing. It also acts as a measure of insulation and helps to

collect the dew more effectively. Some desert plants retain water, to enable it to survive. This is most obvious with the Saguarro cactus. The Saguarro cactus (grand) is comprised of 95% water.

Great strides have been made in finding plants that are adaptable to the desert environment – many of which would never have been believed possible. Acacia is being introduced in some areas to regenerate and restore fertility to desert lands. In the past few decades, China has planted millions of trees and even the Gobi desert now has poplars growing within it. Such situations are reminders that we can adapt to the harshest environments successfully. Such situations remind us that what was once thought impossible now has great potential.

Deserts are places of great beauty and raw power. There is a subtlety of color and a variety of life. They remind us that we can find beauty and success under the harshest of conditions, but we will have to adapt. If we use the resources available to us, we can do more than just survive. We can sustain, succeed and even come out stronger than ever. Deserts have always been environments that invite spiritual revelation. Biblical prophets journeyed into the desert to purify and ready themselves for divine revelation. Its energy is always catalytic, stimulating and awakening clarity to our life or to life situations. From the desert often comes messages about using the resources available and adapting some aspect of our lives.

Forests and Woodlands
Keynote: magnifying of creative forces primal feminine; growth free of controls and constrictions; the unconscious mind

Forests and woodlands have a very ancient symbolism about them. This symbolism is often complex but always connected to the feminine forces within the universe - creation and birth. The kind of forest, its thickness and predominant tree and plant growth will provide specific insight into your life circumstances and lessons and are always part of the message.

Forests are places where vegetation and animals thrive - free of the controls of society and culture. It is hard to find forests that are not touched by human culture in some way any more, but it is always a good point to make occasional trips to forests and wooded lands. It is freeing to our own consciousness. In fact, they are symbols of the unconscious. They reflect the untapped primal feminine and creative forces to which we have access. Individuals who have a terror of forests may find that they are afraid of freedom, their own creative forces, or the perils of loosening the unconscious. The forest, though, is a place where our own creative forces can come alive and thrive without the limitations or restrictions of society and other people in our life. They often serve as catalysts to awaken the creative forces within us.

Forests begin as grasslands and meadows, taking shape when small aggressive trees get a foundation. As the woodland matures, it takes on increasing importance. Forests create a rich soil, and forest soil is as important to the forest community as the trees. Root systems of forest trees and plants are more to the surface where moisture is, as opposed to prairies where roots dig deeper into the earth in search for moisture. The message and symbolic significance of this should not be overlooked. We each need some creative soil in our life, something that is fertile and encouraging to new growth.

Forests and woodlands produce oxygen and absorb carbon dioxide. They aid the water cycle and are water keepers, adding to water tables rather than allowing it to run off in streams. Their trees produce fruits and nuts. They promote biodiversity. There is vast array of wildlife, some year round and some seasonal. The message can be to remind us of a need to be more diverse in our activities or that we are diversifying too much, spreading ourselves thin.

There are different types of forests, many of which are transitional. Transition forests are types that overlap or are combinations. A study of the major trees that make up the different types will provide some insight into your life. The two most common forests are deciduous and coniferous.

Deciduous shed their leaves seasonally and the leaves often take on brilliant color prior to that shedding. Some of the more common are the oaks, maples, aspens, etc, found in moderate and temperate climates. Deciduous forests are often reminders that there is a unique rhythm at play within our life and we should work with it. These temperate forests build up a rich soil (humus) because of the dropping of the leaves, hinting at lessons of fertility from past efforts and sacrifices. One of the more common deciduous forests is the oak-hickory. In fact, oak-hickory forests comprise more than ¼ of the forests east of the Mississippi River. Both trees produce nuts, which are always symbolic of seeds and potentials. Both of these are covered more specifically in the section on trees.

Coniferous forests contain trees that retain leaves (for the most part and which are needle-like). They also produce cones and flourish in harsher climates, including scorching deserts, mountain peaks and even the tundra. Their trunks often have an anti-freeze of sap and an extra thick bark to insulate. Some of the more common coniferous trees are pines, spruce and fir. They all have a small surface area to their leaves (needles) and thus retain moisture. The needles also have a waxy coating reducing water loss. Coniferous forests often help us see how best to insulate and protect ourselves while we grow and strive – regardless of the conditions of our life.

Coniferous forests (also known as needle leaf and/or evergreens) dominated the earth for millions of years before flowering plants. There are two main types of these: the spruce-fir and the pine. The difference between spruce and fir is that spruce cones hang down while fir cones point up. Spruce and fir have sloping branches that allows heavy snows to fall off before breaking. Spruce-fir and pine needles are coated to prevent moisture from escaping. Their needles have a fanlike spray to "comb" dew and fog moisture, which then drops to the ground to feed the roots. Pine needles have a similar process.

The rainforest is a third type of forest, not as common as the deciduous or coniferous, but powerful and important in its own right. Rainforests are moist humid forests, found most commonly in tropical regions. Many of the rainforests contain plants and animals that have not even been discovered. The rainforest is the realm of mystery - of the hidden secrets of life. They produce tremendous amounts of oxygen for the planet and create their own climactic conditions. These forests recycle their nutrients through their own bacteria and insects. Connection to rainforests is often a reflection of hidden wonders and mysteries about to unfold.

With all woodlands and forests, only a small part can be seen at a time. No one can see the full expanse. There are three levels in the forest and woodland, and the forest characteristics change with each season, often due to the competition for sunlight. The canopy is the crown or top of trees. It gets most of the light and most of the moisture. Tree leaves are broader and horizontal to capture light, as opposed to prairie plants where leaves are thin and expose as little surface to the sun as possible. The trees often prevent the undergrowth areas from getting sunlight when they are in full bloom.

The second level is the understory. The understory – smaller trees and bushes - compete for the light and water, wanting to take over the bigger tree's position. The third level is the floor of the forest. The floor is the busiest place (place to eat for animals). The light, moisture and temperature can vary here. In the spring, before the trees blossom, more sunlight reaches the floor and ground dwelling plants and flowers blossom. In the fall when the trees lose their leaves there is a second blossoming of floor plants. Because of this hidden aspect, forests always remind us that there are aspects of happenings in our own life that is hidden. We will not ever be able to see everything, but we still must act, based upon what we do perceive.

Whichever part stands out for you can be an important message. Are you at the top or are you competing for the water and sunlight? Are you struggling to get a foothold? The level of the woodlands that captures your attention will often reveal much about your position in some of your activities.

The rules of life in the forest are very different and sometimes alien to people, especially to a city dweller. Sometimes thought to be dark and scary, a place of beasts, monsters and demons, the forest is often misunderstood. But its dark mystery is its greatest allure. The lessons of predator and prey are magnified to a greater and purer degree but it is an environment that can connect us to mystical aspects of Nature in ways that no other environment can. Forests stir within us our own creative energies, so that we can apply them to our life. They enable us to face our fears and awaken the unconscious mind so we can employ it in our conscious activities.

Gardens
Keynote: developing abilities to create and nurture life; opening doors to Nature's wonders.

For the city dweller, gardens and plants are essential to maintaining contact with Nature in some degree. They are a symbolic reminder of growth, Nature in miniature. A garden is a point where Nature is controlled and subdued. It is Nature enclosed. It is also a symbol of the feminine energies, the ability to create and nurture life. The kind of garden you maintain (vegetable, herbal, etc.) and the kind of animal life that visits it can be very insightful. It can often reflect how well you are consciously using your innate creative energies and abilities.

As your garden grows and produces, you will see movement and growth in corresponding areas of your life. If you house an indoor garden, at some point you f may wish to transplant it outdoors so it can grow free and uninhibited. It can also be a means of inviting animals contact. This will strengthen your connection with Nature and animals. Doing this at a time when you wish to expand some area of activity in your own life or to increase abundance is a form of sympathetic magic that has been utilized in various ways around the world.

Caring for your garden is a means of symbolically saying you are open to Nature. You are willing to explore what it has to offer. Developing your garden is a sign of developing consciousness and control of our own life. If allowed to become overgrown, it may be a sign that things are getting out of control around you. If nurtured and cared for, it serves as a catalyst for growth and production in our own life. Your garden, regardless of size, is an outer reflection of your willingness to commune with Nature. It is a simple but powerful way and open doors to communication with spirits and energies of the natural world in a very effective way.

Inevitably, someone will say, "I can't make anything grow. *Every* time I plant something, it dies." Death is a part of Nature and should not discourage you. It may also reflect that you are trying too hard or attempting to grow something of which you are not yet capable. Just like the development of anything beneficial, gardens requires time and effort. Trying to develop immediate communion with Nature or assuming you will pick up augury or animal-speak quickly and easily just by planting a garden is what creates superstition and disappointment.

Remember that seeds need time to germinate and take root. As you work to align with any aspect of Nature, you open the doors to align with all aspects. Gardens are places where Nature is controlled and they serve as catalysts for understanding the signs and messages of the natural world, ultimately inviting us deeper into Nature's mysteries.

Hot Springs
Keynote: Healing; purification

A legend tells of how a great dragon ravaged the earth and the Indian Nations prayed to the Great Spirit for help. The Great Spirit heard these prayers and drove the dragon deep into the earth. Its presence though is still felt at times when the earth shakes, but it does not emerge. Instead, pure water gushes forth. For this act, the Great Spirit asked that this place be neutral so that all souls share in the healing waters. The steaming waters of Hot Springs, Arkansas were a sacred place among Native Americans. Even warring tribes came together in peace at these places to share in the healing waters and mud baths and to hunt and trade. These included Crow, Blackfoot, Choctaw, Sioux, Comanche and others. But this is not so different from other hot spring areas around the world.

The creative energies of Nature are at play wherever hot springs are found. Rain falls, sinks into the earth, minerals dissolve, and heat filters out impurities and then flows out as a healing water source. The mineral content, heat and mud combine in powerful healing vapors, that enhance breathing and which draw out toxins. Visits to hot springs are catalytic for all healing situations, lessening their intensity and opening us to allow for other possibilities.

They remind us that some places should always remain sacred and should be honored, if they are to maintain their healing qualities. Have you forgotten to honor something sacred in your life? Are we not honoring a commitment? Is someone around us not doing so? Is there a need to heal? Do we need to examine our intake (or lack of) vitamins and minerals? Do we need to get back to basics in our life?

House and Home
Keynote: health; consciousness; appearance

Your home reflects and affects you as well. Traditionally, it is the place of wisdom, and it often reflects the human body and thought process. What rooms do you spend the most time in? What are the shapes of those rooms? What are the conditions of those rooms? Neat? Messy? Dirty? Clean? Warm? Comfortable? Apartments and homes have some of the greatest impacts upon city dwellers. It should be where you are comfortable and safe. What feeling do you get when you step through your front door? When you step out into your yard, what do you primarily feel? Your home or house and the plants and animals around will reveal much about the general condition of your life and activities.

If you are looking to move, it is a good idea to look at the flowers, trees, plants, birds and animals that live in that environment. Where they appear can also reflect much. If they are most abundant and frequent in the front yard, this may reflect the "front" you present or that part of you which is open to the public or predominant in the front of your mind. If they are found most in the back, they may reflect your private aspects - that which you have kept hidden, the inner consciousness.

Psychologists have often recognized the importance of house symbolism in dreams. Different levels of the house reflect different levels of our own being and consciousness. What are the main activities on each level or area of the house? In what condition are those areas? How does that reflect what is going on in your life in those areas?

Every aspect of the home, interior and exterior, can provide clues to understanding what Nature is saying to you. For example, if squirrels seem to gather most often in the front of your home, it may reflect that you appear to everyone to be a very busy person - working, gathering, and staying active. If they are most often in the back, it may reflect that you are privately gathering a working on many busy things that most people do not see. Remember that we are always looking for relationships and the symbolic significance of what catches our attention.

Lakes and Ponds
Keynote: **opening to the spirit world; an oasis; nourishment of body, mind and spirit**

Much of the symbolism of lakes is similar to that of oceans, seas and other bodies of water, and the information in those sections of this chapter should be reviewed as well for further insight to the meaning of lakes and ponds. As with all sources of water, the lake is a place of magic, mystery and the feminine in all things and it has found itself in frequently in myth and lore. In the legends of the Holy Grail and King Arthur, the Lady of the Lake gave to Arthur the sword Ex Caliber. In the Egyptian tradition, the lake is a hieroglyph reflecting the mysterious and even the occult. As a bridge to between lower worlds and outer worlds, the occult

significance is clear in this Egyptian association. The crossing of a lake in many traditions was a crossing into and out of spirit worlds and other dimensions. In the Celtic tradition, the Land of the Dead is at the bottom of the lake or ocean. Water has often been the source of life and the source of death.

There are many types and sizes of lakes. Some were formed from glaciers, some from receding seas. Some are associated with rivers and floodplains. All are generally short-lived. Each year lakes and ponds become smaller as vegetation grows and they fill in. Ponds are considered small lakes and their symbolism is often identical. Many ponds may have been lakes at one time. While it may take ages, geologically speaking, for a lake to disappear, a pond may disappear in as much as a century or less because of its shallowness. But the time frame is never fixed for many of Nature's elements can influence it.

Lakes have often been compared to forests in their energies. One is a watery environment, but with the same feminine energies so often associated with the forest. Like forests, the lake has zones, in which different life patterns grow and abide. Shorelines will be different and depending upon its locations the depth and variety of plant and animal life found within the lake or pond will vary.

Lakes and ponds provide an oasis for wildlife. There is food, water, shelter, nourishment within and around it. This is probably its most important energy. Lakes and ponds stimulate an oasis of body, mind and spirit – nourishing us on all levels. For those who become unbalanced in psychic, magical and spiritual endeavors, lakes and ponds help restore the balance. I often recommended to clients in the past to spend time around lakes or ponds when at those times when they felt psychically overcharged. Messages and signs around lakes and ponds often have to do with our own life oasis or lack of them. Are we taking time for ourselves? Do we need an oasis or break from our usual activities?

Plant life and wildlife abound in a variety of species around lakes and ponds. Beaver and muskrats and water fowl often take up residence. Turtles, snakes, fish and other reptiles and amphibians enjoy this home environment. Larger mammals and a variety of birds visit frequently to drink, bathe and eat. Plant life thrives. Duckweed, cattails, grasses, lilies and more inhabit these areas – each with its own unique qualities.

The lake and pond is a place where the mothering, nurturing and nourishing energies come alive. A mother feeds, nourishes and protects her young. This is the energy of lakes and ponds. They awaken a need and a drive for that which will nourish our body, mind and spirit. They help us tap new waters within ourselves and replenish our creativity and our connection to spirit. They enable us to bring forth the magic within the waters of our own being. And the outstanding elements often speak to us of our own creative expressions.

Marshlands and Wetlands

Keynote: Transition; emotions at play; decomposition; new growth/birth.

Marshes, swamps and bogs are all wetlands and they are usually the most productive ecosystems in North America. They are places of life, death and rebirth. Wetlands are shallow bodies of water with encroaching plant life, offering shelter and habitation for a variety of plants and animals. The key to distinguishing wetlands from other bodies of water is that they contain a still and shallow body of water.

There is often great prejudice about wetlands and marshes. Many people still think of them as bug infested "swamps". Communities still drain and fill them in, so that they can build upon the land. They believe they are wasted lands, but they are quite valuable to all surrounding environments. They absorb rainfall and reduce flooding. They capture surface pollutants, protecting ground water. They are also breeding environments for plant and animal life - providing shelter areas for ducks, food for muskrats, camouflage for birds, etc.

Wetlands are just one step in the process of natural succession. Water areas become a wetland, which will become a meadow. The meadow becomes a thicket and the thicket becomes a woods. The woods then become a forest. In the rich soil of marshes and wetlands, a small forest is born. There is a succession of ecosystems. Often messages associated with wetlands provide clarity as to our own stage of progression in accomplishing goals.

A marsh is an area that retains water long enough for herbaceous plants to take root. Herbaceous plants are soft-stemmed plants that can be squashed between your fingers. There are different types of marshes and they appear in a variety of landscapes. There are salt marshes, cattail marshes and more. They can last decades or only a few years.

Marshes are areas of decomposition. They are combinations of water and earth in a passive form. Decomposition is part of the transitional process, the tearing or breaking down of the old is necessary before the new is born. It reflects the alchemical process active within your life, especially if your plant or animal totem resides or is discovered in marshland. In the tales of King Arthur and the Knights of the Round Table, Sir Gawain is one who would finally achieve his quest for the Holy Grail. Part of his journey and testing occurred in marsh landscapes.

Those who have a totem from marshlands would do well to read the story of Gawain. The appearance of a marsh or wetland in our life will provide insight into what still needs to be cleared out before the new birth can occur. What do we still need to shed to enhance the transitions we desire?

Swamps are often considered places of fear, danger and mystery. They are associated with haunting and wandering specters. Swamps and marshlands are areas where strange creatures abound that are rarely understood. To the shaman, marshes and swamps are doorways to the Underworld. The Underworld is connected to our place of birth, the land, our heritage and all of the powers and magic inherent within it. Many traditions speak of crossing through the Underworld to get to some transformational state of being. Contact with marshes and swamps usually trigger a return to the chemistry of our truest essence that may have gotten lost over the years. It can stimulate contact with people and issues of the past that need to be cleaned out and transformed, so we can manifest our truest essence. This is part of an Underworld initiation. Contact with marshlands and swamps can trigger an initiation in some area of your life. There will arise opportunity to cross into new lands, and often, it will be a crossing of faith and fear.

Marshland hosts a wide variety of animal and plant life. Animal life can include waterfowl, reptiles and amphibians, muskrats, red winged blackbirds and more. Water fowl commonly gather in this watery environment. They reflect the ability to move beyond the emotional or passionate stages of life. They can be symbols of bringing fresh air into our emotional life. Other breeding birds often come to marshlands as well, for it is a place of rebirth and regeneration. The plants provide food for mothers and their young.

Algae and cattails are two common plants found in many marshes - as can be duckweed, wild rice, grasses and water lilies. A study of the common plants will provide even more insight into your own transitions and rebirth. For example, algae are the most common plants to all marshes and wetlands. Algae are tiny, aquatic plantlike organisms. They are critical to all new life. At the bottom of food chain, the rest of the life in the wetland depends upon it on some level. Blue-green algae are found in areas with decaying plants. It is also an indicator of the healthiness of the wetland and thus the healthiness of your emotional life in many ways. Too much algae indicates pollution, reducing oxygen and can suffocate fish and plant life. Are you suffocating in your emotions? Are you nourishing healthy emotional expression?

Cattail is another dominant plant of wetlands. It contains an estimated 250,000 seeds, scattering countless numbers yearly. It also spreads through rhizomes or rootlike structures under the thick muck. They are often reminders to spread as many seeds as possible when striving for new growth. Not all will make it,, but many will. And try it in several ways, especially when breaking away from old habits and cycles.

If we are looking for or experiencing transitions in our life, a visit to a marsh can be beneficial. It will stimulate and accelerate this process in our life and it will help clarify what the transitions are likely to impact. It can clarify emotions. It is not unusual after visits to marshes, for individuals to have disturbing, emotional dreams. These dreams often reveal where there is still decomposition within our life of which we may or may not be aware. The dreams help us focus our efforts, so that we can be most successful in all transitions and new births. If we are having difficulty making a transition or seem "bogged" down in the process, a visit to a marsh can serve as a catalyst for movement or at the very least great understanding of why and how we are bogged down.

Meadows and Fields
Keynote: **Abundance, nourishment and fertility; balance of life; place of silent and soft growth**

Meadows are areas of abundant animal life and vegetation. They are usually near a stream or river, so it is good to examine the symbolism of rivers and stream, along with meadows. The water source usually nourishes the meadow. A traditional meadow has some trees, but most importantly it has waves of grass and wildflowers, lending the meadow a soft appearance.

The soil is usually very fertile and well nourished, and the totems and elements of this landscape remind us to awaken and add fertility and nourishment to your own life. They may also reveal places where it is lacking. Be sure to examine the pre- dominant colors, flowers, and the overall shape of the meadow. Remember that meadows are places of silent and soft growth. They trigger a softness in us, replenish hope. They can serve as a catalyst for recovering joy and fun.

In Nature, meadows and fields if left alone will become thickets, which in turn will eventually become a woodland. Common to meadows and fields are grasses which have a unique way of spreading, sending out underground runners. This can often be a reminder to look for a unique way of accomplishing our tasks, that there will be abundance but let a lot of the work be done quietly – underground.

Fields and meadows are often visited by most animals, but a number of species actually live in them. These can be burrowing rodents, a variety of snakes, and rabbits, but most animals are found in the border areas, except for the insects. The insects come for the flowering plants that are often in abundance in meadows and fields. But rodents will burrow. Birds are drawn to feed on the insects and so on. Fields and meadows are meeting places of a variety of natural elements and often reflect a balance. This in turn can stimulate a balance in our life or even reflect a need for it. Meadows and fields are places where the cycle of life is enacted successfully throughout the year. This aspect has been drawn upon by many traditions around the world. In the past and even today groups and individuals perform sacred rituals and celebrations in open fields and meadows to add balance, harmony and fertility to their ceremonies.

A variety of plants and shrubs can be found in meadows and fields and a study of those specific to yours will help you to define some of the energies at play. Pines are common along the edges, as well as bayberry. Black-eyed Susans, Queen Anne's lace, milkweed, ragweed and a variety of different grasses are often common as well. Several of the meadows and fields on my farm have blessed thistle, which I love, along with butterfly weed. These fields in the summer fill with butterflies. They

are fields whose energy combines strength and gentleness in all change. They can be used to invite gentle and fertile metamorphosis.

Meadows and fields are places of renewal. Contact with them or images that capture our attention from this type of environment are important messages. They center around and trigger energies of balance, growth, abundance and fertility.

Mountains

Keynote: discovering our own spiritual powers; overcoming obstacles for spiritual attainment; communion with spirits.

Mountains often have great symbolism and significance. The energies surrounding them are powerful and primal. Stories and legends speak of those who climbed a mountain and returned – no longer the same. Priests and priestesses went to the mountains for inspiration and guidance for their people in the valleys below. They are a place of facing fears and of testing one's purpose. Much mountain lore centers on facing tests and trials. When done so courageously and honestly, there are rewards. Mountain energy brings on the tests and trials of your own life for the rewards you most strongly seek at the time of contact.

Every mountain or mountain range has its own unique energy. They each usually have their own legends and tales, which reflect the hidden spirit and powers of the mountain. And most mountains had their own god or Great Spirit. A study of the lore of native peoples, associated with your mountain, will provide insight.

Mountains often reflect power and a loftiness of spirit. Those plants and animals found around or indigenous to them will reveal ways to discover your own spiritual power. Mountains have height and verticality, which is traditionally masculine in its symbolism. This mass and shape reflects the sexual aspects of masculinity, along with outward expressions or assertiveness. Mountains can reflect the alchemical process active within your live. The plants and animals that you encounter in such environments will reveal the means by which you can best work with this process in your own personal circumstances.

Many myths speak of mountains, which are hollow inside, serving much the same function as an oven-baking and tempering the spirit of those who enter. The hollowness and the interior have been described as the land of the dead and the home of the fairies. Again, it reflects that the totems associated with it are those, which will open new dimensions to us.

The ancient Chinese venerated mountains. They were symbolic of greatness and generosity. Mountain ranges often took the symbolism of dragons. The mountains generated the clouds and thus the rains, bringing and sustaining life. Even today in China the Cult of Five Mountains still exists. These five mountains represented the five directions and were places of sacred sacrifice. Mountains often had spirits, which look like monkeys or little men. In some Chinese tales, the mountain spirits are foxes that live in trees and often have one leg.

The mountain reminds us of the spiritual attainment that is ours as we overcome our obstacles. The height of many mountains gives rise to thoughts of being a world axis, linking heaven and Earth. Castles were often built upon mountains, providing a point where humans could commune with the divine or could draw the heavenly powers out of the sky and into manifestation on the Earth. Mountains are symbols for higher meditation, spiritual elevation, and communion with the blessed spirits.

To climb a mountain was to enter voluntarily into the world of spirit, whose doorway was the sky. It invites greater spirit contact within our life on all levels. This includes greater contact with the spirits of the stars. For those wishing to experience and understand how planets and stars impact us, a climb up a mountain and camping at night where the stars can be seen, can trigger their play upon your life more clearly. Many astrologers could benefit from this simple activity.

Mountains lift our spirit. They give us perspective on things both mundane and spiritual. They open us to hear our own inner spirit and open us to hear the spirits around us. It is not unusual for people to begin hearing spirit after a visit to the mountains. Intuition heightens and creativity flows. Most mountains and mountain ranges have their own unique legends and tales, reflecting the energies of that area. It bears repeating that the study of the lore around the mountain you visit will help you tremendously in uncovering its messages to you.

Ocean and Seas

Keynote: **the subconscious mind and the primal feminine; new tides and depths of possibilities; birth**

The world of the sea is filled with great mystery, power and magic. Some of our most ancient myths revolve around the sea and its creatures. Many traditions tell how all life sprung from the primal waters of life. Water is the archetypal creative source and the creatures that live within the watery realms can guide us to our most primal creative energies.

Most traditions of the world had gods, goddesses and great spirits that lived in and through the oceans and seas, touching the lives of those who came to their shores. Neptune and Poseidon were the Greco-Roman counterparts of the God of Sea. One of the most famous depictions of the goddess Aphrodite is of her standing upon a shell amidst the ocean waters. From Yemaya of Santeria tradition to Tien Hou of China, sacred spirits and heroines are often associated with the ocean. Spirits abound in and around the oceans and seas - from sirens and mermaids to water dragons and other strange sea creatures. Oceans and seas are realms of great mystery and spirit.

Water has a life of its own, and symbolic images and totems of ocean and sea abound throughout the world. It is a world in which many fantastic creatures and beings exist. There are many spirits of the waters and seas, and they often take the form of the creatures found naturally within them. And inevitably, when a sea creature becomes a totem there will be greater contact with the spirit realm of life. As a source of great mystery, every watery realm and its shores had its own unique spirits and energies. Reefs and shoals were often objects of religious awe. They personified giants and aquatic monsters, home to fantastic creatures such as dragons and mermaids. The sea life surrounding them was their children. Reefs and shoals were symbols of enchantment and they are symbols of possible obstruction to our destiny.

Water is an archetypal symbol for birth, death, and creativity. It is the formless containing potential form and possibilities. It is the realm of dreams and the astral. It is the home of emotions, intuition and inspiration. Through the watery elements, plants and creatures within we find healing, psychic ability and heightened powers. Plants, fish and animal life of the water were considered a sacramental substance.

Fish have been a part of all mystery religions. It was associated with the worship of all moon goddesses, all goddesses of the water and the underworld. In the Hindu tradition, the fish is Vishnu the savior. He used the form of the fish when he saved humanity from the flood and founded a new race. The golden fish was Varuna who controlled the power of waters. In Buddhism, fish represented freedom from restraint of desires and attachments. Buddha was the Fisher of Men. Jesus in Christianity was the fisherman. In Christianity, the fish symbolizes baptism, immortality and resurrection. In the Chinese language, the words for fish and abundance are homophones (words that are pronounced alike), and so the fish has come to represent wealth, regeneration and harmony. Also in China, the mother goddess Kuan Yin has a fish as one of her emblems. In Scandinavia, fish was eaten on the Feast of the Great Mother. The day of the feast was Friday, a day of the week named for the goddess Freyja. One of the most ancient images is that of three fishes sharing one head. It was a symbol of divinity, and variations of it were found in Egypt, Mesopotamia, Persian, and France and among the Celts. This symbol of the three fishes even became common among the early Christians who adopted it from these earlier pagan traditions.

Other watery realms had their own mysteries and wonders. Rivers reflect the spirit of time. The lake is an oasis, but the oceans and seas were the most mysterious. They are older than anyone knew. They always changed, and yet they were always the same. Civilizations could come and go, but the great seas were always there. From the great seas came life-sustaining foods, and yet many experienced death through the seas. Water was always shifting, with no beginning and no end. Ponds, lakes and rivers had their own spirits as well - each unique to their environment. A study of the specific environment will provide even more insight.

Water is purifying. Physicians often recommended that recuperating patients make a trip to the ocean shore to facilitate the healing process. This environment is still one of the most healing and balancing we can find. And it is one of the most beneficial for recovering from illness. As mentioned, beaches and dunes are areas of sometimes harsh conditions, but they are areas where primal elemental forces are encountered. When we are ill, our own elements have become out of balance.

Ocean and sea shores contain all of the elements of Nature in a primal form. There is the sun and the element of fire. There is the ocean or sea and the element of water. There is the land with the element of earth and the ocean and sea breezes with the element of air. Spending time in this environment brings our own bodily elements back into balance. It is an environment that can benefit everyone at times and we should seek to spend some time there every year – if not every season. For those who may not have access to these primal energies at the ocean or sea shore, lake and river shores can also provide this same balancing, in a less primal manner.

The sea and ocean has rhythm and movement. It represents time and change – the shifting of tides. The crossing of any water source was often seen as a change in consciousness and even an initiation. Oceans and seas are the womb of life. They are a source of rebirth. At the very least, they are symbols of all that we dream of manifesting. Oceans, seas and other watery realms are the home of dreams and the ethereal realms of life. Thus, the creatures and plants of this realm help us to awaken to our dreams, making them more vibrant and important. They guide us when the waters of our own life become murky. Contact with oceans always contains a message to pay attention to dreams.

Anything of the water implies connection to fluidness, emotions and the feminine aspects of life (the creative, intuitive and imaginative powers). Through the plants and creatures of the water realm, we open to the initiation of water. We learn to use the emotions creatively and productively. We develop our intuition and creative imagination. We open ourselves to healing and the development of our psychic natures. Through them, we will always experience a rebirth on some level, in some area of our life. We learn to re-emerge from the womb more empowered.

Watery realms are always significant. They are the primal life source, containing messages and signs of our spiritual life and our emotions. Many myths and scriptures speak of how all life sprang from the seas. Oceans and seas are symbols of womb, mother, and woman. They have the ability to absorb and concentrate life. They stimulate dream activity, stirring the waters within us, so that we may heal and flow more easily in life. Contact with oceans and seas always brings upon initiation into the element of water. Inherent within this initiation is control of emotions, the imagination and intuition – and even dream activity.

Oceans and all water in general are a dynamic force. They are constantly in transition, and they can reflect the same within your life. The plants and animals of this realm can reveal how best to work with the tides and transitions of our life more effectively.

The ocean is also the sum total of possibilities. The ocean and great seas are symbols of the subconscious mind and even the unconscious mind. They awaken the deeper levels of the consciousness. The quality and activity of the water in seas, oceans and rivers are often signs of these same aspects of us. These are realms of the unknown. They have depths unexplored and encounters with them always contain messages that encourage us to explore new depths within us and within life.

Prairies and Plains
Keynote: abundance; hopeful journeys to new homes and possibilities; new winds and subtle changes.

When plains are mentioned to most Americans, the image of wagon trains and early settlers, heading west across great expanses, often springs to mind. Whether it is the plains in the United States or the great plains of Africa, the crossing of them often reflects hopeful journeys to new possibilities. In myths tales and lore, prairies represent expansiveness and new potentials. Mithras was known as the "Lord of the Plains", through which he conducted souls on their way to heaven.

Prairies are vast open spaces, and while many people assume they are the same as meadows and fields, there is a great difference. Prairies can be home to hundreds of plants, birds and dozens of mammals. The native prairies of the United States are hosts to an amazing assortment of three to four hundred different plant species, as many as several hundred bird species and 50 or more mammal species living in harmony.

When native prairies have not been plowed or farmed, their soil follows a natural cycle of growth. The sod is so thick and compact that seeds of trees and other weedy plants are unable to get started. They are very fertile areas, but most natural prairies in the U.S. though have been lost to agriculture and urban sprawl. Prairies more than any other environment provide great examples of how interdependent plants, animals, and other natural elements are on each other. They provide a tremendous barometer, reflecting the impact of humans on the ecology around them.

The characteristics of prairies are most significant. It is a realm of extremes. The summers are hot and dry, while the winters are cold and wet. This requires plants to adapt and conserve moisture. Plains teach us how to adapt in extreme conditions and find balance when opposition arises within life. Prairie grass seeds will often lie dormant for years, just waiting for the right conditions.

The wind constantly shapes the environment and it is essential to many aspects of life on the prairies. Plants and animals use wind to advantage. Birds of prey soar, insects release chemicals into wind to attract mates, plants develop greater flexibility to bend rather than break. Plants also use wind to scatter seeds and to pollinate. Wind is active air. It is a reminder that movement is necessary in life. We should not remain still or stagnant for long periods. Wind is unseen, but it has great power, and prairies awaken within us greater realization of our own unseen power. For anyone living around or experiencing the plains, further study of the symbolism of wind and air would be most beneficial.

Prairies stimulate movement. They remind us that there are possibilities and potentials in abundance. New winds of change are always near. And change can always be good if we keep our eye on the horizon – to what is still open before us.

Rivers and Streams
Keynote: Creation; the flow of time; shapeshifting; evolution and movement is necessary

In the Chinese tradition, water is one of the five elements. It is associated with the North. Water is soft, yielding and pliant and was often used in China as an example of proper behavior. "Weak overcomes strong, soft overcomes hard" is the power of water described in the *Tao Te Ching*. It is an apt description of rivers and streams as well.

Rivers and streams follow the path of least resistance. They adjust to the environment, flowing around and over objects. They shift as they flow. They are the natural shapeshifters, taking the shape of whatever contains it. Because of this, the messages and signs associated with rivers, streams and creeks tell us something about our adaptability and our flow with life. Through rivers and streams, we gain guidance in adjusting the flow of our life, to help us take on the form that is most suitable for where we are.

Rivers and streams, as with all watery realms, have great symbolism and meaning for us. Water is the creative element of life and is purifying, but it is also destructive. Thus, it is a source of life and death. The crossing of any water source was often seen as a change in consciousness and even an initiation - the death of one aspect of ourselves and the birth of another.

Waterways have often been the most traveled route into places - even into new consciousness. They are paths to the dream world, into the Faerie Realm and even new life. Water realms always link us to the astral dimension where spirit beings operate more actively. The creatures of waters help us in connecting with these subtle realms. Rivers, streams, natural ponds, wells, seashores and creek beds are open doorways and magical places. The creatures of these realms awaken our own belief in magic and wonders. Messages can often lead us back to our own magic and lost beliefs.

Rivers and streams always represent time and change in some aspect of our life. This is reflected in the flow of the river and its correlation to the flow of time from birth to death and beyond. Rivers embody the mysteries of time. Contact with them can be catalysts for past life issues and examination, along with future life revelation. If we feel we are stuck in a repetitive pattern, tapping into the river energy can be a powerful aid to stimulate movement. People who live along rivers often are learning lessons of time in some form or fashion.

Anything of the water implies fluidness, emotions and changes. It has a life of its own, and it is always shifting. Rivers and streams have rhythms and moods. Inherent within their elements are lessons and messages associated with the emotional aspects of life. Through water, we learn to creatively express and use our feeling nature. We learn to use our psychic and creative abilities uniquely, giving them the expression most beneficial for us. Many messages from river and stream habitats provide insight into the use of our own creative and emotional expression.

Those with a predominance of the water element in their astrological charts - or important planets in the water signs (Cancer, Scorpio and Pisces) - usually require intense emotional involvement in life. They also need the presence of water within their life for balance. It replenishes energy and it is healing. Sitting along rivers and streams has a recuperative and strengthening capacity on everyone, but especially those of the water signs.

Rivers have an ancient symbolic connection to animal life, creation and the flow of time. It is where animals gather to drink and refresh themselves. It is a link to their survival and their evolution. The quality of the river water, the speed of its movement, and the animals and plants associated with it helps us to define the areas of our life undergoing evolution. They guide us through that evolution most effectively and with synchronicity. Rivers and streams awaken the ability to shapeshift our lives through creative intuition and imagination.

Valleys
Keynote: Fertility and new life; protection and safety; developing our role in society

In tale and lore, the valley is the place of safety, where one returns after an adventure. It is also the place one leaves to find adventure It is the home of the hero of lore and legend. The valley is home and refuge. It is where we make our living and fulfill our dreams.

Valleys are often equated with meadows, but there is a difference. A valley is more of a low-lying area, often found amid uplands, hills or mountains. It is usually associated with a river system. If you are living in a valley, there is likely a major river impacting it, and this should be studied as well. Valleys are places of great fertility, in contrast to deserts and their energies of purification. Valleys have long been symbols of new life and new fertility. They are a neutral zone beneficial for developing creativity. It is a place of safety. The totems associated with this environment will help you in developing creativity and maintaining protection.

In life, we go out from the valley to learn new things, and then we bring those things back and incorporate them into our daily activities, sometimes successfully and sometimes not. The valley though provides an environment in which we can test ourselves and develop our skills in safety and in a community. In valleys, we learn to look outside of ourselves to the benefits of the community at large.

In legend and lore, valleys were often the home of priest and priestesses of the community. Periodically, they leave the valley to go up the mountain, into the hills, or into the wilderness. Usually, they bring back wisdom, skills and gifts for the community. In the valley, everyone has a role, and part of the lesson and energy of the valley is to help us recognize that role for the good of the community. Time spent in a valley will often trigger opportunities to help others or to become part of something greater than our on goals and ambitions.

Part Four

The Whisper of Trees

"Lightning is good.
When Lightning strikes a tree,
people say that tree has been blessed
and they go to gather that wood
for special purposes."

- Apache Tradition

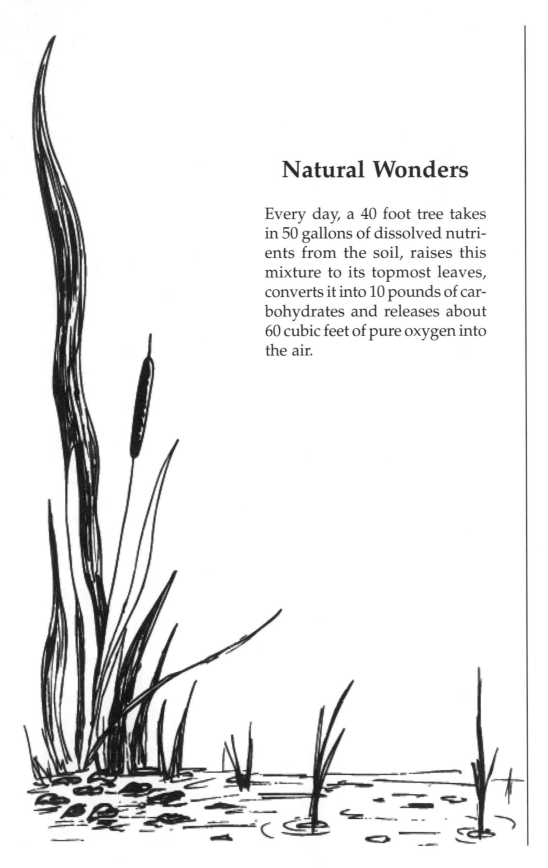

Natural Wonders

Every day, a 40 foot tree takes in 50 gallons of dissolved nutrients from the soil, raises this mixture to its topmost leaves, converts it into 10 pounds of carbohydrates and releases about 60 cubic feet of pure oxygen into the air.

Chapter Eleven

Ancient Mysteries of Trees

A tree is a living creature. It eats, rests, breathes and even circulates its "blood". It also provides a home and shelter for animal life. It provides shade and prevents erosion of soil. Trees are critical for habitat and they are the biggest and the longest living plants on the planet. They help keep the earth's ecology in balance transforming carbon dioxide into oxygen. They make the world livable.

Trees and their smaller woody counterpart, bushes, have a multitude of virtues. These range from beauty to fruit to shelter and beyond. They provide patterns and colors to our life. One of their most important virtues though is their ability to serve as our most frequent and important signposts in life.

Trees speak to the child in us. Most people I've met have their favorite tree(s) just as they have their favorite animal(s).We've climbed them, played in them, hugged them and even built houses in them. And I'm a firm believer that we should periodically climb a tree as long as we are able to do so – regardless of our age. Much of their appeal has to do with their powerful and inviting energy. And although not always understood, every tradition upon the planet has honored the great spirits that inhabit the Earth in the form of trees.

The tree is an ancient life and a powerful symbol. It has a great spirit and it represents all things that grow. It symbolizes fertility and life. To some, it is the world axis, and to others it is the world itself. Its roots are within the earth, and yet it reaches to the sky. It is a bridge between the heavens and the earth, the mediator between both worlds. The ancient mystical Qabala uses the symbol of the Tree of Life as a guide to our entire unfoldment process. Through climbing the Qabalistic Tree of Life, we bridge one level of our consciousness with the next, just as the tree bridges the heavens and the earth.

Three Steps To
Tree Communications

Where do we begin with understanding the messages of the tree? Understanding the messages of trees is accomplished in three steps:

Is the tree deciduous or evergreen?

This will provide quick insight into the overall energies at play in your life in general, or the overall energies affecting a specific situation. It is an overview.

What are the unique botanical properties of this tree?

Much of this is covered for you in chapter twelve for a number of trees. Chapter twelve also provides guidance in determining those unique qualities and characteristics. Primarily, examine the unique botanical aspects, as well as those qualities reflected by the Doctrine of Signatures, discussed earlier in this book.

What are the magical and spiritual associations of this tree?

Most trees have had some magical associations. Often these associations came about through traditions communing with the spirits of the trees. Later in this chapter are exercises for understanding and connecting to the spirits of trees. The spirit and energy of a tree is always reflected by a combination of the botanical qualities and those properties reflected by the Doctrine of Signatures. Determining these will help you to understand and apply the message of the tree to your life more effectively and accurately.

The tree, as the Tree of Knowledge, has been associated with both Paradise and Hell. In Greek mythology, the Golden Fleece hung upon a tree. The Christian cross was originally a tree, and Buddha found enlightenment while sitting beneath one. Druids recognized the energies and spirits of trees, while the Norse honored Yggdrasil, the one great, tree of life. Every civilization and traditions has its stories, myths and mystical legends of trees.

Trees bear fruit from which we gain nourishment. They provide shade and shelter. The wood is essential to the building of homes, and it is essential to the making of paper - a source for communication and knowledge. The leaves of many trees fall in the autumn only to re-emerge again in the spring, reflecting the continual change and growth - dying only to be reborn again. We rake the leaves in the autumn, gathering what has dropped to create mulch for future plantings. Trees also serve as barriers, often used as a windbreak or fence by farmers. They are boundaries, whether separating one piece of land from another or one world from another. Because of all these things, trees contain are often our clearest signposts and message bringers when dealing with life issues.

Most people are familiar with the family tree. This tree has its roots in our ancestors, both familial and spiritual. All that we are lies in the roots of the tree, and thus all of our ancestry can be awakened through the tree. Trees can reveal ancestral patterns, issues and gifts and provide past life information that has helped create and nurture our present life.

The tree has its roots within the earth and its branches extend to the heavens. Because of this, it serves as both a wonderful symbol and a powerful tool for opening the energies of heaven and Earth for us. Trees serve as a home and shelter for a wide variety of animals and thus they are a natural tool of the shaman. Ultimately, work with trees will strengthen your focus, increase your abundance and develop your awareness of all signs in Nature. They mirror so much about us that they will speak to us clearly about our life and what is unfolding within it.

Deciduous versus Evergreen Trees

Determining if the tree that catches our attention is a deciduous or evergreen provides a quick answer for us. This will always be part of the message, which tree signposts provide. It is usually an overview of the situation, initiating guidance. Examining whether your favorite tree in life is an evergreen or deciduous will reveal insight about your own personal energies and patterns in life. For example, a deciduous person finds greater success in working with the rhythms of the seasons when undertaking tasks or pursuing goals. An evergreen person finds it beneficial to use what is available at the time, adapting things to each situation.

Deciduous trees shed their leaves seasonally and the leaves often take on brilliant color prior to that shedding. Some of the more common are the oaks, maples, aspens, etc, found in moderate and temperate climates. One of the more common deciduous forests is the oak-hickory. In fact, oak-hickory forests comprise more than ¼ of the forests east of the Mississippi River. Both trees produce nuts, which are always symbolic of seeds and potentials. These two trees are covered more specifically in the next chapter.

Trees of the temperate forests build up a rich soil (humus) because of the dropping of their leaves, hinting at lessons of fertility coming best from past efforts and sacrifices. Deciduous forests are reminders that there is a unique rhythm at play within our life and we should work

with it. Using the seasonal rhythm will facilitate all activities. Remember that there are times to germinate, times to blossom, times to shed and times to harvest. Some only produce fruit at certain times of the year. Where is that tree in its normal cycle? Where are you in relation to that cycle?

Although most people think of evergreens as strictly pines, this is not so. Magnolias, eucalyptus and rhododendrons are also evergreens. For our purposes, we will define an evergreen tree (also known as a needle leaf and/or coniferous tree) as a plant that holds its foliage even when it is dormant or resting in winter.

Evergreens dominated the earth for millions of years before flowering plants. There are two main types of the conifer evergreen: the spruce-fir and the pine. The difference between spruce and fir is that spruce cones hang down while fir cones point up. Spruce and fir also have sloping branches that allows heavy snows to fall off before breaking. They all have a small surface area to their leaves (needles) and a waxy coating reducing water loss. Their needles have a fanlike spray to "comb" dew and fog moisture, which then drops to the ground to feed the roots. Pine needles have a similar process. Coniferous and evergreens often help us see how best to insulate and protect ourselves while we grow and strive – regardless of the conditions of our life.

Evergreen and most coniferous trees retain leaves (for the most part). And they do have leaves - their needles. They also produce cones and flourish in harsher climates, including scorching deserts, mountain peaks and even the tundra. Their trunks often have an anti-freeze of sap and an extra thick bark to insulate. They bring messages of successful  strength and persistence in difficult times.

When we encounter a tree that stands out for us, the first question we should ask is: *Is this a deciduous or an evergreen?* If it is deciduous then we know that there is a seasonal rhythm at play and by working with that rhythm, we heighten our chances for success. If it is an evergreen, we then know that adaptation and persistence will be necessary for success. Are you using what is available to you? Are you being too sensitive or too insulated? Are you remaining strong and persistent?

Magic and Spirits of Trees

Understanding the magic and spirit associated with trees - or anything of Nature for that matter - will help you to understand the signs and messages to you. The meaning of those signs does not always come solely through the botanical description of the tree. Biology and the mythology often go hand in hand. Study the lore of the trees. Examine the myths associated with the area in which that tree is found. Explore any spirit associations. They add another dimension. Trees have had some of the most ancient, colorful and magical folklore of all plants. Do not chalk it all up to superstition. Remember that the symbolism and message is always a little more than we first think.

Trees have always been imbued with certain magickal and spiritual attributes. Often these have been determined through application of the Doctrine of Signatures to the tree. This doctrine though – although not always botanically correct - is an excellent guide to the energy imbued within a tree. It is also an excellent too for developing better understanding of the communication, when the tree becomes a message or sign for you.

Every tree has its own energy and its own spirit. Every wood has its Lady/Lord of the Wood. We don't have to believe that everything in Nature has a creative intelligence, but we should be able to realize that everything in Nature has some spirit or archetypal force associated with it. And with just a little knowledge and effort, we soon discover that every tree can be a doorway to the Faerie Realm or to other spirit dimensions. In fact, one of the safest ways to open to spirit guides and to stimulate greater spirit contact is through work with trees. All of Nature is filled with devas, spirits and other supersensible beings that assist in the maintenance of life. There truly are worlds within worlds. The more we acknowledge their presence in Nature, the better the communications become for us.

Every tree is a source of energy, healing and creativity in its own unique way. Some trees are healers, some are guardians and others are keepers of knowledge and wisdom. By opening to the spirits, devas, faeries and elves associated with the trees, we invite the energy of the tree itself into our life more strongly. If patient, tree spirits will share their energy and their knowledge of the universe - be it in the form of assistance, compliments, guidance or more.

Each tree and each tree spirit has its own unique qualities, but some generalizations can be drawn from folklore, teachings and experience. Tree spirits are not harmful. In fact, they are drawn to humans and they can also be quite affectionate. Tree spirits are not bound to the tree, although they will often stay close. They can emerge from the tree for a little distance when they desire. Usually, during the day, they are so busy with normal growing activities that they are not as discernible. At night, when the outside world slows down, they are more free. They have greater opportunity to move about.

Many people get jitters when outside at night, especially in forested and wooded areas. Part of this is a physiological response that the energy of the tree spirits triggers in humans, as they begin to emerge from the trees and their presence is felt more strongly. It is easier to feel their presence when the day's activities have slowed. They often have vibrations that are so strong and different that people will get chills and shivers when they are around.

Every tree is also home to a wide variety of elves, faeries, devas and other shining ones. Often these live in communities and are seen in groups. Many of them are tied to the tree for life, and thus they are very protective of them. It is also why it is best to ask their permission before cutting. The tree elves are usually what are first seen by humans around the tree, and are often mistaken for the actual tree spirit. Most of these faeries and elves are earth spirits. Thy often live beneath the surface of the tree, but they are frequently seen running along its branches. A great homed owl appearing in an oak tree can often be a signal of the presence of a shape-shifting wood elf.

The elder tree has the highest elf population. Under its roots live many tiny elves. The elder also has its own faerie personality, sheltering many good elves and faeries. The oak tree has a long history of magic and faerie lore associated with it. It is often the home or gathering spot of many nature spirits, and it always resents being cut. Elms will mourn cut members of their family, and willow spirits have been known to follow travelers on dark nights for short distances, muttering behind them. The hawthorn has long been considered an elf tree, and cutting one will bring misfortune from the elves that lived within it. The lime tree in Denmark is thought to be a favorite of elves.

One group of spirits found beneath trees are known as the moss maidens in Germanic lore. These very ancient beings live within the root systems of trees. They possess the knowledge of the healing power of all plants.

There are other spirits, who also gather and live around trees, in woods and forested areas. To the Greeks, they are dryads. To most people they are simply wood nymphs. They are still found in wooded and forested areas especially those that are somewhat wild. The wood nymphs are usually female, and wear little or no clothing. Glimpses usually show them as dancing in the sunlight that comes through the trees. They sing beautifully, often imitating the birds. They understand the language of animals and of humans. They have a great curiosity about humans, and although they usually avoid direct contact, they will risk it for the opportunity to observe humans. Sometimes the wood nymphs will appear childlike, and they are drawn to certain kinds of trees. They are very playful and rejoice in all expressions of Nature in their environment.

Along with the wood nymphs that are found within forested and heavily wooded areas, there is usually a mistress or lady of the woods. Often in the form of a beautiful woman, this spirit is guardian to entire forested areas or even small groves of trees. Birch groves are intersections in which they often appear. These beings are enchantingly beautiful, and they speak the language of the animals. They are often tending to and tended by deer, and they sing sweet songs that touch the heart and bless the grove. They know all that goes on within their woods, and you only see them if they allow it - no matter how accidental it may seem. To encounter the lady of the woods is a blessing that is similar to those of the traditional faerie patrons and godmothers that we hear of so often in tales and folklore.

Actual tree faeries are rare, but many faeries will attach themselves to a particular tree or species of tree. Wildflowers when found at the base of a tree (especially the oak) often signal the homes of tiny faeries. The wildflowers grow at the foot of trees so they can share in the protection and energy of the tree spirit. The most common wild-flower homes for tree faeries are cowslips, thyme, foxglove and bluebells.

Facility at seeing the tree spirits and elves will vary from individual to individual. Much depends on practice and knowledge of what to look for. The meditation at the end of this chapter will help. Learning and studying about the qualities of the particular tree and its lore will also tell you a lot about the character of its spirit. It also helps to re-establish resonance with the tree's energy. The next chapter will help you attune to some of the tree personalities and characteristics. Spend time around trees. Go to parks. Climb a tree or sit under them. Enjoy being in their presence. Note how each tree makes you feel. Try to determine its inner character and spirit.

And always look for the presence of tree spirits when out in the woods. Do the leaves rustle as you walk by? Do the branches creak and groan? These are comon greetings of tree spirits. Occasionally sit at a distance from trees and bushes and then allow your eyes to half-focus, using a daydream kind of gaze upon the tree. Can you see any forms or faces in the configurations of bark and branches? Don't worry whether you may be imagining it. You are stretching your perceptions. This soft focus helps in seeing the spirit of the tree. It will usually be first noticed peering out from the gnarled bark. With practice and persistence, you will start to see the tree spirits and much more.

Jack in the Box

The superstition of "knocking on wood" originated as practice to ensure no spirits were in a tree before it was cut down and thus inadvertently upsetting the spirits. In some traditions, trees that were cut own were carved into different forms to honor the spirit of the tree and provide a home for the displaced spirit.

In German folklore, the kobolde were spirits inhabiting trees. When these trees were cut, a piece of the tree was carved into a figure so that the spirit would always have a piece of its original home to live. These carvings were shut up in wooden boxes and brought inside of the house. Only the owner was permitted to open it, and if anyone else did, the result would be untold damage. Children were warned not to go near them, and jack-in-the-boxes were fashioned to scare kids and remind them not to touch the real boxes.

Planting a Tree of Life

When asked what he would do if he had only one day left to live, a wise man replied, "I would plant a tree." Trees are bridges between the heaven and earth and thus they are ideal signposts to guide us along our own path. They are powerful allies to both the magical and mystical existence. It requires that we consciously stimulate our perceptions in both the physical and non-physical environments. Planting a tree is a very magical act for re-establishing our connection to Nature, for awakening these new states of perception, for blossoming newer, stronger inner potentials, and especially for recognizing signs and messages through trees. It creates greater resonance with Nature.

The powerful process of attuning to Nature's messages and all of her inherent energies can begin with a simple and fully conscious planting of an actual tree. Some may consider this exercise just another form of sympathetic magic, but it is much more - especially when we consider its symbolic significance. It can be a tree for the outdoors. It can be a tree for indoors. It must be an actual tree though. The kind of tree is individual. Each tree has its own energies and distinct properties. The list in chapter twelve can assist you in your choice. Doing research on the tree, meditating upon it and deciding before purchasing or transplanting the tree is a way of preparing our internal soil. Our consciousness is being prepared to become more aware of Nature's signs, omens and messages.

By planting a tree, we are performing an act of affirmation. We do not have to know all that this tree will reflect. That will unfold as it grows and we nurture it, but we should be somewhat aware of its significance and our goals. Do we want a fruit-bearing tree? Do we wish to bear a lot of fruit in our own life? If so, we must consider that most fruit trees have specific stages of growth, and only bear fruit seasonally. It doesn't mean there is no growth at the other times, but it may be less visible, less tangible.

Learn as much about the tree as possible before choosing. Have some ideas of your own goals - immediate and long range. Then choose a tree that is appropriate for your goals. Never choose a tree simply because you feel it may have more magickal associations. Those associations may not hold true or be as effective for you. Such decisions can be difficult, but there are simple things you can do to help yourself. First, remember that you have all of the time in the world. Then you may find it easier to begin with the tree that is your favorite. You can also go out into Nature and meditate on which tree might be best. Find a quiet spot among a group of trees and perform, what the Confucians call "quiet sitting" (back straight, hands on knees and eyes slightly lowered. This contemplative state will develop a quiet mind-heart, where the intuition can be recognized.

When you have chosen, plant the tree where you will see it everyday, a visible reminder that as it grows and blossoms, so will our own inner tree and your connection to Nature - *"As above, so below. As below, so above."* This planting can be indoors or outdoors. If the tree is planted indoors, at some point we may wish to transplant it to the outdoors so that it can grow free and uninhibited. If so, you may wish to choose another tree for indoors.

The care of the tree is a potent part of this process, for establishing that more intuitive connection to Nature. As you prune and water this tree, you are also pruning and watering your own inner tree, enabling it to take stronger root so that you can extend yourself to the heavens. As you care for and nourish the tree, the care and nourishment of Nature toward you will grow stronger. And even if the tree should die, your efforts will not be for nothing. In Nature, even the dying trees provide shelter and food for insects and other plant life. When working with Nature, every effort is a promise from you to her. And she always rewards the efforts.

The tree that we plant can be a wonderful way of empowering all of the exercises within this book and for heightening our sensitivity to the signs, messages and omens of Nature. Before and after each exercise, we can take a few minutes and give conscious attention to the tree. Adding a little water before an exercise is a way of adding water to the aspect of the tree we will stimulate through the exercise. By taking a few minutes to reflect on the tree, what it represents and how much it has grown at the end of the exercise strengthens its overall effectiveness. It enhances our concentration and focus. Just as a tree planted on a hillside can prevent soil from eroding, this simple gesture prevents the energy awakened from eroding away or being dissipated.

At the end of the exercise, we can turn the soil around it or just place our hands within its dirt at its base. This grounds the energy we have accessed, and it helps to release it more tangibly and solidly within our physical life. Although it may seem silly to some or even mysterious to others, it is powerful and effective.

Inevitably, some will say, "I can't make anything grow. Every time I plant something, it dies!" The planting of the tree is a physical act to release change into our life – to re-establish our connections to the magic and wonders of Nature. Death is always a companion to life, and it is change. It is part of the universal life cycle: life, death and rebirth. If we are unable to deal with this aspect, we will have trouble with all aspects of the natural world.

On the other hand, we must keep in mind that the tree is an outer reflection of an inner energy. If the tree dies, it does not foretell our own physical death. Most often, it reflects that an aspect of us that is no longer vital has changed. Maybe the chosen tree was not the best to start with. Some people choose a tree because of its extensive magickal associations, but many trees are difficult to grow. Are you tending to the tree properly? Magical practices to be effective must be performed consistently and responsibly. Maybe the death of the tree only reflects attempts to undertake too much too soon. Or maybe we are trying to connect with Nature and read signs and omens for the wrong reasons. Regardless, all efforts – successful or not – help strengthen our connection to Nature.

With all work in Nature, we must start simply. We must allow the tree (inner and outer) to grow at the rate that is best for it. One of the tests that everyone must undergo periodically is the test of patience. Nature teaches that the growth cycle has its own unique rhythm for each of us. Forcing growth impairs judgment. Seeds need time to germinate, take root and then work their way up through the soil. Unfortunately, we live in a "fast food" society, and people wish to have their psychic and spiritual development quick and easy. They wish to pull up to the drive-through window, get their psychic unfoldment and then drive on. Often with Nature many assume that nothing is happening until they see the plant working its way out of the soil. Nature teaches us that things will happen in the time, manner and means that is best for us if we allow it.

If the tree does die, give it back to the earth. Thank the universe for its presence within your life - if only for a short period. Then get another tree. And another, if necessary. If we wish to truly bridge and unfold our highest capabilities, we must persist. Everything we try and everything we grow within our life - successful or not - adds to our life experience and our soul development. Nature teaches this daily throughout the year.

Every flower has its fairy,
every tree its spirit.
Every woods has its
Lady of the Woods.
The world is filled with spirits
and energies that play upon us
and dance about us daily.
Through Nature,
we open doors to that often
supersensible world of spirit.

Exercise:

Meeting the Tree Spirits

Benefits:

- **opens communion with tree spirits;**
- **heightens intuition**
- **develops ability to recognize Nature's greetings**

I have spent a good part of my adult life teaching others about spirit and about how to connect with spirit in a safe and productive manner. This exercise is one of the most effective for opening to the world of tree spirits. It is most effective when performed while sitting in the midst of trees, under a tree or in a position to be looking upon the tree itself. Begin your connection with the tree that has always been your favorite, which reflects that it has spoken to you already. If you have no particular favorite, choose a tree that is in your yard or close to your living environment. Because it is in close proximity, you will have already established some kind of resonance with it.

Read and explore as much information about the tree as possible. This can be information from a scientific basis or from a mythical/mystical one. The more you understand about the tree, the more you will understand some of the characteristics of its spirit. This will help you in developing resonance with it.

If possible, choose a day that is sunny - with little or no breeze. Sit within the tree's shade. The shadow of the tree is a border space that facilitates connecting with the tree spirit and any faeries and elves associated with it. (It is beneficial to think of the tree's shadow as an outward embrace of the tree's spirit.)

You may wish to sit against the trunk of the tree so that you can feel it. You may want to sit across from it so that you can watch the bark and other tree formations for the appearance of the spirit itself. Choose your position as it suits you at the time. You will find it varies from tree to tree.

1. Close your eyes and take several deep breaths.
You may wish to perform a progressive relaxation. The more relaxed you are, the easier it will be to perceive the spirit of the tree itself and others of the faerie realm.

2. Read through the following scenario so that you are somewhat familiar with it.

3. In your mind's eye, visualize an image of the tree before you.
Its shadow extends toward you, but not quite touching you. See it standing strong and full. The grass beneath you is soft and lush; the air is sweet and clean. The sunlight that penetrates through this tree casts a soft haze around you. And the following scene begins to unfold in your mind's eye.

As you look around, you see you are in a familiar place. It is a small glen. In the distance is a high mountain and a path leading up to it. On the opposite side of this small glen, the path continues, leading down to the valley below. As you look down that path to the valley, you see your present home within it. And you begin to understand.

This is a plateau, an intersection of time and space – where the finite and the infinite come together. This is a sanctuary - where the real and the imagined meet. It is an intersection of the human and Nature – where all things become possible.

The tree stands strong in the midst of this glen - a singular antennae linking the heavens and the Earth. As you look upon it, you are thrilled by its simple beauty and strength. With that thought, a soft breeze passes through, rustling the leaves in response. And for a moment you are sure the leaves rustled your name.

You gaze upon the tree and see shadows and movements - tiny flickerings - along the branches and at its base. At first, you think it must be squirrels or birds, but you are unable to see them. As you take in the entire sight of this tree, the lines in the bark begin to change and shift. You can see soft gentle eyes peering out from the bark. You are no longer watching the tree; you are being watched by it.

There is a shadowy movement, and a form steps out from the tree itself to stand in its own shadow. It shimmers and shifts with incredible beauty. Around it flicker several tiny lights, and you know they must be faeries. Peering around from behind it, you see a tiny elfin face, shy but curious. Then the spirit speaks your name. The leaves of the tree rustle again, and you laugh with delight.

As you look upon this being, pay attention to what you experience. Are there specific colors? Fragrances? Do you feel a touch or a tingle on any part of the body? Is this tree spirit male or female? Those of the Faerie Realm will often use a form they think you expect.

It begins speaking softly to you. It speaks of its purpose and what knowledge it holds. It tells you its role in Nature and what role it could serve in your own life. It tells you of the mystery of the tree, and why this one is so important to you. See this as a conversation between you and the tree. See it. Feel it. Imagine it and know that it is real.

Don't force it. Let the communication flow naturally. Let this being tell you about itself. Let it tell you why it wants to work with you. Don't be afraid to ask questions. And don't worry that you might be imagining it all and that it's all a product of the mind. You would not be able to imagine it at all if there wasn't something real about it.

The leaves rustle with a singing sound, as this wondrous being speaks. It sends shivers of delight through you. You see specific birds and other wildlife gathering about, and you are told these will be signs of greeting in the future. It holds its palms upwards, and the shadow of the tree extends further outward, until you are encompassed by it. For the first time, you can actually feel a shadow. Its caress is soft and gentle and loving, and you are filled with a sense of great promise.

And then the shadow withdraws. As it recedes, the eyes of the tree spirit hold yours with tenderness, until the spirit is drawn back into the heart of the tree. You can see its form within the natural configurations of the tree itself, and you know you will forever recognize it from this day forth. The leaves rustle once more, whispering your name, and then they are still.

You feel thrilled and relaxed. And as you do, the scene before you shifts and changes, until you feel yourself sitting where you first began this meditation, comfortable and peaceful. You remember all that you were told, and you now know why you have always been drawn to this tree.

At this point, breathe deeply and regularly. Listen and feel. Extend your senses out. Do you feel any touches or tingles on any part of the body? Do you hear the whisper of leaves? Do you hear the presence of specific birds or wildlife? Are there any fragrances that stand out?

Slowly open your eyes, and gaze softly at the tree upon which you were focused for this meditation. Keep a half-focus of the eyes. Do you see any shadows and forms? Can you see the form of the tree spirit within the real tree, just as you did in the meditation?

Observe and note anything that you perceive. You may wish to record observations to honor this meeting and future meetings with this tree spirit. Give thanks for the sharing in some way. The old concept of giving a tree a hug is very effective. Touching or hugging the tree will ground your energies, and it will honor the communication and connection with its spirit and those of the Faerie Realm who call it home. And I have yet to find a tree spirit that did not appreciate it – even if begrudgingly. If you have planted a tree, as suggested earlier, tending to it now will heighten your connection.

Natural Wonders

All of the leaves on a single tree will open on the same day. Similarly, all of the flowers on the Japanese Cherry tree will open at the same time.

Exercise:

Making
a
Sacred Journey Staff

Benefits:

- **Attunement to the spirit and energies of trees;**
- **increases ability to focus and direct energy**

Wouldn't it be great to have a magic staff that could direct and focus thoughts and energies so that we could heal, bless and manifest things more effectively. Magical staffs and wands have come in many sizes, shapes and models throughout the ages. Mystics and shamans used a simple staff. Some Wiccans use the branch of a willow tree. Magicians of the past have used swords, athames and even a finger on their hand. Sorcerers and medicine people have used feathers and bones. Modern psychics make quartz crystal wands or attach crystals to walking staffs to redirect and focus energy.

The magical staff is just a tool. It is not the source of the magical energy but it does help focus and direct it. It can be used like an antenna. It can be a storehouse of energy that we can draw upon when needed. It is a source of protection. It can open veils help us walk between worlds and dimensions with greater balance. It can help us project thoughts and energies to heal and bless, to balance and strengthen.

All staffs are links to the ancient power, energy and spirits of trees. They act in many ways like a satellite of the tree essence and in order to understand how it works we must first understand some of the power and significance of the tree.

Choosing Your Staff

A journey staff can be used for many purposes. There are healing staffs, staffs for protection and even staffs to help open the world of spirit to us. I have a variety of staffs. One is a general all-purpose staff. One draws upon Dragon (and snake) energy for protection. One is for healing and I even have one that is based on my work with the Qabala. It represents the Middle Pillar of Balance. It is a work in progress as I continue to carve into it the various names of God and the angels associated with the Tree of Life.

Choosing and making our own journey staff awakens a powerful process in our lives. It is a commitment to the spiritual journey. It is the taking upon ourselves the path of initiation – especially into the mysteries of Nature.

Although traditionalists will tell you that you must cut down the tree that you intend to use for your staff, it is not something I recommend at all. There are dowel rods that can be purchased at hardware stores and at lumberyards that make effective staffs and wands. They can be decorated and painted with symbols that link to the energies of the tree. The second option I recommend is to find trees that have fallen and/or are lying dead already. Cut a branch or staff off of it. It is a powerful way of keeping the energy of the tree alive. (Even fallen trees and trees we think are dead, still retain their energy until they have decomposed.)

If you must cut down a tree to use as a staff, then get permission from the tree and the landowner on which the tree is found. Taking it without permission is first of all illegal, and second of all, it is dishonoring to the tree. Sit and meditate. Ask the tree for permission. If you must take a live tree, then plant a live tree of the same kind in its place. It is a way of honoring the tree. And do not take trees that are endangered, and I have found it beneficial to use trees that have several purposes, so that it is unnecessary to take endangered trees. The kind of tree is individual. Each tree has its own energies and distinct properties. The list on the following chapter can assist you in your choice.

1. Gather the materials for your staff.

Choose a tree or a piece of wood of a length that suits you. Reflect on its significance and on what you wish it to do.

2. Decorate your staff.

Use paint of colors that amplify and reflect the energies you wish. You may wish to attach feathers to the staff. They are particularly empowering to the energies, as the tree is the natural habitat for birds. You can also carve or paint the images of animals on it. If using a dowel rod to create the staff, you can use a wood stain appropriate to the tree whose energies you wish to invoke. You may wish to attach crystals of specific types to enhance the energies of the staff. As you work and bring it to life, imagine and feel its energies growing stronger. If the tree that you intend to work with is a fruit bearing tree, paint or carve the images of the fruit on it to strengthen the ties.

3. **Charge the energy of the staff and do this in several ways:**
   - Stick it in the ground next to a tree whose energy you wish to activate through this staff.
   - For protection staffs, I will set them outside during thunderstorms, charging them with the power of thunder and lightning.
   - For staffs to serve as an antenna for your psychic abilities, set them outside beneath the full moon.
   - Set my spirit staff outside during times of the years when there will be meteor showers to charge them it with the power of the heavens.
   - Take nature walks regularly with your staff.
   - Have it nearby when you meditate and/or perform ritual.
   - Do not let others handle your staff in the beginning. There may be some staffs that you never want to let others handle.

4. **Offer a prayer and thanks for the energy of this staff.**
   One of the best ways of doing this is by planting a tree. You may also perform a giveaway in the Native American tradition. Hold the staff above your head and lift your face to the sky and offer the staff to the spirits of the heavens and earth to use it through you for their benefit.

Trees are patient. You cannot force the expression of their energy through your staff. When you plant a seed – which is what we are doing when we make our own journey staff – that seed needs time to germinate, take root and then work its way up through the soil. Do not assume that nothing is happening if there is no immediate noticeable manifestation of energy through your staff. Take the staff with you on your walks in Nature. Signs and messages in Nature will become stronger. If we wish truly to understand Nature's messages and omens, we must persist. Everything that we try to grow within our life - whether successful or not – adds to our innate power and wisdom. You will discover in time that your journey staff has become a tree from you fly or under which find shelter. You can follow its roots into the underworld and climb it to the heavens. It will hum, cool or warm when there is a message. It will be your antenna to the communications of Nature.

Healing Staff & Bird Medicine

Many staffs are ideal for use in healing. I have found that they work especially well when working with bird medicine. The following are some general guidelines.

1. If there us a particular bird that you work with in healing, make sure that you have a feather on the staff that is associated with that bird. You should also wear a feather of the bird yourself when calling the bird's energy so it knows whom to come to.

2. Bird feathers used in healing should always be kept with sage when not in use. This keeps their energy clean and strong.

3. Do not allow others to touch the feathers you use for healing.

4. Have the individual sit or recline.

5. Place the staff upright so that you are always between it and the one being healed. It is your antenna and directs energy to and through you. No other person should come between you and the staff. If you move to the opposite side, take the staff along and place it again.

6. Smudge the individual using sweeping motions with your aura duster. As you do imagine and feel healing air brushing in and around you and the person being healed. Imagine great wings of the bird surrounding you and the person being healed. Feel and see their energy being balanced and smoothed out. Work from the top of the head to the feet, clearing all energy around the person.

7. If you are working with owl energy, do not touch the person with the feathers, as it will push the imbalance deeper into the person rather than drawing it out.

8. Then perform any other healing technique that you are inspired to do. Some find it effective to hold the staff over and around the individual, projecting energy directly from it.

9. Offer a prayer of thanks to the bird spirit for the healing.

10. Set the staff aside. Remove the feathers from it and yourself. Set them aside, protected and perform some grounding exercise.

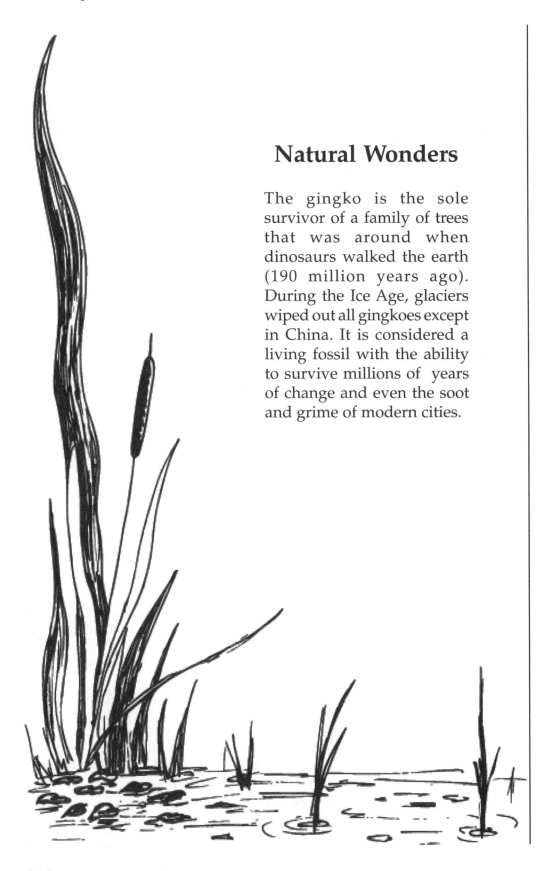

Natural Wonders

The gingko is the sole survivor of a family of trees that was around when dinosaurs walked the earth (190 million years ago). During the Ice Age, glaciers wiped out all gingkoes except in China. It is considered a living fossil with the ability to survive millions of years of change and even the soot and grime of modern cities.

Chapter Twelve

Dictionary of Shrubs & Trees

Trees are living creatures. They even have a heartbeat. In the spring, hold a stethoscope against the bark and you will hear it gurgling and crackling with a steady pulse. (This works best with smooth-barked, deciduous trees.) Trees provide nearly all of the oxygen that we breathe. As a child who grew up with very bad asthma, I was fortunate enough to notice that when I was next to a tree (or in one of its branches) my breathing was always easier. Those with lung problems can benefit greatly by sitting beneath a tree and breathing with it. The area around the tree is an oxygen rich environment.

Trees are the giants of the world and they each have their own unique personalities. (And yes, that is making them anthropomorphic, but it is still true.) I never cease to be amazed by them. They store the sun's energy. They provide nourishment and homes for wildlife – even when dead. They are truly some of our most important totems and signposts. They are adaptable survivors. It is difficult to kill a tree outright. Granted a good lightning strike, a chain saw or a family of beavers can accomplish it, but they can handle the harshest of conditions.

Shrubs and bushes have also had their magical properties. And they often have similar botanical and magical properties to trees. The real difference between a tree and a bush is simply height. Shrubs rarely get over 20 feet in height. While the typical tree grows more vertical, bushes often grow more horizontal. Verticality is often considered more masculine in symbolism, while horizontalness is feminine. This can always be explored symbolically as well when examining your tree signposts. A tree though usually only has one main truck and can achieve great height. Shrubs and bushes have multiple trunks and stems and

their branches and stems do not get as thick as trees, but they are also a bit vinier and fuller with leaves and flowers.

Aside from this height difference, their aspects are often indistinguishable. Both shrubs and trees can be deciduous or evergreen. They are both woody plants, which means their stems and branches survive from year to year. The woody covering gives them resistance to winter cold and snow. Because of this, all trees and shrubs – all woody plants – speak to us in some way about protecting ourselves, when they stand out for us in Nature. The woody plants strengthen our auras so that we are more resistant to outside influences. Individuals, who are very sensitive (emotionally and psychically), can benefit tremendously from working with trees and shrubs.

So often with the Green Kingdom, there is overlap in categorizing plants. Trees have similar qualities to flowers and herbs. Trees flower, so does that make them very tall perennials? Well, maybe, but they are not flowers themselves. Some shrubs, bushes and herbaceous plants produce fruit just like trees, but that does not make a strawberry plant a tree. It can be confusing at times. To facilitate organization and to avoid picayunish disagreements about my groupings – and because the differences are mostly semantic ones - I have included woody plants with trees.

Do not allow yourself to get hung up on the proper classification of the tree or plant throughout this book. The categories that I have chosen for the various plants are simply to facilitate the average person finding information and guidance more easily. If you do not find a plant in an area where you believe it should be. Check the others categories or the index to see where I might have placed it. And please keep in mind that a book of this type cannot hope to cover every single tree, flower or plant. If the book does not contain a member of the Green Kingdom that you seek, use the guidelines that follow to help you determine its meaning and message to you. Remember that what I've provided are simply sketches to help you begin the process of understanding the language and signs of Nature. In developing this book and creating these symbolic sketches for you, I've used these same guidelines over the years, always combining the mystical and scientific. That is when the messages become clearest.

The following are general suggestions for understanding the meaning and messages of trees:

1. Read and study some of the botanical and biological properties of the tree. Start with the initial observations. Is it deciduous or evergreen? Is

it a flowering tree? Is it fruit-bearing? Is it more bush than tree? After the initial observations, make note of its most unique aspects. You may need to consult some books to discover its more unique botanical properties.

2. Read and study some of the lore of the tree.

3. Examine the tree and its qualities from the perspective of the Doctrine of Signatures. What do you suppose its aspects might symbolize for you about something in your life?

4. Take time to reflect upon its meaning and significance. How does the lore and its unique botanical aspects fit with what is going on in your life? At the time you had your encounter with this tree, what was most on your mind for the hour or two before? For the previous 24 hours?

5. Take time to meditate and reflect upon different trees. Sit quietly with it. Hug it. Note its fragrance. Examine its leaves and bark. Make rubbings of its bark. And as you do these things, pay attention to how each tree makes you feel. Doing so with a different tree a week will open communication with a lot of trees in a single year.

6. Spend time around trees. Go to parks. Climb a tree or sit under them and just enjoy being in their presence.

Natural Wonders

The number of rings in a tree can be used to determine the age of a tree. The width of the rings will tell us information about years of drought andrain. Wide rings indicate years of abundant rainfall. Thin rings indicate dry years.

Alder   (alnus)

Keynote: protection during transition; trust prophetic insight

Alders live most often near ponds and marshlands and so those habitats should be explored as well. They usually have multiple trunks, which is very significant. Any tree that has multiple trunks usually reminds us to keep a good foundation in several areas of our life or activities. Do not limit and build something on just a single foundation. Count the number of trunks the alder has and explore it numerologically for greater insight.

Remember that wetlands are areas of transition. Transitional times often make us feel insecure and unsteady. The extra trunks give us a firmer grip during times of transition and thus alder is often a symbol of protection during such times. Its presence is a reminder to stay grounded during times of change and not to keep all of our eggs in one basket.

The alder can endure standing water for a long time and it is able to survive in what is normally infertile soil. Often when the alder catches our attention, we feel like life just isn't flowing for us. We seem stuck in some area of our life. The alder reminds us that we are protected during those times. All transitions have periods of stasis. Nothing seems to be moving. In actuality, there is movement, but we may not be perceiving it. Alder reminds us that we will survive, even when there seems to be no flow in our life.

Alders usually have catkin flowers (scaly clusters) and an egg shaped fruit that look like small pine cones. They are often used in floral arrangements. Folklore speaks of placing the catkins in your pillow to stimulate prophetic dreams. Contact with the alder can stimulate dreams of the changes that are about to unfold around you.

The alder tree is one whose energies provide protection. It can awaken prophecy in humans and it has strong ties to the element of water and its force within the universe – because of its natural wetland habitat. It has ties in mythology to the Celtic pantheon and the blessed giant Bran. It is a good tree to align with in order to overcome unawareness of what is going on around us.

The raven is an animal totem often associated with it, and the raven is a bird of great mysticism and magic. It is a messenger bird of great knowledge and perception. Crows and ravens are aware of everything within their environments. Their association with the alder reinforces the need to examine what is going on around us, which is not readily apparent to us.

A staff made from alder can awaken the ability to open perceptions to the dark void. Through the alder, we can see what is not readily apparent. It is a reminder to pay attention to what might be hidden around us at this time.

Almond   (prunus)
Keynote: **promise of sweetness and delicacy**

The almond is actually a relative of the peach and its blossoms are pink or white. Instead of becoming plump like peaches though, they harden. All nut producing trees are associated with fertility and the hidden fruits of life. And they are harvested in the fall, reminding us that there is a time and rhythm at play within our life that cannot be rushed. You cannot force a fruit or nut to ripen any faster than is normal for it. If we remember that there is this rhythm, we save ourselves a lot of impatient frustration.

Almond trees seldom need feeding. It is usually one of the first trees to blossom and thus late frosts can be hard on it. Because of this is it often a symbol of delicacy, but as a nut t here is a sweetness to it. Almond trees remind us to savor the delicate sweetness of life. Are we appreciating everything that we have?

Sweet almond oil is used as a base for many herbal tinctures and even as a base for massage oils. It is delicate and is absorbed gently into the skin. Almond often reminds us not to push - to be gentle in our endeavors for the greatest success.

Apple   (malus)
Keynote: **time for joyful giving; hidden knowledge, happiness and healing at hand**

"An apple a day keeps the doctor away." This is one of the most famous sayings about apples. And most people are aware of it. Although this saying came from the 19th century, the popularity of the apple dates back much further. The Romans are usually credited with developing the wild apple into what we now know as the apple today. Pliny the Elder described three dozen different varieties. The apple was a fruit popular in Asia and throughout Europe. In fact, an apple was once considered an ideal Christmas treat. Even today, it is one of the most popular fruits in the world with over 7000 varieties.

In America, Johnny Appleseed has become a legendary figure, with the image of traveling across the country with apple seeds in his pocket and a bag of apples over his shoulders. He tossed seeds as he walked, turning America into a country of apple trees. His real name was John Chapman and he cultivated apple nurseries as far west as the Ohio territory.

Apple trees come in many varieties, bearing fruit of differing tastes and at differing times. Different apple trees grow better in different regions, and many of the species of apples have been lost because they are not suitable for large scale marketing. Apples cannot always be grown in the Deep South because they do not get long enough periods of cold temperatures, which they need for a rest period each year in order to grow properly and produce fruit.

The trees have trunks and branches that twist. The fruit is high in flavor, fiber and flavonoids – antioxidants that improve the immune system. They are filled with vitamins and the eating of a raw apple is good for the teeth and gums.

The apple tree has many magical and healing characteristics. It is sometimes associated with the Tree of Knowledge. The apple was the "Fruit of Avalon" that could endow individuals with magical abilities. Staffs and wands made from an apple tree are often painted and carved to help awaken the magic. Most kids are aware of the apple divination technique for discovering who you will marry. As you twist the stalk, you recite the alphabet. When the stalk breaks, the letter you are at is the letter of your future spouse's first name.

Its mythology and folklore is great and entire book could be done on it alone. In Teutonic mythology, the apple tree is associated with youthfulness and beauty, helping to manifest opportunities to learn through choices. It helps us to focus and not divide our energies for greatest success. In Greek mythology, the apple tree grew in Hesperides and was sacred to Aphrodite. Apple is a tree that awakens true desires of the heart. Christianity has often distorted the fruit as a symbol of indulgence in forbidden desires, but its magical and mystical qualities are powerful. Its spirit is strong, gentle, giving and playful.

To the Native Americans, all fruit bearing trees were honored for providing food and more. The apple tree is a loving giver, especially when treated with love and respect by humans. It thrives on human contact and teaches the power of sharing.

The apple tree has had a long association with the Faerie Realm. The blossoms draw large numbers of faeries who help promote feelings of happiness. The apple tree is also the home of the mythical unicorn. The unicorn is one of the most ancient archetypes of the natural world. The spirit of the apple tree works with the unicorn, and in the spring the spirit will often appear in the form of a beautifully enticing woman. Together they open the heart to new realms of love and giving.

Apple blossom is one of my favorite fragrances. I love the short time in the spring when my apple trees bloom and every breeze carries their scent. I use its fragrance when I teach work with the Faerie Realm. I always try to have it when guiding groups in meditation for connecting with the Faerie Realm.

Its blossoms are powerfully fragrant and in aromatherapy, the fragrance of apple blossom promotes happiness and success. Its energies are also cleansing to the astral body. It stimulates the need to make choices within our life, and its energy helps us to realize that we always have choices. Its appearance in our life as a sign or messenger is a reminder that there is abundance and happiness about for us. It reminds us of our dreams and our possibilities. It often heralds contact with spirit and especially contact with the Faerie Realm.

Ash   (fraxinus)
Keynote: **combine strength & wisdom during times of sacrifice; look for connections**

The ash is part of a family of trees known as fraxinus. The leaves are often in pairs on opposite sides of the stem – joining at the stem. This, in itself, reflects its message of bringing opposites together. The ashes are usually noted according to their color – black, blue, red and white. A study of the color will provide some insight to the message this tree holds for you. And all ash trees grow quickly, as long as they have room and light. The black ash is often found in swamps and marshlands. It splits easily into thin tough pieces and the Native Americans combined these strips with other trees (such as cedar) to make baskets. It has an aggressive root system in swamp areas. It is a reminder that even in difficult arenas of life, we must keep our roots strong and extended. The blue ash gets its name from the fact that the sap turns blue upon exposure to the air. It is almost exclusive to the Midwest and in oak-hickory forests.

The white ash is the most familiar to people. In fact, anyone who has ever played baseball knows the feel of white ash, for it is still what most wood bats are made of. It is often used in sporting equipment because it is tough and light. It is not a flashy tree, but it embodies strength that can be relied upon. Although often unnoticed around other trees, its message is often that one doesn't need to be noticed to lead a noble life.

It has had much foklore surrounding it. Ashes were occasionally cut down in their first year and cut into pocket pieces. These were given out for the general well-being of others. it was also considered bad luck to break one of its boughs. it has often been a tree of protection and many once believed that no serpent would ever lie in its shadow.

The leaf of the ash tree has an equal number of divisions on each side. The number of divisions was considered significant in folklore. "Even ash or four leaf clover, you will see your true love before the day is over." But this was not its only folklore, which was often contrary. To break a bow was considered bad luck, but the pieces of it from a cut bow when the sun moved into Taurus would stop a nosebleed.

It is a tree with much mysticism though. It has ties to Celtic mythology and the one known as Gwydion, and it has ties to the Norse traditions as well. The ash is the sacred tree Yggdrasil, upon which Odin sacrificed himself that he might achieve higher wisdom. The Teutonic gods held council under this tree each day. There were nine worlds in Teutonic myth, all located throughout the great Tree of Life. The energy of this tree can open us to the perception of how events and people are linked together.

It has a spirit that awakens great strength and might. It is a universal source of light and life energy, amplifying the innate abilities of the individual. Shamans used staves made from the ash tree in the past to link the inner and the outer worlds and move between them.

The ash is a reminder that all things are connected, even if we don't see the connection initially. They remind us to move forward with gentleness and strength. Sometimes, its message will have to do with learning to be at one with the self, without cutting yourself off from the rest of the world. The ash helps us to become more sensitive to the great and small influences around us.

Aspen   (populus)
Keynote: **face fears and doubts through open communication; shed the old**

The aspen is part of the poplar family of trees, and you should refer to the section on the poplar as well. It is a tall, fast growing tree. The bark is thin, smooth and nearly white. As it gets older, the base becomes black. Throughout the country, it is grows in many habitats. It is one of the most talkative trees around. The slightest breeze sets the foliage into a whispering. Wands made from the aspen can help us to understand the language of trees more easily.

In the autumn, its leaves turn a wonderful yellow. It is almost a visual reminder that there is still color and sunshine, even though the light is diminishing daily. They remind us that there is always light to shine in the dark areas of our life where fears and doubts hide. Although the aspen is relatively short-lived (as most of our fears and doubts are when faced), it is one of those trees which will quickly take root in soil and habitats that are harsh and even burned out. And as trees go, it reproduces itself quickly.

The aspen is a tree whose spirit and essence helps us to face our fears and doubts. It is associated with the Egyptian symbol of the uraeus – the image of a snake coiled around to swallow its own tail, the symbol of life, death and rebirth in all things.

The aspen is a tree of resurrection. It is calming to anxieties about changes within our life. It facilitates entering the subtler planes of life, and it awakens greater soul fearlessness. Its spirit opens us to greater control of dreams and through the dream state, it can bring hidden fears to the surface so they can be faced. Once met with determination, there occurs a rebirth and an increasing ability to overcome impossible odds. It strengthens communication with the higher self.

This tree works well with snake medicine. In the animal kingdom, the snake is one of the most feared and misunderstood totems. And yet, it is a universal symbol for healing and rebirth. It is not unusual for those to whom the aspen whispers, to find new opportunities for rebirth and healing. The aspen will help you to shed the old and move into the new. It will require though that fears and doubts be faced. It is then that everything becomes possible.

Bamboo   (fargesia)
Keynote: balance strength and flexibility; healing of the heart

Bamboo is actually just a grass, but because of its unique qualities, I have chosen to include it in this category, rather than the others. The giant timber bamboos can grow to 100 feet. Bamboo is extremely fast growing and yet it retains great strength and flexibility. And there is often a lot of confusion and disagreement about the name. Regardless of its name, it is both decorative and useful. Bamboo crafts are popular all over the world.

Bamboo was originally one of China's most important natural products, and it is becoming increasingly acknowledged around the world. In the Tao and Confucianism, it is used as a philosophical tool to measure the quality of life. As a functional tool, it is used in housing and even as raw material for paper. It is one of the four noble plants of China, along with plum-blossom, chrysanthemum and orchid. In China, bamboo shoots are still a culinary delicacy.

It is often a symbol for healing of the heart. Its stems are hollow and its leaves droop because its inside (its heart) is empty. But to the Chinese, an empty heart is not filled with ego, and so the bamboo is also a symbol of modesty to them. Bamboo is associated with the element of air and wind. It is used to make chimes and the wind moves little pieces of bamboo to strike against each other gives joy and peace to those who hear it. Bamboo flutes facilitate healing, bring peace and stimulate joy

Bamboo seems to have many personalities and many uses. When it stands out for us, it is a reminder that we can be strong and flexible in everything. Like the bamboo, we can be self-propagating. We can bend with the wind and rise to untold heights, as long as we maintain that balance of strength and flexibility.

Beech (fagus)

Keynote: **time for new expressions of ancient knowledge; find power and nobility through speech and prayer**

The beech tree is a sturdy and imposing tree with a short trunk and a wide-spreading crown. It is known for its smooth, gray bark. It is amazingly tolerant to different soil conditions and habitats. Their shade is so dense that nothing but moss rarely grows under it and for those to whom the beech tree speaks, a study of moss will certainly help in understanding its message.

The beech tree was the favorite host of the now extinct passenger pigeon. They passenger pigeons fed upon the beech nuts. When the great

forests of beech trees disappeared, so did the passenger pigeon. If the beech is a messenger, then pigeons probably are as well - especially the passenger pigeon.

Although the beech tree has not had a great deal of faerie association, it was always considered a holy tree. The almost universal belief that a prayer spoken under it would go directly to Heaven reveals much about the spirit of this tree wherever it is found. The tree spirit of the beech has great knowledge of the past. It knows how to use the past to make changes in the present - which is often what we seek through our prayers. Beech trees hold the knowledge of the power of the written word and can stir within us a love of literature. Many historians believe that it was on the beech tree bark that the first pages of European literature were written. The Sanskrit characters were thought to be carved on strips of beech bark. In fact, the word book comes from the Anglo-Saxon "boc" meaning "letter" or "character", which in turn derives itself from "beece" for the beech tree.

The spirit of the beech tree is one of great strength and grace. She has the ability to awaken and to teach the skills of written communication - for both mundane and magical purposes. No other tree spirit can teach as well how to use words to express our own love or move another to love us. She willingly feeds mind and body. This is reflected in the fact that the peasants of central Europe used the beech tree as a prime fuel source and its nuts as a food staple. .She also teaches and reminds us that we need food for the mind as well as the body - that when we awaken the mind and learn to express ourselves that we discover our true nobility.

The spirit of the beech will awaken opportunity to explore the past (either within the current lifetime or those long past). It helps us to synthesize that knowledge into new expressions This is the tree of discovery of lost wisdom. It reminds us not to discount the experiences, knowledge and teachings of the past. It will soften and balance oversensitivity due to emotional experiences in our life.

The beech is a tree whose energy and essence can awaken old knowledge and new expressions of it. It awakens the soul quality of tolerance, and its essence helps align the individual with the higher self. It can be used in a staff that is beneficial for all patterns of growth. It can awaken greater opportunity to explore the past (immediate lifetime or past incarnations) and to synthesize that knowledge into new expression.

This is the tree of the discovery of lost wisdom, and thus the individual must learn not to discount the knowledge and teachings of the past. It reminds us to soften over-criticalness due to the individual's past and balances oversensitivity. It is often a sign to develop and apply written and spoken communication to accomplish our tasks more effectively.

Birch (betula)

Keynote: **balance and healing is necessary; opening of new dimensions**

Birches have smooth barks, which peel in thin papery plates. The branches are slender. There are many types of birches: paper, yellow, cherry, river. The paper birch is often found among conifers, like old friends and often the message of a birch will tell us something about a friendship of ours.

To the Native American, the birch tree was source for canoes and for snowshoe frames. The canoes could carry twenty times their weight, and their appearance as a sign reminds us that we can carry more if we maintain balance in life.

Birch is the "Lady of the Woods," and she helps connect us to all goddesses of the woodlands. One is never to take its bark or a limb to use as a staff without permission of the goddess. The birch tree is one whose spirit and essence has ties to ancient forms of shamanism. Shamans used staffs of birch to awaken an energy that would enable them to pass from one plane of life to another. It balanced the shamans as they made such treks. The energy of birch staffs should be renewed each year through some ceremonies. Those who take upon a staff from this tree must also learn to renew it and rededicate it each year. This is best done in the month of November, as November was the start of the Celtic New Year.

The birch tree reminds us that new dimensions are opening for us. As they do, balance is necessary for the greatest success in entering them. She awakens the energy of new beginnings and a cleansing of the past. She will help us manifest opportunities to clear out old ideas, those things that are no longer beneficial. She speaks to us of a need to keep our energy and efforts purposeful.

Cactus   (succulents)

Keynote: **adaptation; find and express the beauty and strength in all conditions**

The cactus family is a group of succulent plants with copious juices and numerous spines. Its name means "thistle" in reference to those spines. The flowers are usually congregated around the top of the stem. As a species of plants they have adapted themselves to some of the harshest environments, and yet their flowers are some of the most delicate and beautiful of all flowering plants. It is in this dichotomy that the cactus finds its keynote as a messenger.

The cactus is tied to those energies which help in the manifestation of riches and beauty under all conditions. It helps the individual to rediscover the elixir of life within themselves, in spite of outer conditions. It manifests the life waters wherever one is parched.

There are many varieties of cacti and volumes of books could be written upon them. So why include cactus in the tree grouping. I have chosen to do so because of one particular species, the saguaro. Saguaro is a giant cactus - sometimes 30-40 feet tall. It has enormous branches.

The base of its stem contains long strands of wood that are so strong both Native Americans and Mexicans have used them for centuries in constructing homes. This is a tree that was honored by the Apache for it great strength in harsh environments. Their image with their outstretched limbs lends them a humanoid appearance. This alone gave Native Americans reason to marvel at their spirit.

Because of the unique climate in which it grows, it has adapted in unique ways – even for a cactus or desert plant. Its root system is extremely shallow, but very far-reaching, so as to catch the maximum amount of rainfall, which never penetrates deeply in that desert environment.

The saguaro produce a fruit, called pitahayas by the Spanish. It was one of the most important wild vegetables of the Papago and Pima peoples. Jam, syrups and preserves were made from them. It is also home to a wide variety of animals, which should be studied – especially the gila woodpecker and the elf owl.

The saguaro is an ancient spirit. It has been upon the earth a long time and it knows how to adapt, persevere and find strength and beauty, where none is apparent. Its appearance as a messenger alerts us to adapt and persevere. There is great and ancient energies at play. It reminds us that true growth is usually slow but steady, but we must adapt and not try to force it.

Cedar (juniper & chamaecyparis)
Keynote: protection and cleansing

Cedar is an ancient tree found throughout the world. Cedar trees come in several families. Two of the more common are the juniper and the other is the false cypress. Both are long lived, aromatic and resinous. And there are many varieties in these groups and they all are versatile.

Cedar has an ancient history. In ancient Egypt, it was considered imperishable. Solomon's temple was made entirely of cedar wood, cut from the great cedar forests of Lebanon. Its great cedar forests were decimated and have not recovered to this day. It is a tree of consecration and dedication, and it has ties to Wotan. Tradition tells us also that the unicorn keeps its treasures in boxes made of cedar. These boxes are hidden beneath the apple tree.

The white cedar or false cypress variety was an important part of the American Revolution. Its charcoal was used in the making of gunpowder. It is common to swamps and like all swamp trees, it is extremely resistant to water decay. Water barrels made from it kept water pure, killing micro-organisms. Early American cities used it for water pipes because it would not decay in soil and kept water supplies healthier.

The juniper variety of red cedar is most commonly used in the US. It is a tough survivor and one of the signs of new growth returning to an area. It often found as a windbreak, trooping along fence rows and on hilltops. In the early history of the US, the red cedar bore the brunt of the pencil industry for over a hundred years. Only the knot free heart was used and so nearly 70% of the bulk cut was wasted. The Faber Company used them exclusively.

A fungus-type gall disfigures cedars. These produce spores, infecting the leaves of apple trees with yellow splotches, which in turn re-infect the cedars. In 1918, the easiest solution to save the apple trees was to try and eradicate all of the cedars. Political battles arose between apple growers and the cedar owners. For those to whom cedar comes as a sign, there is usually a message associated with the apple tree as well, and it should be examined.

All cedars have a fragrance that is cleansing and protecting. It has been used in rituals and ceremonies to prepare a person or an area. Native Americans use it for it purification properties. A staff made from cedar has the energy of protection, and it can open opportunities to heal imbalances of an emotional or astral nature.

Cedar is a tree whose spirit and essence will strengthen and enhance any inner potentials of the individual. This is a tree tied to strong healing energies. Its energies cleanse the auric field, especially at night while the individual sleeps. It helps the individual to balance the emotional and mental bodies and can stimulate dream activity, which brings inspiration and calm. Do we need to be more protective of our environment? Do we need to cleanse some area of our life? Cedars will help us to do so.

Cherry   (prunus)
Keynote: **new awakenings and birth; insight**

Sweet and sour cherries have great symbolism – especially when examined from the perspective of the doctrine of signatures. There are a variety of cherry trees, some bearing edible fruit and some not. The trees can live 30-40 years. Of all the cherry trees, the black cherry was considered the most valuable to lumbermen. Its wood is precious to cabinetry making. Appalachian pioneers distilled its fruit into a drink called cherry bounce. When the cherry trees began to ripen, bears would congregate and move to feast on them, creating problems for settlers and others in the Appalachians. For those to whom the cherry is a messenger, study of the bear is also recommended as well.

From the red to the rich black fruit, it has a symbolic aspect associated with the juices of life and new birth. It also has a tendency to produce thousands of stray seedlings, a gift quite symbolic of it ensuring its own rebirth on some level. It is because of this, that it has often been associated with new awakenings.

The cherry tree is the tree of the phoenix, which rose from the ashes. One who aligns with its spirit and essence will find the energy and ability to rise from the fires of their own life in a magnificent manner.

Cherry blossoms have some dynamic qualities associated with them and which will become active within an individual's life that aligns with the tree. It awakens the energies of faith and trust on high levels. It enables the individual to let go of the aspects of the ego which are preventing growth. Its appearance as a sign or messenger in Nature is a reminder that rebirth always follows death. It alerts us to be open in consciousness for new insights. This tree tells us that we are on the threshold of a new awakening. It is up to us though to cross that new threshold.

Cypress
Keynote: **find comfort in the home; new understanding of a crisis**

The cypress tree is one of the wetlands and swamps. It has resistance to water decay and it is tannic in nature. Swamps are often places that lead to the underworld or infernal kingdoms. Going through a swamp was a means of facing ones fears, sacrificing for a greater cause. The cypress tree was dedicated to Pluto, god of the underworld, in mythology.

The cypress tree encourages us to explore the sacrifices that we are making within our life. It guides us to a greater awareness that sacrifice must not always involve pain and suffering, especially when the sacrifice is made for something or someone we love.

Its presence as a sign or messenger can stir the primal feminine energies, the creative forces that are static in our life (symbolized by the wetland or swamp). Cypress will help us manifest opportunities of healing. It helps us in understanding our crises, and it awakens the comfort of home and mother.

Elder (sambucus)
Keynote: **time to regenerate; wish-making & fulfillment**

Elder is one of the most common shrubs along roadways, where it often inhabits moist ditches. Whether the American elder or the European, it is usually best suitable for rough areas of gardens. This is a broad and rounded bush with bright green leaves and white flower cymes. It is a fruit bearing tree and its berries have been used in jellies and wine. The elder is a stemmy shrub that regenerates itself easily. This should not be confused with the box elder, which is actually part of the maple tree family.

Elder literally translates as "old" and its energies are sacred to the followers of the old religions - especially those of Druid and Celtic tradition. This is a tree of birth and death, beginning and end. It is the tree of transition. In the Celtic calendar, it is associated with the 13th month, a brief period just before Samhain or Halloween.

The elder links us to contact with the Mother Goddess in varying forms. It provides energy of protection and healing. The elder tree is the mother who protects her groves and children. And it is always a reminder to protect our own sacred spaces. It facilitates contact with the spirits of the woods, the Dryads, especially at the time of the Full Moon.

Every elder has its own spirit, which shelters many other good elves and faeries. Under its roots live many tiny elves. In fact, the elder tree has the highest elf population of all trees and shrubs. Because of this, it always resents being cut. The elder energy acts as a catalyst to awaken a renaissance and contact with the fairy kingdom.

A wand of elder awakens opportunities to cast out the old and renew the creativity of the new. Elder can serve as a catalyst for manifesting changes, and change is beneficial, even if its benefits are not immediately recognized. . It reminds us that there is blessed protection. It brings magic to even the slightest wish, when the wish is made around it or while holding a wand formed from it. Magic with the elder must be controlled or it will manifest confusion and so working with an elder staff requires practice and care.

Elder signals a time of possible initiation. It reminds us that regeneration is possible and encourages us to explore it in some area of our life. Its essence helps open us to a greater understanding of the ancient burial rites as forms of initiation. The elder's energies and messages are dynamic and can be overwhelming at times. It is important to understand all the significance associated with this tree in order to balance the energies as they manifest within your life.

Elm   (ulmus)
Keynote: strength; trust intuition

Elms are one of my favorite trees. As a child, I was often climbing or sitting in the elm tree in our side yard. Elms have scaly bark and can stand extreme soil conditions. It is a strong and supple wood. Long before the Europeans made their way to America, the Native Americans held council beneath the elm. Elms were council trees that would become treaty-making trees between whites and reds. It has a fountain appearance. The trunk rises up and the branches spread out, dropping just a bit. It is sad that Dutch elm disease devastated the beautiful and stately American elms that once graced the land.

Elm has always been a favorite tree of wood elves. Sitting at night beneath an elm, while singing and storytelling, will invite them close. They are more likely to appear just before dawn, if they trust your intentions. Sometimes they will appear in dreams when you sleep beneath the elm. They have a great feeling nature – sensitivity to the connectedness of life – especially other elms. In fact, elms will mourn cut members of their family.

A staff or wand from the elm assists the individual in "hearing the inner call" in meditation and magical work. It is a tree strongly associated with the elfin kingdom, and alignment with this tree through a staff will assist you in attuning to those more ethereal beings of the Nature Realm. It is important though not to become lost within it or to become "fairy charmed."

Elm is a tree whose spirit is one of the kindest I have ever met. Its essence gently lends strength to the individual. It assists the individual in overcoming exhaustion - especially that which has accumulated over great lengths of time. It helps the individual to access more universal sources of strength so that your own individual strength will not be tapped and expended.

This is the Tree of Intuition and its appearance is always a reminder to trust your intuition. Find strength in listening to your own inner voice. The elm serves as a catalyst to sensing, feeling and even seeing that which is not always visible.

Eucalyptus   (eucalyptus)
Keynote: balance emotions; explore your dreams

Eucalyptus is also the blue gum tree, and although it originated in Australia, it has made its way to all corners of the world. It is actually an evergreen, and there are hundreds of varieties. They all have the ability to absorb great amounts of water and they all have an antiseptic property to them. Thus, they have great medical benefits. The essential oils that are distilled from the leaves have too many medical uses to list here, but one of the primary uses is in aromatherapy.

Literally, the name of this tree means "wrapped, covered." Its oil was used in the Ancient Mystery Schools to wrap the aura in balancing

My First Encounter

I was always very fortunate to have had close contact with a wide variety of trees. Most of my early life was spent in an area in which there was an abundance of woods. My brothers and I played in the woods, among the trees, creeks and ponds. One of the first tree spirits I ever truly encountered was an elm in a part of the woods where we often played tag, hide-and-seek and other games. I remember one time hiding next to an elm, behind a bush at its base. The bush was sparse, I knew if someone came by that I would be spotted. And yet I couldn't move either, for that would surely give me away. I could hear the others drawing close, and I didn't know what to do.

I t was then that I heard a soft voice whisper my name. I jumped, startled at first, and then heard a soft, gentle laugh. I raised my head to the branches above me, following the sound of the laughter. I saw a soft face appear in the bark.

"Just lean back against me," the tree whispered, "and imagine that you are part of my bark."

I was stunned, but I leaned back, making myself comfortable. I heard my brothers' voices and the voices of our friends. I was the only one who had not been found. They drew closer, and I could hear them scouring the bushes for me. I found myself relaxing, and at times, I felt like I was sinking into the tree itself. I even felt like I was peering out from the bark - just like the face that I had seen when I heard my name. I even felt a little sleepy, but I fought it. I was afraid that if I fell asleep, I would be found

They searched all around for me. One of my brothers and one of our friends even stood not six inches from me, and I knew that I was invisible to them. I remember having to stifle a giggle. As they moved off to another part of the woods, I felt myself sitting outside the bark again.

I stood and faced the tree, unsure what to say or do. The face within it was very distinct, and it smiled and again laughed softly. It was the beginning of a wonderful friendship. I would go back to that tree many times to hide, and never was I ever caught there. This beautiful spirit would show me how to see spirits in trees and plants and how to become one with them. I didn't know it then, but I was also receiving my first lessons in shapeshifting.

vibrations, for they recognized that knowledge could bring an unbalanced awakening of the psychic energies of the individual. Its energies are highly protective and dynamically healing on all levels. Its influence penetrates both the physical and subtle energies of the individual, and it stimulates an opening of the brow chakra.

Eucalyptus fragrance is very soothing to highly charged emotional states. When I was teaching school, there were days when I did not think I could handle the intense energy levels of the type of students I taught. On those days, I would sprinkle a few drops of eucalyptus oil in the heating vent so that the fragrance filled the room. As students came in, the fragrance dropped their energy levels down a notch or two. I didn't use it often, so that they would not become acclimated, but it was effective for those days when I needed a little extra help.

Eucalyptus trees are some of the tallest on the planet. Although I have never worked with one in person, I can only imagine that the spirit is also tall as well. Staffs and wands of eucalyptus assist us in walking in the dream world. They help stimulate conscious out of body experiences. Eucalyptus alerts us to the importance of our dreams. It can awaken the individual to full consciousness while in the dream state (lucid dreaming). It clarifies dreams and balances the emotions. These dreams help to bring out healing energies and an understanding of the causes of various illnesses and imbalances within our life. For those dealing with nightmares, it is one of the most calming. Four or five drops of eucalyptus oil in a bowl of water next to the bed, facilitates deeper and more restful sleep.

Those to whom the eucalyptus comes as a totem or messenger should also study the koala. This marsupial has the ability to eat the eucalyptus leaves without being affected by its poison. This animal as a totem –is usually a signal to slow down and detoxify our life. They hold the promise of relief, and this is reflected in the tree as well.

Fig (ficus)
Keynote: **opportunities for abundance; trust intuition**

The fig is one of the oldest fruits known to humans. The trees grow to about 20 feet and they can produce two crops per year, which is unusual among fruit trees. The first crop comes from buds left from the previous season's growth and the second from the new season's growth. This in itself is a reminder that we should build upon past activities for greater abundance.

The fig tree was the sacred tree of Buddha. Under it, he found enlightenment. Its spirit and essence awakens the intuitive insight that enables the individual to put our life and activities into a new perspective. It releases past life blockages, bringing them out and into the open so those new thresholds may be crossed (reflected in the first crop coming from the previous season's growth). It is a tree whose energies help the individual to link the conscious mind with the subconscious and to do so with the correct perspective.

The fig tree reminds us to trust our intuition in order to take advantage of abundance opportunities coming our way. Its message is one of building upon the past.

Hawthorn   (crataegus)
Keynote: patience brings creative success and fertility

The hawthorn trees and shrubs have a scaly bark and usually thorns. They bear a berry or nutlet. The berry has been used as a cardiac tonic, helping with blood pressure and even strengthening other aspects of the heart. The thorn apple variety often plays host to a wide variety of birds – from sparrows to doves to warblers and finches. Beneath its branches, grow wonderful and dainty wildflowers, often considered the personal gardens of the hawthorn faeries.

Hawthorn translates as "garden thorn." It is known as the May Tree in Europe, and it was an important part of most European May Day celebrations with ties to the fertility rites of Beltane. It is a tree symbolic of the energies of fertility and creativity. The hawthorn's essence will stimulate and manifest opportunities for growth on all levels within the individual's life.

It is a tree sacred to the fairies. The hawthorn has long been considered an elf tree, and cutting one will bring misfortune from the elves that lived within it – especially if it is blooming. On the other hand, hanging a branch of it on the high point of a structure would prevent harm through lightning.

The hawthorn staff helps manifests opportunities for cleansing and the development of chastity that strengthens the individual's inherent energies and allows them to draw upon greater reserves. It provides protection against the inner magical realms, but the individual will have to learn not to act too hastily or the new doors will not be opened (and life may bring a thorn prick to remind you).

This is a tree of special magic. Those of the Faerie Realm living near it hold the knowledge of its magic. Its message is a reminder of our own fertility. And it often speaks many opportunities for new expressions of creativity and fertility that are available if we pursue them in the appropriate manner.

Hazel (corylus)
Keynote: time for transformation; act on inspiration

The hazel tree bears sweet flavored nuts or filberts on an easily maintained tree. It is often used for erosion control and for medicinal purposes. Of course, all nut trees reflect something about fertility and the fruit of our life – or lack of it. All fruit and nuts associated with trees are symbols of hidden wisdom, and this tree and its energies can bring out the opportunity to acquire and express hidden wisdom in a unique manner. It is a tree whose name is also a common name used in society by people. It comes from the "hazel nut tree" and indicates the quality of "quiet spirit."

This is a very magical tree. In the Celtic tradition, it was associated with sacred wells, springs and the salmon, which should be studied also by anyone for whom the hazel tree is a messenger. In an Irish legend, the salmon ate the nuts as it swam by a hazel tree next to the shore and it became transformed with wisdom. Salmon is an animal that transforms itself, and this is one of the messages of the hazel tree. It is time to transform ourselves.

Hazel twigs and even the staffs were often used as powerful dowsing instruments, being very sensitive to the electrical-magnetic fields of the earth and of individuals. Hazel tree staffs and wands help us awaken the inner intuition and insight, and it is a powerful tree for stimulating artistic and poetic skills. It is often associated with "skaldcraft" of Teutonic lore.

The hazel tree encourages us to pursue meditation to develop a greater concentration of innate talents. It alerts us to act upon our inspirations if we wish to transform our life or some part of it.

Heather   (calluna)
Keynote: don't look for shortcuts; fertility requires activity

Heather, whose name means "forest", has soft, needlelike leaves with flowers of great shimmering color. This shrub needs well-drained soil in order to survive. It requires flow and absorption and thus is a reminder not to become mired in the past. We should look to new colors, new endeavors.

Heather is a ground cover shrub whose energy can help the individual to awaken closer contact with the inner world of spirit. It can open one to the healing forces of Nature - especially the healing power and magic of herbs. It helps the individual understand that healing begins within and not from without.

The bloom of the heather has an energy attached to it that helps the individual link to the inner self more strongly. It is a universal healing energy which will act in the individual's life in the manner appropriate to him or her. It stimulates self-expression in those who align to its essence, and it alerts us to manifestating inner forces and potentials in the outer world. Its blooms are drawing to bees and these should be studied by anyone for whom the heather is a messenger.

In Scotland, heather brooms were used to sweep cottages and homes. It also had use as thatching and bedding. In northern Europe, heather is important to the environment, providing food and cover for a variety of animals.

In the bloom of the heather are faeries that have a unique ability to stimulate greater self-expression. They are especially drawn and open to those children and adults who are shy and introverted. They can facilitate outward expression and the manifesting of inner abilities. This is a bloom that seems to have a number of faerie spirits that oversee its growth, rather than just one. This may be due to the fact that it is sometimes considered a tree, although I have never seen a tree spirit with it only the flower faeries.

This plant of fertility reminds us that our own fertility can be expressed in many ways. The task of those who take this as a totem will be to learn to build upon a strong foundation. Looking for shortcuts or easy ways will create problems and demand correction of the past and the laying of a new and more solid-foundation. Heather speaks to us abotut this. Heather represents immortality, and it facilitates seeing the immortal soul. When undergoing an initiatory path, heather will serve as a gentle catalyst to unfold inner potentials. It brings beauty into one's life. And it serves as a guide to developing new and creative endeavors.

Hickory   (carya)
Keynote: balance strength and flexibility; persistence

This is a hard and tough tree with compound leaves and often a scaly bark. It is deciduous and a nut bearing tree, and as with all nut trees, it reflects hidden wisdom and messages afoot. There are many types of hickory, and in fact, the pecan is a hickory tree. (The pecan is also related to the peach tree.) The wood of hickories is tough, heavy and resistant to impacts. It has been used to make brooms, skis and sulkies. In fact, the early years of sulky racing was somewhat dependent upon the strength of hickory, which was used in the hubs and was resistant to vibration. It is this same reason that among wood skis, skiers often favor hickory.

Hickory is known as a pushing species, in that it is able to succeed other hardwoods in ecological events, generation after generation, on the same land. This means it can endure poor soil and drier situations better than other hardwoods and it can re-grow in the same area faster than other hardwoods. Because of this alone, hickory speaks to us of our persistence. Are we persisting in our efforts? Are we giving up too soon?

One of the more common deciduous forests is the oak-hickory. In fact, oak-hickory forests comprise more than ¼ of the forests east of the Mississippi River. Both trees produce nuts, which are always symbolic of seeds and potentials. The hickory speaks to us of persisting in the seeds we are planting.

Strength and flexibility will usually get us through difficult times. Hickory reminds us that there is potential in our endeavors, but we must push through and persist for success. But we must also balance this. Are we just being stubborn? If we are unsure if the message is to persist or to quit being so stubborn, the hickory spirit always sends us another sign in the form of an animal. As you sit near the hickory, what animal stands out. Your message will be clarified through it.

Holly (ilex)
Keynote: **time to become the spiritual warrior; be clear about purposes**

Technically, holly is a bush, but it has all the power of a tree. It is one of my favorite evergreens, providing color throughout the year with its leaves and its berries. It has closely packed spiny leaves, white flowers and red berries. And as an avid birdwatcher, the berries always draw them. Even deer like the leaves in the winter.

Holly has often been used as decorations. A crown of holly and a crown of ivy was placed on the heads of male and female newlyweds respectively. It is one of the most recognized plants associated with Christmastide.

Holly has often been used as a drink or an herbal infusion. Native Americans made a drink from the leaves of a holly, called the yaupon or cassina. They believe it is a gift of the Great Spirit. It was consumed like coffee in the morning for its stimulating effect and it came to be known as the black tea. A stronger version was sometimes taken to cleanse the body and mind, providing energy, stamina and clear thinking.

Holly was also sacred to the Druids. They kept it in their homes during the winter to provide a haven for the "little people." Its spirit and essence manifests energy of protection for them and those who treat them with respect. Holly is powerful to use for wands, staffs and prayer sticks. It is magical and can successfully be used by anyone with little effort. It is one of my favorite plants to use for magical wishes, for protection and for connection to the Faerie Realm.

Holly will stimulate an opening of the heart so that true love can be experienced. It awakens compassion, and it assists us in understanding "misunderstood" emotions. It reminds us of the importance of proper emotional expression in our life - especially with those we love. Do we need to be more expressive of our feelings? It has the archetypal energies of love, with its ability to overcome anger and hate. This is a tree whose energies can help the individual to awaken the Christ energies within, and can open one to angelic and faerie contact with time and effort.

Often considered a masculine tree, it holds the energy of the spiritual warrior, an energy that can be drawn upon in times of fighting and disruption. It activates the masculine energy of the individual in a creative manner. It is important for those who align with its energies not to scatter their own energies. Any lack of direction may create problems. And this is always part of its message when we encounter it in Nature.

This is a plant whose energies need to be honed, pruned and watched in order for the highest expression of it to manifest. Once done, it can stimulate a dynamic healing capability, one that can be expressed in many avenues. The message of the holly is usually clear. It centers around issues of protection and asserting energies necessary for protection. Holly reminds us to be clear about our endeavors and to pursue them. Are we hesitant about what we are involved in? Do we need to be more assertive? Are we protecting our endeavors and our creative energies? Is it time to assert new efforts in working with the spirits of the woods?

Honeysuckle (lonicera)
Keynote: **the new is coming so learn from your past; adapt and endure**

Honeysuckle is a shrub that many argue about its worth. It is flowering, fragrant, and long lasting. It is a vining plant and vining plants contain clear messages. Are we becoming entwined in things we shouldn't? Do we need to be entwining ourselves in something new? Are past attitudes and experiences entwined and inappropriately impacting our new activities?

Honeysuckle is an adaptable and enduring plant. Some species are considered "weedy', seeding into woodlands and out-competing native plants. But some of the species are wonderfully aromatic – their fragrance filling the air through spring and summer, alerting us to the presence of the nature spirits. The flower faeries and elves of honeysuckle are powerful. They hold much knowledge about aromatherapy, especially in overcoming the past. Contact with them often stimulates powerful dreams and they awaken greater psychic energy. They can teach how to develop charms and "glamour" so that others are more drawn to you.

Honeysuckle is a shrub with an energy that reminds us to learn from the past (present life or past life) so that mistakes will not be repeated. It may even manifest similar situations we experienced in the past, to enable us to deal with them more productively and to eliminate the karma of such situations. Honeysuckle blossoms are powerful. They remind us it is time to overcome the past and their fragrance and energy will assist us in doing so. They awaken the power in our lost dreams.

Honeysuckle balances the hemispheres of the brain, enabling the individual to draw upon greater power and potential. When aligned to, it creates within the aura an air of confidence that affects others within your life. It helps awaken psychic energy and the ability to become magnetic in avenues desired. Its gentle spirit encourages a strong energy of change, and it sharpens the intuition. The fragrance will open the psychic energies of those who work with it. It can bring revelations of hidden secrets, and assist the individual in developing sureness, while overcoming any tendency toward faltering. Opportunities to develop strong discriminatory abilities are awakened - especially in distinguishing the true from the false.

The honeysuckle wound about a staff, which we use in meditation and magical practices, will help us follow our own beliefs safely. The tree awakens greater versatility and confidence, and its fragrance is "attracting" to those of the opposite sex. It helps the individual to balance the hemispheres of the brain for more powerful expressions of creativity. It increases understanding of non-physical realities and has ties to the Celtic goddess Cerridwen.

Joshua Tree (yucca)
Keynote: **resilience; beauty and survival through perseverance**

Tradition has it that the Mormons gave this tree its name. To many, the shaggy bark and twisted branches give the appearance of an Old Testament prophet. The Joshua tree resides in the high desert environment and only in the United States. In the US, it is confined mostly in or near the Mojave Desert. It is often the pride of the high desert, an important ecological factor to the surrounding environment. This twisted and spiky tree is slow growing - only about an inch a year. They are known for their creamy white flowers, but they do not bloom every year. Joshua trees also do not branch until they have bloomed. It is actually a giant member of the lily family, in fact it is also a part of the family of plants that includes grasses and orchids. It is such a tree like plant though, that I decided to place it in this grouping.

The tree has shallow roots and top-heavy branches. And since the trunk is made of small fibers, it is difficult to tell its age, unlike other trees, it does not have annual growth rings. Although it is not a strong tree, if it survives the rigors of the desert, it can survive up to a hundred years. It also produces steroid-bearing saponins.

Although it provides no shade through the high desert, it gives the environment great expression. One cannot help but be moved by it in some way. And it is a home to a wide variety of animals. Burrowing owls are frequently found near it, as are a variety of other birds. The desert night lizard rarely leaves the protection of this tree, and so it is an animal that should be studied as well.

The Joshua tree is an important part of the desert ecological system and the desert landscape should be studied as well by anyone for whom the Joshua is a messenger. The Joshua tree reminds us that if we persevere we will not only survive, but we will grow in unique ways. Our beauty, though slow in manifesting, will express itself more with each passing year.

Lemon (citrus)
Keynote: Time to refresh; new spirit guides about

All citrus trees have qualities in common. Their energy and fragrance is always cleansing, and the lemon is no exception. Their flowers are most abundant in the spring but only about 2% of all citrus flowers actually produce fruit. The flowers though are usually so abundant that even this small percentage is enough to ensure a good crop. Citrus trees are also long lived. They can last as many as 100 years if cared for properly, and the lemon tree again is no exception.

The lemon tree fruit is very acidic, and its fragrance is cleansing. This tree's energies balance the aura and help to keep it cleansed of negative emotional and astral influences. When it speaks to us, it is usually in regards to something that needs to be cleared up around us. Are we involved in negative activities or with people who are negative? Are we allowing others' negativities to affect us?

Past spiritualist mediums often used lemon to cleanse the energy of a room in which séances were performed. The fragrance helped keep out unwanted spirits and helped close the doors to the spirit world more effectively when the séance was completed. Sometimes the lemon tree speaks to us when we are not being careful about our own work with the spirit world.

A staff or wand made from the lemon tree is especially important for those who are just beginning to develop and unfold their psychic energies. It draws protective spiritual guides and teachers into one's life, and it is especially powerful for anyone who does work at the time of the Full Moon.

The lemon tree is a catalyst for clarity of thought, and its essence can make us more sensitive to using color therapy - in any of its forms - as a modality of healing. It stimulates love and friendship and it is strengthening to the entire meridian system of the body. The lemon always speaks to us of cleansing some aspects of our life. It reminds us that spirit is near, but to be truly open to them requires that our energy be cleaned and cleared.

Lilac (syringa)
Keynote: **balance the spirit and intellect; contact with spirit is imminent**

There are many harbingers of spring, but for me it is the lilac. When the lilac blooms, there is no doubt that spring has fully arrived. It is a magnificent flowering shrub or tree and its fragrant flowers are delightful additions to any garden.

In holistic health practices, both its color and fragrance are tremendously beneficial. It will align and balance all of the chakra centers of the body. Decorating lilac staffs or wands to reflect the chakras of the body in some way is powerfully healing. It awakens mental clarity, and for one wishing to activate the kundalini in a balanced manner, lilac is an excellent tree staff to work with.

Lilac draws protective spirits into one's life. It is a wonderful fragrance to use in meditations to open to your spirit guides. Sitting beneath or near lilac while meditating opens doors to the Faerie Realm. It has a strong tie to the nature spirits as they use the lilac's vibrations to raise their own consciousness. Various orders of fairies have always been associated with this tree.

The flowers of this tree are very fragrant and powerful. The lilac fragrance stimulates mental clarity, and its essence can help us to link more productively with the kingdom of nature spirits. The lilac flower aligns all of the chakras and it spiritualizes the intellect. It awakens the kundalini. It can open us to the ability to explore past lives, and it activates greater clairvoyance.

Although technically a tree, the blossoms of the lilac are filled with faerie and elf activity. The flower is very fragrant and powerful, and as you learn to attune to the nature spirits associated with it, you will find the fragrance also has a musical harmony to it. The faeries of this flower are musical in their communications. They can help harmonize our life and activate greater clairvoyance. They also can reveal to you past lives and how they are harmonized with your present.

Lilac is a great healing spirit. She is a beautiful shrub whose essence activates a play of archetypal energy within our life that helps us to spiritualize the intellect. Lilac will lovingly help us to recall past lives and it will help awaken clairvoyance. Most importantly, it helps us realize that beauty is sufficient only to itself, and that there is a beauty inherent within all things.

The message of lilac is usually very clear. This is a time to be balance spiritual activities with intellectual activities. Spirit is close and willing to work with you. Now is the time to open and develop trust in your spirit guides.

Linden   (tilia)
Keynote: keep the child and dreamer in you alive; follow your heart

The linden tree is a member of the basswood family. It is sometimes called the lime tree but it is not of the citrus variety. In both Europe and America there has been much mysticism associated with it. It is a tree whose spirit can teach healing and the ability to see the beauty beyond outer surfaces. She is the spirit of the mystic, the poet, the dreamer and the child - all of whom have the ability to see beyond appearances. This is reflected in its heart-shaped leaves and in the fact that the underside of the leaves is shiny and not the upper surface as in most trees.

Linden is the spirit that can reveal the sweet honey of all life situations. In the spring, bees are drawn to the linden nectar, and the honey differs from the honey of other flowers. It is lighter. The linden tree spirit reminds us of the dreams we have tucked away to the back of our hearts and it awakens the inner desire and strength to follow them.

In Europe, there has been a close association between the cuckoo and the linden tree. The spirit of the linden will often take the form of a cuckoo to leave the tree itself, and the cuckoo has long been the source of great superstition and inspiration. The cuckoo is often the herald of spring, the time of rebirth. In parts of Europe, it was also the herald of death and marriage, all of which are symbolic of great transformation. The linden tree spirit holds the knowledge to life, death and transformation - and the true beauty and sweetness in those processes, no matter what form they take for the individual. If the linden speaks to you, then you should study the cuckoo as a totem as well.

In America, the linden tree has had much association with the Iroquois False Face Society. Indian masks of North America often represented spirits that influence life. A person could only become a member of the False Face Society if he or she had been cured by someone in it. The individual also had to dream of the spirit, and the dream had to be confirmed by another member of the society. In the dream, the spirit instructs the individual how to make a healing mask that represents the spirit. The making of that mask was very ritualistic. A tree would be picked out, and often it was a linden tree. The bark would be peeled from a section, and then an outline of the mask would be carved into the tree. The mask was then to be cut out of the tree without harming the tree. This reflects the basic essence of the linden tree spirit - whether in Europe or America. She teaches how to work with the inner spirit to heal and transform and to find the beauty and joy in all transformations. She teaches that suffering is only good for the soul if it teaches us how not to suffer again.

Linden trees remind us to follow our heart and pursue our dreams. It is a reminder that our dreams are never lost, only forgotten. It is a reminder that for dreams to manifest, we must pursue them.

Magnolia   (magnolia)
Keynote: recover what has been lost; faith and ideals tested

The magnolia is an evergreen. It has very large leaves and an aromatic flower that is bisexual. All magnolias have a strange, knobby fruit that often looks like a cucumber. The trees are practically free of insect pests and easily tolerate fumes and grime of cities. This reinforces its primary message. If we hold true to our ideals and have faith in them, the pests that seem to be pressuring us will soon disappear.

For centuries, the Chinese have been growing magnolias in many varieties. Herbally, many aspects were considered helpful to anemic conditions. Its blossom symbolizes a beautiful woman. The fragrance of the flower is actually an aid in the opening of psychic energies, and it can enable the individual to use that intuition to locate lost items, lost thoughts and lost ideas and apply them anew.

Magnolia is a tree whose energies help to strengthen and activate the heart chakra, the center of idealism, love and healing. More importantly, it aligns the heart of the individual with his or her higher intellect. Magnolia's spirit strengthens fidelity of all those around it and provides opportunities for developing stronger relationships, based on ideals. Because of this, it is a wonderful tree to have around the home. Magnolia reminds us to be true to our ideals and our heart, no matter the pressure upon us.

Mango   (mangifera)
Keynote: trust your psychic abilities; watch sensitivity

The mango is a tropical tree that produces an oblong fruit. it is actually related tothe cashew and to poison ivy. Todays mango probably developed out of the Asia and India trees and there might be past life connections to these areas for those whom mango is a totem or messenger. The skin contains irritating oils, causing similar reactions to poison ivy. Our skin is our largest sensory organ, and the mango may provide messages about oversensitivity. It may also indicate that what we are "feeling"is a psychic /intuitive response and not just an emotional one.

Although a tree, its flower has a dynamic quality beneficial for all who are working to unfold their psychic energies. It awakens the intuition and stimulates telepathy. Anyone who works with the nature realm in any fashion can benefit by alignment with its essence.

It has ties to the archetypal energies that awaken within the aura the hope of true spiritual realization - one that is attained by alignment with nature. Its scientific name has an exotic sound which reinforces this, when this tree is addressed by this name in meditation and other magical practices.

Maple   (acer)
Keynote: **balance the male and female in you & relationships**

Maple trees are probably the favorite shade and ornamental tree in the US. There are more than a dozen species. They are all relatively tall growing and their leaves are relatively pest free. The flowers and fruit are not very impressive, but most children have found enjoyment in playing with the winged seeds and their "helicopter" type flights. And in the fall, they provide some of the richest colors. From silver maples to sugar maples, they are always a popular tree.

Maple is a tree, whose loving spirit will helps the us to bring a balance to the male and female energies within. This is particularly true of the sugar maple, from which maple syrup is developed. Europeans learned the art of sugaring from the Native Americans, and they each developed their own techniques. For the most part, a tap is inserted into the tree in the early spring, allowing the sap to flow out. It is then slowly boiled down. It takes about 30 gallons of sap to make one gallon of syrup. This insertion of the spout to produce a flow that leads to sweetness has been likened to the sexual act. When the male and female come together there is always a new birth.

The Native Americans have a strong connection to the maple and they often speak of its spirit loving the company of humans. The love works both ways though. Humans love the maple just as fervently.

All maple trees though are associated with the linking and balancing of the male and female. Maple trees balance the yin and yang, the electrical and the magnetic. This tree's spirit and the archetypal energies behind it help the individual to ground psychic and spiritual energies and to find practical means of expressing them within their lives.

It is activating to the chakras in the arches of the feet, which enable the individual to stay tied to the energies of Mother Earth. It was a popular tree for making and using magic wands – especially for sex magic and for awakening the intuition. For men, a staff or wand of maple is often beneficial to work with as it facilitates the awakening and proper expression of the feminine aspects of nurturing, intuition and creativity.

For women, the staff or wand of maple helps stimulate more outward creative expression.

The beautiful maples have the energies of sweet promises and aspirations. They awaken the inner fire, which illumines without burning. Maples remind us to keep a balance between our masculine and feminine side. When they are in balance, our intuition is sharper, our creativity is stronger and we are healthier.

The Magic of Mistletoe

We cannot discuss the oak without also discussing the mistletoe. It is a parasitic plant associated with it. It attaches itself and grows in mature oaks. Birds carry the seed of its berry to branches and forks of trees. (Attempts to grow it in soil seldom work.)

The mistletoe was sacred, and it was a predominant symbol of the feminine energy and sexuality. Its white berries, which grow in pairs, are reflective of the male testicles. This plant has generated tremendous lore and magic. Mistletoe helps us link with all lunar aspects within the universe. It manifests energy of protection, particularly toward children or to the child within. It reminds us to recognize the power and rhythms of change reflected within the lunar cycles, and it also alerts us to important dream activity.

Most people know about the tradition of kissing under a mistletoe as a sign of friendship and good will. In France, this practice is reserved for New Year's Day. For couples in love, kissing under the mistletoe was considered a promise to get married. A man standing beneath a mistletoe can not refuse to be kissed and such a kiss was an indicator of romance or deep friendship. A woman who is not kissed while standing beneath the mistletoe could not expect to be married the following year.

It has been used to develop an "invisibility" or going unnoticed when desired, along with the ability to shapeshift. The mistletoe was a powerful herb of the Druids, used primarily for fertility and as an aphrodisiac. It was a symbol of rebirth and the awakening of vision that could open the secrets of life beyond the physical. Its energy awakens the vision of one's soul life in the future. It can be attached to your staff with ribbon or thread. Some people take the mistletoe from Christmas each year to replace the mistletoe on their staff.

Oak   (quercus)

Keynote: strength and endurance win out; open to new spirit forces

The majesty of a mature oak always gives pause for reflection. They radiate an aura of calm strength. The leaves are green in the spring and summer and turn a bright russet-red in the fall. It has the deserved reputation of being the king of trees. It has one of the widest and most magnificent spreads - particularly the white oak. There are two great groups of oaks – the red and the white. The easiest way of telling the difference is by examining the leaves. The veins in the leaves of the red extend to beyond the edge of the leaf, like tiny bristles. The veins of the white oak leaves never extend past the edge.

The oak tree was sacred to the Celts and Druids, and in the Teutonic mythology it was associated with the energies of Thor. It is a tree aligned with primal male force, which must be controlled and expressed properly. It is a powerful symbol of the male energy, the yang or electrical aspect of the universe or individual. Thus, it is also aligned with all solar aspects of the universe. When a wand or staff of oak is worked with, its energy awakens great strength and endurance - even through the most trying circumstances. It helps to manifest a stronger and more active sense of helpfulness towards others, and it opens us to more easily be helped by others.

Oak has strong ties to the realm of nature spirits as well. The oak tree wand or staff provides the energies to open the doorway to the inner realms and their mysteries in meditation, magic and in real life. It awakens greater strength and security in all pursuits.

The acorn of the oak is a symbol of fertility and fruition and the manifestation of creativity. It may require one or two years for an acorn to mature and they usually drop n the fall. Sometimes the presence of the oak and its acorns is a sign that the fruit of your efforts over the past year or two is about o be harvested.

There are a number of magical practices associated with the acorn. Carving or painting it on your staff helps awaken this energy. It represents the continuity of life. A great many magical practices arose around the acorn, including the placing them in windowsills to prevent lightning strikes.

Oak trees provide strength to everyone and remind us that true strength is also gentle. Now is the time to demonstrate your own strength and endure. The energy will be there to do so and as a result new confidence and new spirit forces will open to you.

Olive   (elaeagnus)
Keynote: look for peace and harmony; trust inner guidance

The olive tree has wonderful foliage and a terrific resistance to harsh conditions. And in most traditions it is the Tree of Peace. It is also known as the Tree of Honor, and it has ties to Athena, Poseidon and Zeus.

There is always peace if we do not allow ourselves to be affected by outside circumstances. The olive tree embodies the spirit and archetypal energies of harmony and peace of mind. Olive trees remind us to manifest greater inner strength and faith as true forces - not just as beliefs. It promises the energies of renewal and rejuvenation - restoring a zest for life.

It is also linked to the processes of regeneration - in physical healing and in spiritual unfoldment. It can serve as a catalyst to access the levels of consciousness that leads to better inner guidance and deeper levels of clairaudience. It increases sensitivity, and renews the individual's hope and will to enjoy life.

Orange   (citrus)
Keynote: trust emotions and dreams; time to release fears

All citrus trees have qualities in common. Their energy and fragrance is always cleansing. Their flowers are most abundant in the spring but only about 2% of all citrus flowers actually produce fruit. The flowers though are usually so abundant that even this small percentage is enough to ensure a good crop. Citrus trees are also long lived. They can last as many as 100 years if cared for properly.

There are primarily three types of oranges. All speak to our sensitivity in some manner. The navel is thick-skinned and sweet tasting. It is often a reminder that we may need to be a bit more thick-skinned as well. Are we being overly sensitive? Or are we being too thick-skinned and insensitive? The common orange is thin-skinned and very juicy. It often reflects how close our emotions are to the surface, and we may need to control them a bit more. The third type is the blood orange, which has a reddish skin and juice, and of all the oranges, it ripens first – usually in the spring. It can be a reminder that our emotions are tied to our physical health and so they must be balanced.

The orange color of the fruit reveals much about the qualities of this tree. Orange is a color associated with emotional energy – positive and negative. The tree, its fruit and its fragrance stimulate clarity of emotions. It can assist us in releasing emotional trauma gently. As a messenger, it is usually speaking to us about something emotional, present within our life.

The orange tree spirit brings calmness to highly charged states. Its energies can aid in the development of counseling abilities, and it can stimulate dreams that provide clues to deep-seated fears or fears of unknown origins.

Orange trees speak of a need to releases tensions held within the subconscious. A wand or staff from an orange tree can be used to create intense thoughtforms. The color of orange should be used in designs on this staff. Aligning with this tree through a staff can manifest an energy that assists the development of conscious astral projection, the rising on the planes. This can help us realize that it is time to release our fears.

Palm   (palmacea)
Keynote: **group protection; maintain peace through past learnings**

Palm trees are tall, unbranched trees. They have a crown of large cleft leaves. They are common to southern areas of warm, often arid climate. The palm is the Tree of Peace. It has a powerfully calming energy associated with it.

Its spirit can provide protection for all members of a group with whom you are connected. It can also provide protection from a group with whom you are connected. The leaves alone have been rumored to prevent evil from entering into an area. Do you need to examine more closely with whom you associate and align? The palm makes a wonderful staff or wand for group work.

The desert palm has become a part of gardens worldwide – wherever it can be grown. In many places, it is now seen as a native plant where it might not actually be. Hawaii is one such place, where it is known as the hula palm. The first European to discover the desert palm was a Franciscan priest, Juan Crespi. He spotted it near Baja, Claifornia. It is different though from the cabbage variety in Florida.

Native Americans would often cut the bud, which gives all of the leaves, and then they would roast it and eat it. Unfortunately, this is one of the ways to kill all growth of the palm. The bud of the desert palm though retains its leaves as long as possible, even when they have died. It clings to them and they become a kind of armor for the stem. This reflects itself in the keynote of protection for this plant. Palm is often a reminder that the past, no matter how long faded, still serves a purpose and will always be a part of us.

The palm tree alerts us to celebrate or to produce something worth celebrating. The wind blowing through them stirs a longing within observers. It is an easy plant to grow indoors, providing a protective energy for the home environment. It is a reminder to look for and realize the divine within. It can be a messenger for members of the angelic hierarchy.

Peach   (prunus)
Keynote: longevity; blessings through artistic endeavors

Peaches are one of the most popular home-grown fruits. Their flowers in the spring though are very susceptible to late frosts. Peaches and nectarines are essentially the same fruit. The only difference is that the peach has a fuzzy skin. The peach tree is tied to awakening hidden wisdom, as with all fruit-bearing trees.

In this case, though, the archetypal energies behind it can help the individual to develop a new realization about immortality and how it can be attained. The peach tree staff alerts us to beneficial activities associated with youth and the prevention of the aging process.

Contact with peach trees renew and re-activate our life force, the kundalini. It stimulates artistic energies, along with innovative applications of them within our present life endeavors. It activates energy within the aura that is calming to our emotions and those we meet.

Pine (pinus)

Keynote: **Balance strength and softness; emotional protection and healing**

Pines have a resinous wood and needles for leafs, usually bundled in groups of 2/3 or five. When doing nature hikes with students, I would teach them to count the number of needles in a bundle to determine if the pine was red or white. If there are five needles per bundle, it is a white pine. There are five letters found in the word "white" and five needles are in a white pine tree bundle. It is a simple way of identifying the pine.

No other tree has had a greater role in American history than the white pine. It was the most abundant tree in the northern range Pioneers used to say that a squirrel could live its lifetime moving through the pines without ever coming down. Trees that stood 150 feet tall greeted early settlers. On the present site of Dartmouth College, a pine tree was measured at 240 feet.

The pine trees were gold to the early settlers. It was the only great export of early New England. The white pine because of its size, softness, strength and light weight was ideal for ship masts, and since England was the king of the seas, it was a valuable commodity. It would eventually become one of the major economic factors leading to the American Revolution. Laws were passed in England to restrict and stop American settlers from cutting and selling what England claimed as its own. In fact, one of the first flags of the revolution had the emblem of the white pine. From ships, to covered bridges, to homes to railway ties, the white pine was an important player in the development of America.

There is a variety of other pines. These include the red pine, jack pine, scrub pine and more. Of all of these, the red pine has always been a companion to the white. It has a more colorful bark of armor-like plates, adding to the idea of it being a tree whose energy helps protect emotions.

But no matter what type of pine it is, they all have energy of protection and their fragrance is always soothing to emotional states.

The pine tree has great mysticism as well. The pine tree was the Sacred Tree of Mithra. It also has ties to the Dionysian energies and mysteries. It is balancing to the emotions, and it awakens the divine spark, which resides within the heart chakra for true salvation as defined through occult and Gnostic Christianity. Pine comes from a word that translates as "pain," and its essence helps alleviate pain within on many levels. It was also a tree sacred to Poseidon, who helped make its essence cleansing and protective against all forms of negative magic. The pine helps to repel evil.

Pine trees are very personable and very communicative. You must be careful what you say around a pine tree or you will hear it softly whisper it to other trees. I used to demonstrate this with groups when I served as a trail guide at Brukner Nature Center. I would take the group to the pine woods and have them sit. I would then tell them that you had to be careful about whispering secrets around pines because the pines would hear and they would pass the secret on. If you hear pines whispering (the sound of the breeze rustling through them), others would soon know your secret. I would then have them all make whispering sounds to each other. WIthin a minute or two, a breeze would always come through and the pines would rustle and whisper in response. And because they are a taller tree, they easily pass those whispered secrets on.

Pine has an archetypal energy and message about eliminating our feelings of guilt and balancing over-emotionalism. The pine spirit is kind and sensitive and loves contact with humans. It soothes emotions and always reminds us that we should make decisions best from as clear a perspective as possible. The pine heightens our psychic sensitivity, while balancing the emotions as well. It reminds us to express our creative energies without feelings of guilt and without allowing others to overly influence or manipulate.

Poplar (populus)
Keynote: endure and pursue your dreams; time to manifest

The poplar tree is a beautiful, fast growing tree with quite an extensive and strong root system. It can grow quite tall and some species have the ability to grow quickly in arid conditions and without much coddling.

The wonderful spirit of this tree has the ability to teach the average individual how to make dreams and projects manifest quickly, yielding great rewards in the shortest time possible (often and noticeably within a year's time). This message is a reminder of the possibilities in life and that opportunities are never lost. They do come back around. This is reflected not only by its quick growth but also by the fact that its leaves turn golden (with all its symbolism) in the fall, and when they drop off, masses of vertical branches are etched against the sky. The spirit of the poplar tree awakens and reminds all people of the possibilities in life. She reminds us all that all of life's experiences have gold within them, and that we all can rise and grow to great heights.

The spirit of the poplar tree is most concerned about the earthly and mundane matters of the people in her environment. She teaches us how to endure the hardships of life and to keep our roots are strong. She will help us overcome our personal fears and self doubts that may block our endeavors. She reveals to us lost and forgotten memories of our dreams through the gentle whispers of her leaves with every breeze.

The poplar message often encourages and leads us to the many avenues and means of manifesting dreams. An old form of tree magic involved planting a wish or a dream with a tree. As the tree grows, its spirit works to manifest and aid the growth of your wish or dream. With no tree is this easier, for the spirit of the poplar loves to show all people that we are never given a hope, wish or dream without also being given opportunities to make them a reality.

Quince (chaenomeles)
Keynote: time to be more expressive of love and nurturing

This is a small shrub that produces spectacular flowers and, a small hard, apple-like fruit that is often jellied. Its flowers are very rosaceous and quite striking in color in shades of orangish-red pastels.It often has a tangled mass of stems that require frequent pruning. The flowers bloom at the first sign of warmth in winter and thus can be damaged by the cold. This can be areminder not to express our tangled feelings too quickly, to allow them to develop more.

Often associated with the goddess Venus, it is tied to the universal energies of love. It awakens the feminine, and it stimulates within the auric field an energy which promotes greater expressions of love and mothering. Its presence reminds us and helps us to balance love and nurturing with power and strength. It draws to the individual opportunities for self-actualization.

Redbud   (cercis)
Keynote: **trust your creative efforts and abilities**

As a small, flowering landscape tree, the red bud is one of the most beautiful with magenta and pink flowers. It is small and low-branching and it is adaptable to various soils. They are scaly barked and all scaly barked trees have something to teach us about our sensitivity or lack of it. The flowers are early bloomers, coming out in the first fine weather, as early as February is some parts of the South. George Washington had a reputation of transplanting redbuds from the woods to his garden

The Judas tree is an older, more foreign name for this tree that has been transferred to the American species. It was so named due to the belief that this was the tree that Judas Iscariot hanged himself from after betraying Jesus. This is one of those beliefs though that in no way reflects the character and energy of the tree itself.

Redbuds love a clay soil, which in itself is significant. Clay has always symbolized the material of life. It can be formed and shaped into a variety of uses. The redbud is always a reminder that we each have the ability to shape our lives in a variety of ways. Its message is often to trust in your creative energies.

The color of the flowers are always part of its message. The magenta is often a color used to stimulate more outwardly creative expression. It is a reminder not to keep our creativity hidden under a barrel. The redbud spirit is one of joyful and creative expression and she stimulates creative expression within us. Redbuds also stir passion especially in regards to expressing love and emotions.

Leaf Beliefs
Leaves and blossoms have always been considered magical signs:
• Leaves blowing in the house was considered very good luck.
• If you catch a falling leaf, you will have 12 months of happiness.
• Every petal of apple blossom that you catch equals a month of happines.
• And if you catch a leaf before it touches the ground on Halloween you will be granted one wish.

Redwood (sequoia)
Keynote: **ancient protection and balance; pursue new visions**

The sequoia family of trees is home to some of the largest and oldest spirits upon the planet. This is reflected in throughout the family of redwoods. They are conifers of great size and age. The General Grant tree is more than 270 feet high and the Boole tree is 25 feet in diameter at a point about 15 feet up from the ground. They live in higher altitudes and the sequoias only grow in groves. These groves serve as a council of spirit, and there is a gentle but powerful sacredness to the groves. One cannot enter them without a stirring of our own sense of the sacred.

They have tremendous resistance to decay and even to fire. The sap of the sequoia contains tannic acid, which has great healing capacity for the trees, as tannin does for humans. This enables them to live longer, but because they are so long lived, they do not produce as many cones as other conifers. There is not that need to reproduce so extravagantly.

Redwoods are practically immune to termites and other pests. Their energy immediately helps put our own life pests into perspective. They strengthen and heal the aura so that we are less affected by the buzzing of the daily pests we encounter. They remind us to look at the bigger picture.

Redwoods live an extremely long time – 1500 or more years. They are ancient and they are direct descendants from the time of evolution known as Lemuria. Alignment with their essence can open one to understanding the evolutionary cycle of humanity. The redwood spirit helps the individual to put his or her life into an entirely new perspective. Its essence awakens a clear insight into our own personal vision of life and what must be done to follow through upon it.

Being around the redwoods stimulates great spiritual vision - especially of the etheric realms. And even after short visits, the psychic amplification continues on, for even months afterwards. It activates the brow and crown chakras, although if not properly balanced, it will manifest as unbalanced imagination and even superstition. It awakens within the aura a vitality that is simultaneously soothing and stimulating. It awakens extended growth periods that will touch strongly upon soul levels.

The redwoods are ancient spirits who try to help us gain perspective about our life. Do we need to step back and take a new look at what we are doing? Is it time for us to pursue our true visions? Redwoods remind us that there is always enough time. Great changes and great growth occurs just a little at a time.

Rowan (sorbus)
Keynote: develop control; time for discrimination and discernment

Rowan trees have smooth bark and twigs that have ring-like scars on them. The leaves are alternate and they produce beautiful berries. The rowan comes to full flower in the early summer, but in the fall, the leaves turn a brilliant yellow and the apple-like berries are a rich vibrant red. It is in the fall that the energy is strongest. For those to whom the rowan comes as a messenger or totem, the fall season will be one of importance, and its significance should be thoroughly explored.

Rowan berries are rich in vitamin A and C and were probably a common staple of people past. They've been used in jams and in herbal concoctions as a laxative. The Welsh once used them in the process of making ale, and the Native Americans made their own drinks from the dried berries as well. Its berries always draw cedar wax wings and other birds that enjoy berries. As an ornamentals plant for the yard, it is wonderful to have if you are an avid birdwatcher because it will bring them in.

The rowan spirit will help you control of the senses - physical and otherwise. Its energy is strong and protective. It is often a reminder that we must maintain control of our emotions and situations for our own well-being and protection. It can be called on as powerful force against intrusion by outside energies (including spells and enchantment). Carrying a piece of the rowan upon you throughout the day is strengthening to the aura, and it prevents intrusive energies from those we encounter throughout the day. Because the aura is partly an electro-magnetic field, contact with others throughout the day results in an accumulation of energy "debris." Rowan reminds us that we are likely being affected by these extraneous energies. It thus helps us as a protective and cleansing spirit.

The rowan has had a number of mystical and magical uses. The berries have a small pentagram at the point where they connect to the stalk. Its essence can also help open one to understand the significance and practical application of the Norse Runes. Its branches are powerfully effective as dowsing rods. They are sensitive to the element of water. Staffs made from the rowan protect a person while traveling. It can also be a connection to the faerie Realm, as more than one legend speaks of it as a gift of the Faerie folk.

The rowan alerts us to the need for developing discrimination, especially in balancing common sense with superstition. This is the tree of protection and vision. Its energies invoke all goddesses and assist the individual in learning to call up magic spirits, guides and elementals. Its energies enhance the individual's creativity.

Spruce (picea)
Keynote: **understanding; attend to your dreams; trust intuition**

There are many varieties of spruce trees. They are evergreens, which are extremely aromatic. They love human contact. When my wife and I purchased our first home, we had a blue spruce tree in the front yard. It blocked a good part of the house. It was tall, broad and it looked dead. There was little color to its needles, and we assumed that it would need to be removed. Within the first month, the color began returning to the tree. Within three months, it was completely healthy and vibrant.

The house had been empty for a long time, prior to our purchase of it and the spruce was depressed and lonely. That spruce was one of the most protective and beautiful spirits I ever encountered. When we moved, leaving it behind was the most difficult part of all. Before we sold the house though, we ensured that the new owners would not cut it down.

Spruce comes from a Russian word meaning "fine, smart." As a link to the archetypal energies of Nature, the spruce is powerfully effective in awakening realizations as to how best to detoxify one's system and to balance one's energies on all levels.

Spruce reminds us that we may not understand what we think we do. This can apply to any aspect of our life, but often it applies to health. The spruce spirit is wonderful at awakening understanding of disease/ illness causes. Spruce always stimulates dreams and its appearance is a reminder to attend to them, for they are providing guidance and greater focus. It can even assist us in developing lucid dreams that lead to conscious out-of-body experiences.

Spruce is a gentle messenger and friend. It amplifies healing on all levels, and it is calming to the emotions. It is a gentle awakener of the dynamic feminine intuition. It is an excellent tree staff to work with for any disorientation or lack of direction.

Sycamore (platanus)
Keynote: **nourishment and beauty abound; new life and new gifts**

The sycamore has thin, grayish white bark and large leaves. It is found in low lying areas, near streams or where water flows or gathers. It likes to soak its feet in the water, and for those to whom the sycamore comes as a messenger, exploring foot reflexology and foot baths can be a tremendous health benefit.

Its name actually means "fig" and it is often called the ghost tree. It is one of the tallest of the deciduous trees and its whitish bark stands out strong in the woods – especially at night when the moonlight is strong. Its thin twigs and branches look like arms outstretched, especially when they are bare of leaves.

The sycamore was the sacred tree of the Egyptians. A sycamore staff can be used to draw the energies of Hathor into one's life and individual energy field. The sycamore is a noble tree and its appearance is often a sign that there is nourishment about.

Sycamore energies help prevent atrophy of higher abilities the individual has brought into this lifetime. It is a reminder to build on old gifts and to express them in new ways. The staff can open communication between the conscious and subconscious minds when used in mediation and magical practices. It strengthens the life force of the individual and opens the opportunities to receive "intuitive and spiritual gifts" from the universe.

The sycamore is also a sign that gifts, which are more mundane, are on the horizon. These gifts may come in the form of assistance, compliments, etc. It is important to receive them graciously, for if we do not receive the little things, the universe will not bring us the big things. It holds the knowledge of the laws of abundance and how to utilize them to your greatest benefit. It also has knowledge of hidden treasures of the Earth.

The sycamore awakens the feminine energies of intuition, beauty and nourishment around us. It can open us to the energies of love and Nature and all their magnificent aspects. The sycamore will augment all connections to Nature, and its appearance in our life encourages us to draw upon the realm of Nature for health, abundance and inspiration.

Walnut   (juglans)
Keynote: **power for transitions; hidden wisdom**

Walnut is one of those trees with strongly aromatic leaves, bark and fruit. There are varieties of walnut trees, each with their own unique characteristics. The butternut variety has a fruit that is a true dye. It will stain the fingers and cannot be washed off. Black walnut wood has been a staple of furniture makers. At one time, black walnut trees were so plentiful that they were even used for snake-rail fences. In some cases, the wood actually changes color when viewed and lighted from different angles. This hints at walnuts secret life and power.

The autumn equinox was a time for the ritual gathering of nuts – especially the walnut. It was an act that was as magical as it was mundane. It provided food throughout the winter and spring, but the gathering of nuts was a way of using the equinox energy to awaken abundance, prosperity and wisdom over the next year. Carrying the nut was a way of awakening fertility.

The walnut has had many uses throughout its history. Its shell made excellent dyes. The nuts were turned into flour and added to cakes. Tea made from its leaves was good for stomach indigestion and other digestive imbalances. Native Americans used the oil in a variety of its ceremonies and celebrations. On the other hand, folklore teaches that eating the walnuts helped to cure and prevent madness.

Walnuts activate hidden wisdom within our own life circumstances. Its appearance alerts us to pay attention. We will begin to hear and see things that have been going on around us but had not noticed before.

Walnut helps us make transitions of all kinds. This is reflected in its protective shell. We are less sensitive to the changes occurring. Its energies are often catalytic in the manner in which changes will manifest. The walnut reminds us that – if allowed to play out - all changes will be of benefit. The walnut cleans and strengthens auric field so we see clearly what needs to be changed and how to accomplish it from the clearest perspective possible. Walnut holds the power of rebirth and when it becomes a totem or messenger, the esoteric aspects of death and rebirth become predominant for at least a year in our life. A staff or wand of walnut in meditation and magical practices reveals apply these mysteries constructively within our life.

The walnut spirit awakens freedom of spirit, telling us it is time to break free of the cocoon. It will even herald the coming of opportunities to follow our own unique path in life. Whether we follow through on such opportunities is a free will decision, but walnut's appearance in our life is often strong encouragement to do so. Walnut is a tree of initiating and initiation. The key is to be true to one's self when aligning with these energies. Self-deception and delusion result in chaotic disruption instead of creative transition.

Willow   (salix)
Keynote: be flexible and look for connections; trust inner visions;

Willows are fast growing trees with a bitter and astringent bark. All varieties have limber twigs and branches. There are a number of varieties, some of which fall into the tree category and others into the shrub category. The black willow is one of the largest in the world. The weeping willow is a favorite among many people for its beauty and it has inspired many a poet.

The pussy willow is also one of the favorites in the willow family. A powerful plant, pussy willow has an essence that can help us in divination and reading signs. In fact, it is good for almost any form of divination. It is tied to the archetypal energies of the future. It reminds us that there are promises yet to be fulfilled. It renews and revitalizes, awakening the inner fires of hope and inspiration for that is yet to come.

All willows grow best in moist areas, and they are often found along ponds, streams, marshes and wetlands. These habitats should be studied as well for anyone to whom the willow appears as a messenger. Willows are water loving, and water is an archetypal symbol of the feminine energies of birth, creativity, intuition and the moon.

Willow is a magical and healing tree. Its name literally means "convolution," and there is a convolution of energies associated with it. It stimulates an energy of healing on many levels, especially though in the areas of herbology and aromatherapy. And its meanings to us are often multidimensional. There is rarely a single message from willow. It is always multiple and many layered.

Willow awakens flexibility and encourages many avenues of exploration when it appears as a messenger. It alerts us to powerful opportunities for communication, and it has ties to all deities of other worlds and other traditions. The willow tree is associated with the goddess Brigid of Celtic mythology, and Willow's spirit can help us invoke and align with those energies. It is also linked to Orpheus who brought to Greece the teachings of music and Nature and magic.

Willows also awaken clairaudience - hearing of spirit. In Europe are tales of travelers being frightened at night while walking through the woods. They made claims of willow tree spirits following behind them, muttering in their ears. When the gift of clairaudience first begins to awaken, the sounds are like a soft muttering.

Willow makes one of the very best dowsing tools. This is partly due to willow's strong connection to water. Just carrying a piece of willow in your pocket can make your more sensitive. When you are near a water source, you will feel that piece of willow. For some people it vibrates. For others, it gets warm or cool, but there is always a response from it around water. Wands made from it are powerfully effective for wish-making and all water magic. When properly worked with in meditation and magic, willow wands and staffs help us realize the very intimate link between our thoughts and external events in our life.

Willow alerts us to new opportunities to learn and explore. It encourages a flexibility of thought, and its energies. Willow is associated with an awakening of the feminine energies, of going into the darkness of the womb and activating greater expression of them. Its spirit opens "night" vision, or vision of that which has always been hidden or obscured. It reminds us to use the rhythms of the Moon to look for dream messages of importance. Willow always stimulates great dream activity. And her message always involves learning to trust our inner visions.

Wisteria (floribunda)
Keynote: **time for clarity; illumination and new learning at hand**

This exotic plant is very powerful, with dynamic ties to archetypal energies. In pagan traditions, it has been a popular name taken by those who are students and scholars. Just aligning with its name helps manifest greater opportunities to learn, especially to learn that which is not normally accessible. It awakens inspiration in the life of the individual, and in fact, it has been known as the "poet's ecstasy".

Occultists and healers have used its fragrance to draw good vibrations. This tree's flower activates the heart and throat chakras. It awakens a realization of the good that is already present within one's life; it clears the fog within the aura. It stimulates creative expression and the "power of the word". It is a rare spiritual influence that can be a passport to higher consciousness. It opens the doors between the realm of humanity and the realm of the Divine. It assists us in contacting other planes of life and higher forms of illumination.

"Trees are living creatures.
Their spirits
are gentle and strong
and they hold great affection
for humans.
They serve as living antennae
between Heaven and Earth.
Prayers and wishes
whispered beneath them
are always
more powerful."

Part Five

Song of the Flowers

"Yet to pursue a purpose in life
so strenuously
that you will not linger
among its flowers,
is to miss the best of it all."

- Donald Culross Peattie

Natural Wonders

Wildflowers are herbaceous plants that grow naturally in the wild. In the US, more than 15,000 flowering plants are found in the wild. Wildflowers must appeal greatly to the free spirit of Americans as half the states have a wildflower as their official flower.

Chapter Thirteen

How Flowers Speak to Us

The story of flowers is the story of humanity. Flowers are found in all mythologies and traditions. Among the Lakota, the prairie rose came up from the heart o f the Earth Mother to face the demon wind of the outer world. She was so beautiful and fragrant that she charmed the winds which softened to a breeze. This gave the other flowers in the heart of the Earth Mother courage to come out and adorn the world. Images of flowers have been painted on cave walls and hang in museums. They are a source of inspiration, medicine and food. And as Ralph Waldo emerson said, "The Earth laughs in flowers."

Flowers are great sources of energy and inspiration. We use them to express love, sympathy, friendship and more. Every aspect of the flower has been used by healers and metaphysicians. The fragrances, the herbal qualities, the color and imagery serve as powerful sources of energy. Flowers - wild and domestic – have been used as divination tools for thousands of years. Many flowers have been associated with gods and goddesses. Individuals looking for a magical name have often taken the name of a flower that is associated with a particular god or goddess, opening themselves to all of the archetypal forces that are reflected by the actual flower itself. Sometimes this is through taking its more common name or even its botanical delineation such as in the case of Sagebrush and Artemisia.

Flowers, in any form, are sources of strong energy vibrations. Even dried flowers continue to be a source of such. It is only decayed and decaying flowers which are not. Both traditional and modern spiritualists are very familiar with the energy aspects of flowers, and they take care to set flowers in the séances room or any room in which there will be spiritual activities. The influence of flowers upon all within that area is

"We should love
the Earth and all things
that grow and live upon it.
We should love the soil
and sit upon the ground often -
feeling close
to its great mothering power,
allowing it
to strengthen and heal us."

very subtle and very real. They raise the vibrations of the individuals, facilitating contact with other dimensions and realms.

Flowers raise the energy or vibration of any occasion. They are always used in rites of passage. A rite of passage is a celebration of a transition in one's life. Births, baptisms, dedications, weddings and funerals are all rites of passages in which flowers are beneficial. For weddings, they invite loving spirits and angels into the celebration, blessing it further. Flowers have an ancient and esoteric role in funerals as well. At the cessation of life, the soul is cut off from the prana or life force that it would normally draw from the sun and through the physical body. In the untangling from the threads of life, it must draw energy from other sources to assist itself. Lit candles and flowers are placed about to facilitate the soul in this rite of passage. The flowers also help prevent the soul from drawing the energy needed from those still living.

Most people are at least superficially familiar with herbal aspects of flowers and plants, but an even newer process of using such has unfolded within the later decades of the 2oth century and is still growing in popularity. Flower elixirs and essences are dynamic tools for healing physical and psycho-spiritual conditions. Each flower has its own unique vibration or energy pattern and this is infused into water which can then be used in a variety of ways. They can even be taken internally to assist with particular conditions of the body, mind and spirit. Although this process of healing with flowers from various plants, herbs and trees was established by Dr. Edward Bach, other groups have taken his research and have expanded upon it

All plants that flower - just as with all fruit bearing trees - are indicative of hidden wisdom and joys that can be brought out into the individual's life. They are some of our most important message bringers. Remember that each aspect of the flower signifies something, and honor it, just as was described with the trees. Buy bouquets of them on a regular basis. Paint and draw pictures of them. Make a drawing of them in your Nature Journal. Plant them in your house, apartment or garden. Make an amulet upon which is a picture of it in which the number of petals of the flower corresponds to the number of your birthdate numerologically. Use your imagination. By aligning oneself with the flower, you are aligning with Mother Nature herself. You are opening yourself to creation, growth and sustenance. It is these qualities of Mother Nature that are symbolized by all flowers, fruits and trees.

How Flowers Speak to Us

Flowers are some of our most important messengers. Because of this, it is important to learn as much about the flower you encounter as possible. How and where does it grow? Under what climatic conditions does it best unfold? Learn all that you can about its growing process and all of its parts: roots, bulbs, stems, leaves, flowers, etc. Each aspect has significance and can help you to define how the archetypal energies working through it will manifest within your own life. A good example can be drawn from the "lily". Its fragrance awakens the divine aspects within us. Its stalk is symbolic of the upliftment of the godly mind. The hanging leaves reflect the energies of humility, and its whiteness awakens the purity of the individual's soul and helps manifest its expression. When a flower stands out for you, begin with the following basics:

1.   What is the flower's color?

Color is a wonderful quality with the ability to touch us physically, emotionally, mentally and spiritually. Some colors are warm, some are cool, some soothe and some excite. Everyone is affected by color. Each color has its own characteristics. We spoke of this earlier, and the study of color is essential for anyone wishing to truly read signs, omens and messages from the Natural world more effectively. We are drawn to those colors we need or those that have a message for us. Often our responses are instinctive, especially when we are out in Nature. We are struck by a particular flower or blossom of some kind.

2.   What is the flower's fragrance?

Fragrance is one of the most powerful psychological triggers that we encounter in life. Fragrance, like color, has its own characteristics. Some fragrances are calming, some exciting. Some fragrances are attracting and some are repelling. Fragrances can be healing or disruptive. Often the fragrance that captures our attention in Nature is one that we most need or which has the most important message for us.

There is a principle at play when it comes to fragrance as messengers to us in Nature. An old occult axiom states, "Like attracts like." When we are out in Nature, our aura, our energy, will resonate with those trees, flowers and their aspects that have a message for us. We will catch the fragrance of a plant that is important to us or something within our life. Noting and identifying that fragrance is an important part of developing nature-speak.

3. What does its shape suggest?

The Doctrine of Signatures is one of the most important ways of determining the message of a plant – especially flowers. The shape of the flower, the shape of its petals, the number of petals, help us get into greater details of the message. Begin by examining the general form and feel of the flower. Touch it, as well as look at it. For example, Lambs ear is soothing to the touch and often contains messages of softening our efforts.

Is the plant soft, rigid, spreading, vertical, and horizontal, etc.? Upward growing plants are open to the sun and usually reflect optimism and enthusiasm. Hanging flowers often reflect issues of harmony that should be focused upon. Horizontal growing plants carry messages of social exchanges, interaction and circulation. Are there many blossoms or just a few? The number of blossoms may reflect things about abundance or limitations in regards to some situation.

The flower blossoms take a variety of shapes. What is the shape of the flower and what do you think that significance is? Is the blossom a trumpet shape? Is it a chalice or cup shape? Traditionally, all cups and all bowls were symbols of the Divine Feminine, the birth-giving energies of creativity, intuition and imagination.

And what about the petals? Are they flat and open or closed? This may tell us something about whether we should be more open or closed in some situations of our life. Are the petals ruffled? All flowers that have a fringe and ruffled petal are soothing and protective. Flowers with ruffles often smooth out ruffles in our own aura, helping to restore balance.

4. Is it a perennial or annual?

When does the flower bloom? How does that time frame fit in regards to aspects of our life? Flowers bloom at different times. The times in which they bloom is often a power time for them and it can reflect a similar power time within our own lives. Often the cycle of blooming reflects a time cycle associated with something in our own life. What is its flowering cycle if it is an annual or a perennial?

An annual is a flower or plant that lives one year or less. The seed germinates, grows, flowers, releases a new seed and dies all in one growing season. Perennials are non-woody plants that live for more than two years. Typically, they bloom year after year. The annual reminds us about renewing our efforts each year, while the perennials remind us about how our efforts often are investments in the future. Whether a flower is an annual or a perennial helps us utilize our energies and efforts in all endeavors more effectively. Annuals remind us that the rewards may be great but they are short lived. Perennials remind us that our efforts should build upon the past and will grow with each new year. More of this will be covered on the following pages.

One aspect of this though begins with determining if the plant is a wildflower, which are often perennials, or if the plant is it a domestic? Wildflowers are typically hardier, but domestic varieties usually have much brighter colors and more varieties of them.

5. Are there animals or insects associated with the plant?

Some species of animals are dependent upon plants. The koala's existence is dependent upon a particular kind of eucalyptus. Certain insects are drawn to certain flowers and are often critical for pollination. Monarch butterflies are dependent upon the milkweed. Butterfly weed (left) draws a variety of butterflies, which is how it gets its name. The animals , associated with the plant, are always part of the message.

A study of the plant and its association to certain animals can also help us identify pests in our life. Certain plants and flowers are associated with certain insects. Some insects are particularly damaging to specific plants. A study of the associated will provide some insight into such things as what we may need to protect ourselves from. Cutworms gnaw on roots and stems. Aphids can have a tremendous impact on both the quantity and quality of plants. Sap-sucking capsid bugs are a serious pest for dahlias and chrysanthemums.

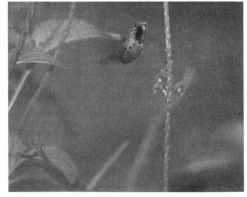

Other animals as well can reflect this message. Moles can create havoc, causing root damage. Birds can be selective in their choice of flowers. Blackbirds and sparrows will sometimes strip crocuses of buds and flowers in the spring. These animals are also part of the message for us - something we need to explore for greater understanding.

6.   What is the mathematical floral plan, if any?

Most plants and flowers grow according to some kind of mathematical plan. Primitive flowers like water lilies and magnolias produce petals and sepals in abundant profusion and confusion. But other less primitive plants have definite, basic numbers associated with them. Daffodils (below), for example, often have six petals.

Succulent plants work with the number five: five sepals, five petals, five orten stamens, five separate pistils. Some develop in conjunction with the number three, like trillium: three petals, three sepals, three stamens, etc. And interestingly enough, in general, the less primitive the plant, the less parts it has. Leaves will often form a polygon shape around a flower. Petals will also take on a particular geometric shape as well. It is always a good idea to examine the botanical numerology for greater depth into the mesagage.

7.   Where does the flower originate?

This does not apply as much to the habitat in which it is normally found but rather to the land from which it originated. Plants come here from other countries and often become a part of our own. Examining the origins of the plant can provide insight into past life influences at the time of the message. Let's say, for example, that we are having frequent encounters with coleus. This is aplant that originally came from Asia and Africa. It may indicate issues of a past life from that area are coming to the forefront. Past life exploration may provide insight. If there is a particular plant that you have always been drawn to, explore its origins to see which past life may be most impacting you in this one - for good and bad. The origins of some of the dominant folklore can also provide clues to past life connections with this messenger.

Annual versus Perennial

An annual is a flower or plant that lives one year or less. The seed germinates, grows, flowers, releases a new seed and dies all in one growing season. The seed left is called a volunteer and when it germinates the following year, it will often differ from the parent flower in color. Annuals remind us that we must renew efforts each year, according to our goals.

Some annuals do better in the fall and spring (cool seasons) - such as primroses and calendulas. Some annuals do better in late spring and summer (the warm season) – such as marigolds. Those that do better in a particular season may be telling you you're your own efforts are more likely to bloom. All annuals are sensitive to frost and so the planting of them is usually well after the last frost and their season ends with the first frost. This provides a time frame by which we can pursue activities more effectively if annuals are our messengers.

When most people think of gardens and flowers, the first thing they think about is the color. And this is one of the most important aspects of flowers and it contains much of the message for us. Annuals are utilized most frequently to add color to a garden of landscape. We spoke a little about the meaning of color earlier in the book and in the bibliography are sources for even further information, If you truly intend though to learn nature-speak, then you must become a little more fluent in the meaning of colors and their effects. Annuals often alert us to the color or lack of it somewhere in our life.

Here today…here tomorrow. That is the essence of perennial flowers. Perennials are non-woody plants that live for more than two years. Typically, they bloom year after year. And they are the mainstays of most gardens. Perennials though differ from other shrubs because they do not have a woody stem – a quality defining shrubs and trees. Because they come back year after year, part of their message has to do investments in our future.

There are three main types of perennials. One group dies down to the ground at the end of the growing season and then re-emerge at the start of the next. Hostas are examples of this type. A second group goes through the winter as tufts of foliage, waiting to bloom again when it gets warmer. Shasta daisies are an example of this type. And then there are evergreen perennials, such as day lilies. Their foliage remains relatively unchanged throughout the year. The type of perennial will guide us as to how best assert our energies in the course of each year for the greatest benefit. Do we need to have periods of activity and rest – an ebb and flow of activity? Do we need to keep our efforts constant?

Whether a flower is an annual or a perennial helps us utilize our energies and efforts in all endeavors more effectively. Annuals remind us that the rewards may be great but they are short lived. The efforts will have to be repeated from scratch each year. Perennials remind us that there is an ebb or flow at play. Our endeavors may not generate as much at once, but they will build and sustain for longer periods of time. We do not have to start anew, but each year rather builds on the previous. Our energies add to the previous years.

Natural Wonders

Where a flower or plant originates may provide some insight into past life influences affecting us when the plant is a messenger or totem for us. For example, poinsettias were first vultivated by the Aztecs and were known as "flores de noche buena".

Spirits of Flowers

Flowers have always been great sources of inspiration and energy. All aspects of flowers have been used by healers, metaphysicians and poets. Many flowers have been associated with gods and goddesses and are often endowed with mystical qualities.

Flower spirits, devas, faeries and elves are some of the most delicate and beautiful of the Green Kingdom. They are as myriad as the flowers themselves, and they serve many functions in regard to the flowers. There are spirits or faeries that help the flowers emit their fragrances. There are those who assist in making them grow. There are flower elves and gnomes who work to create the color of the flowers, and there are field faeries and elves who watch over the entire area in which they grow.

There is also for every single flower one particular faerie or spirit that embodies the essence of the flower itself. This spirit often oversees the activities of the others working with and around that particular flower. Learning to connect with this being is the key to unlocking all of the energies of the flower and opening perception to all of the others working around it.

Flowers in any form are sources of strong energy vibrations. Even dried flowers continue to be such. It is only decayed and decaying flowers, which do not. In the case of decayed and decaying flowers, the elementals work for the breakdown of the flower, to return it to its natural element. All of the energy of the elementals and the flower faeries in such cases are drawn inward to facilitate this breakdown. Thus the energy of the flowers in such states has an inverse energy effect. Instead of giving off energy, they draw it away.

Because of this, it is not beneficial to have decaying flowers indoors or in close proximity to you, as the elementals may draw on your energies to assist the breakdown of the flowers. You may feel energy drains and tiredness as a result. Flowers in the house that are decaying should be removed to an outdoor location (compost area, etc.). Wildflowers that are dying are usually no problem, as the elementals draw from the natural environment to assist the breakdown, and so you will feel little or no effects.

Modern spiritualists are very familiar with the energy aspects of flowers and flower faeries. They take care to set flowers in the séance room or any room in which spiritual activities are going to occur. The fragrance, color and activity of the flower faeries raise the energy vibrations of the individuals and the environment. It is important to note that picking a flower does not stop the activities of the flower spirits and elementals. Part of the reason a rosebud will bloom even after it is picked is because of the continued work of the flower faeries.

As the flower dies however, so will the primary spirit of the flower, along with some of the other faeries associated with that flower. Some may move on to other flowers in that environment and work to assist them to grow. The elementals though remain to assist in the breakdown of the flower and its return to its natural elements. In the case of perennials, the flower faeries withdraw and help protect the plant through its dormant stages until it is time to sprout and blossom again.

There are many who find this very sad, but we must keep in mind that those of the faerie realm have a much better view of the life and death process than humans. They see it as a creative process, filled with joy on all levels. To the flower faeries and nature spirits who have short life spans, the time they have is one that is wonderfully bright, warm and beautiful. While we may have thousands of days, they have thousands of moments in which they rejoice in their life. They also know that beauty will not cease when they die. To them every moment of their life is long and beautiful, full of joy and sweet feeling.

Flower faeries and spirits speak to us often. Most of the time, we don't pay any attention. Have you ever been for a walk and caught the soft fragrance of a flower? The faeries have greeted you. Have you ever commented on the beautiful color of a particular flower? The spirit of the flower has caught your attention. Is there a particular flower that is your favorite? Its flower faeries have something special to share with you. Every time you inhale the sweet fragrance of a flower or comment upon its color, you acknowledge the flower faeries.

Every flower faerie and elf is a wonderfully unique creation. Each has its own energy, its own appearance and often its own personality. Each flower, and thus each flower faerie, can teach us something different. Every flower and faerie will interact with us in their own unique way. Every flower's spirit has its own wisdom that they will joyfully share with us if we are open.

It is not difficult to attune to the flower spirits and faeries. Begin by learning as much about flowers as possible. How and where do they grow? Learn about their growing processes and all of their parts: roots, bulbs, stems, leaves, blossoms, etc. Every aspect of the flower means something and is tied to some faerie activity.

Buy bouquets of flowers on a regular basis. Paint and draw pictures of them. Plant them in your yard, house or garden. Have an area of your yard in which you allow wildflowers to grow freely. Make an amulet that has a picture of your favorite flower on one side and a picture of the faerie on the other. Use the meditation at the end of this chapter on a regular basis; it will increase your connection to the flower faeries immensely.

By aligning yourself with the flower faeries and elves, you align yourself with one of the most creative expressions of Mother Nature herself. You open yourself to creation, joy, growth by all flowers and epitomized by the flower faeries and elves. The descriptions of flowers in the next chapter contains information about the faeries and elves associated with them. It also includes the wisdom and energy they can easily impart to us, if we learn to work with them. Remember that each flower and its faeries are unique to them- selves, but certain groups of flowers and their faeries embody specific characteristics.

The information given is what I have uncovered from my explorations and research into the flowers themselves and my meditations with their flower faeries. If you have always been drawn to specific flowers, examine them first. The descriptions may provide insight into why you have been drawn to them. You will learn how the faeries work through them. Do not limit yourself to my descriptions. Use the meditation at the end of this chapter to open to the flower faeries yourself. That is the joy of discovery.

*"If you have two pennies
left in the world,
buy a loaf of bread
with one
and a lily
with the other."*

- Chinese Proverb

Exercise

The Spirit Garden

Benefits:

- Invites contact with the nature spirits and faerie beings
- Provides a sacred place attune to Nature
- Introduces you to different types
- Helps develop contact with the spirits of plants

Wherever there is an aspect of the natural world, there will be spirit beings from it. Imagine having your own special place to watch and connect with the faerie beings and other spirits of Nature. One of the easiest ways of extending an invitation to them is by creating a magical, faerie garden for them. A special garden, dedicated to them, is one of the best ways of learning to recognize their presence. You can sit in or near your garden and talk to them. It will also help you to tune into the spirits to discover hidden magic of the plants and flowers in the garden.

The faerie beings are Mother Nature's children. They work to make things grow. When you work to make things grow, they will be drawn to help you, especially if you ask them while you are planting the seeds and preparing the garden. Planting a seed and helping it to grow is one of the most magical things you can ever do. What we do on one level always affects us on other levels. Planting a seed is more than just trying to make a plant grow; in this case, it is also sowing the seeds of opening doors to the Faerie Realm.

1. Choose a place for the garden.

It should be in a semi-shady area and it should be placed away from the traffic of the house – a little more secluded area. Being near, but

314

not right under a tree or two will enable the tree spirits to help protect the faerie garden.

If you do not have a yard or an area of your yard to plant, you can make an indoors faerie garden. There are many types of flower boxes and small plant containers that can make wonderful little faerie plots. Smaller pots, planted with herbs and flowers that are faerie friendly, can be kept in the house and can be moved around to suit your purpose.

2. Decide what plants and flowers to use.

In the following chapters are lists of herbs and flowers that are very faerie friendly. They are inviting to them. Most garden stores have a wide variety of starter plants and flowers that are very inexpensive, and those listed are easily found.

3. Layout your garden.

Draw out the garden you would like to have. Choose the shape according to what energies you hope to awaken. The earlier chart on the energies of geometric shapes will help you with this. Mark on the paper the plants and where they will go. In the beginning keep the garden small and simple.

One of the easiest is a small circular garden that is ringed with faerie plants and crystals and the inside is all grass. I prefer a circular area. Faerie circles are small, circular areas where faerie beings like to gather. They are often nighttime meeting places where they gather to sing and dance. Such faerie circles are found naturally in the wild, but you can make your own.

With a shovel or trowel, dig up the grass or weeds in the circle. (Set them aside and start a compost heap from them that you can use in the future for mulch.) Then with a rake or hoe loosen up the topsoil and rake the area smooth.

4. Choose and plant your flowers and herbs.

Use a trowel to dig holes and plant the flowers around the perimeter (the outer edge of your circle). The holes should be about twice as big as the potted plants. Remove the flowers and plants from their pots, place them in the holes and fill in the dirt. Give the plants a good long drink of water.

5. Leave an open area in the middle.

This can be just a small grassy area for the faerie beings and nature spirits to dance. Initially, you may have to plant some grass seed. Once you have scattered the seed in the open areas, cover it with a little straw to protect it until it takes root.

6. Add special touches.

Place crystals and stones about the garden. They have a spirit too and are as much a part of the faerie world as the flowers and trees.

Build a stick fairy house or pavilion type structure for the faeries to play in. Some people use old Barbie dollhouses for this, painting and redecorating them to be more faerie-like. Another nice touch is putting a small, tinkling wind chime in or near the circle somewhere. You will be surprised how the faeries and other nature spirits will let you know of their presence through the chimes – even when there is no breeze.

7. Set up a seat or bench nearby to observe.

This should be outside of the circle, but close enough that you can easily see the whole garden. I recommend about 3 feet back from the garden at first. Once the faeries have gotten used to your presence, you can slowly move in for closer observation. The best times for observations are dawn and dusk but experiment with different times of the day.

When observing, sit quietly and relax. Do not stare intently. Just let your mind go wherever it wishes. Daydreams become quite powerful and magical around faerie gardens. Pay attention to what you feel and even to what you imagine. Perform the acupressure exercise from the earlier lesson before your faerie watching and you will surprise yourself with what you see.

8. Dedicate your faerie garden.

As you work on your garden, focus on it as an invitation to the faeries and other nature spirits. As you plant each flower and/or herb, focus on its qualities and the kind of faerie beings that it draws and how that can benefit you.

Tending to the garden regularly (pulling weeds), keeping it neat, replacing plants that die, watering the garden, etc. is one of the best ways of dedicating it to the faeries. They tend to their creative activities with great responsibility. It shows them that you are responsible and trustworthy.

After the garden is completed, sit down beside it and offer a prayer to the Nature spirits and the faerie beings. Tell them that this garden is for them and that you will watch over it for them. Ask them to help you with it. (In time you will be inspired to unique changes in the garden layout. This is often a sign that the faeries are working with you.) you can do this in your head or say it softly out loud. If you say it out loud and repeat it three times, there is usually a breeze that softly brushes over you. This is a sign that the faeries have heard your wishes.

Then sprinkle a little milk around the garden as an offering to the faeries. Have you ever heard the old saying, "Don't cry over spilled milk"? Well it was originally, "Don't cry over the spilled milk. It's some for the fairies." Spilled milk was considered a gift for the faerie folk, and leaving it for them was good luck.

Even a flower box can be a faerie garden.

Exercise

Meeting
the Flower Faeries
and Spirits

Benefits:

- Increasess awareness of the subtle voices of the spirits of Nature
- Invites more tangible contact with Nature spirits
- Helps with attuning to spirits of specific flowers and plants

This meditation can be adapted and used to attune to all flower spirits and faeries. It can be performed outside in the midst of a flower bed, or it can be performed inside while holding an individual flower upon your lap. When I perform one of my workshops on faeries and elves, I bring to the class a dozen or so different kinds of fresh cut flowers, making sure I have enough for everyone in attendance. In this way each can choose the flower he or she is drawn to-the one in which the flower faerie speaks the loudest.

1. Choose a time in which you will not be disturbed. This exercise is most effective when performed outdoors, but it is not essential. When performed indoors, use a fresh cut flower and have it in your hand or on your lap.

2. You may wish to perform a progressive relaxation. You may also wish to use some music in the background. All faeries and elves are drawn to music. In the appendix are some pieces of music that are beneficial to drawing the faeries and elves out more effectively. You may simply want to use sound effects of the outdoors.

3. Take time to examine the flower. Become familiar with it. Take note of its color, stem and shape. Touch its petals. Caress your cheek with it. How does it feel? Bring the flower up to your nose and inhale its fragrance. Note how it makes you feel.

4. Close your eyes and breathe deeply. Allow yourself to relax. Bring the flower up to your nose and inhale its fragrance again, and then allow the flower to rest on your lap.

As you focus on the fragrance, visualize yourself sitting in a beautiful garden. All around you are flowers and trees. The grass beneath you is soft and lush. The air is fresh and clean. The sunlight that penetrates the trees to touch this garden is soft and muted, casting the area in soft haze. You are relaxed and at peace. You know this place. You have seen it before. Maybe it was in your dreams or maybe in a distant lifetime - it doesn't matter. Somehow you know that this is a place where you can go to heal and refresh yourself. It is a place where all worlds meet.

In the distance, there is a high mountain and a path leading up to it. The path is lined with trees and stones of every color. On the opposite side of this garden is another path, leading from the garden to a valley below. As you look down this path, you see your present home. You understand that you are at an intersection of time and place. It is an inner sanctuary where the real and the imagined meet. It is a place of the finite and the infinite, the physical and the ethereal. It is then that you notice the flower on your lap. It seems to shine, and as you focus on it a soft, pleasing sound is heard. It is as if there was a tiny voice singing.

You bring the flower to your nose and inhale its fragrance, and it makes you lightheaded and you smile because it is so pleasant. As you gaze at the beauty of this flower, the petals begin to unfold. One by one, each petal unfolds, and as it does, the music grows more distinct.

As the flower blossoms before your eyes, you see in its heart a soft ball of light, the color of the flower itself. Pastel and shimmering, it seems to float upon the flower petals. Then it shifts, changing forms before your eyes. As it does, you are filled with wonder. It almost seems to make your own heart sing.

And then you hear your name whispered from that light, and it shimmers once more. Before you now lights a tiny beautiful faerie. Its eyes are filled with joy and love, as if it had been waiting for you for a long time.

As it shimmers and dances before you, you hear it singing within your own mind. Its voice is soft and has a musical quality to it. You are not sure how it is doing it, but you can hear its every thought. It laughs lightly at your amazement.

Then it begins to speak. It tells you of its activity. It speaks of its purpose. It tells you what it will share with you if you work with nature. It tells you of the mystery of the flower and why this one is important to you now.

You are filled with delight. And though a tiny being, its energy as it speaks in your mind sends shivers of delight throughout your body and soul. You gently hold out your hand, and it flies from the flower to your palm, showing you its trust. And then it returns to the flower again.

It begins to shimmer and dance, becoming more vague. And you hear in your mind the promise: "Next time, we will share more." Then as the petals of the flower begin to fold up, the faerie becomes a soft ball of light within its heart. Though the flower has closed up, you can still hear its sweet song.

You raise the flower to your nose, and inhale its fragrance. You brush its petals lightly against your cheek. As you do, you notice the garden scene around you fading, becoming indistinct. Breathe deeply and feel yourself relaxed. You are sitting where you started, comfortable and peaceful. You remember all that you have experienced, and you now know why you were drawn to this flower. Slowly and gently you open your eyes and gaze upon the flower in your lap. For perhaps the first time you are truly aware of the life and energy within nature that surrounds you.

At this point you might want to ground yourself by taking a walk in Nature. You may wish to give thanks to the flower faerie for sharing with you. You may even wish to record what you experienced'. One way of honoring this meeting and all meetings in the future is to plant some flowers or buy a plant that you can take care of in your home.

Blooming Silly

Flowers have had many strange beliefs. Many of these are merely superstitions. Most of them are just plain fun.

- Hold a buttercup under a person's chin and if the chin reflects the yellow, the person likes butter. Or tickle someone's chin with a dandelion. If the person laughs, he or she likes butter.

- If you close yourself up in a room with tuberoses, you will soon die. Many believe that the fragrance of tuberose is the the odor of death and tuberoses have the waxy appearance of death in the flowers.

- It is considered a sign of jealousy to wear a yellow flower.

- If you give a person a fern, you are giving that person sorrow. The person who accepts a fern as a gift will never settle down in life.

- If a woman plants flowers while menstruating, the flowers will die. If vegetables are planted during this time, they will not develop. On the other hand, ferns will grow better if they are sprinkled with the water in which you washed your clothes after menstruation.

- Plant flowers in the sign of Gemini and they will bloom more quickly and be more beautiful.

- Sunflowers growing in your yard brings good luck and good health.

- Flowers grow better if you use the water in which you washed your meat.

- Blow the seeds off of a dandelion puff. The direction the wind carries them is where you will find your fortune.

- Flowers planted in the light of the moon will have more blossoms than those flowers planted at other times.

- If spring flowers bloom again in the fall, there will be a hard or sorrow filled winter.

Exercise

Rose in a Bottle

Benefits:

- **Develops ability to make and use energy elixirs**
- **Increases attunement to flowers**
- **Teaches perception of flower energy patterns**
- **Facilitates meditation**

Flower elixirs are energy medicines. They can be made and used by anyone. They do not interfere with any other form of traditional or non-traditional medicine, and they serve very dynamic functions in the entire holistic healing process. They are particularly effective for opening to and working with the spirits and devas of the natural world. They can help restore the balance necessary to open to new levels of awareness. This includes psychic, creative, and spiritual states of awareness and their integration within our physical life circumstances.

They assist us in attuning to our environment. Because they are made from elements in Nature, we begin to recognize through their use the intricate interplay of Nature and humanity. They assist us in aligning and attuning to our more subtle energies and their impact upon our physical life. They are particularly empowering to all of the exercises within this book.

Flower elixirs assist us in developing a deva consciousness, an awareness of the archetypal patterns of energy which operate in and through Nature. It is these patterns, which enable each flower, plant, stone, and crystal to grow and form in its own unique manner, and yet do so in harmony with humanity.

In the 1930s Dr. Edward Bach of London gave up a very lucrative practice to explore and develop remedies in the plant world that would restore vitality. The flowers were picked from various plants and trees and prepared into medicines that would treat negative states of mind. He strove for simplicity, wanting to first identify the state of mind, mood, or personality, and then to pick an appropriate flower remedy for it.

His original 38 remedies were discovered by trying them on himself. He was considered an extremely sensitive man who was so sensitive that if he placed the bloom of a flower upon his tongue, within a short time he would experience the exact state of mind that it would serve to heal. This reinforced his homeopathic training and its primary axiom of "like cures like."

Unlike medicinal herbology, flower elixirs do not use the physical material of the plant. Instead the energy behind and operating through the plant is extracted in a simple alchemical procedure. The flower remedies are truly "simples," as Dr. Bach referred to them. They stimulate no physical discomfort. They use only pure and beautiful elements of Nature. The plants and techniques used in their making are accessible to anyone.

Ideally they are made from plants grown in natural conditions without chemicals. Flower and gem elixirs are absolutely benign. They can not produce an unpleasant reaction under any circumstance.

There are as many uses for flower and gem elixirs as there are flowers. Every flower has its own personality. Each flower has its own vibrational frequency, its own life energy pattern. They each have their own unique function and effect upon the individual. A study of the flowers, their colors, shapes, etc. can assist you in determining its energy pattern. It is this energy pattern which is infused into a liquid. The liquid is then used to alter, transmute, or create new vibrational patterns for you that will assist you in achieving particular functions and purposes.

For this exercise we will be making a rose elixir. Rose is the flower of love. It has an energy that is healing and will balance and align all chakras. It is especially effective to use with all activities associated with Nature. One of the most sacred plants, this flower is linked with dynamic archetypal energies of love. The energies of this elixir activate the heart chakra for healing and increases telepathy. It awakens a greater love for divination and healing. It can help open one to exploration of the mystery of time, life and death and all that is unknown.

The red rose is a symbol of the sun, of earthly passion, love and fertility, of the divine manifesting in the physical. Its spirit will assist us in all aspects of love and fertility. The white rose is a symbol of the moon and of purity of the inner divine aspects of the soul. The spirit of the white rose can help us develop spiritual purity and awaken our own divinity. The pink rose is a symbol of the blending of the male and female within to give new birth and creation to one's life. Its energy can teach us how to blend the male and female for new birth. The yellow rose can teach us how to recognize and express truth. The blue rose opens one to the energy that makes the impossible possible and the unobtainable obtainable. Using any rose elixir helps you attune to the angelic hierarchy and awaken a greater sense of love. It facilitates telepathy and divination.

Preparing and Using Healing Elixirs

Please Note:
Never use flowers considered herbally poisonous. Although flower elixirs can be taken internally, those made from the method described below should <u>not</u>. Some of the herbal properties can be transferred using the following method and could cause allergic or other reactions. This method is for creating elixirs to anoint the hands and body only - to facilitate meditation and shifts of consciousness. It should not be taken internally.

Flower elixirs are prepared by placing the flowers or crystals in a bowl of water (preferably a quartz crystal bowl) in full sunlight for several hours. This process extracts the life essence or energy matrix of the flowers to form a potentized elixir. This is known as the Mother Elixir. To this elixir is added brandy or alcohol as a preservative.

From the Mother Elixir will come stock bottles. Two drops from the Mother Elixir are added to a one-ounce dropper bottle of good water (non-chemically treated). To this add a teaspoon of brandy as a preservative. From these stock bottles will come individual dosage bottles. The dosage bottles are also one ounce in size.

Two drops of the elixir are taken from the stock bottle and placed in the dosage bottle. To this is added water and brandy. The flower essences actually become potentized in this dilution method, much in the same manner as homeopathic medicines. In traditional flower elixirs, once the dosage bottle is made up, the individual can either take the elixir straight from the bottle or add drops to a glass of drinking water. The essences we make should *not* be taken internally. We will be using them in an anointing method. A drop is placed upon the brow, and the heart. Placing a drop on the palm of the hands is also effective.

1. As for the roses, make sure you pick them in their full maturity, and do so early in the morning. The early sun is more vitalizing. Usually past noon the ultra-violet rays become more intense, and the basic prana

of the air is diminished. If you do not have the ability to pick your own roses, purchase them early in the morning and use them while they are still very fresh. Roses retain their energies for a longtime after being picked and so even purchased roses will create a wonderful elixir.

2. Appropriate water should also be on hand. Crystal spring water that is not chemically treated is most effective for flower elixirs.

3. Set crystal bowl in full sunlight. Make sure it is a day in which there are no clouds. Add approximately 10 ounces of water to the bowl. If it is a quartz crystal bowl, chime it softly. Remember that the more significance that we can add to the process, the more empowered the elixirs become. Chiming the bowl also serves to cleanse the water of any outstanding pollutants or thought contaminates.

4. Pick the rose and float them immediately upon the surface of the water. (Some people recommend that you handle the flowers with a leaf or stem, rather than your hands, and to avoid touching the water.) Do this until the surface of the water is covered, making sure each blossom is touching the water. Use at least one dozen roses. Place the bowl in the sun where the shadows will be unable to touch it for several hours.

5. Wait at least three hours or until the flowers begin to fade. Carefully remove the blossoms from the water. Use stems from the flowers or long crystal points to pick the blossoms out. I recommend the blossoms be laid around the shrubs and plants within the yard as a sign of reverence and as a blessing of the return to Nature.

6. Add brandy (approximately one-fourth to one-half of the amount of the elixir). This is your Mother Elixir. From it you will be able to make stock and dosage bottles.

7. Before use, shake the bottle of elixir. This keeps the energy active, and the periodic shaking prevents it from becoming dormant when not in use. Prior to walks in Nature or to any meditative exercise, sit quietly and anoint your head, heart and hands with the elixir. Breathe deeply, knowing that the elixir is softly and gently balancing all of your energies, bringing you more in tune with the natural world.

8. There are a number of other ways in which this can be used. They can be used in baths, and they can be used as a spritser. We can then sprits ourselves to give us a boost, or to sprits doorways and windows and other areas of the environment to cleanse, balance and protect.

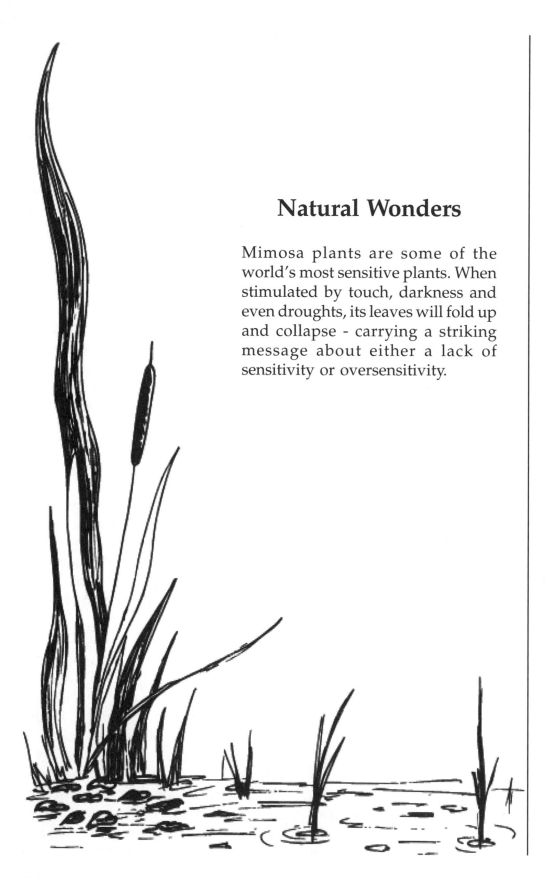

Natural Wonders

Mimosa plants are some of the world's most sensitive plants. When stimulated by touch, darkness and even droughts, its leaves will fold up and collapse - carrying a striking message about either a lack of sensitivity or oversensitivity.

Chapter Fourteen

Dictionary of Flowers

Flowers are the embodiment of color. They are gentle spirits and they reveal their essence through their colors, fragrance and other botanical aspects. The flowers I have chosen to use in this section are most commonly found and are the most accessible. There is a vast variety of flowers and each has its own lore, spirit and energies. Flowers contain many healing energies, properties and symbolic significances. Exploring those aspects of any flower will provide insight into the character of the spirit or faerie associated with the flower as well.

The meaning of the names of flowers often reflects something about its signature or essence as well. For example, pansy, which means "to weigh or consider", is a flower whose message alerts us to think things through before acting. Black-eyed Susan with its yellow petals surrounding the black disc reflects light surrounding the dark. Thus it is a flower that carries a message about hidden things being revealed. We should consider all sides.

Do not allow yourself to get hung up on the proper classification of the flower, tree or plant throughout this book. The categories that I have chosen for the various plants are simply to facilitate the average person finding information and guidance more easily. If you do not find a plant in an area where you believe it should be, check the others categories or the index to see where I might have placed it. Part of the difficulty of classifying is that genus names and listings change. For example, the Shasta daisy used to be classified strictly as part of the chrysanthemum family. Now it is often listed as a separate species, called leucanthemum. This is why I use the more common name in referring to trees, flowers and plants throughout this book.

*"It was a secret
with great power and magic.
It was a secret that would
forever help me to remember.
It would forever remind me
to believe.
It would forever teach me
that wonder is as necessary
to life as the air we breathe
and the food we eat.
It was the secret
of the Green Kingdom"*

Even if you don't know the specific genus name, initially the doctrine of signatures will help you to determine a flower's essence and meaning. And if it looks daisy-like, for example, explore the daisy characteristics described in this book. At some point though, you may wish to get a good flower field guide to help you in the identification process.

And please keep in mind that a book of this type cannot hope to cover every single tree, flower or plant. If the book does not contain a member of the Green Kingdom that you seek, use the guidelines that follow to help you determine its meaning and message to you. Remember that what I've provided are simply sketches to help you begin the process of understanding the language and signs of Nature. In developing this book and creating these symbolic sketches for you, I've used these same guidelines over the years, always combining the mystical and scientific. That is when the messages become clearest.

The following are general suggestions for understanding the meaning and messages of flowers:

1. Read and study some of the botanical and biological properties of the flowers. Start with the initial observations. Is it a wild flower or a domestic flower? Is it a perennial or an annual? What is its color? Is it fragrant? After the initial observations, make note of its most unique aspects. You may need to consult some books to discover its more unique botanical properties.

2. Read and study some of the lore of the flowers. Although many look upon folklore as superstitious fun, there is often much more. Always disguised within the lore are threads of truths. We don't have to take the folklore literally, but when we examine it, we can find truth in it. If nothing else, it reminds us that there is always much more to life than meets the eye.

3. Examine the flower and its qualities from the perspective of the Doctrine of Signatures. What do you suppose its aspects might symbolize for you about something in your life? Count the number of petals and explore it numerologically. What does the shape of the petals suggest? What about the shape of the flower? Some flowers blossom flat-faced and others have trumpet shaped. Some have a chalice appearance. Explore the symbolism of chalices as a reflection of the archetypal feminine, the womb, etc. Ruffled and fringed petals usually have a calming effect, smoothing out the ruffles within our own aura.

4. Take time to reflect upon its meaning and significance. How does the lore and its unique botanical aspects fit with what is going on in your life? At the time that this flower caught your attention, what was most on your mind for the hour or two before the encounter? For the previous 24 hours?

5. Take time to meditate and reflect upon different flowers. Sit quietly with them. Note the subtleties of its colors. Note its fragrance. Examine its leaves and stem. And as you do these things, pay attention to how each flower makes you feel. If you do so with a different flower each week, you will open to the communication and meanings of a lot of flowers in a single year.

6. Create flower planters inside your home and outside whenever possible. Visit botanical gardens. Explore meadows, parks and fields for wildflowers. Delight in the uniqueness of each variety.

Amaranthus (amaranthaceae)
Keynote: **trust in your dreams; precognitive dreams at hand**

In folklore, the amaranth is the undying flower. It blooms eternally. In truth though, amaranthus is a summer blooming plant with long tassels of rich red, tiny blooms. It is this which gives it one of its common names "love lies bleeding". It is an easily grown annual of beautiful foliage. Its leaves and stems are sometimes cooked like spinach when picked young. It also grows better where heat and sunlight is stronger.

Amaranthus translates as "unfading flower", and its color stays vibrant from mid summer through the first frost. Its color is stimulating to dream activity and alerts us to attend to our dreams – both night dreams and day dreams. It is a flower that was associated with immortality to the ancient Greeks, with associations to Artemis, the goddess of the moon. This also reinforces its connection to dreams. It is a flower that reminds us that our dreams are immortal – they may become lost, but they never die.

This is a flower which has ties to those archetypal energies that facilitate an activation of visionary dreams. It assists in controlling radical dreams and helps maintain an alignment of all the subtle energies and bodies. It assists in overcoming fears and thus our bad dreams and nightmares. Now is the time to trust in and follow your dreams.

Anemone   (anemone)
Keynote: work through fears and sorrows for rebirth; new winds coming

To the Greeks, this flower was a gift from the God of Wind Anemos. In fact, its name means "breath, daughter of the wind". It has ties to all magic associated with the element of air. In other legends, it is a flower that sprung up from the blood of Adonis when he was killed by a wild boar. Thus, it is associated with overcoming sorrow and feelings of abandonment. To the Chinese it was a flower of death and thus of re-birth as well. It is a flower that originated in the mediterranean part of the world.

Anemone comes in colors of red, purple, pink and white and it has been used for menstrual cramps and emotional distress. It is a plant that absorbs water quickly and does not like being dry for any length oftime. Water is a symbol of creativity and intuition and thus anemone reminds us to keep ourselves in creative waters for our greatest benefits.

It has strong ties to the Faerie Realm, as many in Europe believed that faeries nested within it. This flower's spirit will help us to align with sylphs (spirits of the air) to overcome feelings of being forsaken. They bring new winds into our life that result in fresh perspectives of our fears and sorrows. Are we hanging on to old fears and sorrows? Is it time for some fresh air and new winds in our life?

There are a wide variety of anemones. It is a spring wildflower with delicatre white blossoms. They are never typical - with blooms that can be starry or bowl-shaped. There are wood anemones, poppy-flowered anemones and more. And the flowering season can be spring, summer or fall. They are related to buttercups and they have soft ferny leaves that frame the blossom.

Because no one's fears or sorrows are ever the same, this is a perfect flower for working through them. Anemone reminds us to see and hear the reality of our fears, But it also alerts us to new winds that are waiting to come - once those fears and sorrows are faced.

Angelica   (angelica)
Keynote: **cause and effects become clear; look for protective spirit contact**

This "angel messenger" flower has ties to archetypal energies, which awaken clearer insight into the cause and nature of problems. One of its more common names is Archangel, and its essence helps us to align with the angelic hierarchy and provides protection against negativity. In fact, using it in an herbal bath will cleanse the aura, making it a stronger against outside influences. This flower was cultivated in Europe for its fragrance. The roots and stems also had some medicinal aspects. The stalks themselves were candied and eaten

It has mythic ties to Atlantis, where some believe it was used to assist in achieving powerful forms of meditation. It draws good energy and fortune, and it balances the aura, so that the individual can radiate more joy. Just being around it helps awaken the inner light, insight and inspiration. It is also associated with the archangel Michael and the Christian Feast of the Assumption.

Angelica has been used as an expectorant and a diaphoretic. It does have sugar content and it has been used to make vermouth and even baked goods. It is a slow growing plant, taking as much as several years to grow from a seed or seedling. This time frame is part of its message. For those to whom angelica is a messenger, there may be a several year span before endeavors come to fruition.

The plant is from the wild carrot family, and though many see it as not that beautiful, the faeries and elves belie such impressions. For anyone wishing to connect more fully with the angelic kingdom, this is a wonderful flower to learn to commune with. The faeries of angelica strengthen the aura and they bring good fortune and strong energy. They hold the knowledge of how to radiate more joy in all circumstances. Their spirit will even leave the flower and follow individuals they are attracted to for brief periods, serving as friends and temporary guardians.

Angelica stimulates intuition and it alerts us to pay attention to cause and effects. The nature and cause of problems in your life will soon become apparent. Everything has a cause and effect, and angelicais a reminder that our efforts may not create the effects we wish for several years. Now is the time to look at causes andeffects in every area of our life.

Baby's Breath   (gypsophila)
Keynote: **move gently in endeavors; time to be confident but modest**

Baby's breath is also called gypsum pink. It is a tall plant with small pink or white flowers. It is called baby's breath because of its delicate odor and bloom. Baby's breath are loose clusters of white flowers – almost cloudlike in their appearance. Its biological name has a sound that is both exotic and enticing. It is a favorite flower among arrangers. It has both perennial and annual varieties. It does have its limitations though. The flowering period is quite short, hinting at the need to take advantage of opportunities while they are present.

This wonderful flower helps us bring out greater modesty and our own unique sweet beauty. It reminds us to move gently into new endeavors. What succeeds now is using our abilities and potentials without undo attention. This is not a time to force anything.

Begonia (begonia)
Keynote: maintain balance in all things; explore enriching activities

Begonia was named after a French patron of science, Michel Begon. It is a tropical plant, often cultivated for its succulent and various colored leaves. This species of flower is quite extensive but all of the varieties have certain qualities in common. It is a relatively easy annual plant to grow with a wide variety of colors that grow in shady conditions. The leaves are fleshy and waxy and the soil does best if enriched with humus before planting. This enriching is part of the message of this flower. Now is the time to enrich our lives a bit more. Are we becoming stuck? Are we experiencing doldrums? Begonia reminds us that it is easy to shake the doldrums of life with just a little effort.

This flower is tied to the energies of balance on all levels. It reminds us to balance the internal with the external, the masculine and feminine - the usual with the unusual. It awakens strong psychic energies, but it reminds us that such abilities need enriching. We must express them in a spiritual manner. The archetypal energies behind this flower are those of integrated balance on all levels and all planes.

Black-Eyed Susan (compositae)
Keynote: change is close but must be properly initiated; hidden revealed

This name is given to any number of plants with a dark center, against usually lighter and yellow blossom petals. It is a plant of the prairies and plains and these habitats should be studied as well if the Susan is your messenger. It is ignored by livestock and it is often a sign of overgrazing, because it will take over a field, growing where other plants won't.

There are several types of Susans as this is a name also given to a member of the daisy family as well. The thunbergia though is an annual that grows rapidly and has showy flowers of golden color, surrounding the black disc. It has an arrow shaped leaf which is very symbolic as a messenger. Arrows point things out, and the black-eyed Susan tries to point out something that is hidden around us. Is there something we are ignoring? Are we suspecting secrets at play around us? Susans often confirm and alert us to this.

This flower also has an energy which will awaken insight into emotional aspects of the individual. It brings light into the dark areas of the soul. It assists us in overcoming resistance. It is dynamically catalytic in opening the intuitive faculties and in increasing the insight. It stimulates and alerts us to the need for change,change must be properly initiated. There is coming insight into the emotional aspects of our lives and those closest to us, which will spurthe desire for change. Light is about to be shed on dark areas of the soul.

Buttercup   (ranunculus)
Keynote: **develop better self-worth; words have greater power**

The buttercup gets its Latin name from a word meaning "frog" because like the frog, this flower likes wet ground. It has its origins in Persia and past life connection to this part of the world could benefit some exploration. And yet it is a plant that people in some rural areas believe causes lunacy. This probably arose because a number of species are poisonous.

As a garden flower the buttercup is unique in that it will grow in every part of the garden. This is part of its message. With proper self-worth, we can succeed in every environment. It is a perennial flower that gets its name from the buttery color of its bloom, but this is not the only color – although it is predominant. It is found in bog type areas and for those with a buttercup as a messenger, a study of bogs and marshes will be beneficial.

This flower has an energy, which can awaken a new sense of self-worth. The individual will come to know his or her special gifts and how to apply them within this incarnation. We will soon discover this for ourselves and have our worth confirmed by others. Other people will express their appreciation for our abilities. Take it to heart. Buttercup heralds a time of healing and understanding. This expressive flower reminds us to be more expressive ourselves. The power of your words, especially when applied to healing, will be increasing. It alerts us to opportunities for new life directions and for sharing your light with others.

This flower's spirit is so compassionate and so empathic towards humans that it will help you come to know your own special gifts and how to apply them in this lifetime. This flower brings tremendous healing energies and greater understanding of the human condition. Because of this, they are reminders of our self-worth and how words can affect all things. They remind us to choose words carefully for they will have greater impact now.

Carnation   (dianthus)
Keynote: love is deepening; new opportunities for love

Carnation comes in both perennial and annual varieties but most carnations are perennial. The Greeks loved them and Elizabethans referred to them as "gillyflowers". Their leaves are grasslike and often tinged with blue or gray and the stems are upright. The blooms have a distinctive fragrance. There are thousands of varieties but they are generally divided into two categories, those of the florist (grown in greenhouses and much less tender) and those of the border (hardy garden varieties with stout stems and larger flowers). Both types are symbolic. The border types grow more quickly and some varieties even have a "perpetual flowering" pattern in summer and fall.

All carnations have distinctive fringed, ruffled petals and they are very fragrant. All flowers that have a fringe and ruffled petal are soothing and protective. The ruffling often smoothes out ruffles in our own aura, helping to restore balance. The color of the flower provides clues as to where in our life this smoothing out is likely to occur. The name means "of the flesh" and its energies is smoothing to stresses of the body.

Carnation fragrance is one of the most ancient and healing in aromatherapy. It was often used to annoint the heads of the sick to hasten recovery - with a dynamic healing energy that stimulates the entire body. It helps to remove blockages within the meridians of the body. , providing protection and strength to the aura. Its fragrance is alsoa refreshing tonic, especially after physical exertion. In Elizabethan times, it was a flower whose essence and energy would help "prevent untimely death upon the scaffold". It restores a love of self and of life.

It has ties to the archetypal forces of pure and deep love.The flower faeries of the carnation will take the color of the flower itself. They radiate strong feelings of deep love for humans. Contact with carnations strengthen the aura and remind us of opportunities to express and experience deeper love. Are we not seeing opportunities for love and healing around us? Are we hesitating taking the next step in relationships. Carnations remind us that the opportunity for love to deepen are now at hand.

Chrysanthemum   (chrysanthemum)
Keynote: open the heart; healing and vitality growing

Although chrysanthemum translates as "gold flower", it has a wide variety of flowers – both colors and genus. Some are annuals and some are perennials. Most of the varieties have all been renamed and now only a few annual species remain in this grouping. Most people are not aware of this and so I am treating this category in the traditional sense – before all the renaming of species.

To the Chinese, this is the flower of autumn and it was a symbol for long life and duration. It was considered to be good luck to pick a chrysanthemum on the ninth day of the ninth month, and a tea made from its dried leaves at this time would help ensure a long life. In Chinese art, it is often depicted with the pine tree - the idea being that they both outlast all other things. Those with a good heart outlast those without. In the Chinese language the word for grasshopper is similar and thus this is an animal that should be studied by anyone for whom the chrysanthemum is a messenger. It is interesting to note also that the Chinese used the first insecticide almost 2000 years ago. Powdered chrysanthemum was used as a flea powder.

This is a flower which has the capability of stimulating the heart chakra into greater activity. It ties the archetypal energies of vitality and suppleness to the individual, and it serves to strengthen the overall life force so that it can be expressed more lovingly and more beneficially as a healing force. It is a reminder to keep our heart open. There i sopportunity to heal issues of the heart. This will then open us to alchemical processes of healing.

The flower faeries of mums easily touch the heart. They stimulate vitality, and they can help strengthen the overall life force of individual. They hold knowledge of how to express our life force more lovingly as a healing force.

Coleus   (coleus)
Keynote: new spiritual path at hand; rely on your own strength, beauty and power

The coleus is a native plant of Java, tropical Asia and Africa It is best known for its multicolored and variegated leaves., and it is often cultivated for its blue flowers. I love its leaf colors, often with a reddish hue. It is actually a member of the mint family. It is a tender perennial that does best if treated like an annual. It has small blue flower spikes. There are several prominent varieties, including a Wizard series.

The flower faeries of the coleus have a strong effect upon our feminine energies. They can awaken the innate healing energies of the individual. They can stimulate vision of a new spiritual path one that will enable you to draw upon your own beauty and power. The coleus flower faeries reveal themselves most readily to those who have ties - real or symbolic, magical or mythical - to the Arthurian legends and the beings associated with it.

This is a flower that has strong ties to the primal feminine energies of the universe. Its name literally means "sheath; scabbard" and this has great symbolism associated with it. While the sword was always a symbol of the masculine, the scabbard reflected the feminine. Ex Caliber needed its special scabbard to protect Arthur from being killed. This is a flower that awakens the innate healing energies of the individual. It alerts us to a possible spiritual awakening. A

new path - one which will allow you to draw upon your own strength, beauty and power - is about to open.

Cornflower   (centaurea)
Keynote: **clairvoyance stronger; new life and energy**

Cornflower has beautiful blue petals. It is sometimes called a blue bottle and with this flower the primary message is found in its color. Its color is the color of intuitive perception and clairvoyance. It is often found in grain fields, and fields and meadows should be studied by anyone for whom this flower is a messenger.

Cornflower is a powerful plant that embodies the energies of Mother Nature and all goddesses associated with her. It has ties to Demeter, Ceres, Artemis and Cybele, and it is a sacred flower of the Mysteries of Eleusis. It is a flower with ties to those archetypal energies, which enable us to awaken ourselves as if entering the spring of our lives. It reminds us to find a balance between things of heaven and of earth. It is grounding to psychic energies, while at the same time stimulating new visionary capabilities and clairvoyance. It stabilizes the auric field of the individual so that centeredness is maintained in spite of the environment. It has the capability of opening the individual to the creative forces of the universe as they play through the flora of Nature. It tells us that now is the time to turn daydreams into a fulfilling vision.

Cosmos   (cosmos)
Keynote: **work with both heart and mind; express your creativity**

Cosmos has graceful flowers, set against feathery, fernlike foliage. It is an annual that is often used in gardens as a border. Earlier in the book, we spoke of the significance of borders as bridges between realms, and cosmos often brings a message about bridging realms in our own life. It grows rapidly and has a variety of colors and sometimes the petals are daisy-like, making a numerological study of the petals beneficial to understanding its meaning for you more specifically.

This small flower has a very dynamic potential when aligned to by the individual. It facilitates a linking of the heart and mind. It also has a dynamic affect upon the throat chakra, stimulating into activity any creative expression which has been lying dormant. It awakens the imagination, and it brings inspiration through the dream state. It reminds us to express our creativity and to work from both the heart and mind. It also alerts us to the development of clairaudience. Are we ignoring our creative ideas? now is the time to act upon them.

Daffodil (narcissus)

Keynote: **focus on inner beauty; time for clarity of thought; find a rceative outlet for eneregies**

Most people can recognize a daffodil or narcissus. It is the perennial flower of spring. The daffodil group of the narcissus usually has the trumpet, which is as long or longer than the petals. The daffodil particularly is recognized by its single or double yellow nodding flowers. There is a tremendous range of shapes, sizes and colors in this family They are easy to grow in any reasonable soil. The corona of the narcissus and daffodil is usually called a cup or trumpet. If it is broader than long, its flower is a cup. If it is longer than broad, it is called a trumpet. Its bulbs are grown for galanthine, a substance used to fight Alzheimer's.

Daffodil can awaken inspiration and creativity. It alerts us to a need for clear self-exploration and for the balance of sexual energies - a quieting of desires and the importance of a creative outlet for them.

This has ties to both the Greek and Egyptian mythologies. Narcissus fell in love with his own reflection, and this flower can break a pattern of self-absorption. It is a flower tied to Isis in her maiden aspect and can invoke the energies associated with her into one's life and aura. Thus, the presence of daffodils may manifest as an aphrodisiac within us, which must be balanced and controlled - re-channeled into productive creativity.

In other folklore, if the first daffodil of the year is seen with its hanging head toward you, there would be twelve months of bad luck. In rural communities, daffodils were not to be brought into a house during the time that ducks and geese were hatching or they would not bring any luck that year.

The fragrance of the daffodil or narcissus was used as a stupefier. - a narcotic. It is very relaxing. it is especially effective for those who have trouble slowing down excessive brain activity at the end of the day. It relaxes the and balances the hemispheres of the brain, easing insomnia.

The presence of daffodila will help us link the subconscious and the superconscious mind (higher self). It reminds us that our true power and innate beauty manifests more strongly through surrender to the Divine. It opens deeper forms of meditation. Daffodil reminds us to maintain clarity of thought and vitality of the body. It facilitates true contact with the higher aspects of the soul. Have condifence in your own inner beauty. Daffodils are beneficial in teaching us that others will respond to us based on what we feel about ourselves. Even the faeries and spirits, which always have a wonderful glow about them, tencourage us to see ourselves in a new light.

Dahlia   (dahlia)
Keynote: express your own self-worth& dignity; avoid pettiness

The dahlia has its origin with the Aztecs and thus part of its message often has to do with past life issues associated with that period. Through the ages, people have tried different uses for the dahlia, but its most important medical application is in the treatment of diabetes. From its tuber comes a substance called Atlantic starch that was given to diabetics.

Dahlia is considered a tender perennial or a half-hardy annual, originally from Mexico. They bloom most often between the end of July through the first frosts – a time when most other flowers are past their peak. Because of this, they remind us that there is still some fresh opportunity for us, in spite of what other patterns may indicate. Dahlias will grow most anywhere, but they prefer sunshine

Dahlia is a flower whose essence will help manifest the archetypal energies of higher development in a unique manner. It awakens a true sense of self-worth and dignity (regardless of one's profession or position in life). Are we not seeing ourselves as we truly are? Are we being falsely modest? An innate sense of inner nobility begins to grow within the individual when dahlia is a messenger. It awakens a strong realization of our psychic ability, but with no sense of psychic "pettiness". It is a flower which reminds us to overcome pride and false ego, so that the true potential and nobility of our soul can manifest undistorted.

340

Daisy

Keynote: Nature spirits at hand; open to their contact for creative inspiration

"He loves me; he loves me not." Most people are familiar with this divination technique of pulling petals from a daisy to determine the love of another. A version of this was "Rich man, poor man, ploughman, thief." Whichever was plucked last was the kind of individual a woman would marry.

The daisy has an ancient history. Images of it were painted on Egyptian ceramics and the Assyrians believed that awash with daisies, could turn one's gray hair back to its original color. And in the Celtic tradition, children who died in birth became daisies to provide comfort for those who mourned. It mythology it has been associated with the goddess Freya of Teutonic lore and also the Dryads of Greek lore. It is associated with the energies of love and strength.

This flower is literally "the day's eye". It has an "eye" in the center, and it was because of this signature that physicians once used the daisy to treat eye conditions.. There are now a large number of daisies and daisy-like flowers. They are most noticeable from their round , yellow disc in the center, surrounded by petals. It is symbolic of the sun and the light shining out from it. Examining the color combinations and differences between the color of the disc and surrounding petals will provide tremendous insight into the specific message for you when daisy catches your eye.

A lot of daisies are known as biennial, meaning they live for two years. This unique cycle often reflects that this same cycle either is or has been at play in your life, in regards to some activity or endeavor. Are you coming to the end of a two year cycle and need to re-plant? Are you starting something new right now? If so, look for it to have a two year run for you.

This is a flower which alerts to the individual an energy, which increases creativity on all levels. There will occur a greater synthesis of ideas, and there will also occur a greater understanding of the archetypal forces in Nature and how they manifest with individual lives. This is a flower that is drawing to fairies and nature spirits, so those who align themselves with it can open themselves up to commune and work with them more fully. It stimulates a spiritualizing of the intellect.

Daisies are drawing to all faeries, elves and nature spirits. Where it is found, nature spirits, even those not associated specifically with the flower will also be found. It is one of the best flowers to work with to begin communion with the faerie kingdom, as its faeries have no fear of humans and are very open to contact. They stimulate great physical awareness of the presence of nature spirits. The daisy is a favorite flower of dryads (wood nymphs), and simply sitting among the flowers invites contact. Daisy faeries help awaken our creativity and inner strength.

Edelweiss   (leontopodium)
Keynote: past life connections at hand; maintain sense of nobility

This flower is the symbol of the Alps, and for many people it became known through the song from the musical "Sound of Music". It grows high on the slopes. It is often considered mistakenly a more interesting flower than beautiful. This white flower sits upon short stalks and its name means "noble white". It can reflect past life issues from a time in which you may have live in alpine areas.

This is a flower tied to the archetypal energies of spiritual purity. Asa messenger, it alerts us to manifesting situations that will enable the us to develop and express spiritual nobility within the confines of our life. Arewe not seeing ourselves and our activities for what they are? Do we need to raise our efforts to a higher standard? Edelweiss reminds us of and awakens the spiritual beauty that lies within all. It encourages a sweetness of personality and an almost otherworldly purity that is necessary for entrance into some of the higher planes of life.

This is a flower which can open the memory of the past - including past lives. It helps us synthesize all the experiences of the past and enables us to see them from a new perspective. Where we are now is a result of the past. Edelweiss alerts us to explore and understand the karmic connections at hand.

Faerie Lantern   (digitalis – foxglove)
Keynote: stay grounded; imagination sexual energies powerful now

Foxglove has gone by many names: fairy lantern, fairy cup and other associations with the Faerie Realm. It is a biennial plant, which when planted in the autumn flowers the following summer. It is always a messenger of this time scheme at play within your own life. Starting endeavors in the fall, ensures greater success the following summer.

Faerie Lantern grows best in shady areas. It gets its name from the fact that it grows in tall spikes with bell-like or lanterns flowers, above downy leaves.

The energies of the faeries around this flower are very strong. It is important when working with this flower to stay grounded, as you may find yourself becoming "faerie charmed." They have a strong effect upon the imagination, and they are wonderful to work with for anyone wishing to re-awaken or reconnect with the inner child. They awaken the feminine energies that are strong in all prepubescent children. They hold knowledge of re-awakening and re-expression of sexual energies. in a healthier, more beneficial and creative manner.

As a messenger plant, it stirs the imagination and helps to restore a childlike innocence and approach to the world. Are we ignoring our creative imagining? Do we need to act on them? Are we becoming too fanciful and not finding practical outlets for our creativity? Foxflove or faerie lantern alerts us to a re-awakening of sexual energies - our life force - and to the coming opportunities for expressing them in a new and creative ways. This is a time of active imagination. Use it in in all your endeavors at this time for your greatest success. Find a practical outlet for it.

Forget-Me-Not   (myosotis)
Keynote: explore karmic connections and past from new perspectives

Forget-me-nots are filled with folklore of lovers, trying not to be forgotten. This little blue flower has five petals and a yellow eye and its leaves are so bitter, its taste is never forgotten. Some believe this is how it got its name. In spite of its taste, it was used medicinally all the time - including for snake bite. It has small clusters of blue flowers, although some newer varieties come in other shades. It has been used throughout the ages as a symbol of constancy in love.

This flower is often used as a ground cover but it needs a very moist area.This bridging carpet reflects a lot about its meaning to us. It is a very hardy biennial and as such, it often reflects that there is a two year period of past life and karmic connections. Now is the time to look at relationships - personal and business - from new perspectives.

The flowers are actually red in bud but ultimately turn blue which is very significant from a symbolic aspect. It reflects an energy that is raised to a higher level. It is a re-expression of the plant. this has ties to its message for us. People in our life are often re-expressions of a previous life. Arethere lessons we still need to learn? Are there unresolved issues that must be dealt with in this new environment? If we don't learn from the past, we will repeat it.

When this is a messenger in relationships, it can reflect the initial passion and connection being raised from a physical to a deeper - even spiritual - level. It also reflects a connection that goes beyond just a single incarnation (red). This flower is a messenger of past life connections, and it often triggers a soul memory - especially through dreams. It is also a reminder that loved ones who are no longer alive, can come to us through our dreams.

This is a flower which can open the past, including past lives. It reminds us to synthesize all of the experiences of the past and to explore them from a new perspective. It opens us to an understanding of karmic conditions. In meditation, it increases the spiritual experiences and brings greater contact with one's spiritual guides, be they our ancestors or not.

Frangipani   (plumeria)
Keynote: have faith in yourself; aspire for more

This is actually a flowering shrub, whose flowers have been used in perfumes. The fragrance has a bit of an almond scent to it and and a study of the arometherapy qualities of almond might provide further insight. As a fragrance, it has many applications. It strengthens the aura so that others see us as more confident. It balances the throat chakra so that we speak more truly and others speak to us more truly as well, often sharing confidences and confiding secrets. It is a beneficial fragrance as an aid to meditation.

Powerful asa messenger, this plant has a strong ability to stimulate the energies of the individual, so there occurs deeper meditation experiences. It is the flower of the microcosm of the universe - in which all energies are reflected. It is a flower that has five petals, which in numerology is the number of man and the universal life forces expressed through humanity. It reminds us to have greater faith in ourself and in higher forces of the universe. It speaks of a need for greater sincerity within our life, along with a greater sense of devotion and aspiration.

Its fragrance strengthens the aura so that others see you as more confident. It stimulates the throat chakra and thus people have a tendency to confide secrets. When it appears as a messenger, it urges us to act confidently, but it also reminds us to keep confidences to avoid difficulties.

Gardenia   (gardenia)

Keynote: emotional protection; avoid strife; telepathy is strong so trust it

This flower is often cultivated for its fragrant, waxlike white flowers. It was named after theAmerican physician Alexander Garden. Contact with it activates an energy, which helps us to align with almost any plant that can be found within a garden, along with any of the nature spirits that can be found there as well. Alignment with it creates a radiation of purity of action and purpose. It is a very protective flower towards one's emotional well-being. Are we being protective of our feelings? are we allowing others to take advantage of our emotional side?

Gardenia in the environment helps prevent others from creating strife within your life. As a messenger, it alerts us to others doing so. Are oothers truly our friends or are they creating strife behind our backs? It repels negativity. The fragrance of gardenia is strengthening to the electrical aspects of the aura so that we are less sensitive to the energies of others. It is a fragrance that I have recommended to healers, counselors and psychics for years, as it helps prevent them from becoming emotionally tied to their clients. It is very stabilizing to those who work with disturbed people. It affects the auric field in a manner that helps one to remain objective. It awakens and increases telepathic abilities - especially with nature spirits. It draws vibrations of peace, love and healing to the individual and it draws good spirits during ritual work. It has a very high spiritual vibration.

Faeries of this flower hold knowledge of telepathy and the flower reminds us to trust in our own telepathic abilities. They can help us increase telepathic abilities with all of the nature spirits. They stimulate feelings of peace, and occasionally the faerie spirit of this flower will follow individuals around for brief periods to raise the spirits and provide protection. These flower faeries are very protective toward children, and it is beneficial to have them growing where children play.

Geranium   (geranium)
Keynote: new happiness and vitality; take advantage of new opportunities

Geranium is a perennial that comes in many colors. They are usually found and grown as groundcover in woodland gardens and rockeries. Some varieties suppress weeds through mounds of their leaves and flowers. They are easy to grow and the blooms are saucer-shaped. They are a summer blooming plant, making this a messenger about efforts coming to fruition having greater success in summer

Geranium means "crane's bill". In southern Africa, a variety of it is called stork's bill. The crane, the animal to which this flower is also associated by its name, is a symbol of the solar deities and the bridging of the spiritual and physical realms. This flower and its energies awaken a greater sense of happiness and stir the heart chakra into greater healing and a renewed sense of joy in life. It vitalizes the aura of the individual which strongly repercusses on all those within one's life. It helps one to pinpoint and grab life's happiness. In most geranium beds, there will be an elf who oversees the entire area.

Geraniums as messengers foretell new happiness and vitality in our life. They also can show you where you may be missing opportunities for happiness. And they alert us to take advantage of new opportunities when they arise. Are we hesitating? Now is the time to act.

Gladiola   (gladiolus)
Keynote: follow spiritual impulses now; pursue higher aspirations

Gladiolas are native to Africa and they are bulb plants, most often recognized by their sword-like leaves, In fact, the name translates as "sword lily". The size of the flowers and the stalks do vary greatly. The colors span the rainbow and the blooms often have a ruffled edge.

The gladiola is a reminder to make ourselves more receptive to divine will. Now is the time to assert your strength and follow your inner spiritual impulse. This flower activates an energy, which makes us receptive to more light within our life. We begin to reassess where we have been placing our life efforts. It raises the lower emotions to higher aspirations, encouraging us to follow our own spiritual impulses now. It is time to move from psychic energies to spiritual energies.

Goldenrod   (solidago)
Keynote: **be true to yourself and your dreams; look for the positive**

The bright yellow flowers of goldenrod are most noticeable in late summer. They are often tall and weedlike. They are reminders that a new Year of the Soul is coming. The plant bears numerous, small yellow flowers and a study of the number of blossoms will provide some insight into the number of months at play within a situation of our life - for fulfillment, resolution, etc. Goldenrod was believed to have many healing powers, and it was often powdered. It is likely that in such cases it was mistaken for goldenseal.

Goldenrod helps us discover our own "Quest for the Holy Grail" - a quest, which reveals our true essence and how best to manifest it. It strengthens the aura so that the individual can remain true to his or her essence, once uncovered. Goldenrod reminds us to be true to ourself and to our dream. Now is the time to look for the positive. Are we putting on a false personna? it will limit your awakening creativity, intuition and great healing abilities. Trust in your dream. Look for the "gold" within all people and all situations. Now is the time to be true to yourself and follow your own path.

Hibiscus   (hibiscus)
Keynote: **new youthfulness; rebirth of sexual energies**

Hibiscus is a relative of the mallow family. Although they have perennial relatives, this annual flower has a very brief life – sometimes only a day at the most. But they do appear freely and continually on bushy plants for many weeks. Thus they are a sign of rebirth and youthfulness. Take advantage of opportunities while they present themselves - even if only for a short time.

In China, the hibiscus symbolizes fame and riches and its scent is compared to the attractive power of a girl. Hibiscus always stimulates positive feelings of sexuality and warmth. It is the flower of new creation and it reminds us of our own ability to create anew. It has ties to agni yoga and the process of spiritual purification. It will assist us in integrating new sexual energies within our life circumstances. It is the flower of promising new youth, and it reminds that we can attain control of our inner power and enlightenment.

Hyacinth   (Hyacinthus)
Keynote: **overcome grief and jealousy; use gentleness as a power**

Hyacinths are one of my favorite plants. The fragrance is soft, sweet and enticing. Its fragrance relieves grief and depression and it is good for the conception meridian of the body, temporarily balancing the electrical and magnetic properties of the body. Oils made from hyacinths have also been used to ease the pain of childbirth and to treat insomnia. Hyacinths have bulbous, bell-shaped flowers. It has a long flowering period and they do best when planted in the autumn in preparation for the following year's flowering. This time frame will also be more successful for us, when hyacinth is our messenger.

With ties to the myth of Apollo and Hyacinthus, this very fragrant flower has some powerful energy associated with it. Hyacinthus was fought over by Apollo and the wind god Zephyrus who killed him when Apollo won his favors. This flower can open us to an understanding of many of the ancient rituals of burial and the esoteric mysteries within them. It is effective in overcoming feelings of grief and jealousy, and it awakens a strong sense of inner beauty. For men, it is a flower whose essence brings lessons of gentleness and expression of feminine energies in creative and productive manner. Are we not moving on from our grief and jealousy? Do we need to be more gentle in treating ourselves and others.

Attuning to the faeries of this fragrant flower is like attuning to a sweet song of youth - a song that restores belief that all is possible. These faeries hold many answers to the mysteries of death and burial, and they can help us overcome grief. They remind us to awaken greater gentleness, and they can teach how to use gentleness as a dynamic power.

Iris (iris)
Keynote: **maintain hope; sense of peace restored; new birth at hand**

This flower is sacred to all who worship and reverence the virgin goddess in any of her forms. As a flower, it is associated with creativity and self-expression. It is a flower which draws to us higher inspiration and psychic purity. Iris was the Greek goddess of the rainbow who led souls to the Elysian Fields. Alignment with the flower named for her awakens within the auric field a strong sense of peace and the hope for new birth, and thus as a messenger, it reminds us to maintain hope for a new birth and new peace will soon be at hand.

The iris, in the form of the fleur-de-lis ("flower of the Lily"), was an important symbol of the French monarchy, although it is now just considered an ornamental design. It was a symbol of france for over 600 years and for those to whom this flower is a totem, there is likely a past life connection to France. and the revolutions.

Orris root was a staple of perfumers and it was used to flavor brandies. The orris root in the United States was also used in the treatment of syphilis

The faeries of this flower manifest in all of the colors of the rainbow itself. They can open the entire Faerie Realm to your vision. They stimulate great inspiration, creative expression and psychic purity, bringing a strong sense of peace and the hope for new birth.

Irises are a large group of flowers that span the rainbow in color, and the flowering season extends from November through July, following the usual course of the Year of the Soul. It is a wonderful flower to plant for anyone wishing to align more powerfully with the rhythms of Nature as discussed earlier in this book. All irises have similar foliage and the same basic flower structure. Their swordlike leaves overlap to form a flat fan, and the blossoms have three true petals or standards and three petal-like spears or falls. Because of this, the significance of the number three should also be studied when Iris is a messenger. It is the number of new birth.

There are two main groups, rhizome and bulbs. The rhizome group spreads underground by a thickened stem. It can be a reminder to keep our efforts out of sight until preparations are fully underway. This kind develops fleshy hairs in the fall and the leaves are flat and broad. The bulb group is smaller, but they can bloom in winter, spring or summer – again alerting us to the Year of Soul being predominant and promising new birth.

Jasmine   (jasminum)
Keynote: dreams are prophetic; be discriminating in all transitions

Jasmine is the sacred flower of Persia, and it held great symbology and significance to those within the Persian Mystery Schools. The spirits associated with it are both ancient and wise. The faeries of the individual flowers are linked to ancient devas who oversaw the mystery schools of ancient Persia.

To those whom the jasmine comes as a messenger, it draws good spirits. It stimulates energy within the auric field of self-esteem. It is also a flower which stimulates our ability to manifest prophetic dreams. It also activates the God-spark within the heart chakra. It awakens greater discrimination, manifesting opportunities to develop such, along with mental clarity. It is a powerful flower fortelling major transformations.

Jasmine is a flowering shrub with a seductive aroma. Its oil has been used often in aromatherapy to help nasal and lung conditions, stimulating mental clarity. It has been known to ease insomnia, and it is best not to use it before going to bed as it does stiulate nasal drainage.

They foretell of dreams that are precognitive and even prophetic. They remind us to develop discrimination and mental clarity in all transformations at this time. If unsure what to do when transformations and changes are upon us, one can do no better than to connect with the faeries of this flower.

Lily   (lilium)
Keynote: time of new birth; purity and humility win

This is also a flower associated with the goddess Hera. Zeus drugged her and allowed his son Hercules to nurse at her breast to instill immortality upon him. When Hera awaoke, she flung hercules from her. Some of her breast milk sprayed across the sky, forming the Milky Way. Some of it also fell to the earth and the lilly sprang forth.

This is a large and diverse group of flowers. The fragrance can range from sweet to disagreeable. The colors vary, ranging the entire spectrum of flower colors – except for blue and that should be explored. Examine the significance of the color blue and apply it to your life? Are you needing blue energy in your life? Or is there too much blue energy in your life and thus the importance of the lily? Are you needing some peace and mental activity in your life?

Rarely does the lily produce abundant blooms in its first year and it must have well-drained soil or the roots will rot quickly. In fact, the most important factor for growing lilies is to have well-drained soil. This is often a reminder not to get bogged down in the old. Take what you need and let the rest run off. And remember that each year, the blooms will become more abundant.

Lily was a sacred flower to the Assyrians. To the Chinese, the day lily helps us to forget our troubles. It was known as the "Bringer of Sons" and thus it was given to a young woman on the occasion of her marriage. In rural traditions the eating of irises was a way of prolonging life and it was considered a repellent of evil when hung over the door on the fifth day of the fifth month.

The lily is the flower of birth. It has many mythical ties. Its name and essence aligns one with the Archangel Gabriel and the power of the winter solstice. It is also tied to St. Leonard, a slayer of dragons. Tradition tells us that this flower sprouted from the blood of his wounds as it touched the earth. Sometimes, it is the lily of the valley.) As a messenger, the lily always alerts us to opportunities for new birth. It reminds us that there is no need to blow our own horns. Humility is the key; let others speak of your good qualities.

This is a flower which is a favorite to fairies and nature spirits, and those who align with it are also aligning themselves with them. It awakens the energy of new birth on all levels. The stalk of this flower is the symbol of the godly mind being awakened within the individual. The hanging leaves are the humility that comes to life, and its whiteness is the purity being activated. Its fragrance opens the individual to the divine. it is a sacred flower of great power.

The activities of the faeries of this flower are most powerfully connected to during the winter, but especially at the winter solstice. This flower are links to the archangel Gabriel. These faeries will help connect you with the mysteries of new birth and the development of purity and humility.

Lily of the Valley   (convallaria)
Keynote: awakening of mother energies

Lily of the Valley is a wonderful spring flower. Its Latin name means valley and the symbolism of valleys should be studied by anyone for whom this flower is a messenger. It is often considered an additional thing for brides to carry, along with something old, something new, something borrowed and something blue. It is often included in bridal bouquets and its blossoms are worn in May Day celebrations in France.

This plant has small pendant bells on arching stems, cupped within large lance shaped leaves – like a valley cupped within the folds of the mountains. It grows best in cool shade and in moist environments. Its fragrance is sweet – opening the heart and it reminds us of a need to have our own creative environment.

An old superstition warns about planting a bed of lily of the valleys, as the person doing so will probably die in the course of the next twelve months. It was also considered unlucky to bring them into the house. It was as if you are trying to keep their sweet fragrance to yourself. One legend tells us that this flower came to us from St. leonard. He was wunded while slaying a dragon, and this flower grew wherever his blood touched the ground.

Lily of the Valley has been used to treat high blood pressure and its association with the heart is the key to its message. Lily of the valley speaks to us of keeping the heart open. It reminds us that no love its greater or more true than a mother's love.

Lotus   (nymphaea)
Keynote: spiritual, higher knowledge at hand; new vision coming

In Greek legend this was the jujube plant that produced a fruit, which induced a state of dreamy and contented forgetfulness. In truth, it is a member of the water lily family and that should be studied as well. The lotus is also known as the sea rose. And it is of important symbolism in Chinese folklore. It comes from the Buddhist idea that it grows from the mire, but it is not sullied itself. It is used in much of artwork and depending upon how it is placed, its significance and meaning changes.

For example, a picture of a lotus next to a boy with a fish was a wish for abundance.

In extensiveness of symbolism, the lotus is to the East what the rose is to the West. The number of petals is highly significant when it is used in mandala creations. The thousand-petalled lotus is a symbol of ultimate realization and revelation.

A sacred flower of the orient, it has been associated with many ancient masters, gods and goddesses. These include Isis, Osiris, Hermes, Kwan Yin, Brahma, Buddha and Horus. It is the flower of the avatar, the one striving to become the master. It stimulates high visionary states, and alignment with it opens one to healing on all levels.

As a messenger or totem, it encourages greater spiritual openness.Higher knowledge is coming and we should be open to it. It activates a higher sense of grace, harmony and synthesis in all areas of life. It aligns and balances all the chakras, and it is especially activating of the brow and crown chakra. It stimulates energy of calm and serenity within the auric field of the individual. It spiritualizes the psychic energies, and it alerts us to a newer vision unfolding for us soon.

Marigold   (calendula)
Keynote: **words have healing power; sacrifice out of love if necessary**

This flower used to be a common kitchen herb and many herbalist still make a calendula salve that is tremendously healing. It is an annual and is often popular with children learning to grow things. This annual flower grows from seeds. Within ten weeks, masses of flowers begin to appear from those seeds. They will even  continue to bloom through the heat of summer. When marigold is a messenger, within ten weeks our endeavors will begin to truly grow and continue to bloom long after.

It is a flower of love and sacrifice. One tradition tells that it sprung from the blood of the natives of Mexico after they were slain by the Spaniards. This is also the flower of fidelity and longevity. Its essence is tied to the feminine master of the true Christian Mysteries - the one known as Mary.

Marigolds remind us to trust our intution and psychic sensitivities - especially about health issues. They alert us to the coming of important dreams. Its presencecan open us to an understanding of the power and use of words in healing processes. Our words have greater power now to harm or heal with ties to the archetypal forces of consecration and the blessing of all departures.

Its spirit has the ability to open one to the mysteries and magic of thunderstorms. They have knowledge of the mysteries of love and sacrifice, especially those that will be made in the coming months. They are reminders also that sacrifices made will be for the best, although it may not appear so at the time.

Morning Glory   (ipomea & convovulus)
Keynote: **break old habits; be spontaneous**

Place a morning glory under your pillow and your sleep and dreams will be more peaceful. This is one of my favorite climbers. The flowers only last for a day, but they are borne continually throughout the summer. By late afternoon and evening they have begun to close up. The flowers are trumpet shaped. As a child, I frequently would pick the flower and suck the nectar out of it through the small end. It is also recognized by its heart-shaped leaves. Their appearance always stirs the heart to more spontaneous activities.

This is a fast growing vining cover, and older varieties are only open from dawn to dusk. It has funnel-shaped flowers, which are very symbolic. Funnels can be used to draw things in or help express things outward. Eaither way, it carries some message about how we are or are not expressing ourselves effectively. Is it time to to be more spontaneous in our expressions?

This flower comes as a messenger frequently to encourage the breaking down of old habits. Old ways of doing things will no longer work. It is time for fresh life forces and spontaneity. Morning glory heightens our overall sensitivity. It builds within the aura an energy of creative and fun spontaneity. Old ways seem boring and dull, especially in work relationships. It reminds us that we will be able to increasingly draw upon and use our inner resources with greater effortlessness in the weeks ahead - with great success.

Orchid   (orchidacaea)
Keynote: **sexual energies strong; control and balance your energies**

In China, an "orchid room" is the dwelling place of a young girl or the bedroom of a young married couple – its significance having mostly to do with its scent. Orchids are the largest family in the plant kingdom with over 20,000 species. The flowers last over a month on the plant and for several weeks when cut. When they appear as messengers, they alert us to an important 2-4 week period at hand.

Orchid is a flower with ties to the Satyrs of mythology, some of whom were teachers of the healing arts. There appearance always speaks to us in some way about sexuality. In mythology, Orchis was born of a nymph who had been seduced by a Satyr. For those into the spiritualizing of sexuality, tantra and such, this flower will be an asset.

Our sexual energy is a reflection of our creative life force. This flower is often a messenger that our sexual energies are growing. There is an activation of the kundalini. Sexual energy is our most primal essence and thus its energies are strong. They must be controlled or they will become unbalanced, affecting all areas of our health and life. This flower reminds us to develop and control the positive expression of our sexual energies.

Wherever orchids grow, you will always find nature spirits, elves, faeries and even some of the fantastic creatures and beings associated with the faerie realm. Afterall, this flower was named for a nymph who was seduced by a satyr, and thus this flower and its environment is often watched over by nymphs and/or satyrs. These spirits have a dynamic effect upon sexual energy, and they possess knowledge of the spiritual aspects of sexuality, as well as techniques of sex magic.

Pansy (viola)
Keynote: think things through before acting; consider all possibilities

Violas or Pansies are one of the largest groups of low-growing plants. The flowers are flat-faced, reflecting openness – thus the keynote of being open to all possibilities. These flowers always have five petals – the number of the perfected human. There are two upper petals, two side petals and one lower. (Be sure and study the violet as well.)

Pansies are short-lived perennials. It is possible, with the right care, to have pansies in bloom every month of the year. Again this is a reminder that we should always be open to considering other possibilities. They add tremendous color in cool-season gardens. Pansy, which means "to weigh or consider", is a flower whose message alerts us to think things through before acting, for actions now will have long-range effects.

Pansy is a flower with strong connections to various orders of devas and nature spirits. For those wishing to work with them, it is an excellent flower to work with. One source associates this flower with Lemuria and the birth of the black race upon the planet that would sow the seeds for great civilizations upon the planet in the ages to come. It is tied to those archetypal energies which help one to create and magnify thoughts into stronger more productive bands of energy. It helps in the creation of thought forms, and its energies touch the core of the mind to assist the individual to turn his or her thoughts to the divine.

Peony   (paeonia)
Keynote: healing and artistic abilities strong now

Peonies are old-fashioned favorites of many gardeners because of their spectacular late-spring blossoms. Each spring new shoots rise up from below the ground and develop into clumps of large leaves. Its name means "healing", and this embodies its protective energies. That protection lasts a long time. If left undisturbed, peonies have been known to live 100 years or more, often outlasting the homes they once graced.

In spring and summer the buds on the top of stalks open to produce blossoms of vast bowls of petals up to eight inches across. This perennial is thought of as the aristocrat of many gardens. They enjoy a sunny spot, but they do best when planted where they do not get the early morning sun. This allows them to absorb the most dew possible.

The peony does have some interesting folklore. Its roots were used to carve amulets because of its protective energy. If stormy weather arose while on a boat, a peony was burned like incense and the rough weather would calm. To the Chinese, the peony is the queen of flowers and was always associated with the summer season. They have grown peonies for 2000 years. The red peony is still the most admired and valued and it is often a symbol of young girls who are distinguished as much by their wit as by their beauty. It almost became synonymous with flower because of its popularity.

Some traditions tell us that the peony was created by the goddess of the moon to reflect her light at night. Just as the moon reflects the light of the sun, alignment with this flower helps your own inner sun reflect out into our life more distinctly. It helps to cleanse the aura of negative energies and it reminds us that the manifestation of any healing and artistic abilities will be beneficial now and that opportunities to use them are at hand.

Periwinkle   (vinca)
Keynote: moving into a new life and rhythm

Periwinkle, the "virgin's flower", is a small blue/purple flower that has been used by many people as both an herb and as a symbol of one's beliefs. It is a trrailing evergreen plant with bluish and white flowers. It is often used as a ground cover. Trailing plants often encourage us to extend our efforts and not get stuck in a rut. This is periwinkle's message as well. It speaks of opportunities to move into new rhythms.

Periwinkle was once known as the sorcerer's violet. It was often planted on the graves of children to protect their spirits. Its essence is linked to thought forms associated with Wicca and all of those known for healing and magic in many villages and towns of older times. Its essence awakens a renewed sense of coming into a new life. It is protective to the aura, and it has ties to the energies of love and immortality.

Petunia   (petunia)
Keynote: demonstrate proper behavior; be enthusiastic

There have been many changes in the petunia family over the years. Now there are a wider range of colors and sizes than ever before. Each year seems to bring new colors to this annual, making it a popular bedding plant – especially for those who make window boxes or who have little room for expansive gardens. Petunias thrive best in hot and dry conditions and they are fairly hardy. This makes it an even better plant for individuals who are just learning to grow things. In cool or wet summers their blooms are often disappointing, but this can also be a good barometer about our own endeavors in various climates of life.

Petunias are known for their long blooming period – from late spring through the fall. Single flowers are trumpet shaped and doubles look a bit like carnations. The plants are adaptable to a wide variety of climates and water conditions, and the flowers are usually quite fragrant. they also have funnel shaped flowers which are always symbolic. Examine what we use funnels for: to draw things in, to express things out, to separate, etc.. Petunias remind us to become more expressive, but to be careful of how we express. They remind us to be enthusiastic about our activities but to demonstrate proper behavior and consideration in all things, and like thepetunia we will be more successful in all environments.

Petunia reminds us to make a change in mental attitude, one more appropriate to our environs. Petunia stimulates a greater, more solid fusion between the higher self and the outer personality. It awakens within the aura energy of enthusiasm. Asa result, there will begin to manifest an integration of joy and vitality in all areas of life.

Phlox   (phlox)
Keynote: focus on developing your skills; productive and creative time

Phlox is a favorite plant of my wife, who always seems to be planting some variety throughout the spring and summer in a multitude of places. They come in wonderful colors that work well together, forming soft and beautiful carpets. These perennial plants do best in full sun. Their name means, flame, and when they spread and bloom, they alight the ground with bright flames of color. Phlox is a native of Texas and its blooms can continue through the summer. It is most often used today as a flowering ground cover. All of the species have the same flower composition. A slender tube flares out into a flat flower, circular in outline with five segments. And most have vivid coloration.

The presence of activates the universal forces for the unfoldment and development of skill and craftsmanship in some area of our life. Its message is to attend to any latent artistic abilities, and to focus upon them to become more productive in all of our endeavors.

The spirit of phlox often takes the elf form, although there are many phlox faeries. The elf spirit seems to be more of an overseer and guardian. This is not its only form, but it is one that is most commonly experienced. The phlox elf can help you awaken latent artistic energies, and it is not unusual to find them occasionally taking up residence in a house to assist us in developing skill or craftsmanship in some area. As a messenger, this flower alerts us to a more productive time at hand.

Poppy (papaver)
Keynote: new creative energies; don't hold back

Poppies have been found in Egyptian tombs and to the ancient Greeks, poppy seeds were mixed with a honeyed wine for fertility and strength. In the Greek tradition, the goddess Demeter created poppies so that she could sleep after the death of her dauther, Persephone.

The opium producing plant (oriental poppy only) is still a valuable pharmaceutical plant and is different from the common field poppy. It is still used in the making of morphine and codeine. The field poppy (corn poppy) is antecedent of the popular modern Shirley poppy, and it is a brilliant red color. Fire, creativity and energy is what this flower awakens – all of the best qualities of the color red. Now there are variations, but the red seems to speak the loudest.

This is a charming little plant that is one of the easiest to grow. Most are annuals but there are some perennial varieties. The annuals have a daintier appearance, but they all have strong bright colors, which carry the most important part of their message. Many varieties are red or orangish red, reflecting new creative energies at play. The buds seem to bow their heads on tall stalks and the petals will flutter in the breeze of open flowers. They thrive in dry weather when other flowers are wilting

Used as a flower essence, it makes you more perceptive to encounters with the Faerie Realm and facilitates visions of the subtle energies of life. Because of their bright colors, poppies are reminders of new creative energies at play within our life. This is not a time to hold back. Your creativity and imagination are your strong points.

Rose (rosa)
Keynote: healing and love at hand; look for a new birth

Walk into a rose garden on Midsummer Eve and pick a rose without saying a word. Wrap the rose in clean white paper and put it away until Christmas day. Then wear it to church. The first man or woman to speak with you or to notice it will be whom you marry.

Aphrodite presented a rose to her son Eros. It was painted on the walls of temples in Egypt and it was a favorite flower of Cleopatra. Nero was also crazy about roses and because of his devbauchery, the rose became a symbol of paganism and lust to the early Christians.

One of the most sacred plants, this flower, its name and essence is linked with dynamic archetypal energies of love. In mythology it has been associated with Cupid, Venus and Adonis. It has also come to be associated with the blood of Christ within the Christian tradition, but even more so with the feminine expression of the Christian mysteries - Mary. Alignment with its energies activates the heart chakra for healing and increases telepathy. It awakens a greater love for divination and healing. It can help open one to exploration of the mystery of time, life and death and all that is unknown. It is tied to the energies of "strength through silence".

The rose is the queen of flowers, used by perfumers. Its oil was used to wash the ceilings and walls of ancient Roman banquet halls in to remind diners not to reveal what was said or done in the course of the evening's celebration. It is one of the most healing fragrances, soothing all of the yin meridians and balances the heart. It can be used to annoint the head and heart to facilitate greater expression of love.

The red rose is a symbol of the sun, of earthly passion, love and fertility, of the divine manifesting in the physical. The white rose is a symbol of the moon and of purity of the inner divine aspects of the soul. The pink rose is a symbol of the blending of the male and female within to give new birth and creation to one's life. The blue rose opens one to the energy that makes the impossible possible and the unobtainable obtainable. All roses speak of healing, new birth and new love at hand.

One of the most sacred flowers, its faeries and spirits have strong ties to their elder brothers and sisters, the angels. Attuning to them can help you awaken a greater sense of love, as well as attunement to the angelic hierarchy. They can teach the crafts of telepathy and divination. They hold the secrets to time and its exploration. The faerie of the white rose can help us develop spiritual purity and awaken our own divinity. The faerie of the red rose can assist us in all aspects of love and fertility. The pink rose faerie can teach us how to blend the male and female for new birth. The yellow rose faerie can teach us how to recognize and express truth.

Rose of Sharon   (althaea)
Keynote: look to the higher in all things; triumph in transformations

This flower is related to the hibiscus and there is also a St. John's Wort variety. It is a plant mentioned in the Bible in the seductive Song of Solomon. And it is this which most reflects its message. There is love and transformation at hand.

This flower can stimulate a play of energy into our life that facilitates bringing the personal will into alignment with divine will. It reminds us to look to higher purposes when dealing with all obstacles right now. It awakens the soul power to be at the divine's service. This flower reminds us that we have the strength, ability and power to live a higher form of life.

Shooting Star   (dodecatheon)
Keynote: keep your feet on the ground as you open to the new

This beautiful perennial gets its name from the shape of its flowers. They sweep backwards to reveal golden anthers. Like stars in the night sky, they form in clusters on an upright stalk. It reminds us that we must kep our feet on the ground even while we look to the heavens. This is an herb of the prairies, also known as cowslip. For those to whom this comes as a messenger, a study of the significance of the prairie to your life will help greatly.

Shooting stars are meteors and there is tremendous lore about meteors andcomets all over the world. For thousands of years the Egyptians and Chinese kept track of meteors. Drawings of them were found upon cave walls. One of the most common beliefs worldwide is that wishing upon the star will help the wish come true. This plant reminds us to keep our wishes and dreams alive, but it also tells us to be practical and pragmatic when pursuing them.

This flower is tied to those archetypal energies which will help us feel more at home on earth. This is especially effective for those who have feelings of alienation - from home, family, study groups, etc. It manifests an energy that helps our energy field connect more fully with the magnetic fields of the earth. There occurs more grounding and a sense of security.

It awakens sensitivity to the stars and opens us to greater knowledge and insight into astrology, encouraging us to explore it for answers. It helps develop sensitivity for dowsing the ley lines of the earth. This is a good flower to have appear when a new group is beginning to form. It reminds us that we do not need to feel isolated. We are integral to the group process.

Snapdragon   (antirrhinum)
Keynote: **protection; assert your will**

The snap dragon is known to most everyone. As a boy I enjoyed pinching off the lipped flowers and squeezing them, to watch them open and shut – just like a dragons mouth. The corolla resembles a dragon's mouth, hence its name. This is a fairly hardy annual and there are some "snapless" varieties but they come in all colors from white to near black.

They are fantastic in form and bloom abundantly, often a reminder that the wonders of dragons and mystical energy are always abundant around us. They are native to the Mediterranean area and in milder climates they can be perennial, but they are most often treated as annuals.

Snapdragon is a flower that makes a powerful inner talisman and totem. It has ties to the energies of all dragons - those which are meant to be controlled and not slain. Ancient magicians used to invoke etheric dragons into their environments for protection, guidance and strength. The snapdragon has ties to those same energies and more. It awakens the throat chakra, stimulating the will force into greater creative expression. It can help open one to clairaudience, and it assists the individual in discovering the true power of expression and it ability to manifest. It protects the individual against all unwanted influences.

Just like its name, this plant and the environment in which it grows are often watched over by tiny etheric dragons. The spirits of this flower have connections to the energies of all dragons. They encourage us to assert our own will force and creative expression. They remind us that we are protected. They help develop clairaudience and it is not unusual when snapdragons appear as messengers to begin hearing spirits.

Spider Lily   (lhymenocallis)
Keynote: **time to weave something new; avoid entanglements of the past**

This flower is related to the amaryllis and has fragrant, tubular shaped flowers. Its petals and leaves hang, giving it the appearance of a spider. Because of this the spider should always be studied as well when spider lily is your messenger.

Spiders have had a tremendous mythology about them throughout the world. They are the master weavers, weaving illusions, magic, life spans and even languages. It is an animal which teaches how to spin something new into our life or how to avoid becoming entangled in the webs of life. And this fits well with the message of the spider lily.

Spider lilies hung in the bedroom will stimulate dreams of totems. important to your life right now. They alert us to dreams that may solve problems for us.

Legends of the spider woman permeate societies around the world. The spider woman was one who spun the web of life. One either had to learn to walk the threads or be caught within them. Such is much of the energy of this plant when aligned to by an individual. Its message is for us to to spin new patterns within our lives. Opportunities to do so are at hand. Spider lily teaches versatility and suppleness. This is a plant of alchemy and transformation and of learning to move more freely - in new realms or within the old.

Sunflower   (helianthus)
Keynote: **time of happiness and well-being; healing energy strong**

The sunflower always turns its face toward the sun. This behavior is called phototropism and it is actually controlled by hydraulic pressure in the stem in response to light. Water builds up in the cells on the shady side of the stem and the pressure forces the blossoming head in a steady arc toward the direction of light. Facing West at sunset, the flower swings around to the East at sunrise to greet and honor the life-giving light of the sun. This is one of its most significant aspects, a constant reminder to keep our eyes on the higher light in all we do. It is because of this that the major spiritualist organizations used the sunflower as its symbol.

A sunflower is not one blossom, but a cluster of small, five-pointed flowers. It is a native of the Great Plains and the significance of the plains should always be studied when sunflower comes as a messenger. The gigantic sunflower is grown for its seeds, which are edible and have been used for oils and other health products. In fact, a mature flower yields 40% of its weight in oil. Sunflowers carry the energy of the sun within them. All sunflowers are vigorous, erect and fast-growing plants.

The Incas recognized the sunflower as a symbol of the sun and the Native Americans cultivated them. Sunflowers were also planted by early settlers to ward off malaria and other illnesses. This flower was also sacred to the Aztecs, and thus can align the us with the gods and goddesses of them. Its presence helps open us to the influence of energies associated with all of the sun gods.

Sunflower comes in annual and perennial varieties and they are always reminders of the cycles of the sun within our life and of a time of well-being. Sunflower is a plant with dynamic energies, associated with the archetypal masculine forces of the universe. Its botanical name makes for a wonderful magical name to align with this flower's energies. It manifests opportunities which help us find our inner sun. It reminds us to find our own power and our own means of self-actualization. It increases a sense of happiness and well-being within the auric field. Alignment with it can draw protective lions and fire dragons into one's environment. Its appearance alerts us to coming opportunities for happiness, healing and well-being.

Sweet William (dianthus)
Keynote: **protection if we look to higher will; face fears**

This is a biennial plant, blooming the second year, unless planted indoors first in the late winter. it reminds us that our efforts may not produce the most benefits until the second year. It has broad, lancelike leaves. Its flowers are born in clusters atop a short stem. It is always good to count the flowers in the cluster and explore the number numerologically.

Sweet William is a flower who carries a message about greater obedience to divine will. The name William means "brave and protecting". When we align to the divine will, we are protected and can walk without fear. The presence of this flower releases energy within the our life that creates opportunities to reveal the gold of our soul in all of our mundane life. It alerts us to a time of higher forms of intuition and psychic sensitivity, along with creative fires. It is a reminder to face fears, for we are protected by a higher will.

Tiger Lily (lilium)
Keynote: maintain balance and strength in all you do

Tiger Lily is a flower of great strength and it reminds us to maintain balance in using our strengths. It awakens the energy of the soul to overcome the lower self and the baser emotions in the daily situations of life. It balances the auric field when aligned to by the individual. Its presence brings harmony to the male and the female aspects of our personality and soul.

This flower helps us understand the equal but distinct power that resides within both aspects of themselves, the male and the female and how both parts together make us stronger. Its message is one of greater strength and balance creates greatest success. When it appears as a messenger or totem, we should also explore all the energies associated with the tiger, as these will also be experienced when aligned to. In factm this flower can be invoking to etheric tigers.

Trillium (trillium)
Keynote: look to the big picture; small sacrifices may be necessary to achieve dreams

The trillium or wood lily is not a common plant. It requires a special environment. It will flourish only where there is woodland, giving it shade above and leaf mould below. When I worked at Brukner Nature Center in Troy, Ohio, one of the favorite trails to walk with school groups was one known as Trillium Trail. Trillium grew in abundance along this trail. It has a thick underground rhizome which  produces fleshy stems. On these stems the leaves and flowers form in threes - three leaves and three petals per flower, hence the meaning of its name "triplet".

A study of the number three is important with t his plant. Three is the creative number. The number three has great symbology. The trinity - in some form or another - has been a major symbol of most of the ancient mystery schools. It is the symbol of the male and the female coming together creatively to produce the "Holy Child" within. It is new birth and in more modern times, it has taken on Christian symbolism of the Holy Trinity. Among some pagans though, it is symbolic of the three aspects of the Divine Femine - the maiden, mother and crone.

This is a plant that is endangered in many areas, and yet it has always had ties to very dynamic archetypal energies. Native Americans made an eye wash of this plant and often used it in love potions as well.

Trillium reminds us look to the big picture.. Sometimes small sacrifices are necessary. It brings the energies of sacrifice for higher causes and goals. It is purifying to the auric field, and it activates the seat of the kundalini so that it can be given new movement and expression within our life. Its presence opens opportunity for greater service. Trillium also awakens any healing abilities latent within the soul and brings a sense of peace to one's life, regardless of the circumstances. It is a plant that links the physical and the spiritual into new forms of expression and it reminds us of our ability to do so as well.

Tuberose (polianthes)
Keynote: new love about; time to be creative

Tuberose means "swelled or raised area". It is a seductively, fragrant flower, related to the amaryllis family. It produces a spike of creamy white, lily-like flowers. Its message is almost always about new love and creativity coming into our life.

It seems that the more exotic the plant, the more superstitions arise around it though. And the tuberose has had its share - mostly centered around death. One of the more common superstitions is that if you close yourself up in a room with tuberoses, you will soon die. Many believed that the fragrance of tuberose is the the odor of death and that tuberose flowers have the waxy appearance of death.

This is the flower of new creation - of being pregnant with new life. It has strong ties to the archetypal energies of love and attraction and the new creations that come from it. As a fragrance, it was once known as the "mistress of the night" as the most virtuous were supposed to succumb to its influence. Its fragrance brings peace of mind.

In meditation, it increases sensitivity so that we can more easily see the connections between the emotions and physical states of our

366

bodies. Part of its message is often about looking to the emotional cause and effect relationships of issues in our life.

Tuberose promotes serenity and peace of mind. It is stimulating to the crown chakra and it energizes all of the bodies, physical and subtle. It increases our sensitivity and psychic capabilities. It manifests opportunities to turn our vital energies toward the light.

Tulip   (tulipa)
Keynote: keep your feet on the ground; trust in your own efforts

The word tulip means"turban" but it is a corrupted form of a Turkish word. It grew wild in Persia and was associated with love and it was a symbol of the Ottoman Empire. For those to whom the tulip is a messenger, there is probably a past life connection or issues from a past life in that area, which is surfacing.

Tulips are one of the most recognized plants and it is one of the most popular of the bulb plants. It became so popular in the Netherlands that during the seventeenth century they even became used as currency. It is a species that has both soft and brilliant colors and combinations of them. The flower is a larger bell shape of shiny petals on top of a leafless stalk. And the flowers blossom singly on that stalk, a reminder to trust in our own efforts. Each seems to stand out on its own. Color is one of the most important aspects of the tulip's message. for us.

The star tulip has ties to archetypal energies that can make us more receptive to the spiritual realms. It tells us to pay attention to dreams because our recall will be much better. It alerts us to spirit contact through the dream state. Its essence can awaken opportunities to develop abilities at clairaudience. Its presence is vitalizing to the auric field when aligned to - so much so that it can manifest direct contact with one's spiritual guides. There occurs increasing dream awareness, and clarity of the inner voice. The star tulip alerts us to the presence of spirit guides and reminding us to look to stellar influences at play in our life.

Encounters with tulips draws to us an energy of trust and success. It is clearing to the mental faculties, and it is a reminder of the need for greater discernment and discrimination. Tulips come in various colors, each with its own distinct energy, which must be explored. Many vary in the number of petals as well, which is quite significant. This flower assists us in staying grounded and reminds us to work on any "air-headed" tendencies. It stimulates greater vision in meditation, and it facilitates seeing the hidden significance of events, people and things.

Inside the cup of the tulip sits a beautiful flower faerie. This beautiful being awakens trust and helps to clear the mental faculties. These flower faeries can stimulate greater vision, and they hold knowledge of the hidden significance of events, people and things.

Violet (viola)

Keynote: keep things simple; lucky opportunities about

Some of the information on this species is comparable to that of pansy, which is of the same genus, and the dividing line between pansies and violets is not always a clear one. Violets are generally shorter and more compact. The flowers are usually single-colored, where a pansy flower may have several colors on the same bloom. Violet is also usually a perennial and I am looking for them as soon as the weather begins to warm. To me, the tiny purple flowers are one of the harbingers of spring.

Wild violets are an early spring flower that have accumulated a tremendous amount of myth and lore about it. An established patch of sweet violets will bloom in the early spring and remain colorful for as long as a month. They prefer shady and wooded areas. The sweet violet plants grow like strawberries, sending out runners that produce new plants. This is part of its message, to continue to add new growth, based on old growth – creating your own opportunities. Keep things simple and keep stretching out.

There are often two types of violets in a single year. The first blossoms in spring and are fragrant, drawing insects for pollination. The second growth occurs in late summer and early fall and they are self-pollinating. They set the stage for next year's growth. When does the violet speak to you? If in the late summer and fall, you may have to rely on yourself in your endeavors and may not see results until the following year.

Violet is an occult symbol of twilight, a magical time. When used in baths at this time of day, it awakens a general sense of well-being. As a healing oil, it has been used to also ease stomach pains by rubbing the oil on the area. Medicinally, violets have had wide use. They are rich in vitamins and used in salads. Their flowers have even been candied.

Violet is a traditional symbol of simplicity and modesty. One myth tells how it came from the nymph Io. Zeus changed her tears into sweet violets. It is the occult symbol of twilight, the power time when the sun has set and the light still remains, although diffused. It is the occult time of peace.

Many legends speak of the violet being sacred to the Fairy Queen, and gathering the first wild violet in the spring brings energy of luck and the assistance of the Faerie Realm into your life for the fulfillment of your dearest wish in the year ahead. The violet is the flower of simplicity and modesty, two of the best qualities to develop in attuning to faeries and elves. Violets can alert us to attend to dreams of Nature, as their spirits will often reveal themselves through such dream scenarios.

This flower reminds us to keep things simple for opportunities are about. It can also remind us to be discerning in relationship with groups. It awakens a psychic sensitivity - one that reveals itself strongly through dreams. This flower can open the dream state as a source of information, making them more clear and understandable.

Water Lily   (nymphaea)
Keynote: trust your psychic sensitivity and creative energies; new opportunities for money and wealth

This flower is common to ponds and lakes and watery lands, growing within them on the surface. Because of this, the meaning of lakes and ponds should be studied as well by anyone for whom the water lily is a messenger.

Plants always express the creative process of manifestation. Aquatic plants, like the water lily, often reflect primal and new birth –
a coming forth out of the waters of life. Their message is one of trusting your own creative waters in all new opportunities - especially those involving money and finances.

The lotus flower is part of this family as well. In extensiveness of symbolism, the lotus is to the East what the rose is to the West. The number of petals is highly significant when it is used in mandala creations. The thousand-petalled lotus is a symbol of ultimate realization and revelation. A sacred flower of the orient, it has been associated with many ancient masters, gods and goddesses. These include Isis, Osiris, Hermes, Kwan Yin, Brahma, Buddha and Horus. It is the flower of the avatar, the one striving to become the master. This flower was discussed earlier in this chapter and it should be referred to as well, whenever an y water lily appears as a messenger.

The water lily has ties to great psychic energies. It is associated with the water element, which is the psychic sensitivity within us. It reminds us that our own psychicabilities are more empowered at this time. It can help link us to all the energies associated with the water nymphs of myth and lore. It is powerfully - though subtly - healing. It makes our energy more magnetic - activating receptivity toward that which is most strongly focused upon. It alerts us to and opens up opportunities for wealth in various forms. It is tied to the feminine forces of the universe, bringing them into greater activity within our life.

Ylang Ylang   (carangium)
Keynote: hold to the simple truth; doubts will pass

Ylang Ylang is actually an aromatic tree of the Phillipines. Its blossoms are enticingly powerful. The fragrant, drooping flowers produce a volatile oil used in perfumeries.

This exotic flower is probably best known for its effects in aromatherapy, but as a totem or messenger plant, it encourages us to hold to the simple truth. It tells us that the doubts will soon pass. It heralds a time of greater productivity - especially in spiritual and meditative practices. It widens our perceptions, and it is strengthening to the will aspect of the individual.

It tells us that it will be easier to hold to our truths without distortion. Sometimes, when it appears as a messenger, it can often indicate that the truth is being distorted – either by us or someone around us. Examine what others are sayingto you or how they are showing themselves to you. Trust your instincts. This plant is cleansing to our aura, cleansing the fog of doubt from it. It stimulates greater clarity of thought and perception, and the intuitive senses become more specific and more easily recognized.

Zinnia   (zinnia)
Keynote: maintain childlike sense of humor; have courage

Zinnias are annuals that comes in all colors but blue. because of this the significance of blue and its absence should be explored in regards to your life. Do you already have an excess of "blue energy"? Or are you missing "blue"? Blue has ties to peace, mental and spiritual activities and healing activities. (Refer to the color blue discussed earlier in this book.)

This is a flower of large blooms and strong stems. They bloom through the heat of summer, lasting into the late summer and early fall – reflecting a time of power for it and you. They are a multipurpose plant in gardens, and they even have a Peter Pan variety that blooms early and stays in bloom til late in the season.

This wonderful flower has an essence that is beautiful in the manner in which activates the play of archetypal energies within the individual's life. It touches aspects of oursoul where the child-like humor and innocence still resides. It encourages us to re-awaken and express the energy of the inner child, the child that can see all things new, bright and beautiful. It reminds us to trust in our sense of humor, and it awakens within us the opportunity and ability to touch and heal others more effectively with that soft humor. It strengthens and instills a strong sense of encouragement and hope. It releases the energy of endurance and courage in all things. The beauty of the world is about to be re-discovered.

Natural Wonders

Insects do prey upon plants, but some plants are meat-eaters, preying on insects. These plants are often found in wetlands. They eat insects. The voodoo lily (left) is one of these, but there are others. Sundew, a wetlands plant, catches insects on leaf hairs which curl down and digests the m. The Venus Flytrap, found in bogs, snaps its clam-shell leaves around insects. Pitcher plants elicit a sweet fluid that entices insects down the throat of the leaf, from which there is no return.

Part Six

Homespun Wisdom
of
Plants and Weeds

"There are no temples or shrines among us save those of nature. Being children of nature, we are intensely poetical. We would deem it sacrilege to build a house for The One who may be met face to face in the mysterious, shadowy aisles of the primeval forest, or on the sunlit bosom of virgin prairies, upon dizzy spires and pinnacles of naked rock and in the vast jeweled vault of the night sky!

A god who is enrobed in filmy veils of cloud, there on the rim of the visible world where our Great Grandfather Sun kindles his evening camp fire; who rides upon the rigorous wind of the north, or breathes spirit upon fragrant southern airs, whose war canoe is launched upon majestic rivers and inland seas - such a God needs no lesser cathedral."

- Ohiyesa

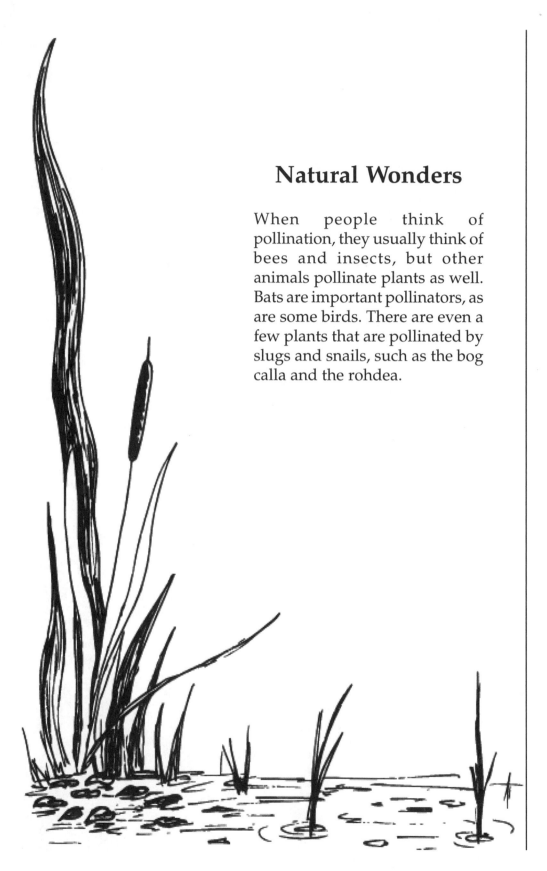

Natural Wonders

When people think of pollination, they usually think of bees and insects, but other animals pollinate plants as well. Bats are important pollinators, as are some birds. There are even a few plants that are pollinated by slugs and snails, such as the bog calla and the rohdea.

Chapter Fifteen

When is a Plant not a Weed?

My entrance into the woods in the early morning was always heralded by the soft cooing of the morning dove and the whistle of the bob white. It was a special time to be in the woods, and so it was a greeting with which I would become very familiar during my childhood. On two of those occasions, the experience would be even more special than at other times. And they would set the stage for my relationship with Nature.

Behind our house was a creek that separated the woods from our backyard. The woods were dotted with pockets of clearings that were fun to seek out. I looked at each one as a secret world filled with hidden treasures to be sought out and uncovered. Beyond one small clearing was the pond. At night, the pond was alive with the voices of frogs, but in the early morning they were comparatively quiet. If you walked the edge of the pond, the stillness of the water was always broken by the splashing of frogs scattering into the water out of the path of footsteps. Dragonflies danced about like flying rainbows.

On the far side of the pond was a fallen sassafras tree with most of its roots still in the ground. Until the pond was filled by bulldozers and the surrounding woods cut to build new houses, it was a favorite place for solitude. I would sit at the base of the tree, watching the dragonflies race and soar about. Occasionally I would snap a small branch from the sassafras tree and inhale its wonderful fragrance. To this day, the smell of sassafras transports me back to that time and place.

In the spring, just a year or two after my family moved to this area, I arose early on a Saturday morning. As I stepped out the front door, I heard the morning dove and the bob white greet me. Even though

Magic and Medicine of Plants

Green medicine is ancient, going back more than 5000 years and in every society and tradition upon the planet.

China (3000 BC)	-	had over 365 herbal remedies, including the use of ginseng
Sumeria (2500 BC)	-	Tablets of Hammurabi listed 250 medicinal plants
Egypt (1500 BC)	-	Ebers papyrus listed nearly 900 recipes and prescriptions
India (1500 BC)	-	sacred Vedas contained more than 8000 herbal remedies & Ayurvedic system of healing
Rome (23 CE)	-	Pliny the Elder wrote 8 books which dealt with medical botany
Europe (900-950CE)	-	Saxon Leech Book of Bold was the first English herbal written

I knew that I could not be seen from the woods, the child within me - with that instinctual wisdom that resides in every child - knew that both the dove and the bob white were well aware that I had stepped out of my house.

The air was sweet on mornings like this, and being a child of asthma, it was much the sweeter, and I would take a moment or two and inhale deeply the freshness, feeling the air alive within my lungs. The moon was faint but still visible in the morning sky, and the dew glistened heavily upon the grass.

I jumped off the front porch and angled across the side yard toward the woods. As I reached the creek, I glanced back across the yard. I grinned, seeing my footprints clearly in the wet grass. Already I could feel the dew soaking through my shoes and socks. It made me feel that much more alive. I imagined that it was a special elixir that the grasses had given just to me. Sometimes that elixir could make me fly. Other times it would enable me to become a deer or a wolf. It could help me do or become whatever my heart fancied at the time. And what better place was there to act it out than in the woods.

I leaped, tip toe style, across the creek to keep from getting my feet any wetter, using stones left over in the creek from a dam my brothers and I had built some time ago. I avoided the heavier, taller weeds on the opposite side, following the creek bed for a little ways. I then cut across the weeds to a path toward the pond that I felt would be less likely to soak my shoes further. Not that it would do any good. Already I could hear them squishing. I made it a magical sound - the song that the dew would sing to tell me its magic was being awakened for me.

The earth beneath my feet was damp and springy, making me feel as if I were light enough to bounce to the pond. As I approached the pond, I knelt down at its edge, peering for frogs hiding near by. Occasionally on days like this, I would try to catch one. I never succeeded. I'm not sure I ever truly wanted to. Even though I had held them before, they felt funny to me, and I always felt that my brothers and friends suspected my uncomfortableness. I wasn't about to let them know for sure. That would have been fuel for teasing. It didn't matter that I was only seven or eight years old. That would be no excuse. I half-heartedly convinced myself that if I could catch one, it would prove I was just as brave as they were, and then I wouldn't have to worry about being teased.

On this day I didn't even feign catching them. I just looked at them. To my surprise the frogs seemed to be looking back at me. There big round eyes held me fixed, and in that moment it no longer mattered if I ever caught one again or not. I straightened up, puzzled by that feeling, but just like a kid, brushed it aside, accepting it. I walked around the edge of the pond toward the sassafras tree and perched myself upon its bent trunk, wedging myself between several of the larger branches, my feet dangling, toes barely brushing the top of the overgrown grasses beneath it.

I leaned back against the trunk of a smaller tree that had grown, butted up against my sassafras perch. It suited my small frame. The morning dove and bob white were no longer audible. Even the dragonflies were quiet in their flight. My eyes were half closed, and I enjoyed the morning quiet. My breathing and the rustling of my jeans whenever I moved were the only sounds.

A breeze brushed softly across me, and I heard a faint tinkling sound, like tiny bells being shaken. I sat up, tilting my head slightly and listening a little more intently. No sooner had I sat up when the sound faded. I shifted a little, telling myself it was the wind playing tricks on me. I leaned back once more, and it was then I heard the rustling of weeds on the opposite side of the pond. At first I though it was just someone else who had gotten up early to enjoy the morning by the pond. I peered across the pond, trying to see through the tall weeds and trees. My heart jumped. I caught a glimpse of a pair of hoofed legs.

I held my breath, trying not to move at all. Although deer frequented the area, it was unusual to ever see them up close. You had to catch them by surprise. I tried to contain my excitement, thinking that

I was about to become very lucky. I watched the shadowed form moving, silently through the weeds. Finally I would get to see one close up!

I didn't blink. I didn't breathe for what seemed an eternity. All I could see was a faint form through the tall weeds. It froze, holding perfectly still, just beyond my sight in the tall weeds. I could make out what I assumed was its own head tilting slightly as if listening before stepping into the open at the pond's edge. I held my breath, sure that the beating of my heart would give my presence away and send it back into the woods without an actual appearance.

The weeds rustled softly, and I could hear the faint tinkling of bells again. Then it stepped out to the pond's edge. I gasped. My eyes widened. It was not a deer that stepped from the tall weeds. It was a magnificent unicorn!

It's head turned toward me at the sound of the my gasp, and its sparkling, blue eyes held me fixed. I didn't move. I didn't blink. I didn't breathe. I just stared, wide-eyed. In that moment, a soft breeze brushed across me, carrying the fragrance of apple blossoms and sassafras. I could hear the tinkling of the bells. This time it was distinct. A soft tiny chiming brushed over me as if the breeze itself carried within it invisible bells.

It stood, frozen at the edge of the pond directly across from me. The eyes were so expressive, and I was sure I saw recognition in them. Some distant part of me knew I was not to speak or move.

The horn stood strong in the center of the head and with what seemed a spiral marking. It shimmered with a silver tint in the early morning light. The unicorn's coat seemed to shift in color and brilliance, depending upon how it caught the light. Sometimes, white and sometimes silver. A soft haze surrounded it.

Keeping its eyes fixed upon me, it bent its front legs, and lowered its head to drink. As it did, the horn touched the surface of the pond. As it did, I heard the soft tinkling of the bells again, and I heard the haunting, sweet song of a young girl singing in the distance. The surface of the water bubbled, like it was being brought to a boil, and ripples spread outward from it. The fragrance of the trees and weeds nearby grew stronger and clearer. The smell of sassafras swirled around me, as if being freed from the tree itself. Hundreds of dragon flies began to circle, their iridescent wings reflecting a multitude of colors dancing in the air.

As the unicorn raised its horn tip from the water, stillness fell over the pond once more. Its eyes continued to hold mine. It tilted its head slightly, and although now when I think about it that just seems too Disney-like, I am sure that it smiled. Before I could blink or respond in any way, it turned and vanished once more through the weeds and into the woods beyond. I do not know how long it was before I moved, but it was not until a dragonfly lighted upon my arm.

I stood and moved slowly around the edge of the pond to where I had seen the unicorn. All that remained of its presence was half of a hoof print, and several weeds that were bent but unbroken. I watched as they rose to their former straight position. I cocked my head every which way, listening. There was no sound. There was no sign.

I knew no one would believe me. But that did not matter because I would not tell a soul. There was something in the unicorn's eyes that told me this was secret. This was special. This was not the time to tell. The telling would come later. A part of me knew this, accepting without understanding. For the time being, I would hold the encounter close and treasured in my own heart.

Looking back now, I know that this was when I experienced how tangible the sacred could feel and be. At the time, there was nothing to which I could relate the experience - no dream and no church experience. Nothing. It was new. It was strange. It was all encompassing. It filled me with such an intensity of wonder and awe - so strong and so powerful - that even today when I think upon it, my heart jumps and I hear my blood roaring into new life through my body.

And yet at the same time, there comes with it such a tremendous sense of calmness. Something was being awakened in me. Or born. From that day on I knew the reality of miracles. Beyond myth. Beyond fantasy. Beyond promise. From that day forward, a part of me would always know that dreams are never lost - only forgotten. And that to be remembered, all one had to do was spend some time in Nature. And although I did not know it at the time, my own sacred adventures in Nature were only just beginning.

Magic of Mortar and Pestle

Every good herbalist, naturalist and magician should have a mortar and pestle. In herbal preparations, it is used to grind and mix various herbs. The mortar is the cup and the pestle is the grinder. There is great symbolism in them. The mortar is the female, the womb and the pestle is the male part. Together, as whenever male and female come together, there is birth. The juices created by it are sometimes called "green blood". It is very powerful in herb magic. The act of using them is an act of creation and healing. It also develops focus and concentration.

A Weed by Any other Name

How does one define a weed? It varies from individual to individual. A weed to many people is any plant that is unwanted in a particular environment. The Random House dictionary defines a weed as "a valueless plant growing wild…any useless, troublesome or noxious plant that grows profusely." The problem with such definitions though is "who decides the value of that plant?" Or an animal? Or of any aspect of Nature? There is so much about the natural world that humans still do not understand. It seems logical that we should reserve judgment, but humans are often anything but logical.

We return to where we began this book – with a need to look at Nature in a new way. At the very least, plants and animals are messengers, guides, brothers and sisters. They are living gifts of the Earth. And even if we do not understand their "value", it does not diminish their role as gifts and messengers.

Plants - even those we consider weeds - do so much for us. They sustain the living world. Plants produce oxygen. They stimulate the senses, heal, and inspire. Plants are alchemists - providing lessons of growth, synchronicity, and relationship. They are forecasters of change in the weather and changes in the environment and they have unique rhythms, powers and cycles. Plants are very self-sufficient. They produce oxygen and food. Without plants, animals could not exist. They are the fabric of our landscapes. They travel and they colonize. They are the life-givers and life-support of the planet. They are living, sacred treasures.

Plants are the only living things that make their own food. They take in light, CO2 and water, converting them into energy - photosynthesis. It is a complicated process and scientists still do not understand it. Green plants are living things that contain chlorophyll – a green pigment. It is a grouping that contains trees, shrubs, herbs, grasses, moss, flowers, and yes, weeds.

Plants – including what we consider weeds - still provide most of the staples of life that we need and use. More than 10,000 plants have been used by humans as food, drink and flavorings. Plants provide pest control, clothing and housing for us. They are even essential to liquors and beer. They are the source of fuel alcohol, and most importantly, they provide the oxygen that we breathe every minute of every day.

Plants are sources of medicine and drugs. One fourth of all prescription drugs include plant extracts. And although science has the ability to duplicate synthesized versions of the plant chemicals, complex molecules of many plants that are beneficial to us cannot be created artificially.

To Native Americans plants were the primary method of fighting illness and injury. To neutralize snake venom, snakeroots (Chicory family) were used. Their milky liquid could be taken as a drink and their leaves used as a poultice. Wild cherry tree bark was used as a cough syrup and the bark of willow trees treated aches and pains. (It is interesting to note that salicylic acid is a commonly found within willow bark and is the basis of modern aspirin.) They also combined extracts from a type of cedar flower and false wild indigo as a disease preventative.

Each day, we are learning more of what indigenous people have known for ages. Extracts from bamboo inhibits bacterial growth. Bee venom can treat arthritis. Foxglove, a source of digitalis, is used to treat cardiac conditions. Oil from cashews fights tooth decay and bacterial infections. It is an amazing time to be living, as we are learning more about plants and their benefits than ever before – especially those often considered weeds or pests at times.

And yet, plants are still taken for granted in the modern world. To many, they are little more than part of the view, but they are unique among all life forms. They alone contain chlorophyll, which allows them to derive energy directly from light (photosynthesis). They are living symbols of the Earth's life force. Every plant is a complex chemical factory. Every flower appeals to a pollinating insect, and there is often a symbiotic relationship between the insects and the host flowers – even if we don't understand it and can't assess a value. And there is life, spirit and wonder in every aspect.

Nature's Myths

• Holding a spade on the shoulder while in the house may presage death or calamity.

• Where rosemary grows the woman rules the house. (Sometimes it is parsley: "When the missess is master the parsley grows faster.")

• Hydrangea planted too close to the house will prevent daughters from marrying.

• Never pick up a flower someone else has dropped. It brings bad luck.

• A flower blossoming out of season blossoms heralds bad luck and even a death. Don't bring blossoms that are out of season into the house (They have been touched by the devil who wants his influence brought into your home.) Apples flowering out of season is a sign of death (especially if there are blossoms and fruit on the tree together).

• Sleeping in or near a bean field will bring nightmares and make you go crazy.

• Place a bean into a pea pod. The first to get it will be the first married.

• Mistletoe cut at the full moon and twisted into a ring will cure headaches.

• Passing under arched brambles (both ends in the ground) three times invites good health and cures of illnesses, such as whooping cough and rheumatism. It is known as the "Circle of Cures".

Exercise

The Unicorn
and the
Wood Nymph

Benefits:

- **Strengthen intuition and communication with Nature**
- **Opens you to the spirits of nature**
- **Ttransformation of feelings about nature**

This exercise is based upon the old tale by the same name. I have changed aspects of the tale to make it more beneficial. It is a good idea to perform this exercise at least two days in a row in the woods. On one day visualize yourself in the role of the individual who falls in love with the beautiful woodland being, and on the following day as the woodland being.

I have tried to make the exercise as non-sexist as possible. The wood nymph in the original story is now a woodland being, so that you can visualize it as male or female - however you desire. When you switch the role, and you see yourself as the woodland being, the mortal (the person of the outer world) can be male or female as you desire.

Performing this exercise in each of the roles will elicit different effects. As the mortal who falls in love with the woodland being, you will find in the weeks that follow how other people perceive you and the changes you are going through. You will find that opportunities to break out of outworn patterns will surface within your life. The choice is always yours, but the opportunities will surface. If you are not ready for them, you may wish to avoid this exercise.

When you perform this exercise as the woodland creature, you will begin to see how your life is affecting the world around you. Choices will also arise as to whether it is time to commit to that which is new or to stay with old habits and patterns.

This exercise will stimulate the sexual energies in you. That is one of the gifts of Nature – stimulating your own creative energies. You will probably find that others will become more strongly attracted to you, and you will find yourself responding with stronger sexual energies to others as well. In the week or two that follows you will find yourself encountering others who are of more like mind to you. New horizons will open.

This exercise also stimulates heightened perception and empathy especially in regards to the Green Kingdom. You will feel what plants, flowers and trees are feeling. You will be more aware of how they perceive and feel you. This exercise can also stimulate greater passion for and empathic communication with all of Nature, including animals. Remember that nature spirits and woodland beings can help open our senses more fully to the wonders of Nature.

This exercise involves working with one of the archetypal images of Nature – the unicorn. This is one of the four sacred beasts and a guardian of the natural world. Some study of this creature will benefit, and sources are listed in the bibliography that will help.

As in the other exercises, make your preparations. If possible, at some point, perform this exercise in the woods. Make yourself comfortable, breathe deeply and relax. Allow our opening scenario to unfold. Allow yourself to see and feel the wonders of love about to open for you:

The Unicorn and the Wood Nymph

A scene begins to unfold for you. You find yourself standing within that beautiful meadow that has now become so familiar to you. The sunlight sparkles off the water, and the sound of the waterfall is soothing.

Today you decide to enjoy the green woods at the edge of the meadow. There is a sense of quiet anticipation, as if the woods themselves are waiting for you. You cross the edge of the meadow and step into the woods, and a soft quiet settles around you.

You spot what looks to be a deer path through the thick underbrush, and you follow it. As you walk along, you feel yourself coming more alive. Your can smell the wood and greenery about you. The ground is cushioning, and then you hear something in the distance. You pause, tilting your head, listening more closely.

At first, there is nothing, but then...yes...a soft voice, faint and indistinct, but there is no doubt it is a voice. You step further into the woods, pausing every few feet to listen. You realize someone is singing, and it draws you further in into the woods. The song rises and falls in a haunting, enticing manner.

Soon you are standing behind a large tree at the edge of the clearing. In the center of this clearing, a small bubbling spring rises out of the heart of the earth itself. In the trees and at the edges of this clearing are a myriad of forest animals, drawn to this spot by the haunting song, just as you were.

In the center of the clearing, you see a figure dancing around that spring, singing that haunting song. This figure has wreathes of wild flowers and greenery upon the wrists and in the hair. The sunlight shimmers off this figure, casting a soft glow.

The figure turns to some of the animals, and walks toward them. You are surprised when they do not scatter. Then each is softly and lovingly touched by this figure. As the figure turns from the animals to face in your direction, your heart jumps and you catch your breath. Never have you seen anyone so beautiful! And in that moment, you realize that this is a being of the woods.

There is such a youthful vitality to this being, and yet the eyes tell you that this being is much older than the appearance would indicate. It is a primitive wildness that you can feel, although it is masked. And you feel twinges of sexual arousal. A part of you would love nothing better than to spend the rest of your life just watching this being dance and listening to that song.

Then you realize that this being has seen you. The eyes only hold yours for a moment, and goose bumps rise all over your body. Then the figure turns and darts into the shadows of the woods on the other side of the clearing, disappearing from your sight. Your heart sinks, and you step from behind the tree into the clearing.

Sadness comes over you. In just those brief minutes, that being had filled your heart. It was like meeting one of your favorite dreams. You look down at the small pool of water. There in the grass beside it is a small flute. You pick it up, and you realize that it must be the flute of that magnificent being.

You bring it up to your lips and tentatively blow on it, making a soft sound. A breeze brushes over you and there is a soft tinkling of invisible bells within it. You smile. Sitting softly in the grass, you begin to play the flute. You are surprised that you are able to do so, and you immediately decide that the flute must be enchanted.

With each note, you feel yourself growing more tired, and in just a few minutes, you are drifting off into a soft sleep. The sleep is filled with images of Nature – wild and tame. You see flashes of animals, trees you climbed, flowers that peeked out at you from among brambles. Then you begin to see those things you loved as a child and that gave you great joy. You see trees that you loved and you smell the fragrance of favorite flowers. And you realize that these were plants that spoke to you. You remember when you believed in faeries and spirits in all things – even in trees and flowers.

Then you see yourself getting older and forgetting your dreams. You see the times you have walked in Nature and did not notice the greetings. You see yourself acting more grown up, and you the things that you knew were true as a child fading. Then you see lights dancing around flowers. You see faces appearing in the bark of trees. You feel the presence of beings that live within Nature and you feel yourself beginning to believe once more. Your heart soars and you remember forgotten dreams.

Then you see others in your life looking at you funny - as if you've gone a little crazy. You hear voices telling you to grow up, that this is no way for an adult to behave. They tell you to look at what you will be giving up. They tell you this is no time to be chasing rainbows. But there is something strange in their voices. You realize that it is fear and sadness you are hearing beneath their words, and you know that there can be no other choice for you.

It is only then that you wake up, lying in the grass next to that small pool of water in the clearing. You raise your head, and the air smells sweeter and fresher than it has ever been. You seem to be able to distinguish a myriad of smells. The individual flowers, animals nearby, traces of everything within the woods is in the air about you and you recognize them all! You are amazed.

The sounds of the woods are sharper. You hear a mouse moving in the grass 100 yards away. You can even hear the sound of your waterfall beyond the woods. And the colors about you are so much brighter. It's as if the dream has awakened your senses for the first time. Never have you felt so alive, so sensual, so vibrant. You see faces appearing behind trees, gazing in wonder at you. And you realize that the woods are alive with life and energy not always visible.

You lower your head to drink from the pool, and your eyes widen. Your heart jumps. You close your eyes, shaking your head. Surely this can't be! It must be the light. You open your eyes and stare at your reflection in the pool. What looks back at you is the face of a magnificent unicorn.

You twist your head to look at your body, and you see the white fur and the four legs. You look to your reflection, and the horn – the alicorn - in the middle of your head shimmers, casting a soft glow of light about you.

You leap to your feet, and find yourself halfway across the clearing in that single leap. It is almost as if you were flying. You are so light, so airy. Never have you felt so free. You begin to do leaps back and forth across the meadow, and you begin to laugh. The sound of that laughter becomes the sound of soft bells within the breeze.

You walk over to the stream, and leaning over it you gaze at your reflection. This time you see your own face inside that of the unicorn. Then the sound of the flute is heard, and as you turn to look in its direction, you see that magnificent being, that step from the woods into the clearing.

Your heart jumps, and you are filled with great love. As you gaze upon this being, you can see and feel everything this being sees and feels. You realize that your love has returned, and ever so softly, this beautiful woodland being caresses your face with a touch that sends shiver through your body. You lower your head to give this being access to your horn. With a touch as gentle as a breeze and as loving as a mother with her newborn child, the alicorn is stroked from its tip to its base. You shiver and then rear up, filled with joy, your blood hot and pulsing with new life.

Then this beautiful being steps back from you and bringing the flute up, plays a haunting series of tones. It is repeated three times, and then the flute is laid upon the ground. The air around this being begins to shimmer, and you watch as the figure begins to shift and change. Your eyes widen with joy and surprise as this magnificent being becomes an even more magnificent unicorn before your eyes.

Slowly this unicorn steps toward you and caresses your horn with its own. Again, you rear. You are filled with a sense of promise. All truly is possible! The other unicorn seems to smile and you both swing around and gallop silently into the shadows of the deep forest to share the wonders of the world together. You leave whispers of bells and the fragrance of apple blossom behind as a promise of hope to others who may follow.

 # Philosophical Conundrums of Plants

Do rubber plants need to be patched regularly?

Why do dandelions renounce sex and choose to live as outcasts?

Before talking to our plants, should we give them names so that they know to whom we are talking?

Was Moses the first person to talk to plants?

Are Wandering Jews reformed or orthodox?

If your cat sleeps in the plants, do you have to worry about your plants getting fleas or your cat getting ladybugs?

Why do so many of the names of plants sound like Latin vulgarities and cursing (fagus sylvatica)?

When plants lose their leaves, are they as embarrassed as when men lose their hair?

Exercise

The Unicorn Boy

Benefits:

- **Strengthening relationship with Nature**
- **Affirms your role as a guardian of Nature**
- **Brings others into your quest**
- **Reveals deception and dishonesty around you**

This is an exercise that can strengthen our connection Nature and help us in recognizing the presence of Nature's spirits. It is a magickal storytelling. The tale is adapted from an Indian epic called *THE MAHABHARATA* (circa 200 BC). It means great story in Sanskrit.

I have used variations of this tale in several kinds of exercises. I have used it in my own magical dance work and I have used it when teaching shapeshifting, especially when working to align more fully with the fluid energies of the Faerie Realm. I have also employed it in the manner that follows. All of which elicit their own unique results.

When used in the manner described below, several things will occur as a result. It will help you to recognize the signs of Nature and the presence of Nature spirits. In the week that follows, you will uncover much about your relationships with others and with Nature. You will find information unfolding, revealing whom you can trust and whom you cannot. You will unfold clues that reveal deception in friendships and more personal relationships. You may even uncover clues as to where you have jumped to the wrong conclusions.

Opportunities will arise to strengthen old relationships and/or to develop new ones with the natural world. Opportunities to heal the riffs of the past will often surface as well. It is not un usual to find that

390

you also manifest opportunities that test your own trustworthiness. Confidences may be shared more freely with you.

Again the unicorn imagery is used in this exercise, as it is a powerful archetype for attuning to the messages and communications of Nature. Remember that the unicorn is a creature of tremendous trust and innocence. Nature demands both from those who will become true guardians and who seek initiation into her mysteries. It will provide opportunities to heal aspects of the Natural world or your own relationship with it. To heal something of such magnitude requires compassion beyond emotions.

Follow the scenario. Although it is written as a male protagonist, it is easy to switch the roles of the male and female to suit you. This is a powerful but subtle exercise, and you will be surprised at the effects that unfold for you. Remember to read the story through several times to familiarize yourself with it.

The Unicorn Boy

You are sitting next to the pool in the open meadow. The sound of the waterfall is soft and soothing. A soft breeze brushes across you, and you hear the soft sound of tinkling bells within it. The sunlight sparkles off the surface of the pool, and as you gaze upon it, you see the image of a unicorn rising within the waters. The unicorn appears to be looking out from this pool. As you gaze upon it and into its eyes, the meadow begins to fade from around you.

You see yourself now standing at the edge of a river. On the opposite side of this river is a hut and an old man is working around it. Though you are standing in the open, he doesn't see you at all. It's as if you do not exist to him. But he exists for you, and as you watch him, you feel the strength of his life. With each passing moment, you seem to know more and more about him.

You know that this man is Kasyapa and that he lives alone. You know that he is a Hindu holy man. You even know that by his own choice, he left the civilized world to live alone in the wilderness of the ancient forests.

Then to your amazement, you see a beautiful unicorn doe step from around the back of the hut. A soft golden glow surrounds the unicorn doe, and you watch as the old man speaks softly and lovingly to it. The doe nuzzles his hand affectionately, and the golden glow about it grows stronger. It raises its head and looks across the river in your direction. You are not sure at first if it sees you or not, but the golden light around it grows stronger still. Then the appearance of the doe begins to change.

For a moment, in place of the doe, stands a beautiful maiden, her hands softly folded over her swollen stomach. You realize she is with child. Her eyes fix upon you for a moment and she smiles at you. Your heart jumps. You feel such strong love coming from her. The blood rushes to your head, and you feel yourself blacking out.

As your eyes open, you are bewildered and confused. The bright light of the sun is gone. In the air is the smell of a cooking fire. As you look up, you see the gentle, worn face of the old man. Several tears run down his cheeks. And you realize that he is holding you - that you are a child in this holy man's arms.

You look across the room and there on the bed is the young maiden. Though the light is strong around her, a part of you knows there is no life left. As you gaze upon her, her image changes, becoming the unicorn doe once more and then it also fades into the golden light. And the bed is empty.

You feel something wet upon your forehead, and it begins to tingle. You turn your head to gaze into the eyes of the old man. You realize that it is his tear that fell upon your forehead. And the old man's eyes widen as that tear brings out of your forehead a single horn. Although you cannot see it, you feel it growing from your forehead.

The old man raises you up above his head and calls out, "This is my son. He shall be called Risharinga, antelope horn."

You see yourself growing up in the ancient forests with the old man. Except for the single horn growing from your forehead, you appear as human as anyone else. But you are different. You feel things more strongly. You see things that others would not see, and with the guidance of the old man, you come to know the forest unlike anyone ever before. You are at one with nature. You understand the language of the animals, and you learn how to make life grow. You learn to work with the forces of nature. You speak with the flowers and commune with the trees. You know each of their spirits by name.

In the world beyond the forests, the people and land were experiencing a great drought. Life was drying up and dying. The king in the world beyond was in great distress for it was his own misdeeds that had caused the drought. Of this you are unaware, for all seems right with your world.

The king's advisors had heard of a forest and the child within it who could make things grow, and they told the king. They also warned the king that the child of the forest could see what other humans could not and so great care would be needed to lure the child from the forests to the outer world.

The king thought long and hard upon this, and finally asked to speak with his beautiful daughter. He told her of the forest child, and since all humans fell under the spell of her beauty, why wouldn't this child. The daughter did not like the idea of deceiving anyone, but the people were dying. She agreed.

For weeks she sailed up and down the river through the ancient forest, looking for this strange person.. She was amazed at how green and beautiful the forest was. It made her realize how even more desperate conditions were in the outer world. Each night she would sail further in, and during the day, she would walk and explore, hoping to encounter this mythical forest child. And all the time she is being watched from afar.

Her beauty stirs your heart in so many ways, and finally you realize that just watching her is not enough. You must develop the courage to approach her, and as you walk out of the woods and into the meadow in which she wandered, she catches her breath. It's true! Her eyes widen, and she stares at the single horn growing from your forehead. Only when she sees how her staring makes you feel awkward does she pull her eyes from it.

Over the following days, you walk the woods together, you telling her about the animals and plants and her telling you about the outer world. It isn't long until you realized that you are truly in love. Although she finds the horn unusual at first, she soon sees past it, and realizes just how strong and handsome you truly are.Then one month to the day that you first spoke to her, she places a small wreath of flowers over your horn and professes her own love to you. Before long, you are talking about going back with her to the outer world.

You return to the hut of your father Kasyapa, and even he can not fail to see that something is truly different. Although you had been asked not to tell, you share with your father the story of your new found love. In your telling and in the intensity of your own feeling, you fail to notice the change come over your father.

His face clouds. "This can not be! You cannot be with the outer world. It is not what you think. You are being deceived!"

You are shocked. Never have you seen your father angry. You are confused. Why would he not be happy at your own happiness. And in your shock and confusion, you run.

When you reach the river, the king's daughter sees your distress. She holds you and listens without saying a word as you describe your father's reaction. And her heart begins to ache over her deception. All that she can say is, "It will all work out. It will all work out."

You walk onto the boat your hand in hers, and as the boat pushes away from the shore, she holds you, not saying a word. Her heart is torn between her love for you and the need to maintain the deception to save the land of her people.

Only when the boat has sailed beyond the borders of the ancient forest does she speak. She cups your face in her hands, and speaks softly to you.

"Your father is right. There is deception. I was sent here by my father the king - to lure you with my beauty away from the forest to the outer world. The outer world is dying, and you are our only hope. But when I got to know you, I also came to love you. Though my reason for coming was false, my love is not."

You stare at her wide-eyed. Your hand clutches at your heart. Never have you known there can be such deceit. You begin to understand why your father has warned against the outer world for all these years.

The king's daughter sees your innocent heart breaking and she begins to weep.

"I had to do it for my people. They are dying. Look about you. Risharinga. Look at how our land has withered upon us!"

Slowly, you pull your eyes from hers, and as you look about, you gasp. Trees are withered and lifeless. Branches, like old skeletons, extend out to you, pleading. The earth is dry and cracked, and you can see that even the river was coming to an end. The devastation is immense.

There is such sadness at the devastation, that your first tears begin to flow. As you weep your tears, a soothing rain begins to fall. The river beds begin to fill. The trees and ground drink of the rain. Flowers begin to work their way from the soil once more. Leaves begin to cover the trees. It is as if the earth is drinking in new life and is being born anew.

You begin to understand. You look at your love, and you see her as you first saw her with the eyes that see beyond the surface. You see her heart filled with love and gratitude. And you embrace.

And the images begin to fade from around you. You find yourself sitting next to that pool by the waterfall. You are gazing into the pool itself. You see the images of a wedding within that pool. You and the king's daughter are being married. Upon her head is the crown of her father who gave it up because of the shame. Upon your horn is the wreath of flowers that your she made for you out of love. Behind you, stands your father Kasyapa, and as these images fade, you see the reflection of the unicorn upon the surface of that pool.

As you raise your eyes, you see it standing upon the opposite side of the pool. A soft golden glow surrounds it and its eyes look upon you with great love and promise. It then turns and walks from the meadow into the woods beyond. And the rest of the images fade from around you.

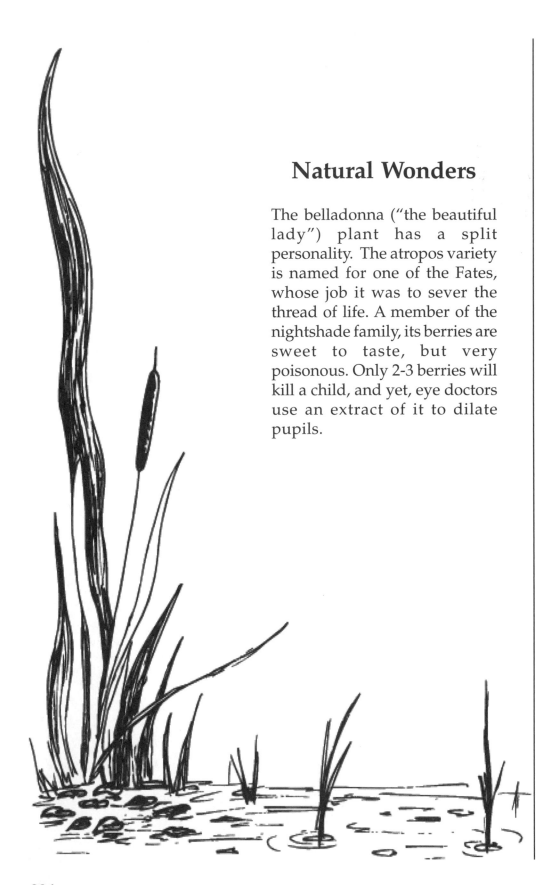

Natural Wonders

The belladonna ("the beautiful lady") plant has a split personality. The atropos variety is named for one of the Fates, whose job it was to sever the thread of life. A member of the nightshade family, its berries are sweet to taste, but very poisonous. Only 2-3 berries will kill a child, and yet, eye doctors use an extract of it to dilate pupils.

Chapter Sixteen

Dictionary of Plants, Herbs & More

Within Nature are many secrets – magical and marvelous – that have yet to be uncovered. There are uses for plants that are healing and can make us strong, psychic, and powerful. Some plants can heal. Some can open the heart to love. Some will comfort sorrow and some can bring prosperity. Some will protect us and some will open up vision of other worlds and wonders.Many uses of plants have become lost, were never recorded or are yet undiscovered. The Nature Spirits though still possess this secret knowledge and they may hold the keys to the natural cures for diseases.

To those who demonstrate a reverence and respect for Nature, the Nature spirits will reveal the healing and magical qualities of their plants and they will guide you in their uses. They are the experts at making things grow. They will show you the magic of planting seeds so that they grow faster and stronger. They will show you how to sow seeds of hopes and wishes, so that they take root and are fulfilled. Theirs is the magic of weaving new life and new growth in the world – whether it is through plants or through activities. They can show you how to grow your dreams like a plant in the earth or grow strong like the roots of a great tree.

Again, do not allow yourself to get hung up on the proper classification of the flower, tree or plant throughout this book. The categories that I have chosen for the various plants are simply to facilitate the average person finding information and guidance more easily. If you do not find a plant in an area where you believe it should be, check the others categories or the index to see where I might have placed it. Part of the difficulty of classifying is that genus names and listings change. For example, the Shasta daisy used to be classified strictly as part of the

Weathercasters

"Red sky in morning, sailors take warning. Red sky at night, sailors delight."

When wild berries are plentiful in summer, a hard winter will follow.

Bay protects from thunder and lightning.

If stormy weather arises while on a boat, burn a peony like incense and the rough weather will calm.

Tornadoes are signs of tremendous cleansing and creative energies out of control.

Thunder storms are cleansing for the environment and are often good signs for new projects.

Halos around the moon usually indicate that rain will soon come.

To cut a fern will bring the rains.

Seeing the puff of a dandelion blown from the head of a dandelion indicates rain is coming.

chrysanthemum family. Now it is often listed as a separate species, called leucanthemum. This is why I use the more common name in referring to trees, flowers and plants throughout this book.

Even if you don't know the specific genus name, initially the doctrine of signatures will help you to determine a flower's essence and meaning. And if it looks daisy-like, for example, explore the daisy characteristics described in this book. At some point though, you may wish to get a good flower field guide to help you in the identification process.

And please keep in mind that a book of this type cannot hope to cover every single tree, flower or plant. If the book does not contain a member of the Green Kingdom that you seek, use the guidelines that follow to help you determine its meaning and message to you. Remember that what I've provided are simply sketches to help you begin the process of understanding the language and signs of Nature. In developing this book and creating these symbolic sketches for you, I've used these same guidelines over the years, always combining the mystical and scientific. That is when the messages become clearest.

The following are general suggestions for understanding the meaning and messages of flowers:

1. Read and study some of the botanical and biological properties of the plants. Start with the initial observations. Is it a wild flower? What color are its blossoms? In what habitat is it most likely found? What is its color? Is it fragrant? After the initial observations, make note of its most unique aspects. You may need to consult some books to discover its more unique botanical properties. And examine where the plant originated and how it was used medicinally and magically.

2. Read and study some of the lore of the plant. This should include the meaning of its name. Many plants were given names that reflected their characteristics. Some were named for mythological characters, providing insight into the personality of the plant.

3. Examine the plant and its qualities from the perspective of the Doctrine of Signatures. What do you suppose its aspects might symbolize for you about something in your life? Count the number of petals and explore it numerologically. What does the shape of the petals suggest? What about the shape of the flower? Some flowers blossom flat-faced and others have trumpet shaped. Some have a chalice appearance. Explore the symbolism of chalices as a reflection of the archetypal feminine, the

womb, etc. Ruffled and fringed petals usually have a calming effect, smoothing out the ruffles within our own aura.

4. Take time to reflect upon its meaning and significance. How does the lore and its unique botanical aspects fit with what is going on in your life? At the time that this flower caught your attention, what was most on your mind for the hour or two before the encounter? For the previous 24 hours?

5. Take time to meditate and reflect upon different plants. Sit quietly with them. Note the subtleties of its colors. Note the fragrance. Examine the leaves and stem. And as you do these things, pay attention to how each plant makes you feel. If you do so with a different plant each week, you will open to the communication and meanings of a lot of plants in a single year.

6. Create planters inside your home and outside whenever possible. Visit botanical gardens. Explore meadows, parks and fields for wildflowers. Delight in the uniqueness of each variety.

Alfalfa   (medicavo sativa)
Keynote: be cautious concerning finances; don't stress them

This is a plant most often found on the borders of fields. We have spoken earlier about the significance of borders as doorways or bridges between worlds and dimensions. For those to whom this plant is a messenger the significance of fields and meadows should also be examined in relation to what is going on in your life.

This perennial plant can grow to three feet in height. It has a deep taproot, which has significance of our need to maintain deep foundations in some area of our life. The flowers are a soft blue to shades of yellow and they bloom through the summer. Because it is a perennial that spreads, it has associations with increasing abundance. Planting it around one's home is a means of protecting your wealth and finances.

Its leaves make an excellent tea that has a tonic and strengthening effect upon the body. It helps restore balance to stressed organs and systems of the body. Are we stressing over money needlessly? Do we believe there is no abundance in our life? Alfalfa reminds us that there is always flow, but our own worries and stress can block that flow.

Aloe   (aloe vera)
Keynote: **time to heal and smooth over irritations**

Aloe is found naturally in Africa, but it is cultivated in other tropical areas. It is a plant that I often recommend be one that every home contains because of its healing capabilities. In ancient Egypt, it was used as a cosmetic and it is believed to be one of the secrets to Cleopatra's beauty. It has a tradition of symbolizing honor for Muhammad.

Aloe is the burn plant. It has been one of the most powerful treatments for burns of all kinds. It is actually related to the lily family. The leaves and stalk contains a jelly-like substance, which is very healing to skin conditions in particular. The skin is our largest sensory organ and most things we encounter register upon us through the skin. When Aloe is a messenger, it is time to soothe the irritations we are encountering. Are we being too sensitive or are we ignoring our sensitivities?

Basil   (ocymum basilium)
Keynote: **time for discipline and protection; express your devotion & have strength**

Although feared in western society, dragons are powerful and protective energies found in the universe. In the East, they control the climate, both in the sense of the weather and the climate of our lives. Many tales and myths exist about their protective energies and abilities. They travel in all worlds freely. Because of this, they are especially helpful and protective when working with the spirit realm.

There is an herb, which is particularly inviting to dragons. It is basil. It draws the basilisk form of dragon to you and into your environment. The basilisk is a powerful dragon, very serpent-like. It breathes fire and has deadly venom. It can kill with a look from its eyes. The basilisk has great magical abilities. Its skin repels snakes and spiders. Through the basilisk dragon, we can learn to read the true souls of others simply by looking into their eyes. It protects against negativity from both the physical world and the spirit world.

This is one of the main forms of dragon that I use to protect my home. It protects the house and all within it. It repels the negativity of others and even those who think about doing negative to the environment are made to feel uneasy. Should negativity be projected, it repels it and returns it to the source like poisonous venom.

The spirit of basil often shows itself in more of an elf form. It holds the knowledge of dragons, of which part of their mystery is the integrating sexuality and spirituality. Wherever basil grows, there is usually a dragon to be found in that same environment, serving as protector. It also draws dragons, when burned as incense. The faeries and spirits of basil help us awaken greater discipline and devotion.

Basil means "royal" and it truly embodies a royal power. It is native to Asia and Africa. It is also one of the plants that everyone should have in their home. It is an annual, and thus it is a reminder to renew our efforts yearly. Its leaves, when bruised, emit a soft, rich fragrance. This fragrance is cleansing and strengthening to the aura. The flowers are small and white, sometimes with a purplish tinge. This herb has been used for culinary, medicinal and magical purposes. And its presence always serves as a catalyst for strength.

Basil was sacred to the deities of the Hindu religion and evoked within ceremonies to elicit an aura of romance. It awakens a higher sense of discipline and devotion. As mentioned, it has ties to the invoking of dragons of protection into one's environment. Its use as an incense was employed for such purposes by ancient magicians.

Basil reminds us to be protective of our environment and our endeavors. It helps us to express our energies more strongly and effectively. We can control the climate of our life with proper discipline and devotion. This is always part of the message of basil.

Bay   (laurus nobilis)
Keynote: clear out old emotions; open to your true feelings

Bay has a history in the Graeco-Roman traditions. Bay was used in laurel wreathes, a reflection of honor. It was associated with Apollo. When one he loved turned herself into a bay tree to avoid his advances, Apollo declared the tree sacred. At the Oracle at Delphi, the priestesses used bay oil in the development of their mediumship and divinatory abilities.

On the eve of Valentines Day, take 2 bay leaves and sprinkle with rose water. Lay them across each other beneath your pillow. You should have clean sheets and sleep wear. As you get into bed, cross your legs

Dragon Protection

Dragons are one of the most powerful and ancient archetypes found within the natural world. We can use plants to invite them into our environemnt for protection. Basil is a plant that is drawing to the basilisk form of dragons.

1. You will need nine basil plants.
Nine is the number for the dragon and helps keep the power of it strong and balanced.

2. Plant the basil in nine areas surrounding your house, yard or property.
If you do not have a yard, place nine individual basil plants in their containers around your room or house.

3. Focus on the power of the dragon.
As you place the plants, focus on the dragon energy opening up and nine dragons encircling your environment to protect you and everything in it.

4. Tend to the plants.
As you tend to the plants know that you keep the dragon energy strong around you. As the plants mature, you can dry some of the leaves and burn them as an incense as a thank you to the dragon and to open up to its magic more strongly.

5. Feel the protective energy of the dragon.
Know that you are encircled and embraced with the protective energy of the dragon. When you do your spirit work, always take a moment to visualize your sacred space in the protective circle of the dragon.

and ask St. Valentine to show you in your dream who you will marry. A variation is to pin bay leaf to each corner of your pillow and one in the middle. You will dream of the one you will marry.

Bay fragrance is very penetrating. It is often used for treating lung conditions, healing and balancing to the heart and throat chakras of the body. It has an antiseptic and decongestive effect. And in this lies its message. Bay reminds us it is time to clear out old emotions and put them into perspective. It is time to open and demonstrate our true feelings, regardless of the result.

Bayberry   (merica cerifera)
Keynote: time of abundance; objectively examine worries and fears

Bayberry is a handsome shrub, with dark green leaves. Northern species are amazingly tolerant of salt and infertile soils. The berries ripen in the fall and can remain until the following spring, a reminder to us of that being a fruitful period in our own life that we can take advantage of. It has been used herbally to treat dysentery and diarrhea and it is a stimulant to the circulatory system.

Bayberry is a fragrance that has come to be associated with the Christmas holidays. It is a fragrance that has the ability to ease emotions - especially worries and fears about money. It is used frequently in department stores, subconsciously easing customers' worries about over spending – especially around the Christmas holidays.

Bayberry is balancing to the entire aura and in aromatherapy, it helps alleviate physical problems resulting from unbalanced emotions. When bayberry speaks, we need to put our fears and worries into perspective. This is the time to be objective. Are we being too emotional about our worries, making more of them than they are? Are we not heeding our emotions enough, ignoring their nudges? Does the worry or fear have any validity or solid basis?

Blackberry   (rubus fractious)
Keynote: protect sacred spaces;

Blackberries should not be eaten after Michaelmas (sometimes All Hallows Eve), the devil has touched them and defiled them. It's difficult with a book of this type to decide which plants to include and which to leave out. As I was putting together this chapter, I had a dream about blackberries. I knew then I needed to include it in this book.

Blackberries grows abundantly on my farm and I have found that it grows quickly around areas that are sacred. My grandfather once told me that blackberries grow to keep humans out of certain areas and the sweet fruit is a distraction to us. And if that doesn't work, there are always the thorns.

This is a brambly, wild growing plant, with branches stretching in all directions and with great length. The leaves usually grow in threes. The thorns are sharp and usually thick. Herbally, this is a powerful herb, excellent for indigestion, diarrhea and a tonic for colds and the flu. It makes an excellent gargle.

Folklore teaches that to crawl under the blackberry is a way of protecting yourself. The thorns will prevent negative spirits and unwanted energies from following. And this is the blackberries message. It is just not time to enter into some new areas. We may not be prepared yet or if we enter into endeavors prematurely, we may have to deal with some thorns. If we are patient, the time will come and in the meantime, we can enjoy the fruit of what is before us.

Burdock   (arctium minus)
Keynote: protect your heart; stick with things that are secure

My brothers and I used to pull the burrs off and throw them at each other or try to stick them to each other without the other person knowing. Burdock is a biennial, reflecting a two year cycle at play within our life. The first year, it has only basal leaves, but the second year, the plant grows along stem - as high as six feet. This is often a reminder that the second year of endeavors is when we will  often see our greatest growth and success. Its leaves are large and heart-shaped.

Burdock has purplish pink flowers that bloom late summer to early fall, and when mature, it develops a burr which can be painful to touch. This gives it a protective nature, and it is often a reminder that as our endeavors unfold, we should be protective of them and tend to them, rather than leave them to others.

Burdock is now a "weed" throughout the US and it is often found along fences and roadsides. In Japan, it is cultivated as a vegetable. The stalks are peeled and eaten raw in salads. The root is the most important part of the burdock from a medicinal aspect, and it is only good the first year. Burdock root is used in teas and other applications as a cleanser with a diuretic effect.

Burdock reminds us to protect things of the heart – the things we love and the things that are dear to us. It reminds us to stick with things that are secure, at least for now. Within two years, things will change, opening new opportunities.

Butterfly Weed   (asclepias tuberose)
Keynote: look for transformation; try a new creative approach

This plant is part of the milkweed family and the description of milkweed should be explored as well. This member of the milkweed family though has no milky juice within it. Native Americans ate the pods and stems and even the root, which was cooked before it was eaten. Another name for it is pleurisy root, and I have used tinctures of pleurisy root at times for breathing difficulties.

This plant got its name from the fact that butterflies are drawn to it. It is wonderful to use in any butterfly garden. This perennial is found in fields and open meadows. Its orangish flowers are significant, because they are a shade that is associated with creativity and artistic endeavors.

Because this plant is associated with butterflies, its message has to do with transformations around us. Butterflies are the masters of transformation; they go through a distinct metamorphosis. They remind us that there is always work, effort and time involved in any change or metamorphosis we are wishing to make. It cannot be forced. The butterfly weed reminds us that metamorphosis is part of life and now might be the time to try a new creative approach.

Catnip   (nepeta cataria)
Keynote: time to face fears; open to the magic within you

Catnip is a member of the mint family. It is a perennial that spreads from year to year. It is often found in fields and on dry banks and gravely soil. It has a long leaf stalk with whitish hairs and the flowers form in clusters and are usually white or light blue. The leaves are dried and used as a tea. The tea itself has a mild taste and is used to calm nerves. It has been used to help treat children who are hyper and have difficulties with attention deficit

This is an herb with a long association with cats and anyone working with a cat familiar or any cat totem (wild or domestic) can benefit from using catnip incense or aroma to facilitate meditative connections. When burned as an incense, it can be drawing to the Egyptian goddess Bast, the daughter of Isis.

Cats have always been associated with the night, a time humans usually associate with fears. Catnip brings the message that it is time to face our fears. Night time is also a time of magic, and catnip reminds us that there is magic waiting to be born out of the dark within us and into our life.

Cattail   (typha latifolia)
Keynote: spread the seeds for new growth; don't limit your endeavors now

Cattail is a plant of wetlands, ponds and even lakes. It requires water in order to live and grow. This, in itself, is part of its message. Water is the source of creativity and birth, and those for whom the cattail is a messenger need an environment that is creative and nourishing. A study of wetlands, marshes, bogs will also provide some insight to this plant's message for you.

Cattails grow to about six feet and a seed end terminates the long stalk. The seed head contains tens of thousands of seeds, that will begin to scatter in the fall. They are reminders of the potential growth and seeds of growth within our life.

It is a plant that is the favorite food of the muskrat and this animals should also be studied if the cattail is speaking to you. The root is often peeled and made into a flour and even the white sprouts that appear in the early spring are edible.

Cattails make a wonderful source of activity. In the early spring, take a green cattail stalk and peel the outer layers. Inside you will see a soft, white center. It can be eaten raw or cooked like any other vegetable. You can tell others that you eat the same food as muskrats. In late fall, blow the seeds of the cattail head into the wind. You are helping to spread their growth.

Cattail is another dominant plant of wetlands. It contains an estimated 250,000 seeds, scattering countless numbers yearly. It also spreads through rhizomes or rootlike structures under the thick muck. They are often reminders to spread as many seeds as possible when striving for new growth. Not all will make it, but many will. And try it in several ways, especially when breaking away from old habits and cycles.

Chamomile   (anthemis nobilis)
Keynote: **renewed health and energy; a new sense of peace coming**

Chamomile is a native of Europe but it is commonly found now throughout the US. It is a perennial plant, usually with 8-12 single flowerheads. The number of flowerheads will be part of Chamomile's message to you. The flowers have yellow disc with white petals surrounding it, very daisy–like in their appearance. It is a common plant in dry fields.

Medicinally, the flowers are used as a tonic tea and for its aromatherapy aspects. (It is related to the ragweed family, so caution should be used by anyone with allergies.) Chamomile fragrance though augments the entire nervous system. It helps release emotional tension that may be causing physical problems. It is calming to the stomach – easing aches and indigestion. The tea has been used as a remedy for colic in babies and young children.

This is a plant that brings health and life to other plants and to other people. It helps keep insect pests away from garden areas and it was a common addition to English gardens because of its scent. While many fragrances do not carry the herbal effects of the plant itself – due to the distillation process, this is not so with chamomile. The fragrance does contain many of the herbal properties that relieve stress. Again though, it is part of the ragweed family, and so care must be taken when using it on someone with allergies.

Chamomile brings the message of new health and energy. We will soon experience more vitality and more peace. Those things that have been irritating or pestering us will soon pass.

Cinnamon   (cinamomum zeylanica)
Keynote: time to increase efforts; people will see you as stronger now so show leadership

Cinnamon fragrance is often used to augment the effects of other fragrances and incenses. When mixed with sandalwood, it facilitates deeper meditations, which is beneficial for anyone having difficulty meditating. It is strengthening and protecting, stimulating the electrical aspects of the aura and body.

In the Courtyard of the Palace Moon grows a mythical cinnamon tree. If left to grow, it is so beautiful that it will overshadow the moon. It is considered an autumn tree in China and thus this is a powerful time for those to whom cinnamon comes as a messenger.

Cinnamon alerts us to a time to increase our efforts. Now is not the time to hold back. People will see you as stronger more leader-like, so step up to the opportunity.

Clover   (trifolium pretense)
Keynote: new luck unfolding in endeavors; situations of fidelity at hand

Most kids know that finding a four-leafed clover is good luck. In fact many believed that having one would help you to see the faeries as well. Traditionally, the first leaf is for fame, the second is for wealth, the third is for a faithful lover and the fourth is for glorious health. There is even a superstition about putting a two-leafed clover in the right shoe. Then the first person you meet, you'll marry him or her or someone of that name. To hand another a red clover stalk is a way of asking for fidelity in love. If it is not accepted, faithfulness in love should not be expected.

Red clover is a perennial and it is often one of the most easily recognized field flowers. The flowers are a fragrant red to purple and have a globe-like head. It is found in a variety of environments, growing equally well in most soil types. Although it is believed that Native Americans of Arizona and California ate the red clover, it is not very digestible. The whole plant has been used though for its antispasmodic properties.

Clover has had much mysticism about it in regards to the Faerie Realm, particularly one of the most treasured creatures of that realm – the unicorn. Unicorns have a great love for wild flowers and clover is one of the unicorn's favorite. It particularly likes to lie in fields of red clover. The spirits and faeries of clover often reveal themselves readily to those who display kindness, so there is great compatibility and fondness between unicorns and clover. During the full moon, the unicorn is drawn more to meadows with white clover and the meadows with purple and red at other times. Washing the eyes with clover water was once believed to promote seeing and feeling the presence of faeries and the unicorn.

The faeries of clover often have an elfin quality about them. It is not unusual to find the occasional leprechaun somewhere in a field of clover. The clover faeries assist in finding love and fidelity. They can aid in developing psychic abilities. The clover faeries reveal themselves readily to individuals who display kindness toward nature. They often first show themselves through flickering lights around the clover itself. The faeries of white clover are most powerful and apparent around the time of the full moon. Ordinary water can become enchanted by infusing it with clover found at the favorite haunts of faeries. Washing the eyes with this water can awaken sight of the closest faeries.

Clover has an essence that draws positive energies. It awakens a vibration of "luck" within the auric field. As an herb, it has magical ties to love and fidelity. It aids in psychic development and intuition, and it balances the hemispheres of the brain. The white clover is tried to the energies and goddesses associated with the full moon. It opens the individual to the kindness of nature. Clover speaks to us of new luck in our endeavors and that now is the time to show fidelity.

Comfrey   (symphytum officinale)
Keynote: **take action; don't wait for better time or place**

Comfrey is one of my wife's favorite herbs. We have used it for many medicinal purposes. It is a perennial with a black root and large, tongue-like leaves. Comfrey root powder has great benefit for healing wounds with little or no scarring. It can thrive in most soil conditions, but it does best in moist and shady areas. Part of its message is that you can do your work anywhere and still succeed.

Placing a leaf of comfrey in your shoe will ensure a safe journey and will prevent your feet from getting sore if you are on them along time. Its ability to soothe and heal wounds is almost legendary among rural folk. It is rich in vitamins and nutrients, which accelerate the healing process.

Comfrey reminds us that we have all that we need to heal or succeed in our endeavors. Trust in your own abilities, start where you are at and just do it.

Corn (zea mays)
Keynote: time to merge the sacred and the mundane; new life and abundance

The Pueblo people thrived because of their ability to grow corn, doing so as far back as 1000 BC. They developed 19 varieties. Corn was part of their daily life and it was also sacred, revered in story and myth. The Corn Mother planted the seeds of all flora and fauna. To this day, Pueblo children are given a perfect ear of corn when they are born – their own symbolic Corn Mother In the Southeast, the Green Corn Ceremony celebrated the ripening of the corn. There was a fast, followed by a feast.

Dolls made of corn husks from the last harvest can be hung in the house for abundant harvest the following year. In some rural communities, the last handful of corn reaped from a field and given to a maiden who became the Queen of the Harvest. Corn was always sacred to the goddess Demeter in the Greek tradition. She was honored as bringing forth a healthy crop, a true sign of prosperity and fertility. Hanging the corn was away of inciting her blessing.

Even the corn silk has had its applications and meaning. The corn silk has been used as a diuretic and because of its hair-like appearance, it has been used magically for growing hair and for stimulating mental activity and intuition.

Corn occasionally appears as a messenger if we are becoming a bit too "day-dreamy". It reminds us of the need to be practical and pragmatic, while holding onto our dreams. Are we just dreaming and fantasizing without acting or doing enough to make them a reality? Corn teaches us that if we merge the sacred and mundane, we will experience a great harvest. Corn reminds of the importance of being grateful.

Dandelion   (taraxacum officinale)
Keynote: find beauty where you haven't looked; look beyond the surface

Most people today think of the dandelion as a pest in the yard. It has deep roots and it spreads quickly. And yet this is a plant that has great lore and many wonderful qualities about it. It is filled with vitamins and minerals. It makes a good addition to salads and it has even been a source of wine. The juice of the dandelion has been used for treating skin conditions – acne, eczema, etc.

And it has a tremendous amount of folklore about it. Dandelion has often been a divination tool. Wishes were made and then the blossoms blown off the stem so that the wish could be carried on the wind to be fulfilled. However many puffs it took to blow off all of the seeds would also tell you how many years until you married. When separated from one you love, hold the dandelion puff in your hands and charge it with tender thoughts. And the message would be carried to your love. After puffing the ball, if any seeds remain your loved one is thinking of you at that same moment (The more seeds remaining the stronger he or she is thinking of you.)

Dandelion teaches us that there is worth and beauty beyond what is visible and apparent. It teaches us to look beyond the surface of things. Dandelion is a weed with great qualities – including color and vitality. Is there something of color and vitality that we are missing around us?

Ferns   (pteris, adiantum, botrichium)
Keynote: open your heart to the Faerie realm; look for wonders

There are a wide variety of ferns and they have had a lot of folklore and superstition surrounding them. Rural folk thought it bad luck to gather them or even to touch them. Possibly this is due to the belief that ferns are one of the signs of faerie folk close by and to disturb their home

412

would invite bad luck. In Wales, it was customary at one time to place a bunch of ferns on the halter of your horse to keep the devil and other bad spirits away. Some believed that to place a fern in the left shoe of a husband on St. John's day would keep him lovingly faithful.

This is a plant associated with St. John the Baptist. A legend speaks how an angel foretold the birth of John at the moment in which the fern seed, at other time invisible, fell from the plant. This is the sources of one of the most common beliefs about ferns. It is the idea that fern seeds were invisible, except for the one instant in which they appeared and fell to the ground. Because of this, catching one could make you invisible. This is do partly to the fact that ferns produce no seed, and many believed the seeds were just invisible.

Ferns are also associated with one of the most dynamic archetypes in Nature – the unicorn. Tradition teaches that unicorns enjoy ferns and green moss for sleeping. Matted but unbroken ferns often indicate the presence of a unicorn as only unicorns could walk upon the grass without breaking them.

Ferns are reminders that we need to keep our hearts open to the Faerie Realm. We are about to experience wonders but we must remember how we believed when we were children. If we do, our beliefs will be rewarded.

Garlic   (allium sativum)
Keynote: protection and cleansing

Garlic is both cultivated and found wild in damp pastures and woodlands. It is a perennial that is used for both culinary and medicinal purposes. It is probably the most widely used herb in cooking, and most people can recognize it by sight and smell. It grows from a bulb and its flowers are normally white.

Garlic does have its lore. One of the more common is that it is repelling to vampires. And yet to hang a group of garlic in the kitchen is to invite good health and well-being. One legend says it sprang from the footsteps of Satan when he walked the Earth. This was God's way of protecting people against the evil influence.

A lot of study has been done on garlic in the past decade or so. Its ability as a natural antibiotic is well known. The Chinese used garlic to treat leprosy and other societies have used it in conjunction with tuberculosis and arthritis. It lowers blood pressure, and is good for the heart.

Garlic is a reminder that we need to protect and cleanse ourselves and our environment periodically. No matter how spiritual we may be, we are exposed to imbalances and negativities that require special efforts. Garlic alerts us to those times that we can eliminate them as easily as possible.

Goldenseal   (hydrastis canadenses)
Keynote: be careful of sensitivity to others; be a bit more protective throughout the day

Also known as Indian paint, this wonderful herb is actually a part of the buttercup family. Because of this, a study of buttercups in chapter fourteen will provide further information. It is a perennial herb with a hairy step and two leaves near the top. The flower, small and white with thin petals, blooms in the early spring and is found in rich woodlands.

Goldenseal has a powerful antiseptic quality to it. It promotes healing of wounds. A powder is made from the root, which is best picked in the fall. It was once considered the most beneficial plant for modern medicine and it has been used by healers since the mid 1800's, especially popular in rural Appalachia.

The thin white petals are significant, appearing almost fringe-like. Fringe was worn in many traditions as a means of fending off negative energies and spirits, protecting the wearer as he or she went about their daily activities. Goldenseal reminds us that we must protect ourselves in all environments and in all activities to some degree. It is part of the responsibility of caring for oneself responsibly. Goldenseal often shows up as a messenger when we are more likely to be sensitive to outside influences.

Ivy   (hedera helix)
Keynote: time to stretch; build upon the past; balance t he old and new

Ivy has smooth, shiny, evergreen leaves and small yellowish flowers. It is often a climbing or trailing plant and these types of plants remind us that we must keep stretching and growing. It has clinging tendrils that provide support for it as it climbs. And this is very symbolic. Are we not moving? Are we stuck? Are we trying to do things before we have established support?

This plant has tremendous folklore. The Greeks wove it into wreaths of victory and celebration. It is associated with the wreath that the God Bacchus wore to prevent drunkenness during his celebrations.

Ivy should only be placed in outer passages and doorways for good health and luck. To bring ivy indoors was considered ill luck. To pick ivy from a church would invite illness. And if the ivy on the house wall died, it foretold of the death of someone living there soon.

Pick an ivy leaf without anyone seeing it and place it inside the shirt, near the heart. The first person who speaks to you shall be a true love. On New Years Eve at night, place an ivy leaf in a dish of water and leave for one day. If it stays fair and green, it foretells good health. If there appear any spots, it foretells illness throughout the year.

Ground ivy is not really ivy at all. Ground ivy is a creeping perennial with stems that lie on the ground. It prefers moist soil. The flowering branches can grow to 6 inches and from April through July, bluish-purple flowers emerge. Poison Ivy is also not part of this family, and I have chosen to treat it separately later in this chapter.

Ivy reminds us to keep stretching, using the past as a support for new growth. We must cling to the old as we open to the new – both aspects have viability and are necessary for success.

Lavender   (lavandula vera)
Keynote: keep emotional and physical balance; deal with frustrations of others in a stable manner; karmic issues at hand

Lavender is a hardy, fragrant herb. Although it has a shrubby growth, it is a colorful plant of purple flowers and almost needlelike, gray-green leaves. The flowers are grouped in small spikes sitting well above the stem. It does well most places, except in humid warm environments.

A very sacred flower, it has many magical properties. When aligned to its essence, it activates energy of stability within one's life. It assists the individual in making any magical operation permanent, and it was a powerful flower, used in rituals associated with Midsummer Eve (a dynamic time to assume this magical name). Lavender was used by Solomon to clean sacred circles, as it activates an extremely high vibration that is impenetrable to lower thought forms and astral entities.

Lavender oil should be a part of everyone's medicine chest. It is relaxing to the entire body, relieving it of stress. It is beneficial for headaches, insomnia, pains, arthritis and depression. Bathing with a couple drops of lavender oil restores physical and emotional balance. It is a powerfully healing flower, and it activates the crown chakra and the chakra above the medulla oblongata which stimulates mental clarity, keen awareness and alertness.

It stimulates the aura to a degree that spiritual beings are more visible to the naked eye. It helps integrate aspects of the higher self into the personality. It stimulates visionary states, connecting people to their higher self and helps to manifest situations for the removal of karmic blockages. It establishes emotional balance and it has ties to the kingdom of nature spirits. It can be aligned with to overcome certain emotional blocks and conflicts that hinder spiritual growth.

As an herb, lavender has been responsible for many healing and magical practices. Much of this is due to the strong activity of the faeries surrounding it. Wherever lavender grows, there will always be great faerie and elf activity - and not just associated with the plant itself. The faeries of lavender can help you to open physical vision of nature spirits. One of the most powerful times to connect with them is on Midsummer Eve. The faeries of this flower and the other nature spirits it draws are very protective. There are many faerie tales about individuals who suffered cruel treatment by spouses, and as a result incurred some problems themselves. It draws love and protection, and it was considered a good remedy for cruel treatment by spouses. The faeries of lavender can bring healing and protection, and they can assist us in overcoming emotional blocks.

Lavender reminds us to maintain emotional balance. Now is the time to deal with issues objectively. Maintain your stability, even if others are not. It is a reminder that issues at hand are probably karmic and so it is best to deal with them now.

Milkweed   (asclepias syriaca)
Keynote: time for transformation; do things in your own unique way

In general, all milk producing plants are poisonous to humans. This includes the milkweed, but it is essential to the life of the monarch butterfly. For those to whom the butterfly is a totem, the milkweed should be studied. For those to whom the milkweed is a messenger, the monarch butterfly should be studied as well. The milkweed gets its name from the fact that all parts of the plant contain a milky juice or sap.

Milkweed is a common perennial, growing easily to three feet or more. For those to whom the milkweed is a messenger, a study of the number five is essential. The flowers have five upright hoods. And there are five stamens.

It is one of the easiest plants to identify. If you break a stem, and it oozes a white substance, it is a milkweed. Although not considered a handsome plant, its flowers are quite large. It is also essential to the monarch butterfly. Monarchs lay their eggs on the milkweed plant. The emerging larvae eat the plant and no other. When they go into their pupal stage, they hand their chrysalises from milkweed leaves.

The monarch, by eating the milkweed, makes itself taste bitter, which is their natural defense against predators. Birds stay clear of the foul tasting butterfly. Other butterflies, like the viceroy, are colored similar to the monarch, and this protects them from birds who think they may be monarchs.

Milkweed reminds us that this is a time of transformation. And if it is to be truly successful, we must do it in our own unique way – even if no one else has done it that way. What works for others may not work for you. What works for you may not work for others.

Mugwort   (artemisia vulgaris)
Keynote: open to the world of dreams; spirit is strong around you

Mugwort is known as a visionary herb. It is related to the wormwoods. The top of the leaves is shiny and the bottom is soft and it produces masses of flowers. They are often reminders to look beyond the surface. Not everything is at it appears (the soft, hidden behind the shiny).Medicinally, Mugwort has been used to help women with menstrual pain.

One of the primary sources of visions – available to each of us is dreaming. Mugwort is one of the most powerful herbs for anyone wishing to do advanced dreamwork. Its appearance as a messenger is always a reminder to pay attention to our dreams. It alerts us the coming of important dreams and helps us to remember them.

Mugwort also reminds us that spirit contact is often initiated through dream activity, and its message is often about loved ones who have passed on and are coming around to visit. Mugwort alerts us to lucid dreams that are important to our life and reminds us that dreams are also messages that apply to what we are doing daily.

Mushroom   (basidiom ycetes)
Keynote: **Recycle; try a different approach**

Mushrooms are amazing. They come in a variety of sizes and colors. Some are edible and some are poisonous. While most people think of them as plants, they are actually a different type of organism called a fungus, but we are including them in this area for simplicity's sake. They do not have chlorophyll and they do not produce their own food like plants. They do not have a vascular system like plants and thus pass water and nutrients from cell to cell in a sponge like fashion. They do not flower but they do reproduce by spores rather than budding.

Mushrooms are the visible, above ground portion of an underground fungus. They are part of a grouping that includes rust, mold, mildew and yeasts. Mushrooms are often called toadstools, at least the inedible or poisonous ones are. Mushrooms often are the reverse of an ordinary plant, and those for whom it is a messenger may want to examine doing the reverse or taking an upended view in accomplishing tasks. Where it would not work for others, it will for you.

418

Mushrooms recycle and assist life. They help break down fallen logs, branches, fallen leaves, helping to return them to soil. Mushrooms and plants have been described as the yin and yang. Plants help feed other living things, and when they die, the mushrooms convert them back into soil for new plants.

Mushrooms serve a wide purpose, including medicine. Penicillin came from a fungus, and new research is exploring the use of fungus to convert toxic substances into harmless matter.

There are many types of mushrooms, each with their own unique qualities. People have known for hundreds of years that mushrooms are poisonous, and most cases of poisoning are from children picking small toadstool mushrooms in their own yards. There are actually over 250,000 species but most poisonings stem from only about twenty. The truth is that more people are struck by lightning than die from eating poisonous mushrooms, and fewer than ten species are actually deadly poisonous. Wide spread, with spores carried by the wind, Amanita mushrooms are one of these. They start out as a small white colored egg. From this, come the stem and a hamburger shaped cap (usually white). Most have a skirt or ring about middle of the white stem. Do not even touch or of you should, wash your hands immediately after.

Witches Butter Jelly mushrooms look like jelly. They grow on wood and range in color from black to yellow to orange. They can be rubbery to very jelly-like. When it is golden yellow and grows on wood – most often oak and beech trees, it is called witches butter. It can be found year round. If you press one, you can watch its jelly-like liquid ooze onto your finger.

Mushrooms remind us that we may need to recycle what we are doing and take an entirely different approach to our endeavors. Are we doing things in the same old way? Let's recycle that old way into something entirely new.

Nettles   (urtica dioica)
Keynote: issues of oversensitivity at hand; be careful what you say and how you say it

The more common name for this plant is stinging nettle. It is a very stout perennial that can grow as tall as four feet. It can grow in shade or sun, often along streams. It is distinguished by the erect square stem covered in stinging hairs. Its leaves are heart-shaped and have sharp, deep cuts. The plant is irritating (stinging) to the skin, causing stinging and itching. The leaves do not sting if picked from the underside. And the herb is one of the few that is excellent at stopping or slowing the flow of blood.

One of the cures for stinging nettle is yellow dock, which usually grows near it. "In dock, out nettle." Rubbing the nettles sting with yellow dock while chanting this three times removes the sting, according to folklore. Folklore aside though, yellow dock does have herbal qualities that will soothe the sting of nettles.

Anything that has to do with stinging and irritation reflects issues of oversensitivity. The skin is our largest sensory organ and when nettles show up as messengers, we need to ask ourselves some questions. Are we being too sensitive? Are others around us? Do we need to be more sensitive to others? Do we need to develop a thicker skin? Nettles remind us to be careful of what we say and how we say it, because our words will have a stronger impact now than at other times. Things expressed more loving will be felt more loving. Things expressed more cutting and irritating will be felt more cutting and irritating.

Parsley   (carum petroselinium)
Keynote: **journeys ahead; move forth**

In European rural areas, it was bad luck to give parsley plants away. It was also bad luck to transplant parsley. Sometimes parsley was an indicator of who was truly the head of the house: "When the mistress is master the parsley grows faster."

To the Greeks it was a sign of victory and was worn as part of a wreath. It was also sacred to Persephone and came to be associated with the crossing of the River Styx. This was eventually transferred to St. Peter and his role in determining who would cross into heaven. There arose from this the custom of planting it at burial sites.

Parsley can grow for several years and was often planted in gardens to ensure that there would be thick green growth. Parsley's primary use is in the kitchen. Medicinally though it has been used as a diuretic and it has been used in the treatment of jaundice.

Parsley speaks to us of journeys and smooth crossings. When it appears as a messenger, it reminds us that the journey ahead will succeed, even if it is a long one.

Pennyroyal   (hadeoma pulegoides)
Keynote: **free yourself of unbalanced emotional attachments; be objective**

Pennyroyal is an annual with a mint-like fragrance, but it is not a member of the mint family. It has blue to lavender flowers that are barely visible throughout the summer and into early autumn.

The fragrance is soothing to nausea and headaches. It has also been used in aromatherapy for menstrual cramps. The herb is an abortive though and it should never be taken by anyone who is or attempting to become pregnant.

The herb and its fragrance is powerfully protective to the aura, strengthening it, so that negative thoughts and expressions of others are repelled. For those who work in the health field or do psychic work of any kind, this is a beneficial plant to have in the environment. It prevents you from becoming attached to the other's problems. Having a pennyroyal plant in the bedroom eases sleep and provides protection against nightmares. It stimulates dream activity that is strengthening.

Peppermint   (menthe piperita)
Keynote: trust in the process of life; all will be well

All mints are "friends of life". When grown indoors they cleanse and energize the environment. Peppermint fragrance is stimulating to the mental faculties. It can be an aid to directing and controlling the kundalini energy – our basic and most powerful life force.

This is a perennial herb with reddish flowers. The leaves are dark green and lance shaped. They are found in moist soils throughout the US and Europe. The leaves are dried or used as flavorings.

They are also distilled to make a strong oil. Peppermint oil has an antispasmodic effect. It has a sweet scent that is lightening to our mood. It is refreshing and helps us to overcome fatigue – emotional and physical. It is also beneficial for conditions of asthma and indigestion.

Peppermint reminds us to trust in the process of life. It may be hectic but it will work to our benefit. Keep a child's excitement about you and trust that all will be well.

Poison Ivy   (rhus toxicendron)
Keynote: protect yourself against irritants; handle everything gently

Poison ivy, also called poison oak, is actually a vertically growing shrub and also a creeping vine. It has a reddish, slender rootstock. The leaves are composed of three leaflets each and they vary in color from

light to dark green. The small greenish white flowers are in clusters. They flower in June and then are followed by a cream-colored fruit.

Poison ivy is widespread throughout the US. It grows frequently in dune and beach areas, one of the few plants that grows strongly in those environments. The fact is that poison ivy can grow anywhere. It is found in creek banks, rocky crevices and climbing trees.

All parts of the plant are toxic and the irritating substance of the plant can rub off on cloths, hands or anything it comes in contact with, causing irritations, blistering and itching. Because this is often a creeping vine, poison ivy speaks to us about not allowing irritations to creep and spread in our life. They should be dealt with strongly but gently. If not, just as the oil can be transferred from clothing to skin, so to can the irritations that are ignored be transferred to others around us, creating more difficulties. Be cautious about irritations building and creeping up on you. Handle everything gently and with care, but do not ignore them when they arise.

Rosemary   (rosmarinus officinalis)
Keynote: protection and healing; be positive

Rosemary is shrub that looks much like an evergreen. It is native to the Mediterranean region and was once a traditional symbol of remembrance. The leaves and the twigs are most often used for a variety of purposes.

Rosemary has always had a tremendous amount of lore associated with it. Most it has to do with fending off bad luck. Rosemary was often hung over the doors of houses to keep negative energies and spirits away. Even into the late 1800's and the turn of the century it was a common practice at funerals for all mourners to carry a sprig of rosemary. After the service, the sprigs are tossed into the grave to bring peace to the soul and to assist its passing. And many believed that where rosemary grows the woman rules the house.

This herbal flower is one of the most powerful herbs against any form of black magic, hatred and evil. It aligns the individual with those archetypal energies that protect and strengthen the individual auric fields. It is linked to the kingdom of nature spirits and elves. It promotes the awakening of healing potentials, and it draws opportunities to explore various avenues of healing within one's own life. It stimulates creativity and it brings clarity to the mind. It increases the individual's sensitivity, and alignment with it assists in integrating spiritual and soul warmth with the outer personality. It reduces the ego, and it assists in the development of out-of-body experiences.

This herb has a long history associated with elves and faeries. Sprigs of it are hung on Christmas trees in England as an offering and expression of gratitude to the elves for their assistance throughout the year. The faeries and beings of the rosemary plant were often used to help combat any form of black magic or hatred. Their energy is very powerful and positive. They stimulate clarity of mind and creativity. They can also help teach and facilitate out-of-body experiences.

Rosemary reminds us that there is protection around us. This protection is enhanced through a positive attitude. It alerts us to be aware of others who may not have our best interests at heart.

Sage   (salvia officinalis)
Keynote: open to higher states of consciousness; spirit communication

An old folk custom for divining one's future spouse involved going into the garden at midnight and picking twelve leaves of sage, while the clock is striking twelve. Before the clock strikes one, you will see your future spouse, if you are to have one.

This shrubby-looking plant is grown primarily for culinary use, but as a herb it has benefits medicinally and spiritually. The typical leaves are gray-green with a corrugated texture, and the flowers come up off the stem in spikes. Sage grows best in full sun and is very hardy with a strongly branched root system. This is a reminder to always keep our roots and foundation strong.

One of those flowers whose botanical name can be adapted and assumed for greater mystery, sage is a dynamic flower and herb. Alignment with its name and essence stimulates an energy which facilitates achieving higher states of consciousness. It aligns the subtle bodies so that a greater flow of spiritual energy can occur within the physical. It helps integrate spiritual inspiration with outer personality. It awakens psychic faculties and mediumistic abilities. It releases tension that is accumulating within the auric field of the individual. It slows the aging process, and it awakens a newfound sense of immortality and wisdom within the confines of one's own life. Alignment with it creates an increased interest in spiritual matters.

The faeries and elves of sage have great energy, and just being around the plant can induce light altered states of consciousness. Attuning to them can help you facilitate mediumistic abilities. They have knowledge of how to slow the aging process, and they can awaken a newfound sense of immortality and wisdom within your life. They also stimulate an increased interest in spiritual matters.

Sage is a catalyst for spirit communication, reminding us that spirit is no further from us than we allow. It reminds us to keep our roots strong, that we can open to spirit realms and still be part of the physical world. Sage teaches the importance of expressing spirit in what we do.

Spearmint   (menthe spicata)
Keynote: emotions will settle; do not overreact

Spearmint is sometimes known as the sage of Bethlehem. As with peppermint, it is a perennial. Its nearly hairless stem, bright green leaves and its strong fragrance distinguish it. The flowers are pink and as with peppermint, its oil is antispasmodic.

The fragrance has more of an emotional impact, rather than physical as in the case of peppermint. It soothes emotional imbalances. The easiest way of distinguishing spearmint from peppermint in the wild is through their scent. Peppermint in the wild always has that scent we associate with candy.

Spearmints are reminders to keep our emotions controlled. Overreacting at this time will only create more problems. If controlled, situations will ease on their own and quickly pass.

St. John's Wort   (hypericum perforatum)
Keynote: there is good in what is happening, even if we don't see it immediately; attend to your dreams

This perennial plant appears very shrub-like and it always has two raised lines of stems. This is a reminder that there is always two ways of looking at things. Is your glass half-empty or half-full? The flowers are a golden yellow with five petals, which have tiny black spots along their margin.

Sleep, Dreams and Nightmares

Place a morning glory under the pillow of a child and it will restore peaceful sleep.

Hang a sprig of rosemary above the bed. It will drive away nightmares, drawing members of the Faerie realm to protect the child.

For children whose nightmares are the result of fears brought over from a previous life, sprinkle the pillow with thyme.

Burn huckleberry before going to sleep. Dreams will become more precognitive.

Ferns placed about the room work like dreamcatchers, filtering and waving off bad dreams.

Spider lily plants will stimulate problem solving dreams and dreams of animal totems.

Take a bath in lavender oil before retiring for the night and your sleep will be deeper and more restful.

Myrrh fragrance stimulates dreams of past events that are still affecting you.

Eating blackberries before going to bed eases fears of going to sleep. It also stimulates problem solving dreams.

Sew an ounce of yarrow into flannel pouch and place under your pillow to dream of a true friend or true love, asking as you close your eyes for the spirit of the yarrow to bring you the dream.

This plant reminds us to look to the positive. We all encounter negativity and difficulties from time to time. St, John's wort reminds us that the sun shines in spite of those times. It is a reminder to be positive. Regardless of what is happening, good will come from it, even if we don't see it immediately.

As an herb, St. John's wort is being used to treat depression and it is a powerful aid to anyone working with dreams. It alerts us to important dream activity, sometimes serving as a catalyst to release hidden fears into our dreams so that we can confront them and eliminate them on that level. It also alerts us top past life connections appearing in our dreams.

This herb is also beneficial for awakening lucid dreaming, where we become aware in the dream that we are dreaming. At that point, we can then change the dream, thereby changing what stimulated it. Lucid dreaming is also one step away from a fully conscious out-of-body experience. St, John's wort always carries a message about attending to our dreams. It eases our nightmares and reminds us not to give into worries.

Tansy   (tanacetum vulgare)
Keynote: keep the pests at bay; stand tall in spite of others efforts

Tansy is tall, hardy plant with a purplish-brown stem and dull golden flowers - very button-like in appearance. Although native to Eurasia, it now grows across the US, often found along roadsides. It is a natural pest control, helping to repel mosquitoes and flies. It was an herb used in the embalming process and medicinally, it was used at one time frequently as a treatment for worms.

Tansy reminds us to keep the pests of our life at bay. Don't strike back; just hold them back. Stand tall like the tansy in spite of others efforts and the tension and difficulties will soon pass.

Thistle   (cnicus benedictus / centaurea)
Keynote: keep sense of pride; protect yourself against criticisms of others

Thistle can be perennial or biennial (every two years). All thistles have leaves with spiny margins, a globe like flower head and spine-tipped bracts and they are common to meadows and fields. It originated in Mediterranean countries. And it is most often used in the treatment of liver conditions.

The thistle is the national flower of Scotland and it is a plant that has tremendous mysticism associated with it. It combines a sense of pride and defensiveness. According to Scottish tradition, a group of Danes tried to invade Scotland and they crept in by night toward a slumbering camp. One of the invaders stepped barefoot upon a thistle and cried out, alerting the Scots who were able to fend off the invaders.

The milk thistle (Marianus) derives its name from the Blessed Virgin Mary. It was once known as "Our Lady's Thistle". It was often recommended by herbalists to stimulate the production of mother's milk. Although farmers think of it as a pest, herbalists think of it as a gift. It contains a chemical sylibin, which is powerfully effective in treating liver conditions.

The liver is a glandular organ that contains bile salts, which have a detergent effect, breaking down and cleaning the blood so that the kidneys can filter out that which needs to be eliminated. Symbolically, the liver problems reflects strong negative emotions. And this reinforces the message that thistles bring to us.

Are we being too defensive? Are we exposed to constant complaining and criticism? Are we doing everything we can to help ourselves? Do we need to clean up some aspect of our life? Thistle reminds us to maintain pride in who we are and not be afraid to defend ourselves. There is such a thing as righteous anger, and we do have the right to defend ourselves from the criticisms of others. When thistle shows up, it is time to do so.

Thyme   (thymus)
Keynote: explore the mysteries of time; study the past so that you can shape your future

Thyme has tiny oval leaves that have a pungent aroma and when bruised or crushed. The foliage is dense, mounding up and spreading wide. It has many branches off of a single root stalk and its flowers are pale blue to purple. Thyme comes in various fragrances and several colors.

Thyme fragrance was used in the 19th century too help fight typhus, because of its disinfective properties. It is strengthening to the immune system, quickening the healing process. Thyme is beneficial for use in past life recall and future life exploration. It can be used in meditation to seek out origins of chronic problems.

When used as a bedtime fragrance, thyme draws the wee folk into your sleeping chambers. This stimulates dreams of creativity and opens dreams of past lives. Thyme reminds us that our present is the result of the past and the more we understand the past, the easier it is to shape the future.

Tobacco   (nicotiana tabacum)
Keynote: look to the power of prayer; our thoughts and words shape our lives

In China, a man was devastated by the death of his wife, and he visited her grave everyday. One day a plant grew up out of the grave, which was the tobacco plant. He smoked the leaves and got over his grieving. And the tobacco plant came to be known as the "Thinking of Each Other Weed". In China, tobacco came by way of the Philippines.

To the Native Americans, tobacco is a sacred weed. The Cherokee squeezed its juices on bee stings and snake bites. It was placed in post holes to keep evil spirits away. More than 1000 years before De Soto, Native Americans were smoking a variety of it in soapstone pipes. It was used to clear the mind, heal the sick and calm the soul, and most importantly it served to carry their prayers to the Great Spirit.

Tobacco is an annual herb with a shrubby base and a long root. The leaves can be a foot or more long. The flowers are diurnal, only open during the day. It is a native of tropical America and wild species have caused death. All parts contain alkaloid nicotine.

Tobacco reminds us of the importance of prayer in life. It alerts us to remember that our thoughts and words have great power to shape our health, our life and our future. – for good or bad. Thoughts are things and they do have power.

Unicorn Root   (aletris farinose)
Keynote: gentle healing and magic about; now is the time to believe

The unicorn is an archetypal force within the natural world. It is one of the gentlest of creatures – with the ability to walk upon grass without breaking it. There are certain environment factors that are drawing to the unicorn. They have a great love of wildflowers. Clover, apple blossoms, ferns and unicorn root are some of the most important.

True unicorn root is also known as colic root and star grass. This plant is part of the lily family. It is often found at the edge of woods and fields – especially at the edges of swampy areas and wetlands. It is one of the indicators of unicorn presence. The flower stems are tubular, about one to three feet high and topped with tiny bell-shaped flowers. The fresh root in large doses can be somewhat narcotic, but when dried, those properties are lost.

Meditating with this plant can facilitate unicorn encounters. It is a plant that reminds us that magic and miracles are possible if we believe. It reminds us that healing is always best when gentle. Now is the time to trust your heart and keep the child in you alive. If unicorn root comes to you as a messenger, explore the magic and wonder of unicorns.

Yarrow   (achillea millefolium)
Keynote: pay attention to the signs; trust what you are seeing

Yarrow has a long association with divination. It is said that the yarrow grew upon the grave of Confucius. One of the oldest Chinese methods of divination is the I Ching. Traditionally, there are two versions of it the coin and the yarrow stalk method. The I Ching is a tool I use to give me perspective when I truly need it, but I have never used the yarrow stalk  method. Many believe that when you see the first blossom in a yarrow patch, you should make a wish and it will come true.

Yarrow is a perennial herb that can grow as tall as three feet. The flowers are white or a pale yellow, looking like minute daisies. It is found all over the world in fields, pastures and along roadsides.

Yarrow has been used to stimulate specific dream that will reveal your love. By sewing up yarrow in a small piece of flannel and place it under your pillow. Then ask this herb of Venus to tell you who your true love or friend is by tomorrow's dawn. Some say that the yarrow must be picked and used on the night of the new moon. Pieces of yarrow were placed in the nose, causing it to bleed and thus easing the pain of migraines. Carrying yarrow on you was also a way of protecting yourself.

Yarrow reminds us that we receive signs everyday. It alerts us to pay attention and to trust in them - even if they do not seem logical.

Conclusion

Guardian of Nature

Take a walk in the woods after a rain. There will be a smell to the woods – a smell of something happening under the wet leaves. It is the smell of next spring. And that is the wonder of the Green Kingdom. Plants do the same delicious things year after year in numerous ways.

Every year though, more and more plants and animals become extinct or endangered. Many plant species are lost even before being discovered. Thousands more species of plants and animals are threatened. Millions of acres of natural land are destroyed every year. We have separated the natural world and all of its wonders from ourselves. Nature has become something to be studied, examined or used for personal gains.

Too many people assume that destruction of wildlife and habitat has no affect upon them, either individually or as a society because the affects are not readily apparent. There is so much that we don't know about the world that we should be careful about destroying aspects that may be beneficial to us in the future - both physically and spiritually. In the Amazon River area alone, 30-50% of the plants and animals are still unidentified and any one of them might hold the key to curing cancer or any number of diseases. But more importantly, with the disappearance of natural lands and wilderness comes the disappearance of many beliefs about the natural world - especially those considered fantastic and mystical. With the loss of natural lands and wilderness comes a loss of belief in the wonders of the world. And when we lose wonder, a piece of our soul is lost as well.

Nature's plan is often very different from humans. Everything in Nature, even that which many may believe is fantastic, serves a purpose. We may not understand that role or purpose, but we should be careful not to dismiss it because of that. Do we truly need to justify the existence

430

of a plant or an animal any more than we should justify the existence of humans? Our ability or willingness to believe in anything should not be based upon a presumed level of intelligence, worth or productivity. Who among us is qualified to determine such?

People often raise their eyebrows to my approach to life. Should I approach life from such a mystical and fantastic perspective? I think so. You don't have to believe all of the mythology or accept all of the mysticism and folklore, but by merely examining it and keeping an open mind, we stir ancient primal parts of our soul, a part of us that can see and truly experience the many wonders of Nature on a level rarely experienced in the modern world.

We must remember that Nature is part of our heritage. Plant hormones are similar to human. In fact, plant hormones have been found in human saliva, pepsin and urine. And though it is part of our heritage, there is symbiosis in Nature that is not often found in modern human activity. Every plant and animal has a life and form unique to itself, while still being part of a greater whole.

Sometimes in life, it is more important to feel than it is to know. When we spend time in Nature, we stir ancient embers, remembering what we felt as children. We become explorers once more – journeying into strange lands and new mysteries. The Realm of Nature is a path of initiation, ripe with mysteries, magic and wonders.

So often people do their meditations and visualizations, and then they proclaim, "The most amazing thing happened. It worked!" The amazing thing would be if these activities didn't work. Magic and miracles are supposed to happen. And no where is this more evident than in the realm of Nature. Through the Green Kingdom, we discover once more that enchanted worlds exist and that magical possibilities still abound.

"Yet, if you enter the woods
Of a summer evening late,
When the night air cool on the trout-ringed pools...
You will hear the beat of a horse's feet,
And the swish of a skirt in the dew,
Steadily cantering through
The misty solitudes,
As though they perfectly knew
The old lost road through the woods...
But there is no road through the woods."

- Rudyard Kipling

Bibliography

Andrews, Ted. *Animal-Speak.* St. Paul: Llewellyn Publications, 1993.
_____. *Animal-Wise.* Jackson, TN: Dragonhawk Publishing,1999.
_____. *Dream Alchemy.* St. Paul: Llewellyn Publications,1991.
_____. *Enchantment of the Faerie Realm.* St. Paul: Llewellyn Pub,. 1993.
_____. *Healer's Manual.* St. Paul: Llewellyn Publications: 1996.
_____. *Magical Name.* St. Paul: Llewellyn Publications, 1991.
_____. *The Occult Christ.* St. Paul: Llewellyn Publications, 1996.
_____. *Treasures of the Unicorn.* Jackson, TN: Dragonhawk Publishing, 1996.

Arnott, Kathleen. *African Myths and Legends.* New York: Oxford University Press,1989.

Bailey, Alice. *Esoteric Astrology.* New York: Lucis Publishing, 1975.

Besant, Annie. *Path of Discipleship.* India: Theosophical Publishing, 1980.

Benyus, Janine. *Beastly Behaviors.*New York: Addison-Wesley, 1992.

Beyerl, Paul: *The Master Book of Herbalism.* Custer, WA: Phoenix Publishing, 1984.

Bright, Michael, Ed. *Exploring the Secrets of Nature.* New York: Reader's Digest, 1994.

Caduto and Bruchac. *Keepers of the Earth.* Golden, CO: Fulcrum Publishing, 1988.

Campbell, Joseph. *Mythologies of the Primitive Hunters and Gatherers.* New York: Harper & Row, 1988.

Carrier, Jim and Bekoff, Marc. *Nature's Life Lessons.* Golden: Fulcrum Publishing,1996.

Christa, Anthony. *Chinese Mythology.* New York: Peter Bedrick Books, 1983.

Cirlot, J.E. *Dictionary of Symbols.* New York: Philosophical Library, 1962.

Cornell, Joseph. *Sharing Nature with Children.* Nevada City: Dawn Publications, 1979.

Culpepper, Nicholas. *Culpepper's Complete Herbal.* England: Foulsham Co. Ltd.

Dillard, Annie. *Pilgrim at Tinker Creek.* New York: Perrenial, 1974.

Dirr, Michael. *Dirr's Hardy Trees and Shrubs.* Portland: Timber Press, 1997.

Doore, Gary. *The Shaman's Path.* Boston: Shambhala Press, 1988.

Frazer, James George. *The Golden Bough.* New York: Collier Books, 1950.

Graves, Robert. *The White Goddess.* New York: Farrar, Strous & Giroux, 1948.

Grieve, M.A. *A Modern Herbal.* New York: Dover Publishing, 1971.

Gibbons, Euell. *Stalking the Healthful Herbs.*Brattleboro, VT: Alan Hood & Company, 1966.

Edroes and Ortiz. *American Indian Myths and Legends.* New York: Pantheon Books, 1984.

Hall, Manley. *The Secret Teachings of the Ages.* Los Angeles: Philosophical Research, 1977.

Harlow and Morgan. *175 Amazing Nature Experiments.* New York: Random House, 1991.

Heindel, Max. *Ancient and Modern Initiation.* California: Rosicrucian, 1986.

Hessyon, D.G. *The New Flower Expert.* New York: Transworld Publishers, 1999.

Hoeller, Stephen. *The Gnostic Jung.* Wheaton, IL: Quest Books, 1982.

Hoffman, David. *Holistic Herbal.* Rockport: Element Books, 1996.

Huxley, Anthony. *Green Inheritance.* New York: Anchor Press, 1985.

Jung, Carl. Psychology and Alchemy. New York: Princeton Un. Press, 1953.

Malin, Edward. *A World of Faces.* Portland: Timber Press,1978.

Moulton, LeArta. *Herb Walk.* Provo: The Gluten Co., 1979,

Monaghan, Patricia. *Goddesses & Heroines.* St. Paul: Llewellyn Publications,1990.

Palmer, John. *Exploring the Secrets of Nature.* New York: Reader's Digest, 1994.

Peattie, Donald Culross. *A Natural History of Trees.* New York: Bonanza Books, 1966.
_____. *Flowering Earth.* Indianapolis: Indiana University Press, 1991.

Peterson, Roger. *How to Know Birds.* Boston: Houghton Mifflin, 1957.

Price, Shirley. *Practical Aromatherapy.* Wellingborough: horsons Publishing, 1983.

Rezendes, Paul. *Tracking and the Art of Seeing.* Charlotte, VT: Camden House Pub.,1992.

Shanberg, Karen & Tekiela, Stan. *Nature Smart.* Cambridge: Adventure Publications; 1995.

Steiner, Rudolph. *The Festivals and their Meanings.* London: Steiner Press, 1981

Stone, Merlin. *Ancient Mirrors of Womanhood.* Boston: Beacon Press, 1979.

Sutton, Ann and Myrin. *Eastern Forests.* New York: Alfred A. Knopf, 1997.

Tanner, Ogden. *Urban Wilds.* Alexandria: Time-Life Books, 1975.

Tompkins and Bird. *The Secret Life of Plants.* Perrenial: New York, 1972.

Watts, May T. *Reading the Landscape.* New York: MacMillon Press, 1957.

Index

N

O

P

Also by Ted Andrews

The Animal-Speak Workbook

**2002
Visionary Award Winner
for:**

Best Non-Fiction Book

Best General Interest Book

**$1795
ISBN 1-888767-48-0**

Explore The Wonders of the Animal World!

From the author of the best selling and award winning books, *Animal-Speak* and *Animal-Wise* comes a companion manual to connect you more fully to your animal guides and guardians and to help you understand animal messages.

- Use pets to bridge to wild totems.
- Explore hawk and owl medicine.
- Develop animal communication and telepathy.
- Make and use medicine shields and sacred journey staffs.

Available from Dragonhawk Publishing and all major distributors.

Also by Ted Andrews

The Animal-Wise Tarot

**1999 Visionary Award
Runner-Up
for
Best Spirituality Book!**

The Animal-Wise Tarot contains 78 full-color cards of actual animal photographs and a 248 page, soft cover guide book.

**$34.95
ISBN 1-888767-35-9**

Discover the Language of Animals!

All traditions taught the significance of Nature - particularly of animals crossing our paths, whether we are awake or dreaming. Use *The Animal-Wise Tarot* to develop your intuition, strengthen your connection to the animals world, and to find answers to your most puzzling questions in life.

Whether an experienced tarot enthusiast, a shamanic practitioner, or a novice to psychic exploration, this tarot's ease of use will be a refreshing surprise. Anyone can use this tarot from the moment it is opened and you will find yourself becoming truly animal-wise!

Available from Dragonhawk Publishing and all major distributors.

Also by Ted Andrews

Treasures of the Unicorn

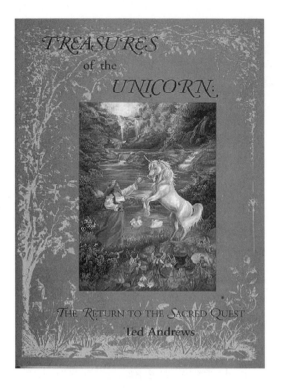

**As seen on the 1998
"Ally McBeal"
Christmas episode!**

*"An enchanting work wthat will
light up your book shelf!*
- **NAPRA ReVIEW**

**$12.95
ISBN 1-888767-35-9**

You will believe once More!

There is still a place where enchantment lives,
Where streams sing and winds whisper,
Where caverns lead to nether realms,
Where trees speak and the flowers tell tales,
Where unicorns dance in the morning dew!

Best selling author Ted Andrews guides you once more into Nature on the sacred quest for the unicorn. And on that journey you will find what was lost, heal what was hurt and restore to life what you thought had died.

Available from Dragonhawk Publishing and all major distributors.

About the Author

Ted Andrews is an internationally-recognized author, storyteller, teacher and mystic. A leader in the human potential, metaphysical and psychic field, he has written more than 30 books, which have been translated into two dozen foreign languages.

Ted has been involved in the serious study of the esoteric and occult for more than 35 years. He has been a certified spiritualist medium for 20 years and he brings to the field an extensive formal and informal education.

Ted is schooled in music and he has composed and produced the music for ten audiocassettes.

Ted, along with his wife of 27 years, holds state and federal permits to work with birds of prey. They conduct animal education and storytelling programs in classrooms with their hawks, owls and other animals throughout the year.

In his spare time, Ted enjoys ballroom dancing, riding horses, hanging out with a menagerie of pets, and yes, occasionally climbing a tree or two.